W9-BNY-971

THE CHURCH TODAY

Emmanuel Cardinal Suhard

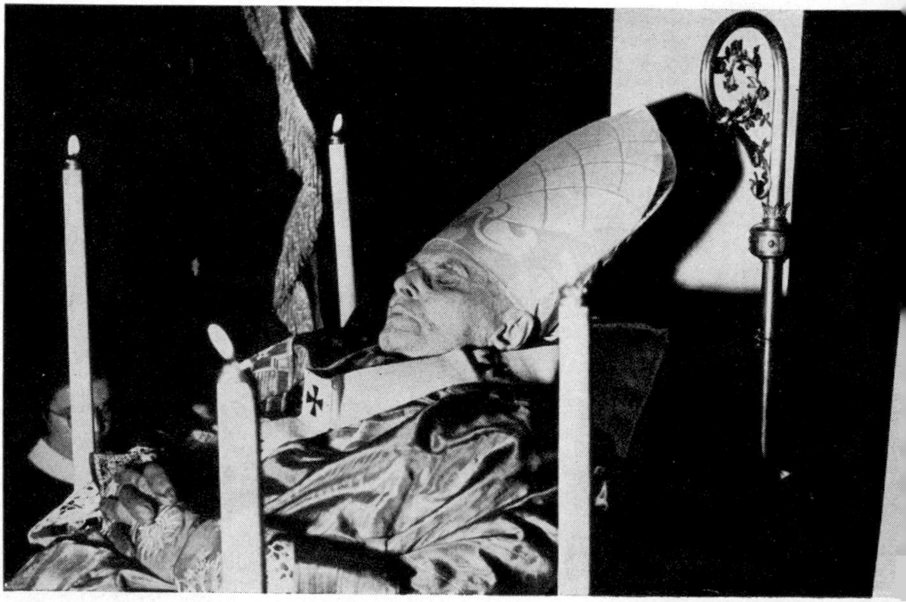

THE CHURCH TODAY

The Collected Writings of Emmanuel Cardinal Suhard

Introduction by
John J. Wright, D.D.

Fides Publishers
Chicago 10, Illinois

American Book - Stratford Press, Inc., New York

55

CONTENTS

Publisher's Note

The writings of Emmanuel Cardinal Suhard have been collected and edited under the editorship of the Rev. Louis J. Putz, C.S.C., University of Notre Dame, and Vincent J. Giese.

Assistance in the preparation of the translation of new material was generously given by Dr. Charles Parnell and Mr. Frank Gwyn of the University of Notre Dame.

New translations of the three previously published pastorals, "Growth or Decline?" "The Meaning of God" and "Priests Among Men" were obtained through the courtesy of the Rev. John Fitzsimmons, editor of "New Life," 43 Offley Road, London, England.

Foreword

When Cardinal Suhard died the Catholic community felt a shock. The Archbishop of Paris was known in America largely because of his two great pastoral letters, *Growth or Decline?* and *The Meaning of God*. To some he was known as the protector of a revolutionary movement of worker-priests. A few of us had the opportunity of meeting him, of hearing his quiet voice, of quickening to his dynamism, of living in his Paris.

Born in 1874, in stanchly Catholic Brittany, Emmanuel Suhard had the usual career of a French bishop. Noted for his intelligence in the preseminary, he was sent to Rome for his major work, coming back to the major seminary as professor once the S.T.D. had been conferred. Almost none of the French hierarchy have had pastoral experience; the steps in the ladder are nearly always "professor"—"secretary to the Bishop" —"Bishop."

Emmanuel Suhard was named Bishop of Bayeux-Lisieux in 1928. Though he remained there only two years, Lisieux was marked as the future center of the *Mission de France*. The Bishop already had made his reputation as a discerning student of men, as a pastor acutely aware of the personal vocation of each of his priests.

He established a special position, "Adviser on Ecclesiastical Affairs," and charged this adviser with the spiritual formation of the younger priests. They could come to him with full confidence and he would plead their cause before the diocesan authority. Suhard said, "For a long time a bishop in *curia* has had a chancellor charged with dispensing justice. It is good that he should have another priest charged with dispensing mercy."

After a term of ten years as Archbishop of Reims, in 1935 the cardinalate was bestowed on the man who in 1940 was to step into the great Cardinal Verdier's shoes. Difficult enough to be the Archbishop of Paris, greatest though not the oldest of Gaul's dioceses; to be the successor of Verdier (the man who gave Paris a hundred new churches, who gave thousands of workers jobs during the height of the depression), but worse

* The foreword appeared in October, 1949, issue of "The Catholic World." FIDES acknowledges the kind permission to reprint it here.

still, Emmanuel Cardinal Suhard became Cardinal of Paris during the height of the debacle, the year of France's shame.

During the occupation Suhard made no spectacular name for himself. Only old, ailing Archbishop Saliège of Toulouse kept the name of the French hierarchy from taint of collaboration. Many were those who were dissatisfied with Suhard's role, which was simply to enable the Church to endure, to survive the onslaught. His quiet, precise letter about Conscript Labor was not vigorous enough for them: no ringing phrases, no audacious challenge. Cardinal Suhard was looked upon at best as non-political, a man of prudence, unwilling to take a stand in France's greatest crisis.

With the liberation, a cardinal's hat was sent to Saliège, and a few outstanding Vichyite bishops withdrew into monasteries. Emmanuel Suhard stayed in his place, enduring the scorn, often the open disrespect of younger resistance heroes—uncomplaining, humble, suffering.

Only now that he is dead do we know that he protected the underground Catholic Action movements, the clandestine newspaper *Témoignage Chrétien;* that he risked his life interceding for Jews, hostages, and deportees; that he repeatedly refused to denounce Communism publicly without at the same time denouncing its twin, totalitarianism.

Almost imperceptibly, the Church of France began to stir. Paris was the center of this activity. The wise said, "The Cardinal is allowing this activity because it would go on despite him; he is trying to redeem himself by letting the young act. They, the pride of the resistance, will bring back honor to the Church in France."

Now we know that in the midst of the occupation, Suhard had read a report of two of his priests on the de-Christianization of France. (This report was subsequently published as *France, Pays de Mission;* in English, *France Pagan?*) Now we know that this sexagenarian spent three sleepless nights wrestling with the awful weight of this new realization and rose up transformed. The prudent, gentle man became a Paul calling for audacity, for confidence.

The great Prince of the Church continued his functions.

Mass in celebration of the liberation of Paris, the reception of General LeClerc and his staff, the trumpets of the great army which redeemed France blaring forth at Notre Dame were unforgettable experiences.

But the old Cardinal began to appear in quite other surroundings: young couple's homes, workers' kitchens. Priests and militants of the proletarian missions had ready access to him. They were told: "My life as Archbishop cloisters me here and cuts me off from humanity in its sufferings, hopes, sins and virtues. You must help me, inform me, make me know my people and meet them. How can I be the guardian of the city, the Good Pastor, if you don't help me to know my sheep? Do you realize that you are responsible with me for my bishopric, my diocese?"

The story goes that his secretary would call up and say, "Come when you can: early in the morning, after supper, Saturday afternoon. The Cardinal of Paris will adjust his schedule to your free time." Abbé DePierre himself tells of arriving late for an appointment, and being told, before he had time to excuse himself, "Your role is to serve the workers and to be completely ready to help them. My role is to serve you and to be ready to help you."

Was this simply an imprudent about-face, a flaunting of all traditional roles, the vagary of an old man? What was this living paradox of prudent youth and audacious old age? Cardinal Suhard showed an amazing confidence in his priests and militants, saying, "Go ahead, go ahead, don't stop. The life of the Church is at stake. She asks you to take this step into a world so much in need of unity and collective kindness."

Wise and prudent pastor, he demanded of them charity, piety, devotion, and total giving of self, prudence, doctrine, discipline. He gave them a superior, the wise priest, Abbé Hollande. Only two rules bound them: absolute obedience to the hierarchy and to the laws of team life.

The Cardinal would say: "Together you have the grace of your state of life to enable you to decide about the demands of your apostolate. As long as they do not touch the laws of the liturgical, spiritual, canonical, or doctrinal life of the Church

. . . you know that there are permissions that you must not ask of me. Have you not received the Holy Spirit? What is the use of your baptism and confirmation, your interior life, and your team life?"

Cardinal Suhard exhorted his priests to live in such a fashion that their lives "could be understandable only if God exists . . . witnesses not by superficial change of habits, but by a firm desire to share the destiny of the disinherited masses. A life which was neither an evasion, nor a study of customs, nor even a conquest . . . it is a vocation of redemption. Work for them is not a pretext, or propaganda, it is the naturalization act of the priest in a people where he is only a stranger, it is the suffering and penitent sharing of the worker's condition in life."

He was always careful to make clear his confidence. For example, in his warning to the Christian Progressives against "habitual and profound collaboration with the Communists," he ended by saying, "we count more than ever on our priests and militant laymen. Living with the workers, they share their anxieties, their worries, and also their hopes. They have our confidence; all the faithful should know this, and we are happy to reaffirm it."

Few things made Cardinal Suhard more angry than pot shots at the *Mission de Paris,* the apple of his eye. He was an unusually tolerant man who bore with many outdated diocesan institutions and revivalist Catholic movements that he disliked, saying, "there is place for them in the Church, if they allow others to exist. I don't think that I should be more severe than the Pope." An undiscriminating attack on the *Mission,* the integrity of the militants or its action, occasioned some of the few holy rages the Cardinal vented during those years.

Suhard's sense of urgency for the proletarians was only equaled by his concern for the intellectuals. He thought both groups vital in the rebuilding of Catholic France.

The Cardinal awakened the Catholic intellectual institutions (associations, universities, and research institutes) out of their Rip Van Winkle sleep. Under his benevolent interest and protection, Catholic intellectuals began to bestir themselves about the university apostolate. Groups of eminent men with varied training met together about a common problem, and the *Centre Intellectuel des Catholiques Français* became a veritable hive of activity, conferences and incisive debates recalling the flash and thrust of the medieval defense of theses.

The intellectual militants were freed by Suhard from the perpetual look-over-the-shoulder, am-I-orthodox fear. His pastoral letter, *Growth or Decline?*, could be called the Catholic intellectual's Magna Charta. In it the Cardinal affirms that intellectual work "remains independent. [The Church] has no mission to solve directly technical problems. She recognizes the legitimate autonomy of competent authorities."

He allayed the intellectual's twofold fear, "Must I give up my professional integrity in research," and, "Is my research really worth while?" by maintaining, "Your research must bear first on pure truth and disinterested science . . . you must not involve any consideration of interest be it even apologetical in your work: you must seek only what is. Your integrity must only be equaled by your open-mindedness and your effective co-operation with all those believers and unbelievers who pursue the truth with all their soul. Do not hesitate to give yourself entirely to the joy of knowing, to your vocation of scholars."

Cardinal Suhard's last public address was made at the annual meeting of Catholic intellectuals where he said, "We live in a great epoch where Catholic intellectuals play a more and more important role. . . . We do not find ready-made answers in the Gospels, in the domain of science, philosophy, social doctrine, art and civilization." He warned them against "premature, *a priori* synthesis," and said that perhaps the next synthesis to illumine future ages as did Augustine's and Thomas's would be a work of another order, the collective work of a group of intellectuals, the end product of many different projects.

Yet the apostolate, the rebuilding of the city, must be the work of all men of good will, not only that of proletarians and scholars. It is the living of Christ among men, the bearing witness, not the retreat into fortresses, or a propaganda campaign.

Cardinal Suhard traces the essential lines of this universal Catholic vocation. It must be "based on Catholic Action," that is to say, be fundamentally the responsibility of the laity. It must be "based primarily on the working class" for two reasons: this is the class most cut off from Christ and the class which is just arriving at adulthood, beginning to take its rightful place in the City. It must be based in the community, because "militants cannot without danger or futility stay alone," and second, because the apostolate must be that of the team, its aim to penetrate groups, institutions, with the life of Christ.

Finally Suhard gives the marks of a true apostolate. It must be realistic, competent, sensible. It must be filled with a "supernatural sense of souls . . . a spirit of faith and humility." It must have persevering charity and, most important of all, "a profound love of the Church."

—*Sally Whelan Cassidy*

Introduction

One of the most pathetic stories to come out of the French chapter of the history of World War II was a story which a Colonel of the French Army told me personally. It concerns a young man, a partisan of the resistance movement, who was killed by a bullet which ricocheted in the Rue du Bac.

The fatal bullet felled the *maquis*, described as being in his late teens, in the gutter not far from the convent where St. Catherine Labouré saw with her eyes of flesh the Blessed Mother of God. Within a square mile of the spot there are world-famed churches, shrines and other hallowed places which pilgrims journey from afar to visit. Within sight of each end of the street are monumental evidences of the Christian faith that has been preached in Paris these seventeen centuries and more.

And yet, when two Catholic sisters drew the dying body of this boy into a doorway which might shelter his last moments, they were sickened at heart by the answer the young lad gave to an earnest effort to prepare him for an eternity that was then but seconds away so far as he was concerned.

"Do you love God with all your heart?" one of the religious asked the gasping partisan. *Aimez-vous le Bon Dieu?*

The answer came in accents of pain, embarrassment and confusion. *Comment dirai-je que je L'aime? Je ne Le connais pas de tout, ce Bon Dieu dont tu parles!*

"How shall I say that I love Him? I don't even know who He is, this God of Whom you talk!"

Where was he dying, the mortally wounded young soldier? Not in Borneo, nor in the Arctic, nor at the furthermost ends of the earth beyond the reach of priests or the influence of the Gospel. Not in "mission" country in the usual sense of that too restrictive term. Not in one of the lands which the Propagation of the Faith magazines describe as "pagan" and for which they ask our apostolic alms and prayers.

Not at all. He was dying in the Archdiocese of Paris, *la ville lumière*, capital city of Christian France, rival of Rome itself among the centers of Western Christendom as the centuries since the thirteenth, certainly, have understood Christendom.

He was dying within the shadow of a chapel to which the devout flock by the thousands. He was prostrate in a street along which saints have walked, a street in which many of us have seen great preachers come and go and pilgrims gather for prayer.

Whence did he come, this lad who could not bring himself to declare his love for God because he did not know enough about Him to call upon Him in the hour of death? Was he from the French colonial empire? Had he been born and brought up in the remote wildernesses of the Senegalese? Again, not at all. He was from Paris, where the very stations of the underground railroad, the *Metro*, more often than not bear the names of Catholic saints, so that the stops called out in his ears as he went to and from his school or work were a veritable litany of the saints and catalogue of the Christian dogmas. His home was Paris, a city in which it would be impossible to walk a half mile and not see in one direction or another the towers of a cathedral, the domes of a basilica or the spires of a great church. In all probability, he himself bore the names of two or more saints; it is even likely, too likely, that if he swore in his moments of youthful anger or violence, he invoked the titles of Catholic devotion and blasphemed with the phrases of Catholic faith.

But when he lay dying, with two Catholic sisters striving to comfort his body and elicit the act of charity by which he might save his soul, he cried out in empty, perhaps even bitter agnosticism, his ignorance concerning God. "How shall I say that I love Him? I don't even know who He is, this God of Whom you talk!"

Is he not exceptional, this tragic young man of the Rue du Bac? We who love France, and who love souls even more, wish that we might think so. Alas, he is all too typical of those unnumbered throngs of people, young and old, who comprise the so-called "de-Christianized" populations of France. Paris has them in multitudes; almost every corner of France has some, certain parts of the country have them in frightening numbers.

Each of the great cities is heavy of heart, sometimes almost perceptibly so, with its host of unbelievers, the *non-croyants* among the sons and daughters of this land so beloved of the Mother of God and so fruitful in martyrs, missionaries, saints and devout souls of every class and condition.

The dying young man who did not even know who God *is* and who could not muster enough of grace to call out to Him in love seems to some critics of contemporary France to be the type of a nation which has suffered so many ravages in her body at the hands of militarists and in her soul at the hands of philosophers (of a sort) and politicians. These critics can make out an impressive case for their thesis that France has become "pagan," that the eldest daughter of the Church has proved wayward and derelict. But their case is specious, for all its evidence, and their requiems over the dead soul of Catholic France fortunately are premature.

The France of King St. Louis still lives. So does that of Saint Joan, St. John Vianney, St. Margaret Mary, St. Therese of Lisieux and all the company of the Catholic French saints. France has become the testing place of certain of the most inhuman and disastrous ideas of modern times, from those of the atheists among the political revolutionaries to those of the degenerates among pseudo-intellectuals. All this is true, and its toll is tragic; typical of that toll is the boy dying in bewilderment and disbelief in the Rue du Bac.

But France remains nonetheless the cradle of the most valiant, the most humane and divine of the cultural, social and spiritual programs by which the unchanging Catholic ideals are translated into terms intelligible to each changing generation. If it be true that France has suffered greatly, physically and spiritually, at the hands of her scoundrels, it is also true that she is continually transfigured by the supernatural wisdom and the divine energies of her own sons and daughters among the saints. No criticism of contemporary France is worthy of our notice which fails to take into consideration the Sisters and the Catholic bookstores in the Rue du Bac as well as the bewildered agnostic boy who died there.

Only against the background of these two sets of facts—the sad history of how France has become de-Christianized and the glorious history of her Catholic revival in each generation—can one grasp the true significance of the work and words of the late Cardinal Suhard. No one will understand the extraordinary interest in the Cardinal's pastorals and other pronouncements throughout post-war France unless he is aware of how the Holy Spirit finds eager and ardent response at all times and places in France. No one will understand the emphasis and the overtones of the Cardinal's teaching unless he has some idea of how far advanced was the work of Satan in the nation to which Suhard addressed himself.

Some of the techniques by which the Cardinal sought to re-Christianize the paganized areas of life in his diocese have been the object of classroom criticism and round-table debate among a few theologians and critics of the French scene. Quite possibly a few of the programs which he sponsored and emphases which he stressed were ill-advised, though the time for the final word is hardly yet. This much is certain: all of them were part of the effort of a mighty man of God to bring back to the Holy Catholic Church a people whose best genius has always flourished in happy communion with that Church.

Even if some few of the many apostolic programs of the Cardinal disappointed his own high hopes, the impact of his teaching, particularly through the medium of his exalted pastorals, has been wide and mighty. The encyclicals of the modern popes have been cited as evidence of the clear operation of the Holy Spirit in our generation. The pastorals of Cardinal Suhard are certainly warm with the same divine fire and have given the apostolic witness within a nation (and indirectly beyond) which the Holy See has given before all the world.

The de-Christianized community which confronted the late Cardinal of Paris and which called out to everything that was Christlike in his apostolic mind and heart is not so peculiarly French in either its origins or its developments that any of us can consider it with detachment and complacency. The boy in the Rue du Bac is a type of France's tragedy and of a particular moment in her history; but he is not exclusively French. *Res nostra agitur:* the evils which have befallen one great Christian nation are not without their roots and unwholesome flower even in fields close to our homes, cities and sanctuaries. Secularism here is inevitably destined to produce a parallel to the paganism there. We can only pray that the counteracting apostolic vision and spiritual energy among us will be anywhere near as powerful as they are proving to be among the French.

We do well, therefore, to read the writings of Cardinal Suhard with great care and searching, not only because they record lofty moments in the Catholic French resistance to modern paganism, but also because they shed abundant light by which we in America can chart our course whenever and wherever Godlessness may seek to detour the progress of the Church among us. The time of our testing is bound to come; many of us think it is closer than any of us would wish. When it comes we shall undoubtedly be found to have been blessed by God with Suhards in our own hierarchy and with apostolic souls in our laity; such is the mercy of God. But it will also be good if we have profited from the wisdom of France's great champion of the faith in the face of paganism; that we can so learn is one of the blessings of the communion of saints as it operates on earth in the Holy Catholic Church.

The zealous scholars who have translated these works of Cardinal Suhard into English have paid the Church in France an affectionate tribute of gratitude and friendship by their work; at the same time, they have done the Church in America and the English speaking world an apostolic favor for which they deserve high praise and prayerful thanks.

✠ *John Wright*
Bishop of Worcester

GOD'S PROVIDENCE

These are times of adversity.

Are we a pawn of chance, subject to an inexorable fate, at the hands of a blind brutality of material forces? Or is there above everything here below another power, full of intelligence and love? Is there a Providence?

Let us see under what conditions we can be collaborators of God and how we can act in conformity with His plans.

Contents

Page

God's Providence

In times of adversity each one seeks help. "Shall we find help this side of the earth?" We all are seeking, waiting, asking! Whatever the merit of the efforts expended, or whatever the value of the results obtained, can we hope for a permanent solution? Are not human things fragile, more fragile than ever in these hours of uncertainty and of inextricable difficulty?

We must, therefore, look higher. We must lift our eyes to heaven. Will help come from there? Are we a pawn of chance, subject to an inexorable fate at the hands of a blind brutality of material forces? Or is there above everything here below another power full of intelligence and love, which sees all and judges all? Is there a Providence?

The answer of certain people to this question is doubt. Many, I am happy to say, and you are among them, my brethren, know that the answer is yes. Discerning minds see in Divine Providence the supreme rule of life, and they make of this certitude a first principle for guidance.

A blessed certitude, alone capable of bringing happiness to our life! What repose can we find outside it? In the midst of so many dangers and hardships, what can our hope be except to see things in the light of God and to know ourselves guided by His hand? Blessed those who know this. Still more blessed, those who, knowing it, draw the consequences which flow from it for themselves and for the guidance of the world.

For, if there is a Providence which watches over us, our attitude must reflect it. If there is a Providence which watches over us, we have duties of faith, of gratitude, of devotion out of respect to it. If there is a Providence, which makes use of us as instruments to realize its ends, we have a duty of docility towards it. And if in its action Providence chooses certain means, or directs us in certain channels, we must try to be faithful to it without evasion.

We would, therefore dear brethren, at the beginning of Lent, help you to re-quicken in yourselves this certitude which we have from the hands of God. We would like to tell you what our attitude towards Divine Providence should be and "at what price we can help ourselves through its designs."

I. THE ACTION OF GOD IN THE WORLD

It is useless to hide the difficulties to which our faith in Divine Providence is subjected in such an age as ours. Really, we are in the midst of thick darkness. Need we enumerate the sufferings which the world bears? Who could do so? Even if we could enumerate the physical hardships of those who suffer hunger, cold, misery, and captivity, even if we could calculate the sufferings of those who fall in the field of battle, we still could not compute the principal sufferings: the moral sufferings, often hidden and therefore that much more intense since they cannot be expressed, the sufferings of hearts tired of waiting and uncertainty, broken by the sorrows of death in the family; the hardships of the country. And yet suffering still is a lesser evil than sin . . .

Suffering and sin, a sea of physical and moral illness, cover the entire world with a violence rarely experienced in the course of ages. Can we still talk about "a world order?" Can we still talk about "a supreme Wisdom," Who administers suffering and sin?

We can and we must, dear brethren. World history can bewilder us at certain times: the world exists, and it is not its own reason of existence. Events must not hide realities from us. The simplest realities, such as the flowers of the field, the birds of the air, of which the Gospel speak, testify to the existence of a Creator.

And what can we say of man's existence—his intelligence and will, at once so feeble and so great? Whence comes our indignation in the face of evil? Whence comes our thirst for justice and happiness, if we have not received them from God, our Creator? But if God creates, if He creates intellects and wills, He does so because He Himself is supreme Intelligence and supreme Love.

Furthermore, the Creator came amongst us. God became man. More than that, He became our victim and our savior. In order that we be unable to reproach Him for being indifferent to suffering and sin, He took upon Himself the suffering that would deliver us from sin: Jesus Christ, Jesus Christ crucified! This is the supreme testimony to the existence of God, and to the merciful love God bears for us.

But then there is no more room for doubt: everything God has created He protects and governs by His Providence, reaching from one end to the other with power and sweetness. Everything is naked before his eyes, even things which happen through the free action of creatures.[1]

"He is our God. Our destiny is in His hands." [2] He takes care of the little and the great. He takes care of all things, for He created all things according to His Wisdom.[3] For something to escape His Providence, it would have to exist without Him.

It is not that history, which is at times so disconcerting, hides Providence, but it is Providence which alone explains history. Without the wisdom and mercy of God, history cannot explain its own conduct or its beginning and end. God did not create the world in order to abandon it to itself, as though the world could continue to exist without Him. Nothing exists unless God wishes it—and nothing happens without His ordaining it and permitting it. For He knows all, sees all, He can do all things. We know that His knowledge is Wisdom; that His will is infinite Love and that His unlimited power is embraced by His Love.

God takes care of His creatures: "See the birds of the air, they neither sow nor reap; they do not gather into barns, yet your heavenly Father feeds them." [4] "The eyes of all are turned towards Him, and He gives to each creature food in its time. He opens His hand and fills with plenitude all that lives." [5]

Would man be the only one in whom God is not interested? "You," says Bossuet, "whom He has made in His image, whom He has enlightened with His knowledge, Whom He has called to His kingdom, can you believe He has forgotten you, or that you are the only of His creatures whom the vigilant eyes of His

[1] Council of Vatican. (Denz. 1784).
[2] Ps., 30:15-16.
[3] Wisdom, 6:8, 11:21, 12:13.
[4] Matt., 6:26.
[5] Ps., 144:15-16.

paternal Providence do not cover?"[6] "Consider the birds of the air . . . are you not worth more than they?"[7]

We know it well: we are worth more than they. Our value is such that the Son of God has given His life for us! "We," says St. John, "have known, and have believed the charity, which God hath to us."[8]

My brethren, you also believe in the love that God bears for you. You believe in Divine Providence. May I ask you to clarify your faith?

You understand that Divine Providence works unceasingly for the world and for each of us, for to love is to wish well to the one we love. God, therefore, Who loves us, does not cease to love us well, and since He does not stop acting, He does not cease to work for our good.

God's action in the world is a secret action. God is powerful enough not to have to make a personal appearance. His invisible action manifests itself in the ordinary course of events. Hence, it does not exclude the possibility of evil. Hence, too, His action permits evil to exist and to grow, certain that the last word rests with Him and that He can draw good out of evil itself.

Have we not often seen this in history? Have we not often seen the happy result of a series of events which seemed at the time to culminate only in catastrophe? Still better do we not often see arise from catastrophe new life more splendid than what preceded it? On the ruins of the past God builds the future. He uses for this a thousand means which we do not possess and which are for this very reason the only efficacious means. Let us not ask God, therefore, to act according to our limited vision. Let us be confident in His wisdom even when it is hidden. "For my thoughts are not your thoughts. Nor your ways my ways, saith the Lord."[9] Should we be astonished that

[6] Bossuet, Sermon on Providence.
[7] Matt., 6:26.
[8] I John, 4:16.
[9] Is., 55:8-9.

His designs are inscrutable in many of their dispositions, especially the greatest of all, the redemption of the world?

After all, evil will never triumph as much as it triumphed on Good Friday, on top of Golgatha when the crucified Christ succumbed. It was the worst catastrophe of all: Israel, the chosen people, climaxed a history of infidelity. Israel, prepared for many centuries to welcome the Messias, rejected the Messias. But even this God, Who permitted it, had foreseen and announced by the mouth of the prophets; and redemption was fulfilled through this catastrophe so disconcerting in appearance. Consenting to the sacrifice of Christ, God redeemed Israel and the entire world.

If world history corresponds in the eyes of faith with the history of redemption, if the world exists only in order that God might adopt children who will partake eternally in His beatific life, must we then be astonished to have a Christ Who must suffer before entering His glory? Can we afford not to complete in ourselves His Passion in order to gain with Him new souls for Divine Life? For Divine Providence uses each of us to attain its goals and to save the world. God acts in the world by making His creatures act, each according to its nature. He did not want merely to create inanimate creatures, or living creatures without intelligence, whose unconscious actions realize without their knowing it the plan willed by Him. He created beings endowed with intelligence and will in order that they might concur freely with His designs.

If some people abuse their liberty and turn the gifts which they have received from God against Him, God never ceases to warn them or wait for them or solicit them until that moment which He has chosen for their repentence or punishment. For in the final analysis nothing can oppose His Will. Who is more powerful than God? "Who is like unto God?"

Sinners serve Providence without wanting to and without knowing it. Saints serve Providence with a love full of humble obedience, and frequently God makes known His plans to them. Let us, likewise, serve Providence in the spirit of faith, not being perturbed because we do not always see the terminus to which it leads, or even the road on which it leads us. We know that it leads us: that is enough! Peace is promised even in this world to souls of good will.

Let us conclude this first part, dear brethren, that Divine Providence is the great sustainer of the world. Providence wishes to save the world and will save it, for the world can do nothing without it and nothing against it.

This vision of faith will be for us the secret of a better course of action; a calm action, because it leans on God; a strong action, because certain of reaching its goal; an unerringly, fruitful action, because blessed by God, Who, in delaying prepares a richer harvest. Such was the life of the Saints—a St. Paul, a St. Augustine, a St. Genevieve, a St. Joan of Arc, all of whom in the most troubled times of world history worked with Divine Providence for the salvation of the world. They gave of themselves generously; they spent themselves in the completion of their task, unable to measure how far reaching their efforts were. But they called themselves "the collaborators of God"—to Whom was due the essential element of their achievements.[10]

Let us see, therefore, under what conditions we also can be collaborators of God and how we can act in conformity with His plans.

II. OUR DUTIES TOWARDS PROVIDENCE

The first duty of man, dear brethren, is to live in the truth. Nothing solid is built on illusion or deception. Let us live, therefore, in the reality of our being and of our supernatural vocation. Let us live in the truth of our relationship with God Who, having created us, does not cease to direct us by His Providence towards our final end and with us the rest of the world.

As we have said previously, however, the action of God does not suppress the action of His creatures. On the contrary, it sustains and uses it. Divine Providence does not dispense us from personal initiative. It even wishes that events which happen have the appearance of coming from us. It is right, there-

[10] I Cor., 3:6-9.

fore, to act according to His designs and to recognize His sovereignty. We owe to Divine Providence a concurrence of obedience and courage; but first of all, we owe it the homage of our faith and our filial devotion. Let us explain this in a few words.

If we are the collaborators of God, our first duty is to recognize His action with faith and filial confidence. To believe in Divine Providence, to have faith in God's supreme vigilance and His goodness is the homage we owe God and the foundation of all other duties. Acting on our own initiative, we must nevertheless know that we are in the hands of God, Who is our master—the *only* master of world events and our personal lives.

And if we see correctly, our faith cannot translate itself except in "filial devotedness." God is first of all a Father, a very good father to His creatures. His Providence is nothing else but paternal care, full of sweetness and wisdom. We owe Him, therefore, our confidence, and this confidence cannot be better expressed than by total surrender. To trust in one's earthly father is to leave everything to his discretion, to his prudence, and to his affection. How much more are we to do so when it is a question of God, to Whom we confide ourselves, to God of Whom we know "there is no father like unto Him."

What security, brethren, to know ourselves as being in the hands of God. What security, especially, to know that the people and responsibilities confided to us are in His hands. Treasures, which we carry in vessels of clay, are kept by God through our efforts.[11] Particularly in the difficult moments of our life when everything seems lost, it is good to turn towards heaven and respectfully and lovingly seek help from God. "I lift my eyes towards the heavens. Whence will come help? Our help is in the Lord, Who created heaven and earth." [12] "Blessed be the God and Father of our Lord Jesus Christ, the God of all comforts, who comforts us in all our difficulties." [13]

[11] II Cor., 4:7.
[12] Ps., 120:1-2.
[13] II Cor., 1:3-4.

Our faith and our filial devotion would be deceiving if it were not transformed by positive courage and obedience. It is not enough to say "Lord, Lord." [14] We must do what God requires of us. It would be better, having at first refused to do something, to relent and work, than, having said yes, to evade our responsibilities.[15]

Undeniably the present situation demands more of us than ever before. What is happening today? We must create a new order, and for this purpose we must restore our spiritual values. All values, even material ones, are deceiving when spiritual values are lacking. We must restore the spiritual values by cultivating our intellects, by disciplining our wills, by forming our consciences, by developing our moral and religious life. Can such values be restored in any way except through the fruit of our own activity? It requires all of our effort, all of our personal and collective labor. God does not replace our effort. If He consents to help us, He does so to urge us to do the work which is our responsibility, not to dispense us from it. We must help ourselves if heaven is to help us. Would any other course of action be worthy of Providence or worthy of us?

The worst of evils would be discouragement, apathy, bitterness, all of which equally hinder the work to be done. If it is already a mistake not to depend upon Divine Providence in our activity, how much greater damage would be worked if we cowardly deserted our responsibilities? This really would be an insult to God. Especially in tragic times we must beware of this.

Let us be courageous with God; but by being obedient to Him. Let us be courageous by following His impulses, by seconding His action in the world! Obedience to God, thus, is the highest homage we owe Divine Providence. This is the true testimony of our faith and filial devotion. Finally, this is the guarantee that we are not running blindly, that our efforts will be fruitful.

Obedience to God is the true way of serving the designs of Divine Providence and working for the welfare of the world.

[14] Matt., 7:21.
[15] Matt., 21:28-31.

For each of us, obedience to God is our only security, namely, entry into the "order willed by God."

It remains, dear brethren, to answer this very important question: If we are to obey God, how are we to recognize His Will? If our duties towards God are a matter of following His inspirations, by what sign do we recognize them? Let us try to answer with precision.

God manifests His Will, first of all, by His commandments, which outline our strict obligations, then by His inspirations and callings, which solicit our generosity, and finally by events, which reveal His Will. Commandments, inspirations, events—three kinds of signs by which Divine Providence outlines the road over which we are to be led.

It is impossible to be faithful to Divine Providence without being faithful to our daily tasks. Daily tasks are God's way of making us a partner to His plans.

The first commandment is to love Him above all things; the second, like unto the first, is to love our neighbor as ourselves. In consequence certain things are forbidden, others are positively commanded. The commandments of God and the Church make these things precise. They trace for us our duties as men and as Christians, as well as our domestic, professional and social obligations.

Everything is summed up by our duties of justice and charity. St. Paul says, "love therefore is the fulfillment of the law." [16] Are we faithful to these duties? If we do not try to be, we fail Divine Providence. Why be astonished, then, when our failures produce effects which the world must suffer?

God not only orders our life through His commandments and those of His Church, but He also does it through just, human laws. It is our duty to obey legitimate human authority. And St. Paul recommends to the Bishop that he recall this duty to his faithful. In his letter to Titus, "admonish them to be subject to princes and authorities, obeying commands, ready for every good work." [17] Having ordained human society, He

[16] Romans, 13:10.

[17] Titus, 3:1.

wants authority to exist, without which society is headless and soulless. The legitimate, constituted authority holds its mission to govern from God. From God it receives the grace to govern well, and it is God Who commands us to obey it, and to submit ourselves to its legitimate requirements is to obey God.

To be faithful to Divine Providence, let us be faithful to our duties as citizens. It is not sufficient not to oppose legitimate authority; we must recognize the powers which reside in it; we must collaborate in its effort with true loyalty; we must go along with its plans, provided they are not against the natural law and the commandments of God and the Church. Once again, when we place our confidence in the wisdom of our legitimate leaders, even beyond that which they order in strict obligation, we work within the designs of Divine Providence. The wisdom of governors, although fallible, comes from God as a providential grace.

By His commandments, by those of His Church, by the order of legitimate authority, God outlines the essential lines of the road prepared by Divine Providence. He further delineates the lines by His inspirations, which do not impose strict duties but nevertheless solicit our generosity.

For some there is the call to walk the way of the evangelical counsels. God asks them to be amidst Christian people as a light and a ferment, the living example of the pure spirit of the Gospel. All are not so called, although some callings are addressed to all, because they complete the commands of God. These are calls addressed to us by His Church.

The Catholic Church, instituted by Christ, sustained by His special guidance, is the official organ by which Christ communicates His divine intentions. Through the teaching Church Christ Himself teaches. When the Church outlines the road to travel, it is Christ, the supreme Shepherd, Who through His established ministers, leads the way for His flock.

How desirable it would be, dear brethren, if the nations were to be inspired by the thought of the Church! It is time that the world returns to wisdom, if it does not want to disintegrate in chaos. Yet we do not hesitate to say that it is on the condition of listening to the inspirations of the Church that the people will survive a universal disaster and bring the world to the ways of salvation. For in listening to the voice of the Church, especially to that of the Supreme Pastor, the Sovereign Pontiff, they will follow the ways of Divine Providence and will find wisdom.

Finally, if anyone believes himself the recipient of interior light and inspiration, let him control them by aligning himself with the directives of the Church.

God solicits us interiorly and exteriorly, but He demands of us, first of all, the fulfillment of His precepts. And when an inspiration proposes even a good work, but beyond our duty, the inspiration does not necessarily come from God. It may be dictated by presumption, or even by the devil who, under the appearance of a greater good, can turn us from the true path dictated by the duties of our state. Hence, such an inspiration is known to have come from God only if it is accompanied by interior peace and true humility; and humility is, in practice, obedience to the Church.

Finally, events themselves are a means of recognizing the will of God. Providence speaks through facts. As long as events are in the future, they remain the mystery of divine good-pleasure. But once they have happened, they reveal to us God's decisions. God's commandments, completed by those of the Church and legitimate authority, call for our obedience. God's inspirations call for our docility. And God's decisions through events demand our acceptance, although acceptance does not always manifest itself in the same manner. While imposing resignation under difficult circumstances, acceptance does not dispense us from correcting evil when we are able. And if we must accept the accomplished situation which has at its origin human injustice and even our own faults, we must not allow injustice to prevail nor dispense ourselves from a sincere contrition for our faults. We must always try to avoid a greater evil and turn aside as much as possible the evil consequences or change them to a good. We correct only what we accept with patience, without revolt and without useless recriminations. We correct effectively our faults only when we recognize the evil they have caused and accept their salutary lesson.

These are the sign-posts which Divine Providence prepares for us: the only path which is certain because it is the path by which God wants us to travel. Other roads might seem wide and easy. The easier they appear at the beginning, the more likely they are to end at an impasse. To advance stubbornly in this direction is to arrive at certain disaster sooner or later. Some day or another the events will provide obstacles against which there is no resistance. You might hope to by-pass the difficulties, but the will of God cannot be by-passed. Whoever butts against the Will of God will be shattered to pieces.

On the providential road, the beginnings might be very difficult, the paths rough, and Christ has told us they would be.[18] The road at certain times might lose itself in insurmountable difficulties, but always there is a way out: God Who leads us helps us find the way out and gives us the strength to reach the end.

Let us, dear brethren, those of us who have faith in Providence, fit this faith into our lives! Let us think often of Divine Providence. Let us pray to it, and without forsaking our activity, let us lean strongly upon it. We can abandon ourselves to it with confidence, if we serve it with courage.

To those who do not have such faith, let us persuade them at least that the government of the world, of which they can see only the faint outlines, is not the effect of pure chance, but the fruit of a beneficent activity which takes care of us all and expects of us generous collaboration.

[18] Matt., 7:13-14.

THE PARISH COMMUNITY

In our century the Holy See has established the charter of the Christian laity.

A whole world must be uplifted. And the whole Christian Community must give birth to a missionary movement: missionary in spirit and missionary in action.

We appeal for an apostolate. We invite all Christians to labor in bringing the world back to Jesus Christ.

The parish is the best site for the apostolate.

The Parish Community

Each year, at the beginning of Lent, it is customary for the Pastors to address their faithful in terms of the needs of the times. We have regularly fulfilled this duty. The various subjects which we have treated always have had some connection with the apostolate of souls. And it is fitting, too, for our mission among you consists above all in assuring the spread of the Gospel. The fear-inspiring phrase of St. Paul, "For woe is unto me if I preach not the gospel,"[1] applies especially to our responsibilities as Bishop. All those who, in the footsteps of the Apostles, govern the church of God, indeed are charged first of all with the salvation of souls through an enlightening of the hearts and minds of men.

Should not our faithful be kept informed of our thoughts, anxieties and hopes? We do not wish, dear Brethren, that you be ignorant of our plans. And first of all, we desire that you know the exact situation of Catholicism in the society in which you live, for we are relying on you to assist us in our apsotolic charge. You, too, have responsibilities. You, too, can render an eminent service in the propagation of the Truth. That is why the late Pope Pius XI so strongly urged the laity to the apostolate of souls.

To be sure, the faithful in all ages have cooperated with the evangelizing action of the clergy, but only in our century has the Holy See established, so to speak, the charter of the Christian laity. This magnificent work of Pius XI, which his successor, our Holy Father, Pope Pius XII, has adopted as his own, sets all Christianity in motion. It defines the form which the contemporary apostolate should normally assume. This is another reason for Pastors to keep contact with their people, in order to give them the necessary directives for a truly unified apostolic action.

The turmoil which we are now witnessing has confronted men's minds with grave problems. We are engaged in a gigantic struggle. A choice must be made between materialism and Christian or Christian-inspired spirituality. The hour approaches when it will be more difficult than ever to serve two

[1] I Cor., 9:16.

masters. Christians, you must be perspicacious in order to discover evil under the various names by which it goes. You must be courageous, choosing resolutely in favor of the Gospel and its teachings. Now, your all-important choice undoubtedly will be made in terms of your predominant attitudes, but even more in terms of the practical orientation which you have given your life. Thought, but thought complemented and enriched by action, will in the final analysis determine your choice.

We shall indicate the broad outlines of a unified action in which all of you are called to participate. We ask that you give us all of your attention. The success of the apostolic effort, which will influence the salvation of the country, depends in a large part on the answer which you give to the urgent appeal which we address to you.

A whole world must be uplifted. What does that matter, since it must be done! Let us call to mind the famous phrase which expresses the courage of the apostles and of the first Christians who had been sent out to conquer the world; "*Non admittit status fidei necessitates.*" "The state of faith allows no mention of impossibility." [2] That which is necessary must be accomplished. That is why we are launching our appeal! We would awaken in the minds, not only of believers but of all patriots, the salutary anxiety which will prepare the way for the resurrection. We would that all men speak often and in all social groups of the religious distress of the masses. We ask of the pastors of souls, whose mission it is to instruct and to warn, that they be the first to obey this command. We also ask that our word be taken up and repeated by all clearsighted Catholics who, because of their talents, their condition, or the integrity of their lives, enjoy a position of trust and honor in the eyes of the faithful as a whole.

As for our part, we shall strive not to fail in the duty which is incumbent upon us. "For Sion's sake I will not hold my peace." [3] So speaks the prophet Isaias. "Sion" represents the souls, all of whom grouped together make up heaven. "Sion" is

[2] Tertullian, *de corona*, c. 2.
[3] Is., 62:1.

the Church of Christ which affords refuge to the pilgrims we all are and guides us towards our goal. "Sion" is our native land, with its heritage of nobility and moral values, which are its force and the guarantee of its temporal and spiritual future. "*Propter Sion non tacebo.*" It is a misfortune to fall into despair, but it is an equally grave misfortune to base one's hopes on an illusion. Catholic opinion must be shocked out of its lethargy! Our faithful, once they have been warned, must firmly resolve to undertake everything possible to bring to Christ the souls for whom He is waiting.

THE MEANS OF REMEDY

The shock which we desire, dear Brethren, must take place first among the faithful, for the saving movement must radiate out from them. It is the duty of Christians to carry the Gospel to their brothers. It is the whole Christian community which, preserving the flame of its own spiritual life, must thereby become aware of the danger at hand, and devote its forces to saving the most abandoned souls! It must eradicate, within itself the slightest traces of religious individualism! It must give birth from within to a missionary movement, so that, by its united and persevering efforts, the wall of indifference may be broken down.

THE WHOLE CHRISTIAN COMMUNITY

Why the whole Christian community? First of all, because a work of this importance, in face of obstacles on all sides, requires action on the part of all. Also because we need to create a Christianizing environment, an environment favorable to conversions, which could not be obtained by isolated endeavors. On the other hand, these apostolic ideas, shared in common, will create a bond of charity among the faithful, will cause them all to live the Gospel more intensely. At the same time the conquering force of the Christian community will be increased ten-fold. Furthermore, if we are to reach the masses, we must necessarily penetrate all social groups, have direct contact with the individuals, study the habits and the attitudes of our brothers outside the fold, seek to discover by what approach Grace and the Gospel truths can be brought to them. Now, only the whole group of the faithful is capable of maintaining the daily contacts with the masses required by such an adaptation. And finally, if the Church is to make certain the salvation of all men, it becomes the duty of the Christian community—the daughter of the Church—to devote its efforts to the service of reChristianizing the masses.

A TRUE COMMUNITY

What, in this endeavor, is to be the task of the Christian community? First of all and without doubt, it must be a true community, i.e., not merely an artificial grouping of individuals, not a juxtaposition of isolated persons, who are joined together by a mere geographic or administrative tie, but a family, united by the bonds of a living, active charity. Although parish spirit and diocesan spirit do often exist, and even intensely among our Catholics, still we believe that in many cases there is much room for the development of both. We shall have to create among all men that fraternal union which alone can assure the victory of the Gospel: by the same token we must bring an end to rivalries between classes, groups, vested interests, and egoisms, which so often destroy all harmony and paralyze our efforts. In addition, this apostolic action carried out in common will contribute to bringing about a re-grouping of our forces, a new departure of God's chosen ones toward the promised land of a new Christianity. For we intend to ask that the Christian community be filled with a missionary zeal: missionary in spirit and missionary in action.

MISSIONARY IN SPIRIT

Now, those Catholics, who are convinced that they are God's envoys can be called "missionaries in spirit," in virtue of their Baptism and the mandate of their Confirmation. Missionaries in Spirit! Those who remember that the whole Gospel story is a missionary story. The Gospel tells the story of a Divine Savior, Who came on earth to snatch men from ignorance and spiritual death; the story of a God Who spent His life on earth in calling men to penance, i.e., to conversion; the story of a God Who joined to Himself human collaborators destined to continue His work until the end of time; the story of a God Who cures bodies to save souls; the story of a God Who rejoices more over the conversion of one sinner than over the preservation of ninety-nine just men; the story of a God Who will be satisfied only when all men will have returned to the Father in the unity of life and the embrace of heavenly love.

Missionaries in spirit are those who, when observing the disbelief of the masses and reflecting on the consequences of this disbelief, are stirred within as was St. Paul when, entering Athens, he saw the city given over to idolatry.[4]

Missionaries in spirit are those who, following in the footsteps of the Master, have learned to respect and love the men who—if they only had the light—would be true sons of God. Missionaries in spirit are those who note on the first page of their Christian agenda the conversion of souls, especially the conversion of those who are nearest to them geographically.

Finally, missionaries in spirit are those who are not satisfied with desires, regrets, intentions, but who go on to acts, and who have decided to be missionaries in fact—in the practical part of their life.

The whole Christian community must go this far! Only at this price will it find itself again and live in accord with the Gospel.

THE TASK OF EACH

Cannot all members of this community be missionaries, if they so desire? Cannot each Christian take upon himself the task of converting one soul, then another, then a third? By attacking with prayers, sacrifices, kindnesses and timely interventions, cannot he count on success? Is it not possible for any baptized person to aid materially and spiritually the lay or cleri-

[4] Acts, 17:16.

cal apostles whose official mission it is to work for the conversion of the masses? We are thinking here of the groups of Catholic workers, youths and adults of both sexes, whom we should like to see active in all our parishes and who, thanks be to God, are already numerous in our diocese. During the past year did they not in a definitely deChristianized suburb reach and group together more than five hundred working girls? Elsewhere have they not reaped a harvest of scores of Baptisms and retarded first communions? But such actions and the young people who have shown so much zeal for the saving of souls do merit our encouragement, interest, affection and comprehension.

Each Catholic should desire to bring together specialized groups, or at least the various groups of "Catholic Action" (in the broad sense), within which, moreover, all the faithful should assemble themselves, whether they be members of movements or not. Without harming the necessary autonomies of specialization, such a re-grouping of the whole militant Christian community on the level of the parish and the diocese is an indispensable instrument for action. We ask, in addition, that all our groups place on their program a very precise missionary objective. We advise members of our diocese to support and, if need be, to create institutions capable of helping and guaranteeing the success of this evangelization of souls: welfare societies, centers for social and family action. Above all, to our Catholic families as well as to all our faithful we recommend the program for recruiting vocations and for giving the clergy missionary training, which affects the success of any apostolic program.

Finally, we are counting on the wisdom of the members of our diocese and on the reactions of Christians and sympathizing public opinion, in order that—without privilege or favor—France of tomorrow may be endowed with human institutions which are morally healthy and Christian inspired and which make possible the free flowering of religious values while respecting freedom of conscience. We ask that in the future the State consider the Christian faith as a treasure to be safeguarded, not as something superfluous to be eliminated. We ask that Christian ethics become the basis of social life and that, therefore, the problems of recreation, housing, religious civic planning be studied by competent men who are interested in the spiritual future of our country.

UNDER THE HOLY SPIRIT

We have not said anything, dear Brethren, concerning the apostolate, however, if we have not insisted on the fact that the Christian community must of necessity be quickened by a powerful spirit of love and a burning thirst after justice: in short, by that Gospel spirit which makes the true face of Christ shine forth. The most fruitful epochs of the life of the Church were those in which this spirit animated the masses of believers. The whole ecclesiastical community was then on the march.

Let us think of the early times of our Christian era, when young and old, slaves and masters, soldiers and merchants, Romans and Jews, Greeks and Barbarians—all faced with the same dangers of persecutions and martyrdom, rivaled with each other in zeal for the propagation of the faith. Burning with love for the Risen Christ, whose spiritual triumph they wished, they all were conquerors. Their testimony, sealed with their blood, changed the face of the world and vanquished paganism.

Let us think of the times called the "centuries of faith," when one often imagines the Church to have been at rest and enjoying a sort of tranquil hegemony over the world. On the contrary, the Church was menaced, under attack, and owed her force solely to the very bitter struggle which she was forced to wage against a multitude of enemies.

Let us think of the century of St. Louis, which was a century of crusades, i.e., another century of missions, inasmuch as Louis de Poissy, Francis of Assisi, Dominic of Guzman, Thomas Aquinas were convertors more than combattants. In spite of the roughness of their manners, the Crusaders, lords or leiges, rich or poor, priests or laity were all quickened by the same love of Christ and by the same desire to base His royalty on their common effort.

Our troubled times demand that souls once more be moved by the same breath of the Spirit. If it is to subsist, the entire Christian community must become active. A new surge must be imparted to it. Our very trials, through which God warns us to have recourse to His mercy, can make it possible for us to become the artisans of a magnificent religious renaissance.

THE WILL OF GOD

Indeed, if everything commands us to have recourse to God, in this need lies a deep reason for us to turn towards an apostolate of conquest. For, to have recourse to God is not only to pray to God, but it is also to take up the divine cause and defend it; it is also to accomplish, in so far as we are able, that which we know will be the Will of God. Now, there can be no doubt that in the present state of affairs, God's Will is that the world be freed from the materialism in which it is engulfed, and that the moral ruins, which are infinitely more dangerous than the material ruins, be repaired.

God's Will is that we consent to a powerful effort to bring back to Christ a world which is His heritage and which, be it through negligence, forgetfullness or malignity, has been stolen away from His influence. God's Will is that souls should endeavor, in order to bring relief to their suffering, to make use of the supernatural resources of their tribulations to accomplish this renaissance. God's Will is that the Church be defended by all Christians and that at no time and in no place should she be forced to suffer an eclipse which would endanger her vitality. God's Will, above all, is that Christians, following the example of Christ, stop nothing short of the total gift of themselves in the apostolate of their neighbor, since "Greater love than this no man hath, that a man lay down his life for his friends." [5]

That is why, in face of the evils which menace us and aware of the resources of generosity and devotion which are innate in our faithful, we confidently launch our appeal for the apostо-

[5] John, 15:13.

late. We ask that all Christians labor to bring the world back to Jesus Christ.

PRAYER AND BROTHERLY LOVE

In closing let us state more precisely some of the means for carrying out this apostolate.

Let prayer have the first and foremost place in it! The conversion of souls is a divine work. Those who are successful in it are those who are united with God, who maintain themselves in a divine atmosphere. By this prayer let us implore the Almighty for the cessation of the evils from which the world is suffering, the end of discord, vengeance, fratricidal struggle, the trials which are added to the tribulations of war and occupation. But above all let us pray for God to make certain the triumph of Christ and His Church. That is the only prayer worthy of a Christian.

May the members of the Christian community join action to their prayer! The apostle is a witness. When he acts under the guidance of Christ he bears witness to Christ.

To their prayer and their action may the members of the Christian community join a sincere love, a deep respect for their brothers of the working class, who are often separated from us and who must be won back to Christ. Let our faithful recognize the often unjustified suffering, the constantly increasing difficulties, the uncertainty of the morrow, which are the lot of the laboring classes! May these sentiments of brotherly love be expressed by acts, by an interest in mutual aid, by participation in any public or private initiative whose aim is to raise up the conditions of our suffering brothers. In short, may the social teachings of the Church be better known and applied in so far as possible! How can we ask that religion and Christian ethics be practiced by individuals or families who have neither home nor a minimum of material resources needed to make this practice possible.

THE PARISH

Furthermore, all should be convinced that the parish is the best site for the apostolate. This institution—the first cell in the life of the diocese—is providentially commissioned to unite souls to the Body of the Church. In addition it is provided with the required organization for penetrating the masses. From this it follows that a living, active parish community, which is coherent in its activities, and strongly united with the diocese in which the plenitude of the priesthood and apostolic ministry resides, is the incomparable instrument for the expansion of the Christian life. But for all that, the organisms which the parish has at its disposal must be regularly oriented towards the apostolate, and the parishioners must be called often to this primordial task. Further, as important as they may be, especially in areas where religious practice is abundant, the administrative and cultural tasks must never become an obstacle to the clergy and the faithful in fulfilling their missionary duty. Is this not the time to call to mind the urgent invitation of Pope Pius XI: ". . . any other endeavor, no matter how beautiful or good, must give way before the vital necessity of saving the very bases of the faith and of Christian civilization. Therefore, let the priests in the parishes reserve the greater and the best part of their strength and of their activities for the task of winning the laboring masses back to Christ and to the Church and of bringing the Christian spirit into the groups which are most foreign to it." [6]

OUTSIDE THE PARISH

Unfortunately, there are some groups which the parish cannot reach. Let us frankly admit that there is a considerable part of our population which remains impermeable to its influence. Either because of indifference, ignorance, or the individual or collective distrust of the Christian community, the Gospel message cannot be brought to these people by the ordinary methods

[6] Pius XI, *Divini Redemptoris,* No. 62.

of the apostolate. This does not mean, however, that either zeal or sanctity are lacking to those who utilize these methods. The present routine of the parish—the time which our clergy is duty-bound to devote to the service of the faithful—sometimes make it impossible for our priests to seek the most distant of those who have wandered from the flock or are not of it. Thus we insist while the parish will preserve all its rights, and must even be re-inforced in its apostolic resources, that there must be joined to it certain organizations outside the parish which will, however, work in accord with the parishes. Their aim will be to accomplish a work of missionary penetration.

We wish success to all attempts which are going to be made along these lines. We approve them. We encourage them. In so far as the pioneers of these organizations come supported by our authority, we desire that they be warmly received and be given assistance.

If our recommendations are heeded, we have reasons to believe that, since you are equipped with a doctrine, a method, well-adapted institutions and especially with a spirit, the work to which we have called you will be crowned with success.

ALL ARE CALLED

In closing, dear brethren, without forgetting that we base our hopes on the Christian community, it seems we should place ourselves on a broader ground. We turn to all who wish a resurrection of our country; even to those who do not today share our beliefs or do not actively adhere to the life of the Church, we say "Take notice, Reflect, Come to our aid!"

Take Notice. At the beginning of the encyclical, "Mystici Corporis," His Holiness, Pius XII, urges us to open the eyes of our souls: "When kingdoms and states fall, when immense resources and riches of all sorts are swallowed up in the depths of the ocean, when the cities, the villages and fertile countrysides are strewn with gigantic ruins and soiled by fratricidal struggles," [7] and when the bankruptcy of systems and ideologies is

[7] Pius XII, *Mystici Corporis.*

consummated on the ruins of the nations, then men, by contrast, are inclined to contemplate the Catholic Church.

They see this society of souls which remains intact throughout the storms of the ages more serene and more united than ever, preserving intact her God-given doctrine, looking down from on high on our present life while at the same time offering a priceless remedy for the evils here below. They see that she alone offers a solution capable of satisfying the desire for social justice which all of us have. They see that she alone can substitute brotherly understanding for the struggle between classes, nations, races.

Reflect! Does not this Church, so peaceful and shining in tortured times, have the word of life which will bring salvation to the world? Can you not at least consider her as an irreplaceable factor in our national renaissance? Do you not find that social and political materialism has shown its worth? That an era of spirituality must be begun at all costs? To reach that goal, you cannot leave aside the Church! That is why, in the depths of your hearts, which are so moved by suffering, separations, mourning and captivity, you feel that perhaps many standards of values must be revised. Why not, then, shake off the last bonds which hold you far from us? If you are tempted to despair, do you not know that faith can save you? If you have energy and sincerity (and we do not doubt that you have), why not cast off the errors of the past? Why not seek in the light of faith the fervor which can cause an ardor that can give life a full meaning to triumph over sarcasms and doubt?

Then, *Come to our aid!* Come, swell the ranks of those who, by word of mouth, with pen, by influence, by all the means at hand, wish to contribute to a defense and restoration of Christianity in our country!

If it be thus, then the appeal which we are launching will, by grouping in one clan believers, sympathizers, and nonbelievers who are seeking the light, accomplish along with the missionary task, the indispensable though difficult task of working in the service of a cause which is certainly that of our country.

THE CHURCH ON PRIVATE PROPERTY

Private Property guarantees man's freedom. It is the guarantee of the family, and it is required for the welfare of all as one of the fundamental conditions of man's union in a temporal society.

But the common good sets limits to the use of private property.

Whoever will compare the teaching of the Church on Property either with the excesses of Capitalism or with Marxism will conclude a change is necessary.

We look to some reforms of structure.

Contents

The Church On Private Property

In our last letter we invited the Christian community to imbue itself with a missionary spirit in order to give Christ back to the masses who ignore Him. The missionary apostolate of the proletariat must be accomplished through social reforms which change the way of life. Inhuman conditions of life are, for most men, incompatible with the practice of a Christian life. So the Church formally teaches. And this is why we address you today on one of the most important subjects worth considering in any reform of structure in the defense of Christian civilization, namely, the subject of private property.

First of all, we will tell you why the Church defends every man's right to own property; then, how she condemns the present excesses of Capitalism, with all their consequences. Finally, we will tell you what the Church asks of her children.

I. THE CHURCH DEFENDS THE RIGHT OF OWNERSHIP

The Catholic Church defends the right of ownership. It is a right rooted in the dignity of man as well as in the common good.

Inferior creation has been made for man who has the right to appropriate it. We see in the universe that matter nourishes plant and animal life, both of which are infinitely more precious in their fragility than all inanimate things. On the other hand, a single thought and a single act of love are worth more than the whole order of material or even living material things. This is so because God is Spirit; He is Love, and man—created in the image of God—is capable of thinking and loving. God even handed over part of His sovereign domain to man: "The earth and all that it contains is the Lord's,"[1] but the Lord gave the plants to man and wished him to dominate all the animals. All of this is *for* man, so that *through* man, who is capable of knowing and loving His God, material creation might be returned to its Creator.

If man has the right to use material things, plants and an-

[1] Pius XII, *Christmas Message*, 1942.

imals for his livelihood, he has the right to appropriate them. His existence as a man requires it. The animal is content to satisfy its hunger at the moment and with what is at hand, but man, who is capable of looking to the future and endowed with initiative and freedom, gives a direction to his life. To live as a man means to manage one's life, and this first of all by looking after future needs by labor. Each man has the strict right to provide by his labor the wherewithal for his subsistence.

To live as a human being man must look beyond the present moment. Because his intellect can foresee and prepare for the future (and in so doing, conform to the image of Divine Providence) man has a strict right to ownership. In his own right he should possess those goods he uses to live humanly, such as clothes, food, shelter, which are called utilities; and in a civilized country, he should possess the financial means to procure them. To do this he must be able to maintain savings and sometimes even own the tools of his labor, without which he is not assured his next day's livelihood.

No one can live humanly unless he has access to a certain amount of *personal* property. Let us add, *family* property. Man is inseperable from the family to which he is born, and in turn, from the family which he founds. Not only must he assure life to himself, but also the future of his children. Unless he do so he will not be truly the head of the family, as is his right and duty—for the good of his family.

Private property assures the father of the family the freedom he needs to fulfill his duties and look after the physical, spiritual and religious welfare of the family. More than anything else a small piece of land and a house—the living space for a family—are desirable, Pope Pius XII says,[2] which by their stability, moreover, assure the coherence and progress of successive generations. Here is established the right of transmission of

[2] Discourse on the occasion of the anniversary of the encyclical *Rerum Novarum*, June 1, 1941. "Today the idea of "espace vital" and the creation of such areas is at the center of social and political goals: but must one not, before anything else, think of the "espace vital" of the family and liberate these families from bonds creating conditions of life which do not permit it even to conceive the idea of a house for itself?"

material goods by inheritance. Often these material goods bring with them a whole treasure of spiritual, moral and cultural riches, which permit new development for future generations.

We conclude that property, personal and family, and some tools of production are indispensable to the human person. Each person has this right, and the right is rooted in man's nature, i.e., it comes from God the Creator. To cease having this right, man would cease to be a man.

Man is permitted to renounce for a higher motive the rights which he holds from nature. For the sake of God man can renounce his right to found a home; he can also totally renounce his right to personal possession or personal ownership in order to better serve the Lord. This is the object of the vow of poverty. Like the complete chastity of the priest, religious poverty is legitimate. Yet because a real renouncement is envolved, and more than a human one, God does not impose it. He invites men to it in an exceptional vocation which must be free.

On the other hand, one man or a group of men may not take from other men what belongs to them by natural right. The misery of a proletarian, who is often deprived of today's necessities and destitute of tomorrow's reserves—the insecurity to which such a man is condemned, not only his own insecurity but also that of his family—constitutes an inhuman and unjust condition. *No more proletarians; all property owners:* this must be the slogan of those striving to restore society to a true human and Christian basis.

Private property guarantees man's freedom. It protects the family. Moreover, it is required for the welfare of all, as one of the fundamental conditions of the union of men in a temporal society. We must assert this, for the Church must not be understood to protect any form of individualism—be it of persons or of families—in her defense of private property.

Individualism is a type of lie for Christians. An individualist acts as though he were self-sufficient, when he neither can nor ought to be. Is not human dignity, in the first place, based on the fact that man—in the image of God—is able to know and love, and therefore, is called to live with other men? God so wished it both in the order of nature and in the order of Grace. Thus it is impossible for a person and a human family to develop and fulfill their natural and supernatural vocation so long as they are not interested in the welfare of other persons and other families.

Man is too weak to live among his fellowmen without need for them. His destiny is too exalted to be attained without dependence on other men or without serving other men. Private property, therefore, should be condemned when it implies individualism, and such a condemnation is all the more necessary insofar as God has placed the goods of His creation at the disposal of all. Such is the natural end God has given to created goods. All other rights remain subordinated, says Pius XII, to the first and fundamental right which reserves the use of goods to all men. No, private property does not necessitate individualism, but on the contrary . . .

While the common good, first of all, claims the existence of private property, it also sets limits on its use. Sinful man can abuse the right, although the right permits men to serve their fellowmen fraternally. Such is the teaching of the Church. Natural law requires, above all, something other than that all men achieve a state of enjoyment of the goods of the earth. *The common good calls private property the most capable means of assuring, in a manner worthy of man, the distribution of all the good to all the people.*

We must say this, first of all, with respect to *the means of production*. The question is how to obtain from the means of production the best return for everyone's benefit. Experience shows that in most instances private property and private management obtain the best results. Personal interest fosters care and initiative, fixes responsibility, and casts aside a multiplicity of authorities disposed to disorder. Thus the Church decrees that because of the natural end of created goods, private property and privately owned means of production should be the norm. This is the Why of it, then, not only in order that the freedom of man be guaranteed in his work, but also in the interest of the common good, which is better served by an initiative coming from personal interest.

The common good which establishes the "norm," however, may call for exceptions. "Certain categories of goods' require "reservation to collective ownership." There is much current talk of "nationalizing," i.e., of substituting collective public property in the place of private property. If it is a question of gearing certain production in view of the general interest "toward the most production and at the best possible selling price," [3] if, in short, it is a question of assuring the production of goods necessary to the life of the group through better management, nationalization can be legitimate, on the assumption that it can be worked out technically.

Pope Pius XI, moreover, expressly foresees the possibility of nationalizing certain enterprises where private property has a social power which belongs to public authority alone. For example, proposals for nationalizing the armament industry, or public utilities, such as railroads. Since it is an extreme solution, it must be justified in each separate case and it must avoid the double danger of injustice and state-socialism. The dispossessed owners have a strict right to compensation. In these tasks the state must be the watchdog of its proper duty without absorbing economic life.

Finally, the common good concurs with the dignity of man in calling for the private ownership of goods of every category. The ancients discovered that there could be no happiness in the city without friendship, and the Christian "who knows the value of the human person and loves him with God and for God" [4] knows what true friendship is. It is Charity in its highest meaning. Will a certain rationalism which thought to sub-

[3] Muller, *Notes d'Economie Politique*, 1st serie, book 4, chap. 2. Here is the whole definition of Fr. Muller: "Nationalization or Socialization is the gradual transfer of production from the domain of individual economy, ordered toward private interest, to the domain of the national economy, ordered to the general interest, having as its objective the greatest production with the best market price obtainable."

[4] D. Lallement, *Principes catholiques d'action civique*, 3rd ed., p. 103.

stitute justice for charity now substitute hate for social friendship? When this happens, the city will collapse in disorder.

To those who, in their desire for a more friendly city, sometimes dream of suppressing private property as a source of selfish and intolerable hoarding, we say "Beware." Must we suppress everything open to abuse? Must we suppress freedom? Must we suppress life? Beware, lest in combatting selfishness you set up in the economic order an obstacle to the effective exercise of brotherly love, which is the sole antidote to selfishness. What will he give who no longer has anything of his own? In the temporal order private property is the solid basis of social love. Justice renders to another what belongs to him; to each his due. Charity gives to another—treated as another self—what is good for oneself. The worst whittling of human dignity to which certain classical conceptions of collectivism would lead would be to deprive man of the opportunity of being the source of benefactions. Charity would cease in the earthly city, not only because the struggle would build up hatred in hearts but also because love could no longer regulate the use of material goods. And joy would disappear, the joy of giving. "It is more blessed to give than to receive," [5] as Christ tells us. This is, moreover, the joy of the very poor who are often the most generous.

Let us conclude with our Holy Father, Pius XII, who took up the words of Leo XIII and Pius XI that "the whole normal economic social order must rest on the solid basis of the right of private property." The Church has "always recognized the natural right of property and the transmission by inheritance of private goods." She cannot accept "a social order which denies in principle or makes practically impossible or empty the natural right of property, as much for goods in use as for the means of production." There is "a vital function of private property in its personal and social role." The state, therefore, must respect and protect it, and one should be able to work for the real acquisition of property—"all this for the temporal and transcendant ends of life, and as a consequence, for the

[5] Acts, 20:35.

benefit of the freedom and dignity of man created in the likeness of God." [6]

We see the point of view of the Church in such matters. She follows, continues the Pope, "a high objective at the same time social and moral." When she undertakes the defense of property, it is man's life she defends, the possibility for man to fulfill his destiny. The Church wishes man to create for himself and for his family "a domain of just freedom not only in economic but also in political, cultural and religious matters." Private property is but the means to this objective. We should remember this when after having shown what the Church protects, we show what she condemns.[7]

[6] Radio Message, Sept. 1, 1944, *Documentation Catholique*, Nov. 12, 1944, p. 3.

[7] The social and individual aspects of private property were explained by Pope Pius XI in the Encyclical *Quadragesimo Anno:* "First, let it be made clear beyond all doubt that neither Leo XIII, nor those theologians who have taught under the guidance and direction of the Church, have ever denied or called in question the twofold aspect of ownership, which is individual or social accordingly as it regards individuals or concerns the common good. Their unanimous contention has always been that the right to own property has been given to man by nature or rather by the Creator Himself, not only in order that individuals may be able to provide for their own needs and those of their families, but also by means of it, the goods which the Creator has destined for the human race may truly serve this purpose. Now, these ends cannot be secured unless some definite and stable order is maintained."

In his *Petit Manuel des questions contemporaines*, Cardinal Verdier has summed up the Church's thought as follows:

"1) It is from his nature and therefore from God, the author of that nature, that man has received the right of private property.

"Some property is necessary to man:

"a) for the true realization of his individual life, since we can say that man can freely develop his personality only through the objects over which he has control, and on the other hand, he can secure his future, uniting to the present and to the past as his nature demands, only with the enduring possession of some sort of goods;

"b) for the true constitution of the family. Without the possession of goods he cannot in effect secure by *himself* the well-being and the future of his family. Now, it is only thus that he is the true head of the family; because in this way only he is truly the artisan of the family's future.

"c) because without private property the goods of this world would be too *imperfectly managed*. Each of us gives more easily his care and efforts

II. THE CHURCH CONDEMNS THE EXCESSES OF MODERN CAPITALISM

When the Church defends or condemns, she shows no preferences, either economic or political.

Although politicians are inclined to attribute a "human interpretation" to the Church, one would be totally misled if he believed that the Church would ever be opportunistic in order to avoid the worst of popular demands. Nothing resembles a "human interpretation" less than the condemnations of the Church directed against all errors, without fear of making enemies.

Through Pius XI the Church has condemned the excesses of Capitalism; she has condemned Nazism and atheistic Communism. In the field of doctrine she has but one policy, Truth, eternal and for all. Truth is the first condition of her mission of Charity. Hence, she will never cease, for opportunistic motives, to maintain the right of ownership; but neither will she always accept "purely and simply the actual state of affairs." [8] The principle of Truth commands both decisions.

One would also be misled if he suspected the Church of attaching herself to an economic doctrine. For if she did, she would immediately be accused of being either out of date or Utopian, depending on her condemnation of irresponsible projects or abuses of the moment. The Church has no economic doctrine in the modern sense of the term. She refuses to intervene in the technical domain, since, as Pius XI has said, she has "neither the equipment nor the mission." [9] The Church has a moral and spiritual doctrine, with consequences in every

---

to those things which are his own. In addition, the double destiny, individual and social, of this world's goods would not be sufficiently realized. When private property in its social aspect is well managed, it is the most beneficent.

"2) Some private property is *needed for progress*, because the prospect of obtaining for himself and family a greater amount of goods and thus a higher social dignity is after all, the best incentive to work."

[8] Radio message, Sept. 1, 1944.

[9] Pius XI. *Quadragesimo Anno*, 41.

aspect of human life—economic as well as political. In the name of these moral principles, and because she has the mission to sanctify the whole man, the Church raises her voice above competitive interests. By this fact alone she reminds us that the fulfillment of man's vocation must surpass all considerations of technique.[10] Thus it is that the Church questions whether present-day Capitalism permits man to accomplish his proper vocation, and she answers No. She condemns the disorder in the capitalistic system.

Nevertheless, the Church does not condemn Capitalism in itself, but rather the abuse of it. "Its structure is not evil," says Pius XI, but in its actual practice the human dignity of the worker and the requirements of the common good, i.e., of justice, have been sacrificed to Capital.[11] The Church will always rise up against all attempts against human dignity and justice. This is part of her mission. For this reason Pius XII, in his

[10] After Leo XIII and Pius XI, Pope Pius XII thus states the right of the Church to instruct and to judge in the social order. (*Discourse*, June 1, 1941): "The competence of the Church is incontestable in that part of the social order which touches upon morals, so as to judge whether the bases of a given social organization are conformable to the unalterable order of things which God has manifested by natural law and revelation, a double manifestation by Leo XIII in his encyclical." And this with reason: "The principles of natural law and revealed truths come to us through different ways, like two converging yet non-contrary currents from the same divine source; and the Church guardian of the supernatural Christian order in which nature and grace are united, has as her mission the formation of Christian consciences, consciences of those who are called to find the solutions for the problems and duties imposed by social life. The good or the evil of souls depends upon and develops with the form given to society according to its conformity to or conflict with divine laws. Before such consideration how could the Church, a mother so loving and so solicitous for the good of her sons, permit herself to remain indifferent to their dangers, to keep silence or to act as if she did not see or understand the social conditions which, voluntarily or not, make the conformity of Christian conduct to the commandments of the Sovereign Legislator a goal arduous and practically impossible of fulfillment?"

[11] Pius XI, *Quadragesimo Anno*, 101. "The Capitalistic system," writes Pope Pius XI, "is not vicious of its very nature, but it violates right order . . . Leo XIII's whole endeavor was to adjust this economic system to the standards of true order; when it follows that in itself it is not to be condemned."

turn, has said "there where Capitalism . . . claims unlimited rights presumptuously . . . apart from subordination to human rights, there the Church has always reproved it as being contrary to natural law." [12]

The same natural law reasons which underly private property and its defense by the Church also oblige the Church to condemn, first of all, the unjust distribution of riches in present-day Capitalism. Every man must have at his disposal the material goods necessary for his own life and that of his family.

Let us recall the protests of Pius XI. Never before, he said, has such an abundance of riches been created as in our industrial epoch, and yet never before have so many men been deprived of their security. The existence of that "immense sea of the proletariat" in contrast to "a handful of the rich endowed with enormous resources . . . attest to the fact that the wealth is unequally distributed." [13]

Pius XII today denounces "the exaggerated accumulation of wealth which under the cover of anonymity succeeds in deserting its social role" as one of the causes which "practically puts the worker outside the class of those who can actually attain to some property." [14] We cannot repeat often enough

[12] Radio message, Sept. 1, 1944.

[13] Pius XI, *Quadragesimo Anno*, 61. The Church also asks for a better distribution of wealth which permits the ordinary worker to obtain property: it is the sole means of removing him from his miserable condition. "Every effort, therefore, must be made that at least in the future only a just share of the fruits of production be permitted to accumulate in the hands of the wealthy, and that an ample sufficiency be supplied to the workingmen. The purpose is not that these become slack at their work, for man is born to labor as the bird to fly, but that by thrift they may increase their possessions and by the prudent management of the same may be enabled to bear the family burden with greater ease and the security, being freed from that hand-to-mouth uncertainty which is the lot of the proletarian. Thus they will not only be in a position to support life's changing fortunes, but will also have the reassuring confidence that when their lives are ended, some little provision will remain for those whom they leave behind them," writes Pius XI.

[14] Radio message, Sept. 1, 1944. Apropos of the distribution of wealth Pope Pius XI writes in *Quadragesimo Anno*, 57: "Now, not every kind of distribution of wealth and property among men is such that it can at all and still less can adequately attain the end intended by God. Wealth,

that the right of property is not the right of monopoly; that the monopoly is directed against the right of ownership; that the laborer has a right to the fruit of his labor, and that he can renounce this right against a fixed salary, as is the general case today. He cannot, however, renounce this against an insufficient salary which would lower his personal and family living to a sub-human level.[15]

Let us note the categorical affirmations of Pius XI: "It violates right order whenever Capital so employs the workers or the propertyless class so as to divert business and economic

---

therefore, which is constantly being augmented by social and economic progress, must be so distributed among the various individuals and classes of society that the common good of all, of which Leo XIII spoke, be thereby promoted. In other words, the good of the whole community must be safeguarded. By these principles of social justice one class is forbidden to exclude the other from a share in the profits. This sacred law is violated by a wealthy class who, as it were carefree in their possessions, deem it a just state of things that they should receive anything and the laborer nothing."

"It is violated also by a propertyless wage-earning class who demand for themselves all the fruits of production, as being the work of their hands. Such men, vehemently incensed against the violation of justice by capitalists, go too far in vindicating the one right of which they are conscious; they attack and seek to abolish all forms of ownership and all income not obtained by labor, whatever be the nature or function these represent in human society, for the sole reason that they are not acquired by toil."

[15] The celebrated passage of *Rerum Novarum*, 34, to which he refers, must be given here:

"Therefore, a man's labor has two notes or characters. First of all, it is *personal;* for the exertion of individual power belongs to the individual who puts it forth, employing this power for that personal profit for which it was given. Secondly, a man's labor is *necessary;* for without the results of labor a man cannot live; and self-conservation is a law of nature, which it is wrong to disobey. Now, if we were to consider labor merely so far as it is personal, doubtless it would be within the worker's right to accept any rate of wages whatever; for in the same way as he is free to work or not, so he is free to accept a small remuneration or even none at all. But this is a mere abstract supposition; the labor of the workingman is not only his personal attribute, but it is necessary; and this makes all the difference. The preservation of life is the bounden duty of each and all, and to fail therein is a crime. It follows that each one has a right to procure what is required in order to live; and the poor can procure it in no other way than by work and wages."

activity entirely to its own arbitrary will and advantage, without any regard to the human dignity of the workers, the social character of economic life, social justice, and the common good." [16] And showing what higher principles govern his attitude, the Pope adds: "the actual conditions of economic and social life are such that a very large number of men find it impossible to accomplish the one work necessary—salvation." "For dead matter leaves the factory ennobled and transformed, whereas men are corrupted and degraded." [17]

In modern Capitalism the Church does not condemn only the monopolizing of wealth and the oppression of the masses. She also condemns particular interests when they are opposed to the common good. The opposition comes into being on the industrial level. Capital is but one of the contributing factors of business; indeed, it is not the first in dignity. The administration of a capitalistic undertaking, Christian employers tell us, is almost always inevitably directed to the financial interest involved—to the detriment of the workers, management itself, and often the consumer.

Disadvantages on the national and international level are no less. The modern super-capitalistic system gives enormous power to a few, first economic, then political.[18] Once again Pius XI denounces that abuse with an unforgettable vigor:

[16] Pius XI, *Quadragesimo Anno,* 101.

[17] Ibid., 135.

[18] Pius XI writes on this subject in *Quadragesimo Anno,* 105, 106, 107 & 109.

"It is patent that in our days not alone is wealth accumulated, but immense power and despotic economic domination are concentrated in the hands of a few, and that those few are frequently not the owners, but only the trustees and directors of invested funds, which they administer at their good pleasure.

"This domination becomes particularly irresistible when exercised by those who, because they hold and control money, are able to govern credit and determine its allotment, for that reason supplying, so to speak, the life blood to the entire economic body, and grasping, as it were, in their hands the very soul of production, so that no one dare breathe against their will.

"This accumulation of resources and power, the characteristic note of the modern economic order, is a natural result of limitless free competition which permits the survival of those only who are the strongest, which

"This concentration of power has in turn led to a three-fold struggle. First, there is the struggle for dictatorship in the economic sphere itself, then a fierce battle to acquire control of the State, in order that its resources and authority might be abused in the economic struggles. Finally, there is a clash between nations themselves—unbridled ambition for domination has succeeded the desire for gain; the whole economic life has become hard, cruel and relentless in a ghastly way. Finally, the State, which should be the supreme arbiter—ruling in a kingly fashion far above all party contention, intent only upon justice and the common good—has instead become a slave," signed over to "the service of human passion and greed." [19]

If private property has the dignity of the person and the common good as its foundations, modern Capitalism, the oppressor of the masses and forgetful of the common good, becomes its own condemnation. To all, as Pius XI says elsewhere, "it is an unjust economic regime which has played havoc for several generations." [20] We bear the heritage of these errors.

Perhaps one can say that the Church has one last reproach against modern Capitalism, namely, to have generated Marxism, which is another excess no less dangerous. Yet Marxism, in effect, reveals the basic error which it shares with Capitalism, despite other differences: *materialism.*

Marxism presents itself to the uninitiated, first of all, as a counter-measure against the domination of man over man. It makes an effort to liberate the proletariat from those whom it calls their exploiters. It wishes to aid all those whom Pius XII declares are "victims of a deplorable economic and social regime." [21]

---

often means those who fight most relentlessly, who pay least heed to the dictates of conscience. . . .

"Unbridled ambition for domination has succeeded the desire for gain; the whole economic life has become hard, cruel, and relentless in a ghastly way."

[19] Ibid., 109.

[20] Pius XI, *Divini Redemptoris,* (on Atheistic Communism), 50.

[21] Radio Message, Sept. 1, 1944.

Thus Marxism openly enrolls the dispossessed class as the new army of the total revolution, an all-embracing revolution since it strikes at those on the very lowest layers of society who, because they own nothing, have nothing to conserve.

There are, then, some good aspects at the base of this doctrine which, unhappily, can in no way at all be the appropriate remedy for the present social disorder.

As indeed so often happens in fighting a doctrine, the adversary makes use of the inner principle of that very doctrine he is attacking; in his battle he accepts the battle-ground of the enemy and even the weapons the enemy has chosen. In the case in point here, Marxism, in its struggle against Capitalism, borrows the capitalistic conceptions of the world and of human destiny. For both, these conceptions are materialistic.

The Church denounces certain errors in Marxist socialism, which, as Pius XI says, also foster the domination of man over man.[22] Without doubt she condemns the revolutionary method inasmuch as it is based on injustice and hate, that is, sin. The welfare of man, whose destiny is spiritual, cannot be obtained through sin. In Marxism the Church once again condemns the attacks against private ownership, which are effective attempts against the freedom and dignity of the person,[23] The Church insists both on the "Primacy of the Spiritual" and the "Primacy of the Person." But the root of the whole evil is that Marxism, like Capitalism, supposes a human society "constituted only in view of one's material well-being." Is it because the founders of Marxism were linked through their family origins to the German Bourgeoisie, whose economic liberalism made secure in their time its enrichment and social predominance? Neither Marx nor Engels ever doubted that the proper task of man on earth was the exploitation of economic riches in order to transform the world.

As a result, the requirements of production became law. Since production required it, man should "hand himself over freely and totally to society." What mattered was to attain the

[22] Pius XI, *Divini Redemptoris.*

[23] A. Angel, Superior of the Priests of Prado. *Catholiques et Communistes,* Lyons, 1945.

greatest amount of material goods. All will thus be "subordinated and even sacrificed to the exigencies of the best planned production," even the highest goods of man, even his freedom.[24]

An "immense factory rhythm" [25] will reign on earth until the day when, although admittedly far off, selfishness born of private property will have given way to altruism. Man, in that "higher phase," will be transformed through the changing of the economic structure. And because production will be equally perfected, all earthly resources being put to work, a general prosperity will flow over into a society without caste, without law, without government—a true paradise where each will receive according to his needs.

The Church loves her children too dearly it allow them to become entangled in an affair such as this, a reform which she knows is doomed to failure because from its very first phase it does violence to human nature and human destiny. Marxism hardly sees more in man than a producer and a consumer. He is made a slave to production while he awaits to give himself over completely to the enjoyment of material goods, and this without order of any kind. Marxism does not free the dispossessed. It sets man to work at the economic transformation of the world; and what it promises him for the far distant future, when the hoped-for paradise will have arrived on earth, is the enjoyment of the material fruits of that transformation. That is absolutely all. Is it enough?

Man demands more. He has a body endowed with sensibility, like the animal which instinctively seeks its well-being. But man is especially Spirit, endowed with a will capable of love, made in the image of God and made to attain God through a disinterested charity. Thus the Church, which does not contest the value of material well-being, sees in it an added facility which man thereby obtains to practice virtue and fulfill his destiny.[26]

If Marxism forgets this, it is because its materialistic atheism

[24] Pius XI, *Quadragesimo Anno.*
[25] Lenin.
[26] Pius XI, *Quadragesimo Anno.*

fails to recognize such a vocation for man. But materialism thus introduced infiltrates everywhere; little by little it deforms all the elements of social life: the state becomes materialistic, having been reduced to serving material progress instead of assuring justice and equity among its citizens, a state fortified at the same time by the economic dictatorship of a self-interested power and without control. Economics becomes materialistic; no longer subordinated to the authority of a state which remains faithful to the proper ends of government, economics knows no curbs. There is no one left to whom one can appeal from injustices; no power which can bring economics back to a "human mode of behavior." The family can no longer humanize economy, although it is by nature a center of spiritual development for man: the family is exposed to the arbitrary acts of the socialist state, just as the dignity of the human person is exposed. There is no place left at all for any spiritual value, if economics is everything; no place for growth of the soul, except a technical growth; no place for religion, in its claims to influence life.

At bottom we reproach Marxism for the same reason we reproach liberal Capitalism. Both sacrifice man to production. Both provoke the same kind of control of economics over politics, "the financial powers dominating all private and public economy, often indeed, civic activity." [27] At the source of all these disorders is the same disorder: "the excessive love of this world's goods." [28]

We are all aware that there is more than one difference between dialectic, Marxist materialism and the common, ordinary materialism. We are likewise aware that modern Capitalism does not suspect its own materialism, but it does foster a practical materialism, and even a doctrinal materialism when it is built "on the basis of liberalism and secularism." [29] It does not recognize the fact that man has a destiny written into his nature and history; it ignores that man can and must recognize his destiny in order to strive for it; it refuses to admit that man's

[27] Pius XII, Radio Message, Sept. 1, 1944.
[28] Pius XI, *Divini Redemptoris* (On Atheistic Communism), 77.
[29] Ibid., 38.

destiny leads him to God, and that this cannot be achieved without recourse to the supernatural. How could liberal Capitalism be expected to know that "the goods of the earth are naturally and essentially ordained to the life of the spirit and to a perfection higher than that of civil life, a moral and religious perfection necessary to a rational being." [30]

In condemning the excesses of Capitalism and Marxist Socialism, the Church thus invites us to restore the true conception of man's destiny, i.e., the attainment of his last end, his happiness.

God wants the world to accept the light of Christian doctrine. New horizons would open up before its eyes because Christianity brings fortitude with light; a new hope would be given.

"*Whoever owns, owns for himself.*" This is the practical principle of Capitalism and its false concept of property. Marxist Socialism also has no other motif. Hence, it sees but one way to do away with the selfishness of ownership: to substitute collective property in place of private property. Henceforth, society will possess property for itself. An apparently tempting solution, this at times gives to workers, who would be liberated from work at the profit of another, the hope of a personal liberation and a kind of legitimate pride. But in reality the solution simply displaces selfishness, instead of doing away with it. Instead of a fixed number of "big bosses" there would be only one. "All the citizens" will have become "the employees and workers of a sole, universal cartel," the State.[31] Economy will now no more be at the service of man than before, but on the contrary. State coercion will supplant capitalistic profit; selfishness of the collectivity will supplant the selfishness of individuals, with the resulting wars between collectivities: wars of class, race, and nation.

"*Whoever owns, owns for all.*" Here the Christian truth is expressed. It is an affirmation and a statement of obligation. It affirms that private property, as we have said, places the goods destined for all at the service of all. It obliges the property

[30] Pius XII, Radio Message, Dec. 24, 1943.

[31] Lenin, *Marx, Engels, Marxism*, 1935.

owner to use his right of property for the good of all. This is what the Church asks of her members, as we shall next see.

III. WHAT THE CHURCH ASKS OF HER MEMBERS

Whoever will compare the teaching of the Church on property with excesses of modern Capitalism or with Marxism will be obligated to conclude that change is necessary.

This is not a matter of changing a few details nor even some aspects of the structure! Nor is it a question of consolidation, correction, or better management. We are speaking of a whole new structure. A good number of its parts undoubtedly could be used, but it is a radical change of what is most important in an organization, namely, its principles, direction, the finality and purpose for which it is made, that dictates all the other changes.

In short, we must look for some *reforms of structure*. A structure responds to a goal. Now, the question is to change the goal: instead of making a goal of production, we must give all men a truly human existence. In place of Capitalism—a simple "technique of production"—where in the absence of a higher principle, production puts man at its service, we must substitute an economy which is henceforth at the service of men—and not of several men only but of all men. Material goods, natural resources and manufactured articles are made for *all* people.

Something other than a more or less extensive modification of these institutions is needed. More than a revolution is needed, for "revolution" means a reshuffling, and a reshuffled situation is not necessarily better nor truly a change. What is needed is a *total renovation*. To this the Church's teaching leads us; and compared to her teaching Marxism, if we may say so, is a weak doctrine. The Marxist revolution merely hands over the privileged position of the Capitalists to the Proletariat. It leaves men a slave to production, with their hearts in the servitude of greed. Being materialistic, it cannot do otherwise. The Church claims to turn human life away from such slavery.

Here revolution penetrates the souls of men to root out hate and cure greed. This is the revolution of love.

"*Whoever owns, owns for himself,*" according to liberal Capitalism. Marxist Socialism approved this by saying "Henceforth, let the Socialist state possess everything! No more property owners, all salaried men," which means "all proletarians." To this Christianity says No. "*No more proletarians, all property owners.*" "Whoever owns, owns for all," must possess for all, can possess for all, with the grace of our Savior.[32]

"Material well-being, first of all. Production, first of all." This is still the cry of liberal Capitalism, and it accomplishes this to the advantage of some. Marxism repeats the motif, but wants it achieved for the benefit of the masses. "*Primacy of the Spiritual; Primacy of the Person;* Primacy of human existence," according to the social doctrine of the Gospel, is commanded for all: for the proletarians, who must cease being proletarians, and for the Capitalists, who also have need of liberation.

In the search for *well-being,* neither Capitalism, which attains it for some, nor Marxism, which hopes to attain it for all, can find *happiness.* How will man find his true happiness in something counter to his nature and spiritual vocation? Only the truth of Christ truly liberates; it is for all and preached to all: love one another.

[32] In his Commentary of *Rerum Novarum,* Canon Tiberghien makes the following remarks on this subject:

"Thus the Catholic doctrine becomes equally distinguished from the pagan doctrine of yesterday and today and from the socialist doctrine on property.

"In effect, the pagan doctrine concludes that private property is destined for private use only, and that this doctrine could thus be resumed in this way: 'I alone own this, therefore it is for me alone.' Socialism comes to the conclusion that common goods are common property; thus: 'the goods of all belong to all.'

"Following Christian doctrine, the possessor is the true owner as regards man but simply a steward as regards God, charged by him and not by society to administer his property for the common good of his brethren. The exact doctrine affirming private property and the common use of goods is: 'I alone own this for all of us.' Naturally this *us* includes first of all the owner himself who sets aside for himself that part of his goods which are necessary and suitable, and who then distributes the superfluities."

We can understand the recent remarks of a Communist to a Catholic, whose life of all-embracing love of neighbor he had observed: "You are more of a Communist than we are." The "Communism" of Christian love is in effect the only love which is truly fraternal and communal. The advent of Christian love into a world grown old through the hardships of individualism will always be the great *novelty*, the only *novelty*.

Such is the ideal towards which Christ commands us to strive, as He gives us the strength to achieve it. Christ sends His Holy Spirit "to renew the face of the earth," as a prelude to the new heaven and to the new earth which He will establish on the last day: when, according to the words of Pius XI at the end of his encyclical on Communism, "the promises of the false prophets will be extinguished on this earth in blood and tears," and when "the great apocalyptic prophecy of the Savior of the world will burst out: 'Behold I will make all things new.' "[33]

The hour is ripe for the work of renovation. The rigors of a war economy, which forced us to break away from the technique of liberal Capitalism, if not from its spirit, call for the consideration of all. Is it necessary to fall back again to the disorders and economic "crises" of pre-war time? The idea is unsupportable. The sufferings endured by the world during the terrible crises through which we are passing merits a better conclusion. Let us repeat it: a change is necessary, a Christian renewal.

Let us not object that we ought to postpone reforms of structure for the sake of preserving social peace. Peace is "the tranquillity of order." Would you call "order" the present disorder, namely, the existence of a proletariat, International Finance, the seeking of mere material well-being? Defined in terms of such disorders, which Capitalism tends to preserve (since it admits the right of private property, but badly understands it), would not "tranquillity" instead be "stagnation?" In his Christmas message of 1942, Pius XII warned Catholics against "a hard and obstinate immobility, childishly attached to oneself," against "a kind of repugnance, born of ignorance and greed,

[33] Apocalypse, 21:5.

to applying oneself to the problems posed by the rise of new generations with their progress and their needs." He has warned against "an apathetic indifference" and "inertia" in this "great spiritual battle whose goal is to construct society or rather to give it a soul." [34]

And let us no longer object to the necessity of technique, as though technical progress necessarily brought with it the gigantic organizations which would impose super-Capitalism, perhaps even Socialism. Pius XII once again answers: "No. Technical progress does not determine economic life as if it were a fatal and necessary law. It is very true that too often technical progress is deflected by reason of the calculations of selfish men avid for indefinitely enlarging their capital. Why could not technique be bent to the work of assuring private property for all, which is the cornerstone of the social order?" Moreover, technique must not rule over man but man over technique. "Technical progress itself" must be "ordained to and subordinated to the general welfare." [35]

[34] Pope Pius XII, Christmas message 1942, taking up the problem of social peace among classes: "There is a domain of social life where, after a century of most bitter conflicts, a calm, at least on the surface, prevails today; and we wish to speak of this workingmen's world, always more extensive, of this immense army of workers, of salaried men, of *dependents.* If the present situation be taken as a fact, with the necessities of war, one could say that this tranquility is a necessary and a well-justified requirement, but if it is seen from the point of view of justice, this tranquility will remain an illusion only, in so far as the goal which is a regulated and legitimate worker movement is not yet attained.

"The Church, always motivated by religious considerations, has condemned the diverse systems of Marxist Socialism. She continues to hold to this condemnation, since it is her duty and her permanent right to preserve men from influences which endanger their eternal salvation. But she can neither ignore nor refuse to see that the worker in his efforts to better his condition clashes with a social system which, far from being conformable to nature, resists the order established by God and the end which he has assigned to this earth's goods. Also, while recognizing that certain efforts at betterment, having taken a false route, are perilous and worthy of condemnation, what man and especially what priest and what Christian could remain deaf to the cries rising from the heart of the masses, who call for justice and fraternal love in a world of a just God?"

[35] Pius XII, Radio Message, Sept. 1, 1944.

In addition, revolution takes place in men's minds before it affects institutions. Now, a revolution already has been accomplished in men's minds, at least in a negative way. Observers agree that neither the workers, nor happily many employers, especially Christian ones, would turn back the clock. The sole question remaining is with what must the old state of affairs be replaced? Here Christians have a role to play, a necessary role, which is important for them to understand.

The goal of Christianity is not to establish a just temporal order. Its goal is to enable us to share in divine life, to communicate with God. Such is the last end and the supreme value, which needs no justification outside itself. Christianity has its own value independent of human repercussions. The Communion with God which the Church establishes here below cannot be considered as a means for human progress. "Not to desire God for Himself is to despise the divine gift."

If the destiny of man is spiritual, however, and even supernatural, it still has those natural conditions which touch upon matter. For this reason the Christian cannot be disinterested in the temporal order nor even in its economic foundations. The Christian has the duty to create conditions in the world favorable to the Christian life. A true Christian civilization assures these conditions. Pius XII invites us to restore economic life, as well as the whole social and international life "on a plane reconcilable with the religious and moral content of Christian civilization." A more sound juridical order must be created; also an order more responsive to divine law and human dignity must be established in the economic and social field. "The uplifting of the proletariat," adds the Pope, "will be the essential element" of this new order. "Every true disciple of Christ" must apply himself to this energetically and generously; for him it is far more than a question of temporal progress; it is "the accomplishment of a *moral duty*." [36]

The Pope makes it a moral duty for the true disciples of Christ to help uplift the proletariat. This is what the Church

[36] Ibid.

asks of her children, according to each case. Of some she requests that they seek and inaugurate the necessary reforms of structure. She asks everyone to contribute to the Christian renovation of the economic order by their personal life, and in particular by the use which they make of their right of property.

To those whose competence, social functions or professional activities render them more capable, the Church asks that they accept their responsibilities in order to discover and affect new structures. The Church does not indicate the technical solutions, but she urges her members to discover them among the many possibilities which are in accord with her moral principles. We have said that the Church does not have an economic doctrine in the modern sense of the term. Thus it is in the whole temporal order: "She does not wish to legislate in the temporal order: this would be clericalism. She does not wish to cut herself off from the temporal order: this would be spiritual evasion. She brings doctrine to the laity, which will permit them to give life to the whole temporal order." [37]

Nor does the Church believe in taking away the initiative from her lay members, nor deprive the state of any of its rights. Provided that the state remains faithful to its functions of high-level politics, instead of lowering and subordinating it to economics, the Church, on the contrary, calls state intervention indispensable. It falls on the state to order business undertakings to the welfare of the nation and to see that all factors in enterprise have a part worthy of their rationality. Again, the state must leave individuals, families, and subsidiary groups (in particular professional groups) to perform those functions of which they themselves are capable. "The reason is that all social activity of its very power and nature should supply help to the members of the social body, but never may destroy or absorb them." [38]

[37] Ancel, *Catholiques et Communistes.*

[38] Pius XI, *Quadragesimo Anno,* 80.

"The state, then, should leave to these smaller groups the settlement of business and problems of minor importance, which should otherwise greatly distract it. Thus it will carry out with greater freedom, power, and

Here we wish to felicitate the members of our professional groups and Catholic Action movements for their research and initiative. So too our Christian employers who, in collaboration with the members of worker Catholic Action movements, have elaborated a "Communal plan for the reform of business." We have no pronouncement to make either on the technical aspects or on the conclusions of a technical nature which their efforts have brought. We only wish to give by way of example a project which is not the only one and to underline the importance of the problem undertaken.

When Pius XII denounces the exaggerated accumulation of riches which thus lose their social role, he states that this "happens under the cover of anonymity." [39] Is not a check necessary here? Has not the regime of corporations (anonymous societies) effaced man behind capital? "The societies of capital (corporations) are not by themselves societies of persons; despite the efforts of the best employers, who are the first victims of the system, financial considerations are preponderant. Capital monopolizes the management and the benefits; final responsibilities are "limited" or spread out among a great quantity of shares whose holders are not in a position to take the responsibilities which fall to them by natural right.

If these statements are exact, and if these hoped-for reforms do not restore the primacy of responsible administration and the primacy of labor over capital in our corporations, we will need to denounce the abuses with force. Money in itself can in no way be considered as a proprietor, for property is the privilege of the person. Money must remain the servant and cannot command. But neither can man, in seeking only profit, cast off the social responsibilities which are attached to prop-

---

success the tasks belonging to it alone, because it alone is qualified to perform them: directing, watching, stimulating, and restraining, as circumstances suggest or necessity demands. Let those in power, therefore, be convinced that the more faithfully this principle of subsidiary function is followed, and a graded hierarchical order exists between the various associations, the greater also will be both social authority and social efficiency. The happier, too, and more prosperous will be the condition of the commonwealth."

[39] Pius XII, Radio Message, Sept. 1, 1944.

erty. And if he insists on limiting his responsibilites or if he cannot accept them, he must then sacrifice part of his revenue and renounce playing in the enterprise the decisive role, which capital normally plays. When he refuses some of his duties, he cedes some of his rights.

An illegitimate preponderance of anonymous capital in an enterprise is all the more intolerable because it is accompanied by a lessening of the role of management and labor, which are the principal causes of the value of manufactured products, as the encyclicals state. Whereas capital can be increased like a rolling snowball, labor stands the great risk of being treated like pure merchandise, whose human character is forgotten. "The worker realizes that in all these decisions concerning his life (hiring and firing, salary systems, nationalization) it is the idea of yield and profit which will take precedence over the care for his most urgent human needs. We see here the vice of the capitalistic system: "the primacy of money over man, capital over labor. The whole problem is to reverse the order of the factors in putting *capital at the service of human values* and in subordinating its profits to the attainment of just remuneration." [40]

One well knows, moreover, that the worker in particular suffers in his moral situation. Too often in enterprise, he is, as it has been said, "only an interchangeable number and an anonymous accessory of the machine," "without material or moral independence with regard to capital," which keeps the whole economic power to itself. The worker is not treated as a *person*, and it is this that makes him a proletarian.

The harm is more noticeable where the enterprise is larger. This is why Pius XII takes it up again in emphasizing a suggestion of Pius XI. He asks that where the same advantages of big corporations cannot be obtained by small enterprises united in cooperatives, then a means should be found of "tempering the wage contract by a partnership contract." [41] One must per-

[40] Cf. Communal Plan 44, *Contribution à une réforme de l'entreprise.* Equipes patronales, 18 rue Varenne, Paris (7).

[41] Pius XII, Radio Message, Sept. 1, 1944, Cf. *Quadragesimo Anno,* 65. It is interesting to note here the progression of papal thought from

mit the worker to bring something *personal* to the common good of the enterprise and to the general welfare, and make him conscious of his contribution. This can give rise to organizing in some manner the participation of labor in profits and even in the administration and ownership of the enterprise. That this be possible without compromising either the principle of the private property of the enterprise, now enlarged into communal property, or of the authority of the head of the enterprise, so indispensable to the smooth operation of the business, is demonstrated by the "communal plan" which we cited above.

We do not ignore the difficulties of these reforms, difficult in the technical order and even more difficult in the psychological order. But these reforms are legitimate and the stake is worth the effort involved. The workers have been able so far, by a pure and simple salaried contract, to dispossess themselves of some of their rights in exchange for a tacit assurance against the risks involved. The pure and simple wage contract was just, but it was free: no one has the right to impose it on those who no longer want it. Let us seek new solutions with a generous and prudent boldness.

In the same way we encourage that everything possible be undertaken to give *human dimensions* to enterprise, at least to its basic units. There is a limit beyond which an enterprise ceases to measure man's stature: that is, when the administration and especially capital can no longer recognize and deal with the human implications of their actions. Man finds himself almost necessarily enslaved by technical requirements, and he is treated as though he were a machine.

Finally, we must praise all undertakings which will permit the worker to feed himself and his family under the normal

---

1931 to 1944. In *Quadragesimo Anno,* Pius XI had written this often cited phrase: "In the present state of human society, however, We deem it advisable that the wage contract should, when possible, be modified somewhat by a contract of partnership." Thirteen years later, Pius XII expressly referring to Pius XI declares: "And where large enterprise continues to make good progress it should offer the possibility of improving the wage contract by a contract of partnership."

conditions of a *salary*, attain the ownership of the house, furnishings, and family gardens, and progressively to share in the ownership of the means of production themselves.

We urge you, beloved brethren, and with you all men of good will, to a veritable crusade against the regime of money in behalf of the development of the human person, according to his destiny, and in behalf of the development of the dignity of *all* men and not merely a small number. The Church has need, therefore, not only of compctcnt laymen but of all her members.

A renewal of the economic order will not be accomplished without the general atmosphere of comprehension and cooperation. Every organization which is not based on living reality is artificial and precarious. *Institutions* are born of *traditions*, to which they give expression, as well as being formed by them. Each one must try to harmonize his own life with the social doctrine of the Church. Thus the Church demands something of all her children: that they conduct their lives in line with the true ends of private ownership.

Let us once again recall this teaching: Private ownership does not go counter, must not go counter, to the *Universal destination of material goods*. "Every man in so far as living, endowed with reason, holds from nature the fundamental right to use material goods," declares Pius XII,[42] and he makes it clear that if there were conflict between this fundamental right of all men and the right of private property, the right of all must win out.

On condition of this fundamental right, and in order to assure its exercise, the nature of man calls for private ownership; this plays a double role: personal and social.

The personal role of private property is to assure to each what is required as fitting for a normal human existence, individual and domestic. The Church does not mean to reduce each to the minimum essential of the proletariat nor even of

[42] Discourse on the occasion of the fiftieth anniversary of *Rerum Novarum*.

the monk. To the minimum necessary things, she wants to add the element of sufficiency: not exaggerated luxury, which injures the individual even before becoming a scandal to society, but a sufficiency that makes an extensive and free development of human qualities possible.

The social role of private property is to contribute to the common good. It will do this as "an element of the social order," in stimulating people to work; [43] but also by the way in which the property owner, if he is conscious of his responsibilities, will use his rights. The property owner has his personal right; he alone is the administrator of his goods. If the state can restrict his liberty, through taxations, various limitations, and by expropriation with indemnity, it can do so only in view of the common good and without going to the extreme of destroying the right of property. But in *using* his right the owner has the duty to consider himself before God as the *steward of the common good.*[44] Let me outline for you how extensive the Christian demands are.

One who owns might easily think that everything which comes to him legally from his fortune is at his disposal, so long as he supports the Church and gives to the poor. But such is not Christian doctrine. Each has the right to keep for himself and for his family what is necessary and suitable to his life, in the large sense. Yet no one has the right to keep for himself more than is necessary for him to live in true Christian moderation. Furthermore, no one has the right to keep for himself the wherewithal to completely escape from work, or permit his sons to so escape. "If any man will not work, neither

[43] Pius XII, Radio Message, Sept. 1, 1944.

[44] In *Rerum Novarum,* 19. Pope Leo XIII wrote: "Private ownership, as we have seen, is the natural right of man; and to exercise that right, especially as members of society, is not only lawful but absolutely necessary. 'It is lawful,' says St. Thomas of Aquin, 'for a man to hold private property; and it is also necessary for the carrying on of human life!'

"But if the question be asked, how must one's possessions be used? the Church replies without hesitation in the words of the same Holy Doctor: 'Man should not consider his outward possessions as his own, but as common to all, so as to share them without difficulty when others are in need.' "

let him eat," St. Paul says.[45] Finally, if Christ proposes for all times the beatitude of the spirit of poverty, does it not apply especially in our age so consumed with the lust for material goods? We know some Christians, in all social positions, who effectively live this spirit.

Once he has assured himself of the necessities and suitable needs of life, the owner *must* consecrate the rest of his fortune to the common good; and not a part but the totality, and not because he would like to do it, but because he has the duty. This is not a duty of *justice*, except when it is a matter of aiding those in extreme necessity, but it is a duty of *charity*, in the large sense of the word: a duty of love by which we love God, Our Father, and our brethren for the love of God.

To give one's surplus through almsgiving is one means of fulfilling this duty, but there are other ways. To invest in new enterprises, foreseeing that these are useful, is a good way to serve the common good. Pius XI expressly foresees this as a way.[46]

Because it is not a duty of justice, no human authority has the right to impose it by executive order. No one has the right to demand it before the courts, and even less so, to take the matter in his own hands. Yet the obligation of the owner is no

[45] II Thess., 3:10.

[46] *Quadragesimo Anno*, 50 & 51. Here again it is interesting to see the progression of the Papal thought between 1891 and 1931. Leo XIII wrote: (*Rerum Novarum* 19): "But when necessity has been supplied, and one's position fairly considered, it is a duty to give to the indigent out of that which is over. 'That which remaineth, give alms,' (*Luke* 11:41). It is a duty, not of justice (except in extreme cases), but of Christian charity—a duty which is not enforced by human law." Pius XI (*Quadragesimo Anno*, 50, 51): "At the same time a man's superfluous income is not left entirely to his own discretion. We speak of that portion of his income which he does not need in order to live as becomes his station. On the contrary, the grave obligation of charity, beneficence, and liberality which rests upon the wealthy are constantly insisted upon in telling words by Holy Scripture and the Fathers of the Church.

"However, according to the teaching of the Angelic Doctor, the investment of a large income in such a manner that favorable opportunities for employment may abound (on the supposition that the labor employed produces results which are really useful) is to be considered an act of real liberality particularly appropriate to the needs of our time."

less grave for that reason. The state must leave men to their consciences in this matter, but your Archbishop is charged with the task of aiding in the formation of your conscience; he does this in the name of God, the common Father of all men and the source of fraternal love, confiding the rest to the generosity which his people have shown him in the past on many occasions.

Let us conclude.

The detachment from the goods of this earth and the law of charity are more necessary than ever in our age of quasi-general materialism, of "greed for earthly goods and enjoyments";[47] in a world which has not, in spite of grave crises, overcome its greed, since those who own still hold jealously to their goods and those who do not own want to seize goods through violence. We hope that our priests, especially in their own lives, be the first to remember this. We ask the militants of Catholic Action to discover for themselves, each according to his social standing, "a mode of life" truly Christian which is resplendent even in the temporal order.

A reform of structures will be valuable only if it is preceded and accompanied by a reform of hearts. Now, the reign of money not only poisons private property. Money is sought everywhere for the selfish enjoyments which it procures for people who should give themselves, body and goods, to the service of their neighbors. The spirit of service must be everywhere substituted for the spirit of enjoyments. Such is the necessary condition of all true reforms of the inhuman economic order. You cannot love money and your brethren at the same time; you cannot serve two masters. A choice must be made: *God or money?* The Gospel is categorical in this matter. Let each imbue himself with the Gospel spirit daily in order to put it in all of his life.

Let all, then, clergy and faithful (particularly the members of the Christian professions), apply themselves to understanding and spreading the social doctrine of the Church, defined by the encyclicals of Leo XIII and Pius XI as well as by the messages

[47] Pius XI, *Divini Redemptoris* (On Atheistic Communism), 44.

and discourses of Pius XII, whose teachings we hope to see propagated through popular editions.

A new world is being formed. Will you give a soul to it? Its soul will be Christian, or it will have no soul.

We speak especially to the believers and practicing Christians. You are the witnesses of Christ. Christ, Who said: "I am the light of the world," [48] commands you to be the light, since you are His witnesses. "You are the light of the world. Neither do men light a lamp and put it under a measure." [49] "You shall be witnesses for me even to the very ends of the earth." [50]

You will not be witnesses of Christ solely in believing Him. He commands you to think and to wish with Him, that is, to think and wish with the Church. And the thought of Christ and the Church is above all a thought of justice and of truth, which requires that the personal dignity of every man be recognized, that every man be offered the means to develop himself according to his destiny.

Believers and practicing Christians, you are, moreover, the apostles of Christ on earth, sent to bring the Gospel to the masses who do not know it. To reach these people it is not sufficient that you present yourselves before them, nor that you tell them you love them, nor that you flatter them by opposing them to other classes. This would give lie to the very Gospel you propose to bring them. They must be *really* loved, and this love proved to them by seeing to their welfare as well as to your own, and, if need be, by affirming and defending their rights: their right to live, their right to develop their personality, and notably, their right to attain some private property.

To so act, beloved brethren, is to be simply a Christian without skimping on one's Christianity, without strangling it. "Even so, let your light shine before men, in order that they may see your good works and give glory to your Father in heaven." [51]

[48] John, 8:12.
[49] Matt., 5:14-15.
[50] Acts, 1:8.
[51] Matt., 5:15-16.

THE CHRISTIAN FAMILY

In our Christian community, the family is the basic unit. We must restore our families to Christ and draw them into our missionary apostolate.

The home is the crossroad of family life, where all rejoice and grieve, where all are born and where they will die. In the home we meet and take leave of one another; we help one another in daily tasks; we learn to serve and to lead; to undertake and to persevere; there we find the model of our lives; there we are trained in wisdom and forgetfulness of self.

Contents

The Christian Family

The whole world is interested in the problem of the family. Citizens and rulers—and even celibates—have come forth from families or will eventually found families. Civilization itself will depend upon the family. And civilization will either progress or regress, depending on whether the primary unit of society is maintained or ruined. These things are so because the family is not an artificial thing but a reality of nature. Do away with the family and society dies. Experience confirms the theory.

In the first part of our pastoral letter, we shall determine the precise nature of the family and its place in the plan of God. In the second part, we shall indicate the principal errors concerning the family, and in the third part, the conditions for restoring full family life.

I. THE FAMILY IN GOD'S PLAN

In our attempt to bring together the teaching of the Catholic Church on family matters, we were surprised that throughout the centuries there has been very little systematic treatment of the family. We noticed the same when we looked at Revelation. The faith of Moses and the New Testament add little to the traditional concept of the family common to all civilized peoples. Long before she wrote about it doctrinally, the Church lived family life. She did not create the family, but it existed before her. When pagan converts were married—provided the union was monagamus—the Church recognized their bond. In family matters the role of the Church consisted in returning to the natural moral law, then drawing it to its highest degree of perfection. Let us not be astonished, for all of humanity is in accord: "there is no institution more natural than the family." [1] We shall see this as we consider successively *the natural law as the basis of the family; Revelation, which exalts it; and the teaching of the Church, which defends it.*

[1] Leclerq, *Principe de Droit Naturel.* T. II. La Famille, p. 6.

THE FAMILY AND NATURAL LAW

To say that the family is a natural institution is to say that it is spontaneously produced by man's biological structure and his instincts as man. Three factors clearly establish this.

The first is the differentiation of humanity into two branches, male and female, a division which was not a matter of chance but has a meaning. At the same time physical and psychical, the differentiation creates a mutual attraction between men and women which is at the basis of love. Such a union, enriching and complementary, establishes a marriage. Man and woman are joined to each other because they love each other. They are free to unite themselves. In this sense the voluntary consent which they give to each other in their choice of companions is a contract.

Once united they must submit to the conditions of the new state to which their common life has promoted them. From this point of view, marriage is an institution, a pre-established condition which one violates only by denying nature. This double character of conjugal union can be discovered in all peoples at different stages of development. Both history and ethnology confirm the value attributed to such a bond; laws surround it with a guarantee; religions, with sacred rites.

The second basis of the family is generation, which fulfills an evident intention of nature, namely, the propagation of the human race. It is to this end that the union of man and woman is ordained; it is its mysterious purpose and reason of being. From this is derived the all-important principle that their relations should be guided by the need of continuing the human race.

The birth of a child establishes the family by strengthening the union of the spouses; they are made more stable by this expression of the permanent union of their lives. It creates new relations between the parents and the new child who will extend them in life and time. Because the infant depends upon them, parents depend upon him; having brought him to light, they must feed and care for him. Among animals the union is more or less stable and exclusive, depending on the need of the offspring; but among men, where there is a slow, difficult, and complex development of the child, the primary quality of the union of the parents is that of stability. A precarious association would endanger or hinder the life of the child. Procreation is but the first step of his birth in the world, a birth which is fully completed only at the time he enters into adult life.

Finally, in order that the child develop in body, mind, and soul, he needs a *home* where he finds brought together through the heritage of past generations the loving cooperation and double influence of both *the man* and *the woman*. It is only in their equality of rights, if not functions, that this cooperation is achieved. The moral union excludes polygamy.

Thus conjugal love, already exclusive and absolute by nature, receives from the fact of its fecundity the added notes of stability and intimacy. The normal human family is the indissoluble couple. Let us draw out the consequences of this conclusion, which does not call for an act of faith but springs from an examination of the facts alone. The advantage of this method is that on this point every sincere man can agree with the Christian conception of the family. Such an agreement is very important if there is to be a common effort at restoring the family.

THE FAMILY AND REVELATION

To remain here, dear brethren, would be to stop in route, for Christ and the Church have given to the family—without changing its nature—a nobility and a transforming grace in the Sacrament of Marriage. We express this truth when we say that the family, having been instituted by God, has been restored and made divine by Jesus Christ.

THE FAMILY, INSTITUTED BY GOD

In the first pages of Holy Scripture we see that God instituted the family. First, man was created; then, a woman is given to him as a "help like unto himself." [2] These two will be complementary beings so attracted by a mutual love that they will become one. Adam himself says so: "Wherefore a man

[2] Gen., 2:18.

shall leave father and mother, and he shall cleave to this wife: and they shall be two in one flesh." [3] Then Eve bears a son, and her motherly instinct cries with joy: "I have gotten a son through God." [4]

In these few lines, full of divine simplicity, the essential note of the human family is already presented to us. The father: reasonable, strong willed, who nevertheless has need of a woman's company. "It is not good for man to be alone." [5] The mother: intuitive, with a delicate sensibility, forgetful of self, who is the bone of his bone, flesh of his flesh.[6] The child: a fragile treasure, fruit and cause of their love, a new flame lighted from their life to burn after them.

Then, sin came, and the Bible does not let us pass over the fact that disorder entered the passions through original sin, and the family was not spared. Nor does the Bible hide from us the polygamy of the patriarchs and of many of their descendants. It shows us Moses permitting to the Hebrews "on account of the hardness of their hearts," [7] the putting-away of woman by her husband. In spite of these defections, however, the Jewish family lives on together throughout the Old Testament united and virtuous. Yet God wished for it a higher dignity.

THE FAMILY, RESTORED AND ELEVATED BY CHRIST

Hence, Our Lord restored the family to its primitive purity and elevated it to the supernatural order by founding it in a Sacrament.

Christ, first of all, abrogated divorce. St. Matthew shows Christ sending his questioners back to the first page of the Bible with finality: "What therefore God has joined together, let no man put asunder." [8] But the law seems too difficult for human weakness: "If the case of a man with his wife is so, it

[3] Gen., 2:24.
[4] Gen., 4:1.
[5] Gen., 2:18.
[6] Gen., 2:23.
[7] Matt., 19:8.
[8] Matt., 19:6.

is not expedient to marry,"[9] replied the Apostles. Our Lord knows our weakness. He Himself will establish the harmony of the spouses—the essence of marriage—a Sacrament of the New Law, a source rich in the grace of unity and mutual santification, which will aid them in bringing up their children properly.

St. Paul has given us the details of the richness of the conjugal union and has extolled the model: "Let wives be subject to their husbands as to the Lord; because a husband is head of the wife, just as Christ is head of the Church. Husbands, love your wives, just as Christ also loved the Church, and delivered Himself up for her."[10]

THE FAMILY AND THE CHURCH

Thus the love of Christian spouses is not only their natural love, but the whole "love" of Christ; and the spirit of the Beatitudes penetrates and exalts it without up-rooting any of its inherent foundations.

A. THE CHURCH FATHERS AND THEOLOGIANS

In departing from inspired scripture, theologians (following the Fathers of the Church) have indicated the place of the family in the over-all plan of God. God is love. The Trinity overflows with love and wants to share it with us. From this love flows the creation of angels; from this, too, the creation and the Redemption of men flow. God wants innumerable sons, but man is not a pure spirit. By his body he is one with a world having its proper laws. One of these is that life transmits itself from the living to the living. Man is no exception. This transmission of life establishes man's dependence, but also his greatness, since on him—God having so willed it—the number of the elect will depend. God will create as many souls as man provides bodies.

Man rarely acts without a minimum of interest and rarely without love. God realizes this still better. God has infused into man a powerful and spontaneous impulse—conjugal love. He creates man and woman. They will be two in one flesh. With

[9] Matt., 19:10.
[10] Eph., 22-25.

child they will be three in one love. In this way man will be twice created in the image of God as a person and as a family. The one and the other will find in Him their ideal of perfection. The most exalted model of the family is the Holy Trinity. Man, source of life, as God the Father; woman, complement of the man, as the Word Who is the image of His substance";[11] the child, fruit and bond of their love, like the Holy Spirit, Who proceeds from the Father and the Son. Without denying that we have here a simple analogy, let us acknowledge that the family has a privileged status and an origin which places it above all human societies. It is a provider for the City of God in heaven, and a provider for the Church, the Mystical Body of Christ, on earth.

B. THE TEACHING OF THE POPES

In the past fifty years the Popes have given the teaching on the family both doctrinal and pastoral support. We need only mention the Encyclicals and documents of Leo XIII, Pius XI, and Pius XII on marriage, the family and education. While the sovereign Pontiffs have spoken only on the occasions of attacks upon the family, they have given the doctrine depth and adaptation.

II. FALSE NOTIONS OF THE FAMILY *

Where is the family today? Does it live up to the ideal we have sketched? You know that the answer is No. In too many homes the family is completely decadent, to the point of death. The cries of alarm of the past twenty years have at least aroused public opinion.

As for the conjugal link, the first breakdown is in the practice of free love. The number of irregular unions has greatly increased, and it has brought with it more and more illegitimate and abandoned children.

How could family life itself be dragged so low? Has it thus

[11] Hebrews, 1:3.

* Editor's Note: Statistics on divorces and abandoned children in France, cited by Suhard, have been deleted, because of interest in France only.

lost all its dignity and moral conscience? In looking closer, however, one must face the evidence. The families are not themselves the blame, but the blame rests on those who, during the past fifty years, have tolerated such abuse and have sometimes concurred with it. If each individual needs a minimum of well-being in order to practice virtue, is this not more true of the family? It has, in addition, a minimum need of doctrine. Certainly no one can say that the family has found either one or the other. Rather than accuse the family, we must seek the causes of its decline.

We must find the causes, first of all, in the economic and social conditions of the family.

SALARY

One would expect, in strict justice, that the worker—the father of the family—would receive remuneration proportional to the number of his children. For a long time the head of the family has been paid the same salary as a single person. While a good number will heroically accept the inequality of a standard of living which brings misery into their lives and a lower standard for their descendants, the majority of the others retrench from such double uncertainty. Their defense is sterility, which is especially true of the one-child family. Or, the woman leaves the home to take a job.

On the question of salary, the system of family allotments has, on the contrary, brought a remedy, yet so late in coming and on such a small scale, that it is still far from assuring a parity of income.

HOUSING

Again, numerous families, especially of workers, are crowded into over-populated units, ugly and damp, cut off from air and light. Infantile epidemics and tuberculosis do their worst in such places. Worker apartments at a reasonable price, better ventilated, too often resemble barrack-buildings. The life of young couples with their in-laws, which is actually the case nowadays because of a lack of space and the high cost of furniture, deprives them of that legitimate intimacy which normally blossoms into a desire for children.

The mother of a large family, on her side, is absolutely swamped by the daily grind of feeding the family, by caring for the children, for she has none of the material things which would ease her task. When the man leaves the factory, tired and worn out from his daily work, and comes back to a dreary apartment where he is welcomed by the cry of poorly kept children and the grief of an exhausted woman, his reaction is simple: he seeks his calm and joy elsewhere. So do his sons and daughters.

Now do you see why the hovel is the great provider of saloons and the first source of family scourges.

These are all partners—they never go alone: first, alcoholism, then sports and shows which are degrading, finally, organized vice. Up to recent times these victims of vice were aided in their course by scandalous publications and by very clever propaganda threatening them with detection in their unmentionable dealings, while those who promoted it all hid behind legal statutes. With the frightening diseases born of such excesses, and especially with the perversion of souls, a whole nation is affected in its physical and spiritual health.

MATERIALISTIC CLIMATE

But it is essentially the family which finds itself undermined and dislocated. That statement might surprise some—at least those in good homes. They seem to think they are not affected by such deterioration, whose hideous visage is so often pointed out to them. Under this form they are right. But they are greatly fooled if they imagine that they and their children escape from such a materialistic atmosphere. They close the door against it, true, but they breathe it outside and even inside the home. They do not mistrust it, because evil, according to the case, knows how to be discreet, cultivated, elegant, and how to take on the semblance of respectability. To be convinced we need only state the ease with which the Christian attitude accustoms itself to divorce, if one does not guard against it. The danger is to finish by shutting one's eyes to certain moral disorders which are classified as "necessary sex experience." As to the law of fertility, it is so often attacked by popular views, the novel, the theater, the movies and by vulgarization which poses as medical, that some good people come to believe, too, or they revolt against its requirements, which are called impossible of fulfillment.

Such an atmosphere would never have been created if it had not found an accomplice in legislation. The Law is said to be the reflection of morality, but on the other hand, it is also a source of it. There is a reciprocal causality, which strengthens the two individualisms. Public Law, coming from the "Declaration of the Rights of Man," sees in the nation a mere sum of individuals isolated and equal before the law, and thus it suppresses all intermediary groups between the state and the citizen. Private Law, in particular the Civil Code, consecrates this principle. It does not recognize the domestic community as such. It seeks only to assure the rights of each of its members. It limits the authority of the father; gives to the children the means to go to court against one another, or against their parents; divides the family heritage; and little by little suppresses the differences separating the "legal" family from the natural family. In short, the family is placed on the margin of the law and left to abandonment.

Juridical individualism, in its turn, has still deeper sources. It is the expression of a whole current of thought: the morality of free love.

FREE LOVE

The morality of free love finds its literary and philosophic tenets in the eighteenth century with the Encyclopedia and Rousseau. It extolls individualism, that is to say, the freedom of every human being to live as he wishes, in following the intincts of nature. This is opposed to the Christian conception of the Family, and it destroys—with equal coherence once the principles are admitted—step by step the last foundation of the Family.

Let us discuss free love, first of all. Love, as the essential form of happiness, is the supreme law; that is to say, each has the right to live with whom he wishes, when he wishes, and as he wishes. Divorce thus is no longer justified as a necessary evil —the position of its first defenders—but as a beneficial liberation. It becomes a good action which releases the couple from intolerable constraint. This does not mean, we are assured by this second stage of defense, which is that of the post-war literature—that marriage must disappear. No. It has a utility, as every contract, but on the condition of being equally revocable when the "atmosphere" of the first union no longer exists. Each one takes back his freedom—his freedom to go elsewhere.

Even this facility appears insufficient to some people, for they maintain one can desire love without desiring marriage. Marriage calls for certain conditions, financial, civil, etc. Hence, what is more beautiful than to follow nature, declare these modern "moralists"? Nature is always good. Why resist sense appeal since it is natural? It isn't free love which corrupts, they argue, but it is marriage which mixes pure love with social or interested considerations, and which condemns the spouse to perpetual slavery. In particular marriage, they say, places the woman in servitude in her submission to marital authority. "Feminism" gives her sovereign rights to dispose of her life and her being as she wishes. If the impulses of man push him towards several women, what of it? Polygamy is good, since it responds to an impulse. And what of other vices? Why are they "against nature" since they come from instinct?

But, you will object, all instinct is not good! Will not the remedy be to fight against these formidable impulses? Watch out well over yourself, they will tell you, for the sexual instinct is irresistible; to fight the passions is not to conquer them; it is to exasperate them. And in support they go on to cite, very quickly and without appeal, the axioms of "Psychoanalysis." In the name of these new principles, the "Naturalists" preach a triple crusade: war on modesty; group sex education of children; and apprenticeship in sex behavior.

In its main lines, such is the morality of free love. These conclusions alarm you, but did you not recognize them? Assuredly they are not expressed in such a logical order, but are they less dangerous? You know that they are largely responsible for family disorder. These plagues that grip society would not be so destructive—and perhaps would never have been prevalent among you—had not these sophisms been introduced.

If you doubt this, realize that even our adversaries are alarmed as the social repercussions of the current doctrine, namely, they lead to sterility. How will "companions for a day" burden themselves with offspring? Free love—love free of children. This can be understood in two ways. If a child is inadvertently born of such a union, the parents won't object to it. They will keep it as long as it fascinates them; if it becomes troublesome, they will hand it over to the State. The essential idea is to remain free. And the surest way to do this is to remain unattached. Free love denies life. It avoids procreation by all possible means: planned parenthood—in the name of Science, they say. But there is also a cynical attack on the life of the child. A disenfranchised couple is not concerned with childbirths.

FALSE REMEDIES

Thees startling conclusions—especially the last one—have affected public opinion. There has been an effort to find solutions, but solutions purely human; in truth, false remedies, which lead us to two opposing conceptions.

NEGATIVE CONCEPTION: THE CLOSED FAMILY

Some say there is only one way for the family to avoid downfall. That is, shut itself off from the world and be sufficient to itself, to live in itself and for itself. Does not the family have this right? The family is the necessary and sufficient unit of society. Each of its members, therefore, must live for it and if need be, sacrifice his life for it. People matter little—it is the family that counts: its heritage, name, possessions. Save them and you will save the nation.

This conception presents itself both as a solution and as a thesis.

AN INEFFECTUAL REMEDY

As a solution for the decline of the family, the "closed family" idea is ineffectual and essentially negative. It flees the world and retires within itself. There is no better way to destroy oneself: "He who wishes to save his life shall lose it," we read in the Gospel. We have seen it happen to the bourgeois society of the nineteenth century and to the peasant society of the twentieth. In trying to safeguard their material interests—dowry, marriage, or heritage—they ended with an only child in the family. When it concerns large families, they maintain a defensive attitude; they give only lip service to the idea of family allotments or only awkwardly fight against an outraged morality. Such an embittered and complaining attitude discredits the role of the family in society.

As for the thesis itself, let us distinguish. That the family must be a factor of social order and stability is clear. It possesses the virtue of conservation and development which defies the wear and tear of time and men. Not in vain do we call the house a "home." In uniting children, parents and grandparents under one roof, the home peacefully unites the future and the past. The Sacrament of Christian Marriage further strengthens this stabilizing function.

HERESY OF THE SELF-CONTAINED FAMILY

But the error comes when the family stops short with its self-enclosed role, without going beyond itself. It is a social cell, true enough, but not a cell with an end in itself, selfish and idolatrous. "As great as the family is," someone has written, "it can happen that the members love it too much, serving it to the detriment of values which are greater than itself. The family, like the State, cannot be defied without harming the rights of the person." The narrow conception of the "closed family" leads to the sacrifice of the human person; it subordinates the person to a means for serving a temporal institution. We cannot admit this, since the person is the "Chosen One" in the eternal designs of God. The community—as natural and sacred as it is—is still only a means to an end. In denying this, such total exclusiveness destroys the family itself. What becomes of a unit isolated from the whole? It slowly dies. The cell has as much need of the body as the body has need of the cells —you cannot take away from one without killing the other. Just as conjugal love cannot stop short of its purpose by forbidding the basic cell its expected growth, the family cannot mark time and vitiate the hopes of the country. Then, it is no longer a family; it is a "clan" or a "caste" which is closed to society. By its nature the family looks outward, for it is a society of people; only by playing false to its inner law does it close itself.[12]

THE STATIST CONCEPTION OF THE POPULATION PROBLEM

From such a distorted picture—which is presented as a Christian picture—one can see that Statism plays a clever hand in combatting the family. For Statism the family would serve as a brake and stabilize the social progress which other more dynamic organisms, such as unions or political parties, would have succeeded in obtaining. We must not forget this point of view, for it completely dominates Statist theory.

Yet its reasoning is cunning, for it does in fact speak of the home, family salary, domestic duties, the rights of mothers, and especially of births. One could be taken in by it, although in fact the theory is a negation of the family, pursued under the cover of propaganda.

DOCTRINAL POSITIONS: MARXIST SOCIOLOGY

A well-known Sociology says that in the beginning, there was a rudimentary society in which the family did not exist. Gradually by evolution the primitive clan developed into an actual conjugal union of father, mother and children. These, in their turn, are not eternal, but must disappear, for with the industrial civilization "all the needs which it serves will be answered by the State." [13]

The family, invented by man, could be a harmful institution.

[12] S. de Lestapis, *Valeur Politique de la Famille*. Cite Nouvelle, 20-2-41.
[13] Hesse et Gleize. *Manuel de Sociologie* des E.P.S., p. 95.

"The first antagonism of class which appears in history," Engels says, "is that of man and woman in monogamy, and the first oppression is that of the feminine sex by the masculine." In these conditions why maintain a stable and indisoluble conjugal union?

Marxism, you see, here comes back to the doctrine of "free love," only from a different point of view.

MAN: AN ECONOMIC FACTOR

According to Marxism the essential goal of man in society is to procure for himself the maximum of goods and economic power. His first duty, therefore, will be to produce with the utmost efficiency. To do this in modern economy a regime of production controlled by the state is required. To attain its goal the regime thus must free itself of all groups which have a desire to be autonomous. In such perspectives, one sees how a domestic economy appears as a hindrance, an obstacle.

The family under its traditional form, thus, must disappear, but the association of men and women must be encouraged, for the population of the nation is at stake. Let us not be duped here. It is not the life in common which is important, but its fecundity. Just as the state has need of raw materials—wheat, iron, coal, steel—it also needs human raw material—workers for industries, soldiers for armies, etc. It needs many sane and healthy citizens. One of the first duties of the State will be to assure births. A special ministry of "Population" will watch over the increase in births.

RADICAL FEMINISM

To whom shall we look if not to mothers? How can we lead mothers to such a social duty if not by giving them special consideration? The best welcome we can give them is their emancipation from the power of husbands. And with the same stroke we impair the unity of the family. "The independence of the woman," Engels continues, "requires as a first condition their entrance into socially productive labor." In turn this condition calls for the suppression of the individual family as an economic unit of socety.

Can one be any more clear? The Right of mothers is the right to live as their husbands do. Secondly, it is the right to be unburdened of household chores which fetter their liberty as citizens and workers. Should they have children? Yes. Substantial advantage will be drawn from children. Hence, mothers are to get special considerations and all kinds of priorities. But raise their children? No. This is the concern of the State. Nurseries, kindergartens, and schools are provided.

FAMILY WITHOUT A FATHER

What becomes of the family in this vast program? It goes unmentioned, at least in its mission, for its name has never been mentioned. But in reality, a family is in question—a family without a father. Rather, the partners have changed. The State becomes father and husband. The mother is directly married to the State. As for the father in the flesh, it matters little whether he be legitimate or not. He is asked to be no more than pro-creator. We arrive, then, to a well-known phrase. "In space the family is reduced to the mother and the child; in time, to the period of nursing." This is the crowning glory of free love.

THE FAMILY WITHOUT A MOTHER

You see, then, that the State when appealing to the family in reality destroys it. Today it has need of the family; but tomorrow, if national interest would require it, it would restrict births, and this would break the last link, namely, maternity. As a matter of fact, it has already begun, since under the pretext of "unburdening the mother of her family" the State little by little substitutes itself for her. Let us not be duped by certain types of praise. It is not addressed to the family society as such—whose existence the State refuses to recognize legally. It merely wants women to bring more men into the world. The Church also invites them to do this, but for altogether different goals: the State wants more "man power." The Church wants "children of God."

THE CHURCH AND POPULATION

This essential distinction sets apart the position of the Church on the family from the position of the State. To the latter the Church concedes a role: the family normally cannot do without society. "The family," says Pius XI, "is an *imperfect society*, because it does not have in itself all the means necessary to reach its proper perfection." Here is the condemnation of the closed family, while, the Pope continues, "the civil society is a *perfect society*, since it has in itself all the means necessary to its proper end, which is the temporal well-being. It has, therefore, under this aspect, pre-eminence over the family." [14]

THE FAMILY: AN IMPERFECT SOCIETY

An imperfect society signifies, on a juridical level, that the State has the right and the duty to recognize and guarantee the conjugal bond; to protect the offspring; to complete the education of children in the measure in which the parents give it the mandate, and according to the choice they express. Thus, the aid of civil society is indispensable to the full flowering of the human person. It offsets the disadvantages that a life would have if it were restricted to a family circle; it responds to the need of the young to face the world.

Someone has said, "It is a false and dangerous belief to expect the family to be sufficient in everything for its members, and to refuse to the children the right to look outside the family for inspiration, friendship and support. The family is everything for the young children—nothing truly replaces it. But in the eyes of adolescents it nearly always becomes too small a world, whose doors they are impatient to open."

But to conclude from this, as does Statism, that the family is not useful or a nuisance is to play with words. The family is not an artificial invention of society; the historical arguments which support this contention more and more are disputed. Ethnology discovers the domestic society under its actual form among the most primitive peoples. "Historically, the state ap-

[14] Encyclical, "Christian Education of Youth."

pears after the family. It is not the State but the family which first of all came into existence. A nation is but a community of families. The family is the source of society." [15]

The family, one and indissoluble, far from being the impoverished residue of society, is indeed a living source of energy, a force which proceeds from its interior love to diffuse itself. The family is love perpetuating itself in an institution, which the whole history of the world proves.

Let us cite these few clear affirmations of the recent Popes: "The source and origin of the family and of all human society is found in marriage. If one considers its object, God has evidently put in it the most profound sources of the public good and welfare." [16] Pius XI says that "the state is what families make it to be." [17] To inject secularism into this "mother cell" is to infect the whole social body, since his Holiness, Pius XII, states: "the family is not only the cradle of children, but also of the nation." [18] We are far from the "closed family."

Because of your faith, the issue is clear for you, my brothers. It is also clear to every right mind. There is no reason for hesitation. Before such a great reality and before such grave heresies against which we warn you, in face of a dimunition of family life, there is one outstanding duty: we must all contribute to the restoration of the family.

III. RESTORATION OF THE FAMILY

The task before us is immense. Yet it would be entirely false and unjust to believe that nothing has been done about it. Courageous attempts have born fruit. After so much evil these efforts are our hope and our joy. We must recognize that due to them we have undoubtedly changed some things for the better.

When we say that the Christian family has taken on a new vitality, we do not imply that such progress has reached all

[15] Declaration of Cardinals and Archbishops, Nov., 1945.
[16] Encyclical Arcanum.
[17] Encyclical, "Casti Connubii."
[18] Allocution, 1942.

Catholic families, nor even the majority. Nor do we mean to insinuate that something new has been added to the Sacrament of Marriage. We wish only to rejoice in realizing that an increasing number of families are imbued with a family spirituality and are living it intensely. Our gratitude goes out to all the Family Movements which by their object, methods, publications and meetings have sparked this renewal. Our thanks to all the families, young and old, who have taken this spirituality to heart and applied it to their lives. We are happy to cite them as examples.

A DEEP CONJUGAL SPIRITUALITY

Without speaking of the nuptial ceremony, in which the worldly extravagances of late have given way more and more to prayerful Masses with Holy Communion, many spouses today look for and find in their union the secret of true Christian perfection. They realize the two ends of marriage which the Code of Canon Law and moral theology teach them: their homes are united and fruitful. Following St. Paul they especially insist on the sublimity of their union. They give legitimate value to the physical aspect, and that without Jansenism. But they also know the beauty of continence, and generously impose restraint on themselves. Body and soul play their proper role. Union for these spouses is the instrument of transforming graces. Marriage is a vocation and a state of sanctity. Recent inquiries show to what heights a love thus understood can elevate two souls.

FAMILY SPIRITUALITY IN COMMON

These inquiries also show what a family centered in Christ can accomplish. Let us cite solely the happy effects in the religious life of the family: evening prayer in common, reading of the Bible, preparation of and assistance at Sunday Mass, etc. Many parents seek to give the Christian meaning of family living to their children during times spent together in a family way, such as at meals and at evening, at work and leisure, at special times such as births, sickness, funerals. They also seek to create a Christian atmosphere by the appropriate decoration and arrangement of their home, by the participation of everyone in family prayer, and in the daily chores done in the service of the family and by giving a new emphasis to the sacraments, particularly those having a family significance: Baptism, the Eucharist, Marriage, Extreme Unction.

CATHOLIC ACTION AND FAMILY SPIRITUALITY

Such families merit the name of homes. They radiate. In reviving true family living they spread their good influence to the nation as a whole. Family restoration is both an effect and a cause: an effect, because it owes its origin to the Catholic Action movements which have taught their militants to put "the whole Gospel into their whole lives." In return it becomes a cause in giving to this same Catholic Action its modern form—Family Action. In its beginnings Catholic Action counted as its members only young apostles who were single. Today these are the fathers and mothers of families. Catholic Action is no longer in its beginnings; it leaves its adolescence and enters adulthood. It has a family footing at marriage age.

In the beginning the specialized Catholic Action movements were defined as the action of worker on worker, student on student, but now, with much logic, the motif is "conquest of family by family." Do not believe, however, that Catholic Action disavows for this reason its first method of an apostolate for the young. No. It simply follows the movement of life and grows with life. It becomes family action in the home. It evolves in order to remain true to itself—always adapted to new times and new needs.

The cooperation of families in the apostolate of the hierarchy is a fact without precedent. It constitutes a veritable revolution—the progressive victory of the community spirit over individualism, a step forward towards the realization of the Mystical Body of Christ.

It assumes two forms. On the plane of spirituality one sees more and more Catholic homes reuniting periodically in groups for a triple purpose: prayer in common, mutual spiritual and material aid, and the study of family problems. This formation is also sought in days of recollection, at family retreats, through specialized literature.

On the plane of action, they aid in instilling Christian Family ideals in their daily lives and works. They want to Christianize the whole life of the home. To do this they bring the aid of the large Christian Family Movement to bear on the problem; they bring in addition the testimony of their own family, and in each locale they assume the responsibility for bringing families together in a common ideal of mutual aid and restoration.

Here again we are in the presence of a new fact: the restoration of the whole country by the constructive work of united families and then by the testimony of individual families.

THE DUTY OF FAMILIES

Families, first of all, must recognize themselves and become aware of the force which they represent in the nation. Now, it is precisely this which the majority of families do not understand. They have a disdain for family associations, which they view simply as an effort to increase birth rates and which they suspect of political intentions. For such reasons family associations have so few members. Is there need to tell you that when we ask you to participate in such groups, we do not leave the family level? Families that group together have but one aim: to form a Family Corps which could speak in their name and promote legislative and social action which will save the nation while restoring its primary unit, the family. With grassroots strength, this organization will render a great service to the nation in making lighter its tasks and also a great service to the people in restraining state socialism.

SOLIDARITY AMONG FAMILIES

Solidarity among families requires faith. Families must forget their timidity and their inertia and inspire themselves with a militant family spirituality. We address very especally those of you who are heads of families, whatever be your social status, professions, or size of family. We ask you to enter immediately one of the already existing family movements. We do not hesitate to urge you to do this as a grave duty in conscience. We insist on this all the more since the Family Corps is at present the object of sharp competition. You must not let it be turned from its mission. Your only means to do this will be to make your presence felt and to act as militants in the cause of the family. This calls for action rather than words. You will generously undertake the services of your association which best respond to your talents.

In giving you the watchword we again take up the instructions that His Holiness Pope Pius XII addressed to French families on June 17, 1945, and to the Catholic women of Rome, October 21, of the same year.

"Fathers of Christian families, it is your right and your duty to act and to speak in the name of your families." "Catholic women, will you leave . . . to those who become accomplices in the ruin of the home . . . the monopoly of the social organization in which the family is the principal element? The destiny of the family, the destiny of the human community, are at stake; they are in your hands. Each woman without exception thus has the duty to act (under the forms most suitable to the condition of each), to restrain the influences menacing the home, and to organize and effect its restoration. Your hour has come, civic life has need of you."

THE DUTY OF THE STATE

The road has been mapped. The duty of families is to prepare the State for its duty of family restoration, instead of passively awaiting a miracle. Thus facilitated, the task of the State is immense. Its object is not merely to repair flaws in family life—this would be a short-sighted policy, unworthy of the times in which we live. The State must found the whole national reconstruction on the family by developing a family platform.

A CIVILIZATION BASED ON THE FAMILY

This is a large perspective, since the whole new civilization must be conceived, if it is to carry on, in terms of the function of the family, taken as the basic unit.

This means, first of all, the legal recognition by the Constitution of the Family as a social reality and a juridical institution. This quite naturally brings up its representation in the councils of the State. In legislation, there must be a forward step towards the suppression of the divorce law, the energetic abolition of abortion, a fight against alcoholism, immorality, organized vice, etc.

These measures of physical and moral purification will have a better chance of success in the framework of civic pride, conscious of the lessons of the past, in full-bodied, constructive civic planning. Small or medium sized villages are to be preferred to gigantic cities. Lodging is at once spacious and more friendly; work is more wholesome and less nerve-wracking; and life has more of a family atmosphere.

TRUE FEMINISM IN THE FAMILY

The salary of the father ought to be sufficient—with a perfected system of family allocations—to raise the level of existence of a large family to that of single workers and to permit the mother to remain in the home without dire financial difficulties to her family. The problem of Feminism ought to be orientated to this goal. No one asks that woman remain walled in her home, but that the home be given a culture and activities compatible with her family duties and centered on her inherent qualities as wife and mother. In the present actual conditions of a large family, such a balance is impossible.

Not that a lack of maturity kills it, but rather poverty, or a lack of assistance throughout her long sixteen hour day. The State also must consider as one of its most urgent duties the problem of Family Aid. In helping organize it, the State should be on guard not to replace the mothers with a substitute, but provide mothers with social workers who have a philosophy favorable to family life.

Let us also mention that the State must respect the rights of parents in education and make the school a natural complement of the family.

On the role of the civil authority in the restoration of the family we have indicated several suggestions, without a formal listing and without prejudice to a particular technique. These suffice for us to conclude that a family policy, far from being a secondary duty of the State, should be a Welfare Policy looking to the future. Let those who have assumed the heavy responsibilities of government be persuaded of it and busy themselves in effecting it.

THE DUTY OF CATHOLICS

Doing this, we have not resolved the problem. The essential factor remains in the family itself. For if certain economic and social conditions are necessary for the development of the family, they are not the cause of it. You know quite well that certain homes equipped with all home appliances remain engulfed in voluntary stagnation. Why? Because they have no principles. We always come back to the absolute need for a spirituality.

Thus, we count on you, our faithful Christians, to bring about this great "Return to the Family."

To spouses and Christian parents, we ask that they restore the principle of authority in their homes—conjugal and paternal: the husband having the "primacy of government" and the wife having the "primacy of love." Let them not give way, either, to a "fear of life," as plausible as that might appear. Providence is there.

To future spouses, we ask that they prepare themselves, separately at first, then as fiancees, for the work which awaits them. We heartily encourage them to take part in conferences and retreats of formation which have been especially prepared for them. As for Baptism, Holy Eucharist, and Holy Orders, so too does the Sacrament of Marriage require preparation. In this area much yet needs to be done. Parents and educators must see to it.

The movements of Catholic Action find a role to play, too. They have already played it, and played it well. We recommend that they be careful not to separate the movement of young people from the movements of married adults.

Finally, our priests must quicken their zeal and strengthen themselves in doctrine in order to bring about the restoration of the family. It is desirable that in their seminary training they receive the element of family pastoral theology and that they use and deepen these principles in the future. They can become competent chaplains for family groups, in which we see the signs of restoration.

The whole Church—families, Catholic Action, and the clergy —must bring about a great renewal of family life. This is the mission of the Church, and the Christian family lives up to this purpose.

FULL FAMILY LIFE

We all know that Christian families form a front. They are distinguished by a "family attitude" from the eldest to the baby in the crib. Their special family seal is the mark of great love; it is the sign of long patience, the patience of successive generations; the sign of the never-tiring efforts of the two spouses. Their sons and daughters surround the spouses at the dinner table "as young olive plants."[19] No one is rich, since everything is shared; no one is poor, since all is held in common. Love, especially, gives itself abundantly. There is the peaceful love of the grandparents in the evening of their lives; a faithful and deep love of the spouses for each other; a mutual exchange of maternal and filial love. The home is the crossroad of family life, where all rejoice and grieve, where they are born and where they die. In the home we meet and take leave of one another; we help one another in daily tasks; we learn to serve and to lead; to undertake and to preserve; there we find the model of our lives; there we are trained in wisdom and forgetfulness of self. Our home is the school of duty and human virtues.

THE PERFECT FAMILY IS THE CHRISTIAN FAMILY

Who will deny that these virtues are also Christian? They are Christian in their culmination, for supernatural life cannot do without them. They are the foundation of the supernatural life. But they are Christian especially in their origin, for they

[19] Ps., 117:37.

are born only of the cross of Christ. The family is founded on sacrifice.

Only a Christian conscience, attached to its divine origin, is capable of such renouncements. It alone can inspire the couple to fidelity of body and soul during their whole life, in spite of the concupiscence born of original sin. Generous and mortified souls alone can accept the risks and burdens of child-bearing. They alone are capable of raising a large family in honor and making men of them. The happiness which radiates from these families is not of this world. Its source is elsewhere, in a joy which comes from God.

CONCLUSION

The happiness of a family is a joy which comes from Christ. It is He Who blesses them. It is He Who is the soul and life of the family. Grant that He animates them, that He be the source and term of them. That is our wish and prayer. Then, "Christian Families," grouped "by the thousands" to "ardently promote the reign of Jesus Christ" can be confident and say once again with the Holy Father: "Who will match the power of such an army, under such a leader?" [20]

PRAYER ON FEAST OF THE HOLY FAMILY

"O Lord Jesus Christ, Who, in the days of Thy subjection to Mary and Joseph, didst consecrate home life by ineffable acts of virtue; by the intercession of Thy Holy Mother and Thy Foster Father, make us so to profit by the example they with Thee have set for us, that we may be counted members of Thy household for evermore. Amen."

[20] Pius XII. Discourse to French Families, 6-7-45.

GROWTH OR DECLINE?

What is the role of the Church?

The Church is the permanent incarnation of the Son of God. Wherefore, her two-fold nature: the one spiritual, transcendent, divine, deriving ultimately from its most intimate principle of life, the Holy Spirit. The other visible, evolving, adaptable, and dependent on concrete circumstances and human wills.

The world needs the Church for its life. The Church needs the world for its growth and development.

Contents

Growth or Decline?

After the end of the war we know that the peace we had looked forward to will not be what our hopes had imagined. It is not as close as we thought, and it will not be a quiet return to the forms of the past. The crisis now shaking the world goes far beyond the causes which brought it on. The war has contributed its share, with the sufferings it brought in its train. But the upheaval it unleashed has not ended with it; it comes from deeper causes and goes much further. The ruins around us are a tragedy, but they are also a symbol; for something on this earth has died, never to rise again. The war thus takes on its true meaning: it was not an interlude but an epilogue; and it marks the end of a world.

But, and of necessity, the era now before us which will succeed it, appears as a prologue, the preface to a world which is coming to be.

A Crisis of Growth

This conclusion is not imaginary. It is founded on converging signs, and on a unanimous body of evidence. All agree in pointing to our age as an age of transition. The sufferings affecting the entire globe, the dangers threatening its future, the great currents sweeping through it, are less the consequences of a catastrophe than the first signs of an imminent birth. Or, more exactly, the present unrest is neither a sickness of the world nor a decadence, but a crisis of growth, and as such it is a fragile and impetuous adolescence and a crucial moment, when new values are gradually replacing the structures of the old. What is dying? What is coming to birth? It is less a question here of analyzing than of recognizing this to be true; and it is already possible, without being in any way arbitrary, to sketch summarily the main lines this process of development will take.

The first sign, and the one which is the plainest because it is a fact we can experience, is that this crisis is a *crisis of unification.* The stages by which it has come about are well known: the great discoveries of science engendered movement and speed; space has changed its dimensions; the airplane has welded continents and linked up the Antipodes. Communications have multiplied. Everything—production, consumption, distribution, economics and finance—all is done now on an international scale. The humblest object of daily life comes from the ends of the earth. Each of us depends on the rest of mankind for the bare fact of survival. And it is the same in the spheres of feeling and thought. The Press is everywhere, and with it the film; for the cinema everywhere reproduces the same cosmopolitan features upon the screen. And the ether, which knows no frontiers, takes the music, the news and the thought of all to all indiscriminately. Radio and television are the brain and the nerve force which, for the first time in its history, have made the pulses of our planet beat with the same rhythm at the same moment in time.

Outline of a Common Civilization

The results have not been long coming; the barriers on this expanding world of ours are falling, the water-tight compartments are breaking up under the tremendous pressure of this new tide which is overturning and levelling everything. What is happening now to the whole world is what happened on a smaller scale in the Mediterranean world when Rome was at the height of her power: the delineation of a common civilization. But whereas the latter confined itself to language, law and commerce, ours tends to establish a uniform way of life and a uniform type of man—what may be called a "world humanism."

It would be a grave mistake, in this new thing, to see nothing but a composite image, a heterogeneous amalgamation resulting from a sudden hasty fusing of particular differences brought together by the practical necessities of human life. The modern man who is coming into existence seems in truth to proceed from an organic unity and an inner principle of life; and it is the same with the City he is preparing for his use. The most obvious feature of that new humanism is its technical character. Born of scientific discovery and the machine, to them it owes the style it has everywhere assumed, it is based on them, it relies on them to bring the coming order into being.

The scientific outlook is daily ousting classical culture and taking its place. The object of thought has changed; the world of pure ideas has been abandoned for efficient action.

This effort man is making is not individual. Henceforth, each has need of all. The unit of work is no longer the artisan but the team. Bonds are being knit which stretch far beyond the frontiers of province and nation, and reach, on a world-wide scale, a communitarian humanism, a universalist civilization.

These features alone, among many others, are enough to show that the world taking shape, above all during the last twenty years, cannot be dismissed as merely some sort of "turning-point of history." It is not an earthquake, brutal and on the surface, but an inner crisis: for the first time, ever since the world began, the world is "one," and is conscious of it. That collective realization, with the gropings, clumsiness and adherence to past forms that accompany it, is nothing else but adolescence. Society, especially Western society, is going through a structural reform which is breaking the continuity of its traditions, upsetting the working of established rules and questioning accepted values. The resulting disorder and the consciousness of inadaptation, in every sphere, justify the feeling so often and ambiguously expressed by the words: "The world is in revolution."

I. WHO WILL UNITE THE WORLD?

It is here that the crucial question begins. Who is going to provide the inspiration of this common civilization arising everywhere and of itself, in a world hitherto divided—for this sudden unity which has emerged more quickly than we realized —for a world-wide humanism for which we were unprepared? Who will make the synthesis of the new universe? What will be its principle and its inspiration?

THE ANSWER OF THE NON-CHRISTIANS

Not the Church, they say, and that for a very good reason: the Church is about to disappear.

Decline of the Church

The signs of her last agony, they maintain, are only too plain. Take numbers alone: the human race is increasing, the Church decreasing. Although always in a minority, at least until recently she numbered solid blocks of the faithful; but today what she herself calls the "apostasy of the masses" underlines her failure. Her vitality, through countless cracks, is ebbing away; and one after another she sees whole peoples fall from her allegiance. The Church's decadence, they go on, is even more manifest in the spheres of influence and prestige, and in her friendships. From being at one time supreme in culture, the monopoly of which was secured to her by her theology, and in power, which she maintained by holding the people in ignorance, the Church is now nothing but a shadow of her former self. Split into rival factions, decried by her own children, she is paying, in their eyes, the price of her infidelity to her origins, and in the eyes of the world, the penalty of an inborn and incurable archaism. She no longer has the ear of men. Finally, one may ask, what is left to her? And they reply: What she has always upheld, the "ruling class" of yesterday, a liberal economy with which she has become identified. Bound up with the regime of capitalism, she is foundering with it. The Church is dying with a dying world.

Her Misdeeds

Since she is "absent" in this way, she must not be counted on. But it is especially if she were alive that she would have to be thrust aside as enemy number one. And the reason for her harmfulness lies in this, that her ends conflict with those of man, even more with the modern humanism. They and the Church are poles apart. The two systems are not only different; they are clean contrary.

Firstly, this can be seen in the view both take of the world. What, in fact, does science tell us of that? We are shown its unity, in space and time. A dynamic continuity, originating in matter, explains man and society. That growth is not haphazard; it is a "dialectical" and connected process, an ascending and inescapable movement of evolution which, by the constant perfecting of technical knowledge, will result in man's emancipation from myths and other forms of enslavement, and will open to him, in a communitarian humanity, the "possession of the world" which is his right; it is an optimistic doctrine which believes in happiness and which, not content with pursuing it, is building its edifice bit by bit, by the methodical study of the biological, psychological and sociological conditions necessary.

As against such a creative vision, what has the Church to offer? A static and "theistic" world, a dependent philosophy and one frozen in impossible dogmas, a negative and preconceived system of morality in which the snobbery of caste rubs shoulders with a jealous mistrust of science, too ready to dethrone God. As for the human person, they assert, the Christian era has produced a model without strength and without beauty. Christianity has taken the virility from man.[1] By urging him to escape into another world beyond the present, religion takes him away from the tasks of this earth and makes it impossible for him to stand shoulder to shoulder with his fellows in the City he inhabits. Weak in the fight, timid in daring, useless in action, the Christian, by reason of his bourgeois or repressed education, cannot be a "comrade." He cannot be counted on to conquer the world.

Such being her program, how can the Church be other than a stranger in a world which believes in itself and is enthusiastically set on making a future which will be at once more real and more beautiful? It is not to be wondered at if this conquest is going on, not merely without her, but even against her, in the measure in which she threatens its success. Man today, in building his new world, expects nothing from the Church; he rejects and thrusts aside this witness from a past age.

THE POSITION OF CATHOLICS

At this stage, it is the turn of the believers to intervene. They also have considered the question; and their reply is clear also.

[1] Here we would have to cite the whole neo-pagan trend from Nietzsche, Hegel, Marx, &c., whose doctrine is the basis of all the present-day anti-Christian writing.

No, the Church is not dead, and the world will not be re-made without her. Yet a number of conditions must be observed.

But in saying what these conditions are, Catholics diverge in their views, and even contradict each other. Nevertheless, it is possible to set out the positions they hold at present and the many criticisms they have made during the last few years,[2] along two main lines.

The first attitude is that of those who say: "Let us stay as we are." Their argument is the very reverse of that of their opponents. To the atheism of aggression they reply with a dogmatism of defence. It is not the Church which is dying, or at fault, but the modern world. Or rather, the world *tout court*, for it is modern only to us. The problems invoked by it to justify its divorce from the Church are in no way new; they are repetitions of those met with in all past crises. "There is nothing new under the sun." The problems remain; the only thing that has changed is the labels they bear. It is not the Church which is out of step, but man, by his sins or his folly. This system, like all others, will pass; we have only to let the storm blow itself out; truth always triumphs in the end. The Church has lived through other crises; she is not afraid of this one.

The great danger which threatens the Church today is to want to adapt herself; let her beware of this ever-recurring temptation. It is not for her to accommodate her message, but for successive civilizations to assimilate it. She must be more adamant than ever. Let her not give ear to the siren voices with which the Evil One so soon began to whisper in the ear of our Savior. Today, everything invites her to forget her essential mission, which is, uncompromisingly, to give to men "words which do not pass away." If, in the doubtful hope of securing the allegiance of men, she gives up her monopoly of truth, she is finished once and for all. For the Church is not of this world. She is the Kingdom of God; and far from setting herself the impossible task of bridging the gulf which separates her from the world, she ought, untiringly, to remain outside and above the successive fluctuations of society. The only attitude open to the Church is one of separation.

[2] At least in France.

That attitude, in the sphere of doctrine, will be best expressed by an outright return to her traditional forms, by invoking those official documents of hers which guarantee and reinforce the rightness of the positions she maintains. Above all, let her beware of accommodating her message: that path leads to complete surrender. Let her proclaim "the truth," in all its harshness, without any watering down.

In the action they undertake, Catholics must realize that compromise gains them neither esteem nor advantage. They must therefore stand aloof from any form of premature co-operation. Their strength lies in their unity. The sole allegiance to the Creed and the declaration that they belong to the People of God are worth more than advances rashly made. The Church will weather the crisis only by refusing to embody herself in temporal institutions. She is less afraid of Nero than of Constantine.

Those who reproach the Church with her inability to succeed in the temporal order invite her to a reform which is the exact opposite. The Church in the West has not evolved with civil society. She has remained riveted to, and congealed in, the feudal conditions which made her success long ago. In our time, instead of being diffused throughout all ranks of society as she was in the Middle Ages, when parish and township had the same life and the same geographical extension, the Church is "absent" from the City. She is above humanity instead of being incarnate in its flesh and blood. In her message she has all and more than is needed both to give life to the systems of today and to draw up plans for those of tomorrow; but she does not use it. She lets strangers, or enemies, take an initiative which is often decisive in the field of doctrine, culture, and action; and when she acts or speaks it is often too late. Whether it be in scientific research, social laws or humanism, the innovators rarely come from her ranks. It is not in that way that she will win the world for Christ. There is still time for the Church to assert her place, and even the first place, in the shaping of the future; but on one condition, that she becomes incarnate. "God became man so that men should become gods." In that case, and in that case only, will the Church come alive once more.

For the vast majority of those who favor adaptation, thus to merge the Church in contemporary civilization means nevertheless to respect formally the whole content of the deposit of faith. They do not spare the Church and the hierarchy their criticisms, and the suggestions they put before them deal with a variety of subjects. From the daily experience which contact with the deChristianized masses provides, many apostles, both priests and lay, are convinced of the need of modifications, usually of a secondary but pressing nature, for successful evangelization. They wish to see a concrete and adapted religious teaching taking the place of sermons and a catechizing too cut off from the gospel. From Theology which, unlike Revelation, is not closed, they ask for an attempt at synthesis and realism which, without sacrificing anything, will place in the forefront and within reach of the spirituality of this century the major dogmas of our religion. They point out that worship and liturgy are often incomprehensible and, for that reason, that the masses of Christians and often the best among them find their way closed to the great common prayer. If they practice their religion at all, they merely conform to a conventional religion unconnected with the rest of their lives. Cannot the Church come to their help by making easier for them the reception of the sacraments and their understanding of the sacramental rites? They point out that the independence of the laity is often more verbal than real; and conscious that the lay people have reached their majority, they claim for them a wider area of responsibility. There are no questions, not excluding those of finance, in particular as they affect worship, which are not for them matters of reform.

From these views, and from many more which cannot be included here, it is clear that everything points to the same demand, that the Church must adapt herself to the modern world if she wishes to reconquer it.

Shall the Church stand aloof and keep everything? Or incorporate herself and conquer everything? Those are the two poles of Catholic opinion.

The Uncertainty among Catholics

Which of the two is right?

The answer is of great importance. It affects the practical attitude of the majority of Catholics, who have not as yet made up their minds one way or the other. At the same time as they are drawn by these new values, they are disturbed and full of misgiving at so many disagreements; they look on and wait. Some do so out of timidity or a desire to be left undisturbed; others, and quite sincerely, because they fail to see how they can escape from the dilemma which, when they are all considered collectively, has brought about these two groups, and which, when they are considered as individuals, cruelly divides their hearts. They belong to two worlds, and are conscious of it. Loyal to both, they carefully avoid whatever might exclude one or the other. As citizens of this world, they realize their solidarity with and responsibility for, its destiny; as sons of God, they are aware of their mysterious incorporation in His Church and their transcendent vocation. So as not to betray either, they refuse to choose or to commit themselves.

Meanwhile, they see the general state of uneasiness and suffer from it. They are well aware that the world's crisis reacts necessarily on the Church, for her roots go deep in that world. They have no fear for her or of her eventual triumph; but they wonder how she can emerge from the present state of things and by what ways they can help her to do so. In them, and unknown to them, the influence and perhaps the attraction of the progressive idealism affecting their contemporaries is also active. Accordingly, when they see the Church divided and plagued by her sons on whether to remain aloof or fearlessly commit herself; when they see her distracted by disputes and torn between the unchangeable and the actual, her uneasiness becomes theirs; and in order not to lose their balance they seek refuge in prayer or withdraw into forms of escapism.

To stand aside, to adapt, to wait: which of these is right, and what is the meaning of the crisis? What do these initiatives and the prevailing anxiety portend? Are they signs of death or of growth? Do they mark autumn or spring for the Church?

We do not pretend that our answer solves anything. We only say that in the measure that this crisis reveals a division among Catholics it is an evil and must end. If it continues, the mutual condemnation by followers of Jesus Christ would constitute a scandal and be an obstacle to the Church's progress. In the measure, however, that these clearly defined positions are evidence of a passionate love of the Church, they are a proof of her vitality and the sign of a period of growth. The volume of ideas and experiments now being put forward is far more reassuring than a stagnating self-satisfaction. We wish at one and the same time to calm the anguish which, as we well know, troubles the minds of too many Catholics as they confront the coming age, and to shake that far too numerous body of the faithful from the deceptive security in which they are held fast. To both we wish to demonstrate that the one and only explanation of the present crisis, and the one and only criterion of security and action for the Christian today, is to be found in the high nature of the Church such as her dogma and her history make it known to us.

Far indeed from presaging her decline, everything contributes to foretell a new development of her life. We intend merely to set out—and they will form the lines of action we propose for you—what are the conditions necessary at this present time for this Second Spring.

II. THE MYSTERY OF THE CHURCH

It is impossible to judge the part the Church should play in the modern world without going deeply into her nature, such as it emerges from Theology and History.

THE THEOLOGY OF THE CHURCH

The Church is part of a larger whole. She has her place in the "economy of salvation." What is God's plan? It is to give His own life to the world; and in fact the method He chose was the Incarnation of His Son: "The Word was made flesh and came to dwell among us." [3] "These graces He might him-

[3] John, 1:14.

self, had He so chosen, have bestowed directly upon the human race; but He willed to do this by means of a visible Church in which men would be united and through which they would cooperate with Him in distributing the fruits of Redemption." [4]

Spouse and Body of Christ

His mediation does not therefore end at His Ascension: "Christ, now risen from the dead, cannot die any more." [5] It was to be continued on earth by His Church. She is thus not a society of the same kind as others, but a mysterious reality: she was born of the heart of Jesus Christ pierced by the lance, coming like "a new Eve from the side of the new Adam." [6] The Church is thus the spouse of Christ and the "new Jerusalem sent down by God from heaven, all clothed in readiness like a bride who has adorned herself to meet her husband," [7] "and so united to Him that she is one with Him and becomes His own body." [8] "The term 'whole Christ' means 'both head and body.' Now the Church is His body. Or we may speak of 'bride and bridegroom,' two in one flesh." [9] It is Christ who is the soul of His body by mysteriously communicating to it His Spirit which is its soul.[10] From this it follows that the society founded by the Christ of history on the roads of Palestine, on Calvary and at Pentecost, and built upon Peter [11] is not a collection of individuals artificially brought together, but an organic and real thing, the Mystical Body of Christ.

"The Church is Christ"

Spouse and body of Christ, the Church may even be called "Christ." The encyclical *Mystici Corporis* points this out: [12]

[4] *Mystici Corporis*, E. T., The Mystical Body of Jesus Christ, in *Catholic Mind*, Nov. 1943, p. 6.

[5] Rom., 6:9.

[6] Gen., 2:21-23.

[7] Apoc., 21:22.

[8] Col., 1:18; Eph., 1:22.

[9] St. Augustine, *Contra Donat.*, *Cap.* 7. (P.L. 43, XII, 593).

[10] *Mystici Corporis*, E. T., The Mystical Body of Jesus Christ, op. cit., p. 12, 20-21.

[11] Matt., 16:18.

[12] *Mystici Corporis*, E. T., p. 20.

"St. Paul called the Church simply by the name of 'Christ' [13] Indeed, if we are to follow St. Gregory of Nyssa, the Church is frequently called Christ by the Apostle,[14] and you are familiar with the saying of St. Augustine: "Christ preaches Christ.'" [15] The theme was developed by Bossuet: "The Church," he says,[16] "is Jesus Christ spread abroad and bestowed among men, Jesus Christ whole and entire, Jesus Christ perfect man, Jesus Christ in His fullness."

It was not without reason that Our Savior intended this visible renewing of Himself in time: "If the Son of the Most High," says Möhler, "had come down into the heart of man without taking on . . . a bodily form, we would easily imagine that He might have founded an invisible and purely internal Church. But 'the Word, having become flesh' [17] . . . in order to win man once more for the kingdom of heaven, wished to suffer and act as man." And the great theologian goes so far as to say: "Considered from this standpoint, *the Church* is thus Jesus Christ ceaselessly renewing Himself and continually reappearing in human form: *the Church is the permanent incarnation of the Son of God.*" [18]

The Two Aspects of the Church

If this is so, it is natural for us to find two aspects closely connected and present in the Church: "Just as the divinity and the humanity in Jesus Christ, although distinct from each other, are not thereby any the less united, in the same way *Our Savior in the Church is continued in everything that He is.*

[13] I Cor., 12:12.
[14] St. Greg. Nyss., *De Vita Moysis* (P.G. XLIV, 385).
[15] Serm. CCCLIV, I. (P.L. XXXIX, 1563).
[16] *Lettre* 28.
[17] John, 1:14.
[18] Möhler, *La Synbolique*, F. T. Lachat, II.

"The Church," says Lippert, "thus appears not only as an institution founded by Jesus Christ in the past, but also as a present reality; at each moment of time it continually springs from Christ like a vast river, which comes from the invisible depths of the soul and spreads throughout the visible world of its organization, just like the pulsing-rhythmed to the movement of universal history—of a heart eternally alive." *L'Eglise du Christ*, p. 298 seq.

The Church, His permanent manifestation, is at one and the same time human and divine; she is the unity of these two attributes. It is the mediator who, hidden beneath these human forms, continues to act in her; and she has therefore necessarily a divine side and a human side." [19]

TRANSCENDENTAL ASPECT

By reason of this first aspect, the Church absolutely transcends all human societies.[20] "God has made the Church by far the most excellent society of all. For the destiny which she claims for her members is as superior to that of other societies as divine grace is to nature or things immortal to things which come to an end. And so in origin the Church is divine; her destiny and the means by which she achieves it are supernatural." [21] It should be noted, it is not a matter merely of precedence, but of a transcendence given by nature. "Mystical" does not mean "less real." The Church is not an "entity" comparable to any of our moral or juridical "persons." The unity which binds the faithful to God and with each other in Christ and the Holy Spirit is an "ontological" unity.[22]

Thus considered in her substantial reality, the Church has been constituted once and for all and made perfect. She is entirely holy, entirely completed. Because she is the undying prolongation of the Savior in time, in her is enshrined what is

[19] Möhler, *op. cit.*, pp. 313-315.

[20] Tradition insists on this reality of the Church; she cannot be reduced to other societies: "The power of the Church is as far above the civil power in value as heaven is above the earth, or rather it transcends it even more." St. John Chrys., *In II Cor.* Hom. XV, 4-5. (P.G. LXI, 507.)

[21] Leo XIII, *Satis Cognitum*, A.S.S., XXVIII, p. 274.

[22] I Cor., 12:27—Tradition insists on this aspect. The principle which makes the Mystical Body immeasurably transcends all the bonds of unity by which any physical or moral body is knit together. (*Mystici Corporis*, E.T. pp. 37-38.) This uncreated principle is the Holy Spirit who, according to St. Thomas "one and unique, fills the whole Church and makes her unity." (*De Veritate* Q. 29, a. 4 c.). "The summit of the Church's perfection, as of the foundation on which she is built," says Clement of Alexandria, "consists in unity; and it is for that reason that she transcends everything in this world and encounters nothing equal or like to her." (Stromat. VII, 17.)

essential to His Resurrection. "Behold, I am with you all through the days that are coming, until the consummation of the world." [23] And in her dwells, absolutely intact and unchangeable, the sacred deposit of Revelation which Tradition hands down from age to age. She is truly the New Law, not one iota of which shall be lost, and the undying Message: "Though heaven and earth shall pass away, my words shall stand." [24] The Church is therefore a rock and a "norm" which no change can alter, no attack impair, no solicitation corrupt. From that aspect she adds nothing to Christ. She does no more than make Him visible in His infinite "reality."

TEMPORAL ASPECT

But this sublime reality must not blind us to another, namely that the Church is also in time, in history, "*inter mundanas varietates.*" [25] For the Church is a body: "It is because she is a body that the Church is visible to us" says Leo XIII; [26] and Pius XII lays down: "it is therefore an aberration from divine truth to represent the Church as something intangible and invisible, as a mere "pneumatic" entity . . ." [27]

Invisibly governed by her founder and indwelt by His Holy Spirit, the Church is also a visible and hierarchical society in which the Pope and the Bishops wield an authority without which there can be no orthodoxy in the faith and no discipline among the faithful.

Contingent

Because she is the body of Christ, His incarnation in the history and the geography of the earth, the Church is first of all contingent. She belongs to a special time and place. Why here rather than there? Why was she born in Palestine rather than in China? And why during the reign of Tiberius? The Church is as she is, but she might have been very different. The battle

[23] Matt., 28:20.
[24] Matt., 24:35.
[25] Prayer for the Fourth Sunday after Easter.
[26] Leo XIII, *Satis Cognitum*, A.S.S., Vol. XXVIII, p. 710.
[27] *Mystici Corporis*, E.T., p. 6.

of Poitiers for long settled her extension and her destiny . . . and in all such events we can only accept the mysterious outcome of men's actions and the workings of Providence. If such and such a saint had not lived, if such and such a religious order had not been founded or a particular continent had remained unexplored, the Church would have neither the same forms nor the same extension: she would not be what she is today. As a community inside history, the descendant of the chosen people who prefigured her, she must submit to the vicissitudes of the centuries and the laws of human society. She takes to herself men as they are, with their language, their customs and their heredity.

Her Growth . . .

Because she is also a body, the Church does not remain stationary; she develops, changes and grows. To her is applied the parable of the mustard seed: "Of all seeds none is so little, but when it grows up . . . all the birds come and settle in its branches." [28] She is also "the whole fabric bound together, as it grows into a temple, dedicated to the Lord." [29] That growth, however, has certain clearly marked features.

She is first of all "*Catholic*," that is, she extends everywhere. The geographical and ethnological aspect of the Church's extension is frequently commented on, and rightly; because the way she has made her way into the heart of countries and the diverse sociological entities making up the world is an event without precedent. "While this City of God is in exile on earth," says St. Augustine, "it enrolls its citizens from men of all nations and tongues. It does not worry about differences in culture, laws and ways of life." [30] But the Church has proved equally well what we may call her *vertical catholicity*: she has embodied herself in the continuing existence of the world, just as much as in its geography. She has passed through, and put on, all the civilizations of history. She has suited herself to time

[28] Matt., 13:31-32.
[29] Eph., 2:21-22.
[30] *De Civitate Dei*, bk. XIX, chap. XVII.

just as she has suited herself to space. Each age has lent her its "stature" and its features.

. . . . is an Organic Growth

These successive incarnations do not destroy the Church's continuity; they are merely the various "moments" of her growth among men. That development on earth is not principally, or uniquely, quantitative, through the enrolling of new members, but an organic development; and it therefore has a direction. The direction it will take cannot be deduced in advance from her existence as it is at this moment, and we cannot lay down beforehand the "temporal" line in which the path of the Church will run.[31] Life always contains an element of the unforeseen. But on the other hand we know the Church's ultimate goal, to which that growth is directed and which defines her: the Church is meant to "complete" Christ. And at the end she will be His "pleroma."

When we consider her from that aspect, we see, first of all, that the successive "actualizations" of the Church, far from impoverishing her, make for her growth. The civilizations of history, as they succeed each other, no more exhaust the Church than do individuals, by their increase, exhaust the species. On the contrary, each of the societies as well as the social forms in which the Church becomes incarnate, all help to "complete" Christ. The body has need of the Head,[32] but the Head has need also of the body. "And yet it is also certain, surprising though it may seem, that Christ requires His members . . . He wants to be helped by the members of His mystical body in carrying out the work of the Redemption." [33] This conclusion is of the highest importance if we are to understand the relations the Church has with the world, and therefore if we are to see the action to which the Christian is pledged. The world,

[31] "As Christ is a living being, the Church is a living organism which develops under the thrust of her vital principle; nor, before living, does she wait for theorists to define her and lay down the conditions in which they will allow her to live." J. Leclercq, *La Vie du Christ dans son Eglise*, p. 77.

[32] John, 15:5; Eph., 4:16.

[33] *Mystici Corporis*, E.T. p. 17.

for its own life, needs the Church; and the Church needs the world for her own development and completion.[34]

Until the Second Coming

Since the Church is the "pleroma" of Christ, it is understandable that she wishes, uninterruptedly, to enlarge her boundaries and become more perfect. She feels the duty laid upon her to grow, right down the centuries, to the dimensions of humanity and in the whole diverse and concrete rangc which its individuals reach in their ideas and their forms of culture. The Church is not Catholic only in fact, but also in intention. Her "end" is Christ's Second Coming, that is, the eschatological triumph of Christ, "the alpha and omega." She has to make for Him, and be to Him, a finished body: "perfect manhood, the maturity which is proportionate to the completed growth of Christ," [35] intent on penetrating and assuming everything the world has "except sin." [36] "During the whole period between the first coming of Christ and the second, the Church is building, under the influence of the seven-fold grace of the Holy Ghost, until at the end of time, she shall be complete." [37] She can know no rest until she has carried out her unique mission, which is to "make God ruler of the world" and re-establish in His Son the whole of creation redeemed by His Blood. The doctrine of the Mystical Body is completed by the doctrine of the Kingship of Christ.[38]

[34] "Nabuchodonosor saw a small stone—Christ—which, split off from the mountain by a human hand, grew until it became a large mountain and filled the whole earth. (Dan., II, 34-35). Detached from the mountain the stone grew and became a mountain, because this body, which had taken only a microscopic part of the mass of the human race, expands to vast proportions because of the numbers coming to it on every side, and does not stop growing until the end of time and until it has filled the whole earth." Adelmann de Brescia, ed. R. Heurtevent, p. 300.

[35] Eph., 4:13.

[36] Heb., 4:15.

[37] Raoul de St.-Germer, *In Levit,* 1:17.

[38] "The foundation of this power and dignity of Our Lord," writes Pius XI, "is rightly indicated by Cyril of Alexandria. Christ, he says, has dominion over all creatures, a dominion not seized by violence nor usurped, but His by essence and by nature (*In* Luc X.). His Kingship is

Able to Suffer, and Suffering

That goal is sublime; but the Church will not reach it in a day. Incarnate, as was Christ, she suffers as He did; she knows in turn victory and persecution. His mysteries are re-enacted in her, Thabor and Calvary, the joyful, the sorrowful, the glorious. Why should we be surprised if she is ceaselessly withstood, often humiliated, always suffering in some quarter or other of the earth, when we know that the course of her life on earth rehearses the suffering life of our Redeemer? "The servant is not above his master." [39] It can be said of her what Pascal said of Christ: "the Church is in agony until the end of time." Made up as she is of men, she will therefore number sinners and the tepid, faithful, apostates, heresies and schisms. During her pilgrimage on earth the Church is *in via*, moving towards the heavenly Jerusalem; and the road is often a road of crucifixion. The march is exacting; and it is not done without wounds and scars. Her human face, as happened with her Master, is often bathed with sweat and blood; and, like the Holy Face, it is sometimes covered with filth. What Isaias prophesied of Christ's Passion can be applied to certain ages of the Church: "And he shall grow up as a tender plant before him . . . as out of a thirsty ground; there is no beauty nor comeliness in him, and there was no sightliness, that we should be desirous of him. Despised, and the most abject of men . . . his look was as it were hidden and despised, whereupon we esteemed him not." [40]

---

founded upon the ineffable hypostatic union . . . and by reason of the hypostatic union Christ has power over all creatures." And the Pope quotes Leo XIII: "His empire includes not only Catholic nations . . . but also all those who are outside the Christian faith; so that truly the whole of mankind is subject to the power of Jesus Christ" (Leo XIII, *Annum Sacrum*, May 25, 1899) and continues further: "Nor is there any difference in this matter between the individual and the family or the State; for all men, whether individually or collectively, are under the dominion of Christ." Pius XI, *Quas Primas*, E.T., in Social Wellsprings, Joseph Huslein, Vol. II.

[39] Matt., 10:24.

[40] Is., 52:2-3.

The Church, Mystery of Faith

If this is so of the Church, why should we be surprised if she is a "scandal" in the eyes of men? Although it be true that the Church, by herself, is a strong enough reason to make an unprejudiced mind believe, why should we wonder when her divinity is not recognized under her human form, when we remember that in Palestine the crowd did not recognize the Messias [41] in "the son of the carpenter," [42] or in the distorted features of the Victim on Calvary? It is necessary to have the faith of the good thief to pick out fully the divinity of the Church from behind her earthly features. We need the spirit of faith to recognize in them "the Spouse with no stain, no wrinkle . . . holy . . . spotless," [43] the bride "adorned to meet her husband," [44] and to realize that, inexhaustible spring of holiness though she is, she is also made up of the lukewarm and sinners. Christ's Mystical Body, as He was, is a "stumbling block," [45] against which the prejudice and impatience of men trip and fall. How can those who judge her from the outside, and according to the single standards of human societies, understand the mystery of that other society "which is far more excellent than all other associations of human beings, transcending them as grace transcends nature." [46] They have eyes and know not what they see. As with the disciples at Emmaus and the risen Christ, men walk the road with the Church and "cannot recognize" her.[47] They see the body, the visible, juridical and institutional Church; but her primordial supernatural reality, her holiness, her unchangeable and imperishable being escape them. We ask again, need we wonder at it? Two thousand years ago the contemporaries of the Messias refused Him their homage of faith and love. Why should the contemporaries of the Church, which perpetuates and incarnates Him,

[41] John, 1:5-10-11.
[42] Matt., 13:53.
[43] Eph., 5:27.
[44] Apoc., 21:2.
[45] Matt., 21:44.
[46] *Mystici Corporis*, E.T. p. 24.
[47] Luke, 24:16.

give it to Him now? The Church, we must not forget, is a truth of faith: "*Credo . . . in unam, sanctam, catholicam et apostolicam ecclesiam.*" Wc need the light given by grace in order to realize that "untold riches are hidden under such varied appearances."[48] When it is a question of the Church, we have to treat her with the same love and respect as we bring to Scripture, in which the Word spoke and made Himself known, or the Sacred Species of the Eucharistic Christ. It is only from the clarity given by faith that in the matter of the Church the cry of the doubting apostle can come: "My Lord and my God."[49] What had at first repelled becomes a reason which makes the intelligence accept.[50]

Autumn and Second Spring

Two conclusions stand out from the "theandric" nature of the Church.

The first is that the Church not only cannot be reduced to what can be seen of her from the outside, but even that her appearance in time witnesses to the eternal youthfulness of Him who conquered death. Where the outside observer diagnoses the oncome of death, the believer, in no danger of being wrong, sees a re-birth. If the Church is the tree sprung from the mustard seed, it is normal that, like it, she should experience the passage of the seasons, knowing at one time autumn, at another spring.[51]

[48] Feast of Corpus Christi, *Lauda Sion*: "*Sub diversis speciebus latent res eximiae.*"

[49] John, 20:28.

[50] "For those who know the Church is divine her very infirmity and her exertions are the most incontrovertible and definite sign of her truth. When the Son of Man came on earth, was it really his mere bearing and the majesty of his look . . . which made the crowds accept Him? In no way. . . . The Absolute appearing in a particular and contingent form, the Eternal enclosed in time, the Unchangeable walking the roads . . . and God jostled by men, there lies the whole Incarnation, and '*Verbum Caro*' means nothing else." P. Charles. *La Robe sans Couture*, pp. 146-147.

[51] "It is true, there have been seasons when, from the operation of external or internal causes, the Church has been thrown into what was almost a state of deliquium; but her wonderful revivals, while the world was triumphing over her, is a further evidence of the absence of corruption in

The second conclusion is no less clear, namely, that a refusal to grant one of these two elements to the Church is equivalent to destroying her. The error common to the two contradictory attitudes described is at once obvious: they derive from an excess of conservatism or an excess of progress; and each is a denial of the incarnation of the Church. The first upholds the transcendence and lastingness of the Church but throws overboard her contingency and her growth in time; the second, in order to safeguard the human forms of her development, loses sight of what is her eternal essence.

The Church is "Theandric"

The truth is larger than either. It is not a question of choosing: it is necessary to unite and reconcile, giving each element its full importance, and thereby the Christian obtains a remarkably valuable lesson for the action he has to pursue in contemporary society. The Church, as the "permanent incarnation of the Savior," perpetuates His mystery. In Him two natures were united: He was both God and Man. Similarly, two worlds are made one in the Church: the invisible reality, and the visible society or communion of the faithful. If one of these two is left out the Church is destroyed. Without a visible organization—institutions, hierarchy, sacraments—Christ would cease to be incarnate in the world and the Church would cease to be a body. But conversely, to stop short at her juridical organization

---

the system of doctrine and worship into which she has developed. If corruption be an incipient disorganization, surely an abrupt and absolute recurrence to a former state of vigour, after an interval, is even less conceivable than a corruption that is permanent. Now this is the case with the revivals I speak of. After violent exertion men are exhausted and fall asleep; they awake the same as before, refreshed by the temporary cessation of their activity; and such has been the slumber and such the restoration of the Church. She pauses in her course and almost suspends her functions; she rises again, and she is herself once more; all things are in their place and ready for action. Doctrine is where it was, and usage, and precedence, and principle, and policy; there may be changes, but they are consolidations or adaptations; all is unequivocal and determinate, with an identity which there is no disputing." Newman, Essay on the Development of Christian Doctrine, Longmans, 1897, p. 444.

and not to go beyond her external appearance would be to kill the Church and replace the Body of Christ by a corpse.

How immensely sublime, therefore, is the mystery of the Church! At each moment she has, at one and the same time, both *to be* and *to become*. "To be," unchangeably, in her invisible reality; "to become" age by age, in her visible reality. "Because the Church of Christ is a body," explains Leo XIII, "she is visible. Because she is Christ's body, she is living, active, vigorous. Jesus Christ guards and sustains her by His own power, just as the vine nourishes and makes fruitful the branches which it puts forth. But just as in the case of animals the vital principle is hidden completely from our senses though we can be sure of its presence because of the activity of the various members, so where the Church of God is concerned we can be certain that she has a principle of supernatural life by watching how she lives." [52]

THE TEACHING OF HISTORY

The way the Church lives is there for all to see in History, both present and past. History, with its wealth of facts, amply confirms the doctrinal views here put forward. In making this appeal to History we have no intention whatever, even briefly, of telling the story of the Church over again, but only to show that in every age the Church has appeared simultaneously in her two aspects: incarnate, she puts on all the social and cultural forms of the humanity she encounters; out of time and transcendant, she "is," and remains her unchanging self, through the civilizations she traverses; she remains eternally young in the process, because, without ceasing to grow and assimilate to herself, she has never *bound herself up* with their structures: she only puts them on in order to sanctify them.

THE LESSON OF THE PAST

Scarcely was the Church born than she was confronted with a choice. The Jewish world or the Gentile? Her hesitation did not last long. St. Paul made the choice, St. Peter understood

[52] Leo XIII, *Satis Cognitum*, A.S.S. XXVIII, p. 710.

and approved . . . *Duc in altum*[53] . . . and the Church shook herself free of the Law. With the "Apostle of the nations" she became "Greek with the Greeks"; and Hellenic and Roman Christendom was born. Nero and Diocletian obstinately tried to kill the intruder. Constantine submitted and made peace—and the Church lived in the open, prospering in a prospering Empire. Then came the Barbarians and their threat, under which the Roman world tottered. The Barbarians struck; and the Empire had had its day. Would the Church disappear with it? Some there were who wondered; and even St. Augustine was alarmed and pondered the question as he waited for the rising tide of devastation, so that anxiety clouded his last years. Under the general invasion, what would become of the City of God? How could the Christian religion be thought of without the framework of "Roman Culture"? Because, "just as for the Jewish Christians the future of Christianity was one with the future of their nation, so for the Roman Christians it was bound up with the future of the Empire . . . Identified with it, the Christian Church, by that very fact, seemed to be identified with the whole of humanity. She had achieved her ideal, she had nothing further to ask of the future, and her whole ambition should have been to eternalize the present . . . But the Church's vision was steadier and her mind more calm; she did not despair of humanity. She did not think that all was lost because Rome had disappeared. She took in with her eye the whole sweep of the gigantic movement of which she was a witness, and in it she discerned the *accouchement* of a still nameless world. She felt in her bones the coming of a sublime novelty which could have been expressed in no other way than by a monstrous coupling of words: "a barbarian civilization," that is, a civilization which could do without Rome and was destined to be mightier than Rome. Fearlessly, conscious of her eternal mission . . . she walked forward into the future."[54]

[53] Luke, 5:4.
[54] G. Kurth, *L'Eglise aux Tournants de l'Histoire*, pp. 42-47.

The Church at the Turning-Points of History

What became of the chosen people?

The chosen people grew. The Barbarian conquered the Rome of the Emperors; but the Rome of the Popes conquered the Barbarians. The assimilation took time; but that synthesis of cultures, seven hundred years later, emerged in medieval Christendom. Losses there were and perils; the heresy of the Albigensians, "horrible as sin and with the sadness of death," struck at the very principle of the Redemption. But St. Dominic and St. Francis saved the day, and soon after there came St. Thomas; and then was seen the Christendom of the Middle Ages and its "great century," the thirteenth. The Church penetrated the structures of the City, "presided at the birth of townships and universities, saw saints sit in the thrones of France and Castile, and for two hundred years . . . she was the supreme authority in the West, the oracle of the Christian World." [55] It was a happy triumph, which freed her from the shackles of feudalism, but only to confront her with a new alternative; for Western Christendom began to break up and weaken under the deeply-seated pressure of the Reformation and the Renaissance. Was the Church about to perish? Clever men pondered the question: for had not the Christian religion found its perfect expression in a society governed by Pope and Emperor together, and were not its slightest structures informed by the Church's spirit? What could a doubtful future offer as against that perfect achievement? Where could the Christian order be found, if not in Christendom? [56] Since the

[55] G. Kurth, *op. cit.*, p. 82.

[56] This confusion between "Church" and "Christianity" or between "Christianity" and "Christendom" is at the origin of all the troubles of history. It is also the source of a serious illusion. It has been pointed out that in our day that illusion takes two forms. The first consists in thinking that Christianity succeeded in the past because it managed to penetrate peoples wholly and officially. Whence a nostalgia among many Christians for a past to which they would like to "return." This could be disputed on historical grounds (the mutual intrusions by the two powers, of which the quarrel of the Investitures was merely a more acute episode, and the dangers, by no means imaginary, which too close an official protection entails for the faith and the loyalty of the faithful, are well known); but

days of Constantine that has doubtless been the worst temptation the Church has had to face. But she saw the danger and freed herself in time; and when the West rose in its new freedom the Body of Christ was to know an increase. A New World appeared and was baptized; a missionary Church arose and native christendoms were made. The Church was everywhere, and yet had lost nothing of her dogma or her unity; the mustard seed had become a tree. So she entered on the modern world. The religion of scientism, of secularism and the heresy of race, all joined in attacking the Mystical Body of Christ, to destroy from without and to undermine from within. The years go by. The new doctrines grow old and make way for others; her enemies destroy each other and the sword slips from their grasp. One has just come crashing down. The Church remains.

The Church and Civilization

To what does the Church owe her series of triumphs?

She owes them to the eliminations she made in time: for growth involves some measure of dying. At the right moment and without regret she has known how to put off all that was merely her "vesture." Like the "leaven in the lump" [57] the Church has been thoroughly kneaded into the peoples and epochs of History; [58] but, a "salt that does not lose its savor," [59]

---

this illusion rests in addition on a fixist conception of culture and the Church, the origin of which is once more to be found in misunderstanding the Church "in time," that is, her constant and necessary development.

The second illusion contradicts the first in appearance only; it consists in thinking that the Church has failed because her work among men has to be begun over and over again and never leads to a stable and definitive order; whence discouragement . . . At bottom, the error is still the same, confusing the Church with the transient forms she puts on. But, as M. Gilson excellently says, "the Church's task is not to preserve the world as it is, even if it has become Christian, but to keep it so Christian that it never becomes anything else." In short, the Church's task is not "to prevent the world from passing away, but to sanctify a passing world."

[57] Matt., 13:33.

[58] The beneficial action of the Church upon twenty centuries of history is difficult to isolate from the context of other influences. It is none the less recognizable, when we compare parallel non-Christian societies. In

she has never bound herself up with their destiny. One structure succeeds another, another age renews the past; but at no time do they coincide with the total Church: she is larger than they and outstrips them immeasurably. Nor is she ever satisfied with her partial successes. For, as the encyclical *Mystici Corporis* says: "the order of things to which human and civil societies belong does not constitute the whole of the Church, just as the structure of our mortal bodies does not constitute the whole of man." [60] It is one of the consequences of the "mystery of the Church" that the external materializations of her vitality never adequately express the fullness of her inner life and her potentialities of endlessly renewing her youth.

What History tells us of the eternal youth of the Church, by virtue of her independence of the passing forms of civilization, also can be proved for her holiness and from the same sources.[61]

THE BALANCE SHEET TODAY

The Church and civilization; the Church and holiness; in each case the lesson of the past teaches the immutable tran-

---

countries where the life of the community is permeated by Christianity, we find that the family is exceptionally and solidly established and family life good; a greater human dignity; an habitual leaning to action and inquiry, born of the Christian "virtues," &c. Cf. J. Leclercq, *La Vie du Christ dans son Eglise*, p. 165, sq.

[59] Matt., 5:13.

[60] *Mystici Corporis*, E.T. p. 24.

[61] Without dwelling on the question here, let it suffice to point out that the spring of holiness which wells within her from her mystical "Head" is all the time unfailing. Christians have always drawn from it the divine nourishment which can and ought to inflect the movement of the world; and by their efforts, and above all by the saints, institutions which are incompatible with human dignity have disappeared. To sanctify the earth it has been enough—and it will always be enough—to "actualize" in outside tasks the infinite power of achievement which the "immaculate and stainless spouse" can draw upon for her children and her Spouse.—We can then appreciate the margin which separates the essential holiness of the Church from the holiness realized at a particular time. There does not exist in History one Christian civilization to be taken as a type, nor a uniform model of holiness, which have to be canonized and made into a norm. There have only been institutions—or persons—to a greater or lesser degree penetrated by Christianity and its virtues.

scendance and the eternal actuality of the Church, the first being the condition of the second. That she is always unchangeable and always young, faithful to God and faithful to man, these are the signs of life in a Church which does not grow old; and those signs are present, and abundantly present, in our day. Here also it is not a question of drawing up a detailed balance sheet; it is enough to set out the main items.

From the list of charges brought by contemporary atheism against the Church let us in honesty accept one fact, the de-Christianization of the world. But on condition that the meaning of this phenomenon is at once explained, for that evolution is far more complex than many are willing to admit.

DeChristianization . . .

It is a fact that the Church has lost whole nations and that the number of believers in Europe is growing less. But as against this, statistics show that their numbers are increasing in other parts of the world; in Africa, in North and South America and in Asia, whether by reason of a higher birth rate in a particular Catholic country or by the activities of the missionaries, the Church sees new provinces joining her. In Asia, and in Africa in particular, where the native clergy is of recent institution, we should rather speak of the Church beginning than of her growing old.[62] Nevertheless, we will grant that the decay of belief and of religious practice is in the main a universal feature.

It is a characteristic in this sense first of all, that it is met with in every part of the world and that it affects all social entities: races, classes and others; but also, and above all, in the sense that it is a phenomenon common to all religion. A law has in fact been stated to exist between the crisis religion undergoes and the presence of modern civilization. Wherever

[62] The appeal of Mgr. Yu-Pin, Bishop of Pekin, is a recent example: "Without a spiritual reconstruction, China will have a body without a soul . . . She has an opportunity in her hands which will not come again: there will only be one re-building of China. That is why I launch my appeal . . . I want to find engineers, doctors, professors, journalists . . . who, while engaged on a professional career, will bring something more to China, the Christian evidence of their lives."

the latter penetrates, religious belief decreases among the masses.[63] From this two considerations emerge. If technical civilization thus everywhere casts out the feeling for religion, the reason must be that it contains elements which it is high time to neutralize or replace by others; and that provides a valuable line of action for Christians. But if, secondly, it is also true that the loss of ground is common to all religions, it is plainly unjust to place the whole responsibility for that upon the Catholic Church alone. Other causes, objective and subjective,[64] enter in to explain a phenomenon painful indeed, and in the words of Pius XI "a scandal," but one which the mistakes and failures of Catholics cannot fully explain. Catholics have their share of the responsibility; and in our day their examinations of conscience, both public and private, on this head, are not wanting. But is systematic disparagement always well informed? There can be but one answer to the question. If Christ has lost the ear of the masses, if habits and thought have insensibly been built up almost wholly outside the Church, that is often the consequence of remote and external causes. It is well known that the influence of ideas begins to be felt only long after they have made their way among the elites. Ever since the Renaissance, but especially since the XVIII century, the latter have been preaching a completely naturalist worship of the individual, a philosophy of man in which there is no room for God. Two centuries have gone by; and those

[63] It seems that this law is verified most in peoples with no decisive religion of their own, such as China or Japan, which took over the gods of India and where the State in our own day has announced that it has accepted Western secularism. On the other hand, it has been pointed out that in India, in the Arab countries, and in general in countries where adherence to a religious denomination is the predominant factor in national consciousness, Buddhism and Islamism asserted themselves to fanaticize the masses. We can see how extraneous and foreign such a political attitude is to religious values themselves, the only ones under consideration here. But even from this point of view "the religious life of Mahometanism is rapidly declining in Syria, Egypt, and North Africa. In India it has begun to fall off." P. Desqueyrat, *L'Apostasie des Temps, Nouveaux*, Travaux, October, 1946, p. 17.

[64] Cf. Desqueyrat, *op. cit.*, p. 14, sq.

ideas, swollen by the whole materialistic current of the XIX century, have captured the masses.

. . . . and the Church Teaching

As against this, never perhaps has the action of the Holy See been so universally felt as during the last fifty years. The Church has not forgotten her essential mission, to teach: "Going, teach all nations" . . .[65] "By the will of God and in virtue of a mission given by Christ . . . the Church, guardian of the natural and the supernatural orders" has not failed "to remind her children, and in the presence of the entire world and in unmistakable terms, of the unshakeable principles which should inspire human life."[66] The desire to be heard by the modern world, which is concerned before all else with its temporal organization, has not made her lose sight of the fact that the Kingdom of God must be preached above everything else. Recent history shows that those among the faithful who have been best equipped to answer the appeal of their times are precisely those who have shown themselves most eager to follow the counsels of the Vicar of Jesus Christ. The voice of the Popes has gone far beyond the confines of the baptized. Leo XIII gave the Church a new road for arriving at a social teaching in harmony with the gospel; Pius XI opposed an implacable hostility to the doctrines of exclusive nationalism and the conspiracies of the totalitarian States; and Pius XII calls the whole of humanity to join with the Church in freeing the human person, now threatened in his being and in his family, which is his natural extension.

The Church's teaching, at this present time, can be related to the three-fold mission which the official documents of the Holy See and the statements of Bishops have ceaselessly reiterated.

As the representatives of the *Charity* of Christ, the Holy See and the Episcopate have tirelessly raised their voices and tried

[65] Matt., 28:19.
[66] Pius XII, Christmas Message, 1942, *Catholic Mind,* Jan. 1943, p. 46.

to preserve peace[67] by forestalling civil or foreign war; and when hostilities began, they tried to prevent, as far as that could be done, any aggravation in the conduct of war, as well as to alleviate the lot of ordinary people.

As the representatives of *Justice*, they set themselves, in the general confusion, to enlighten the consciences of men on the collective and individual means which are necessary for the founding of a future society on moral principles, without which it cannot endure.

As the representatives of the supernatural *Grace* of Christ, they tirelessly remind men that, beyond what is demanded by human, moral, social and political necessities, there exists a Christian mystery which is supernatural and transcendent.

No one can consider the whole series of documents of the Church's ordinary teaching, emanating from the Pope and the Bishops throughout the world, without admiring the unity of doctrine they contain and their fidelity to it, a unity and a fidelity which are equalled only by their relevancy to the situation of the day. When to this teaching activity is added a multitude of services, as well as the assistance given in the material and the cultural spheres by the Catholic hierarchy for the common good, as well as for the good of individuals, their family and professional activities and the good of the State, we have every reason to see in that a sign of the vitality of a Church manifestly taught and ruled by Christ.

[67] The words of the Pope to the last Consistory will be remembered, when the Church's universality appeared so clearly in the new Cardinals chosen from widely different nationalities: "The Catholic Church, of which Rome is the centre, is supra-national by her very essence. We may understand this in two ways, one negative, the other positive. The Church is a Mother, *Sancta Mater Ecclesia*, a true mother, the mother of all nations and of all peoples, no less than of all individuals; and it is precisely because she is a mother that she does not belong and cannot belong . . . exclusively to any particular people or even to one people more than another, but to all equally." And for exactly the same reason "she is not and cannot be foreign anywhere. She lives, or by nature at least she ought to live, in all peoples." Allocution to the Sacred College, December 24, 1945, on the occasion of the nomination of 32 new Cardinals.

The Loss of the Masses

When we consider the particular religious situation in France, the *fact* of religion stands out at once as both present and vigorous. But more and more plainly it is meeting with a mass of realities which are themselves to some extent outside the reality of religion and place religion on trial in a variety of ways. The influence of the anti-Christian elites, after first gaining upon their surroundings, proceeded to spread, and has given birth to a world built up outside the Church. Deep in this world, by a process which is almost automatic, masses of human beings, who have grown more and more numerous, have been severed from religion. To some extent even, this mass of men has thought it was acting rightly in so doing, and adduces the modern world and its outlook as a form of apparent justification. The masses, to a large extent deChristianized, doubtless preserve in their consciousness many of the demands laid down by the Christian religion in matters of justice and charity among men; but they no longer look to the Church for the nourishment their lives need. On the contrary, they turn away from the Church and try to satisfy their thirst for happiness and their need to serve in the idealism of atheistic systems.

Among these godless masses, to whom the term "pagan" has been applied and who have given to France the title of "A Missionary Country," exists a Christian community which includes many degrees of Christian life and practice. Side by side with large and deeply fervent families fired with the spirit of sacrifice and the sense of duty and rich in religious vocations, exists a borderland of baptized Christians, numerically large, who do not practice their religion, although they remain connected with the Church by a number of important features in their lives: baptism, first communion and so on. There are to be found also those "seasonal Christians," who practice their religion only occasionally, and those others who belong to the "parish background"; they, along with those who are sympathetic to religion, make up the "reserves of moral strength" to which appeal is sometimes made in times of crisis.

The Progress of the Elites

One outstanding fact dominates and explains the Church's recovery, and that is the progress made by the elites. In the XIX century they were few and far between, and limited themselves, in the main, to a negative attitude. But in the course of the last few decades, on the contrary, and in every walk of life, elites have begun to appear who are solely concerned with understanding the new situation and being witnesses to Christ among those of their fellows who are the furtherest from Him. Catholics, whose numbers are continually increasing, have sprung to arms, and have realized that the fact of deChristianization presents a phenomenon which is no longer local but world-wide, which must be dealt with as such. A tremendous effort has been made in this direction, so that now, in every sphere, we are again meeting with those tributes to the "quality" of the Church and her vitality.

In Intellectual Life

Take first the world of thought. The position occupied by Catholics in scientific life, literature and philosophy is a sufficient proof how ill-founded was the incompatibility it was at one time the fashion to proclaim between Faith and Science. Fifty years ago, that achievement by Catholics was true only of a small number of brilliant men, whose names were the more publicized in that they were so far and few between.[68] Today,

[68] The arrival of the working classes at positions of social and political responsibility, which is one of the features of modern society, has been accompanied for the last hundred years by an appetite for intellectual research and creation to which philosophy and contemporary science gave a revolutionary and often an anti-religious air. Part of the strength and skill of Marxism has been to profess to associate the move for research with the revolutionary movement for social demands; and the "materialism of history" has been put forward not only as liberating the oppressed classes but as the philosophical doctrine by whose vision of the world modern man will be able to satisfy his intellectual demands. This confusion was greatly helped, it is necessary for us to recognize, by the position of small importance Catholic thinkers had occupied for more than half a century, for which the genius of men like Lapparent, Branly, Termier, &c., could not compensate.

we see a vast articulated movement, established and preparing to go further; for the Catholic intellectuals are everywhere.[69] They can be found in University Faculties, Academies, research centres and scientific societies, where not only are they not afraid to proclaim their faith, but all, the unknown research worker as well as the scholar of world-wide reputation, by their technical worth and honest search for truth, are a witness to the perfect harmony existing between their vocation as scholars and their vocation as Christians. They set themselves, above all, to show—and such a "positive attitude" is indeed a novelty—that the problems put to their conscience in the middle of the twentieth century world find their overwhelming answer in the Catholic religion. Methodically, their investigations cover all the departments of knowledge, Sociology, History and Psychology, as well as the exact sciences. By the large numbers of Catholics it comprises, as well as by its quality, that intellectual renaissance constitutes both the most indisputable proof of the present-day vitality of the Church and one of her brightest promises for tomorrow.

In Religious Life

That rising tide is no less plain in the life of religion itself. Spiritual life has at the same time been widened and deepened. Its development can be seen in the conversions—often startling—which puzzle and impress the unbeliever. But it can be

[69] "It is a fact that a Catholic Renaissance in literature exists, that it is without precedent among us, and that it continues without anything appearing to announce an interruption or imminent end. The divorce between art and faith is less and less admitted among Catholics. Very few today would dare to adopt the attitude of a man like Montaigne, whose life was Catholic but whose work was pagan. Being a Christian, for us, means trying to 'inform' all our life by the Christian religion. Further, the Catholic writer is no longer, as in the days of Barbey d' Aurevilly or Léon Bloy, violent and isolated. We can never be grateful enough to such illustrious predecessors, who fought alone and who were almost the only witnesses to God during a pagan and materialist period. But in our day, Catholic literature has won its place in the City. Our writers are everywhere. And the tone of Catholic books, without losing any of its rightful pride, has changed to some extent." L. Chaigne, *Anthologie de la Renaissance Catholique*, t. II, p. 5.

seen equally well in the demands which are being asserted more and more strongly in matters which affect the Christian life, such as the return to the great "generating dogmas" of the life of the soul and a religious practice amplified and bound up with the liturgy. The latter has stirred up, and still excites daily, the greatest curiosity, eager enquiry and passionate controversy. The Mystical life itself, of the most authentic stamp, draws and captivates an ever larger number of souls, and of this the remarkable success of Catholic books—spiritual writings and the lives of the saints—is in itself a sufficient indication.

Life, however, provides us with another, and one of far greater moment, and that in the order of *holiness*. For if it be true that never has the mass of men been so far from God, never, it is equally probable, has the world had so many saints. The mere recital of those beatified or canonized by the Church since the beginning of the century would suffice to win for it the tile: "The Century of Saints." But how many others, every day, or in a particular circumstance, have given their lives for Christ or the Church! War and deportation had their heroes and their martyrs; and daily life offers virtues for our admiration which are the more sublime in that they are so humble and so withdrawn. Vocations of lay apostles and militants, vocations to the priesthood and the religious life, the spontaneous appearance of religious orders of a new kind in which the most authentic spirituality is allied with a determination to cleave to the present—all these are further signs of a flowering of life within the Church in our day.

In Action

This mounting of the sap is not a "spontaneous generation." It is due, in large part, to a new reality, one clearly raised up by the Holy Spirit to make of it an instrument suited to the penetration of the modern world, namely, *Catholic Action*. If we restrict ourselves to France alone, it is henceforward impossible to understand the history of the last twenty years without taking account of the new fact which its origin and development constitute. We must confine ourselves here to seeing in it a clear proof of the way in which the Church ceaselessly renews her youth. Catholic Action, which began from principles whose consequences were to reveal themselves as incalculable, in particular the sharing of the laity in the evangelization of the world and in restoring their God-given direction to human values, has today reached every class of society. The usual method of appraising it is to look mainly to numbers; and the figures are already eloquent. In the working-class and rural areas where its numbers are largest, its militants, adherents, and those influenced by it total more than 200,000 for each of the J.O.C. and J.A.C. movements; and the girls' organizations contain even more. If, behind these figures, we remember the work done: the taking over the many *milieux*, the realistic answer made to the problems they presented, the proud and comprehensive assertion of the Catholic faith; we can well realize that the action accomplished reaches far beyond the areas where its successes can be seen. It would, however, be a gross error to identify the structures of Catholic Action with its *mystique*, its "body" with its "life," and to confuse "organization" with "movement." This last word, which has unfortunately become hackneyed with use, does, however, sufficiently make plain that Catholic Action is not "something which has reached its final form" but something which is in process of developing. It is *in via*. Its methods are continually being overhauled, its results analyzed, its future scrutinized. That there should be moments of pause and of unforeseen ebullition is normal and even reassuring; for these are recognizable signs of life. Catholic Action is twenty years old; it is normal that it should experience its growing pains before coming out into the adult stage.

All the time, the seeds which so much prayer, reflection and converging effort deposited in these movements have taken root and begun to grow. The final development of their growth cannot always be foreseen. The guarantee of its safety lies in the fact that Catholic Action is concerned with extending its conquests only by remaining faithful to its essential principles, and in its spirit of loyal and filial confidence in the hierarchy.

Signs of Life

It will be the honor of our generation to have realized that the new situation of humanity called for new apostolic conditions. In addition to the general movements of Catholic Action, both of men and women, which are of the highest quality and peculiarly successful, the great effort which gave birth to the specialized movements drives them in an incessant search for the means of working upon the indifferent masses after the manner of leaven. Today we can see and evaluate the very real influence which the rising generations exercise upon the family, the profession, the natural communities of life, and even the institutions of society. All are working together in that immense task: the parish, which is seeking its communitarian and missionary road; the clergy, who are rethinking their apostolate and inspiring the leaders; the lay apostles, who are making their way into the areas of life; finally, certain new forms—*Mission de France, Mission de Paris*—which, often outside the parish but always in liaison with it, constitute its advanced posts.

But we must conclude. Who can be made to believe, after this enumeration alone, that the Church is dying? Have we good grounds, when confronted with such a ferment, for talking of the death throes? The great forces running through the Church, the waves surging up from the depths and uplifting her, are not the signs of death. They show the rising of the sap, the thrust of spring.

III. THE EXPANSION OF THE CHURCH

We are far, however, from any temptation to illusion. What we have described are merely the buds of promise; they are not the harvest. The growth of the Church depends on God; but that growth will not come without us. His omnipotence has laid upon us the responsibility of creating that triumph; and if we wish to know the conditions which govern it, what History and Theology have already taught us about the Church's nature will provide the guide to our action.

THE ANSWERS TO BE REJECTED

That action will be grounded in the "theandric" nature of the Church and will therefore refuse from the outset to enter on two wrong roads, those same solutions which, if pursued one-sidedly to their logical conclusions, would constitute several clear errors. These solutions, contradictory as they are, have this additional feature in common, that they mutilate the full reality of the Church by excluding one of the two elements belonging to her.

Modernism

A first group of errors is what is called Modernism. Its history is well known. Fifty years ago, dazzled by the conquests of modern thought, a number of Catholics, insufficiently conscious of the transcendental character of the Church, put forward an adaptation which was a doctrinal surrender. What was vital, they thought, was to reconcile the Church with the world; and if some accommodation is necessary to bring dogma into line with reason or morals with science, we must be willing to make it. Everything in this world evolves, and the Church cannot escape that law. Let her accept it boldly and the gain will all be hers. For what matters is not the letter but the spirit, not her inheritance from the past but "Life" and "Progress." "Being" is nothing else than "Becoming"; and if the Church wishes to live she must adapt her dogma, her worship and her discipline to the forms of the present. The Church, however, did not view the matter in this way, and by roundly condemning this wrong view she saved herself from a naturalism which, by emptying her of her transcendence, would take from her the whole of her historical reason for existing. Modernism had indeed seen the "human" face of the Church, but it had misconceived her divine nature. All it had seen was the "phenomenon"; and that is the blind spot which lies in wait for all those who in our day also are still even unconsciously influenced by Naturalism.

It is not by means such as these that the Church will recover her place in the world. In the realm of thought, Catholics must never appear either as sytematically rejecting all that is old or infatuated in principle with "all that is new." First, because a belief in unlimited Progress is naive, as reason and experience show, and a contradiction in terms; for what else but "fixism" is any modernist system which, in the name of indefinite progress, canonizes one of the latter's passing phases? By making "what is" as such into an absolute value and a norm of action, the progressive "freezes" life in one of its fleeting structures. What he calls modern today, another tomorrow will call ancient, and will condemn for that reason alone. And there we recognize the blind alley to which Pragmatism and the short views of Americanism lead. But we recognize above all how right the Church is, in face of the concessions and compromises so often demanded of her, in maintaining an attitude of inflexibility which is not merely a pose, or an instinctive attitude of reserve born of prudence, but a natural result of a dogma and the undisturbed radiation of her being.[70] It is useful to recall here the fine words of St. Vincent of Lerins: "Guard the deposit of faith.[71] But what *is* this deposit? It is a treasure entrusted to you, not an ingenious discovery of your own; it is a gift freely given, not the fruit of intense study; it comes to you by teaching, not by research; it is not something to use as you please but to hand on to others. Hence you must not add new Truths to it, you must guard accepted truth; you must keep the treasure of the faith unplundered and undefiled. Have in safe keeping this gift entrusted to you and pass it on to others. Gold you have received; give gold back; do not substitute lead in its place. Teach others what you yourself were taught, by new methods if you like, but not new doctrines." [72]

[70] From first to last, Christianity, in the course of its developments, has had fixed principles in view, and thereby, without losing anything of what was proper to itself, has been capable of incorporating in it doctrines which were foreign to it. A like continuity of principles and a similar power of assimilation are each of them incompatible with the idea of corruption. Newman, Development of Christian Doctrine, Longmans, 1897, pp. 248-273.

[71] I Tim., 6:20.

[72] St. Vincent of Lerins, *Commonitorium*, Rouet de Journel, 2173.

In this practice, the Christian, face to face, with the world, will never, for any reason whatever, adopt an attitude of surrender. "We are not Christians just to be obliging, pliant and soft, ready to adopt any compromise or stay in the background . . . or to be carried about by every wind of doctrine." [73] "The Christian has his line of truth and uprightness, and can say "no" to evil and error . . . Let us remember that however powerful the world is, it is held in check by a firm conscience."[74]

Integralism

But on the other hand, the Church cannot be reduced to her "out of time" and unchangeable aspect without being mutilated. If the Church, by the mystery of her transcendence, is independent of the world and in that sense is not "of the world," she is, on the other hand, "in the world" and is thereby part of the world by that element in her which is visible and human. That simple reminder differentiates her action from that to which Integralism would like to reduce it. Integralism has a number of forms, all of which, once more, come from a one-sided view of the total Reality of the Church. It is therefore important to point out to the conscience of the faithful the three main forms this wrong perspective takes, each of which is an error to be avoided.

Integralism in Doctrine

In the first place, no one must confuse integrity of doctrine with the maintenance of its accidental trappings. Doubtless—and it is necessary to stress this more than ever before—the revealed deposit of faith is the essential treasure the Church has, and cannot be impaired without suicide and sacrilege. Without doubt also we must scrupulously safeguard dogmatic and defined formulas. But must Revelation be identified with systems and theological schools? If that were so, how can we explain the action of St. Thomas, when he ruthlessly broke away from the Platonism of St. Augustine and adopted the system of Aris-

[73] Eph., 4:14.
[74] Mgr. Blanchet, Pastoral Letter, Lent, 1946.

totle? The "real distinction" upon which he founded his course of action could be justified by a precedent in tradition, namely, the two parallel interpretations of the same doctrinal truths which form the two streams in the Church, the Greek Fathers and the Latin.

Does this mean that the Church may not prefer one system to another? It cannot mean this. To safeguard doctrine or morals and by the voice of the Popes, the Church can propose a particular system to the faithful as a sound guarantee. For this reason she has countless times put forward the system of St. Thomas, for the value of its methods and the proved soundness of its positions. In making "the doctrine and the principles of the Angelic Doctor" [75] her official teaching,[76] the Church plainly advertises the high value she attaches to the "wonderful edifice St. Thomas built up out of component parts, timeless and independent of any age, which he brought in and put together, and which he had taken from the masters of every age." [77] Must it be concluded from this that St. Thomas has said all there is to be said, and that his thought has matched and exhausted the deposit of revealed truth? Has thought for us come to an end since his day? It cannot be so. The saying of Lacordaire is well known: "St. Thomas is a beacon; he is not a limit." The light he provides must be used to investigate ever more thoroughly the two sources of faith, Scripture and Tradition, of which St. Ireneus says: "the teaching given to us by the Church is like the priceless contents contained in a vessel. The Holy Spirit is ever renewing that content, and renewing the jar's youth with his own." [78] "Those who deal with doctrine," says Pius XII, "must express themselves in such ways, both in word and writing, that our contemporaries shall understand and listen." [79]

[75] Pius XII, speaking to the General Chapter of the Dominicans, September 22, 1946.

[76] Code of Cannon Law, can. 1366, §2, confirmed by the Apostolic Constitution, *Deus Scientiarum Dominus,* May 24, 1931.

[77] Pius XII, ibid.

[78] St. Ireneus, *Adv Heres,* III, 24, 1.

[79] Pius XII, speaking to the 29th General Congregation of the Society of Jesus, September 17, 1946, D.C. col 1317.

Tradition, indeed, is quite different from a mechanical handing on of an inert "thing." It is the living communication and progressive manifestation, under the infallible controlling power of the Magisterium, of a global truth of which each age discovers a fresh aspect. In this connection also St. Vincent of Lerins contributes something very much to the point. He is forestalling an objection: "But perhaps some one will say: 'Shall the Church then make no development in religion?' Of course she will, great development. Only a man who envied his fellows and hated God could wish it otherwise. Still, it must be *development*, not change. A thing develops when it realizes more fully its own potentialities: it changes when it loses its own identity and becomes something else. And so there must be growth, great intensive growth, in understanding, knowledge, and wisdom: and this is true of individual Christians as they grow older and of the Church as a whole in different centuries. But essentially this knowledge remains the same, resting upon the same dogmas, interpreted in the same sense and in the same meaning." [80]

The same remark applies to the spheres of discipline and action in the Church, in the moral order, and to institutions. Must we really identify Tradition, which is life, with routine, which is death? Or the Law, which is given once and for all, with its applications, which are not? In order to safeguard life, Modernism sacrificed its forms; and in order to safeguard the forms, Integralism sacrifices the life. "It is impossible at the present day," writes Pius X, "to re-establish in the same form all the institutions which have been useful, and were even the only efficient ones in past centuries, so numerous are the radical modifications which time has brought to society and public life, and so many are the fresh needs which changing circumstances do not cease to call forth. But the Church, throughout her long history, has always and on every occasion luminously shown that she possesses a wonderful power of adaptation to the varying conditions of civil society; and without injury to the integrity or immutability of faith or morals, and always safeguarding her sacred rights, she easily bends and adapts her-

[80] St. Vincent of Lerins, *Commonitorium*, Rouet de Journel, 2174.

self in all that is contingent and accidental to the vicissitudes of time and the fresh needs of society."[81]

Here also an attitude of excessive traditionalism loses sight of the elements of the problem and thereby leads to the same contradiction as Modernism; for just as the latter made the values of the day a norm for the Church, so the former turns the values of yesterday into the ideal for today. Therein is contained a serious error which Catholics must carefully avoid, and that for two reasons. First, because such a negative attitude of mistrust of legitimate change slows down the Church's forward movement, holds up her penetration of the world, and risks pre-

[81] Pius X, *Il Fermo Proposito*, June 11, 1905. (E.T. in The Pope and The People, C.T.S., p. 192). One might thus distinguish a double kind of "adaptation." The first, which we may call "adaptation by tolerance" consists in the desire the Church has to suit her enactments to the different degrees of reception among the faithful: "*Non potest esse aliquis perfectior status praesentis vitae quam status novae legis; quia tanto est unum quodque perfectius, quanto est ultimo fini propinquius. Alio modo status hominum variari potest, secundum quod homines diversimodo se habent ad eamdem legem, vel perfectius, vel minus perfecte; et sic status veteris legis frequenter fuit mutatus, cum quandoque leges optime custodirentur, quandoque autem, omnino praetermitterentur. Sicut etiam et status novae legis diversificatur secundum diversa loca, et tempora, et personas, inquantum gratia Spiritus Sancti perfectius vel minus perfecte ab aliquibus habetur.*" St. Thomas, *Summa Theologica*, t. II, *Prima Secundae*, Q. CVI, art. IV.

Even in her official documents, the Church provides examples of these legitimate changes: Lateran Council, 1215, canon 50: *Non debet reprehensible judicare, si secundum varietatem temporum statuta quandoque varientur humana, praesertim cum urgens necessitas vel evidens utilitas id exposcit: quoniam ipse Deus ex iis, quae in* Veteri Testamento *statuerat, non nulla mutavit in novo.* There follows the cancelling of the prohibition on contracting marriage in *secundo et tertio affinitatis* genere and other concessions of the same kind in impediments of consanguinity. Canon inserted in the Decretals of Gregory IX, book IV, tit. XIV, C. 8.

The second, which we may call "adaptation by development," has been well drawn out by Newman. It will be remembered that it was the study of Catholic dogma which brought about the conversion of the famous Anglican clergyman to the Catholic Church. "The Church of Rome can consult expedience more freely than other bodies, as trusting to her living tradition, and is sometimes thought to disregard principle and scruple when she is but dispensing with her forms." Newman, Development of Christian Doctrine, Longmans, 1897, p. 189.

senting the rank and file of the faithful with a pretext for inaction; secondly, and above all, because such a habit of suspicion, were it to become systematic, would not be Christian, as it would lead to adding a subtle danger of private interpretation to a want of intellectual charity. For what does outdoing the Bishops in the views they come to, criticizing them for the initiatives they authorize, and appealing "from the Pope to the Council" amount to, if not to a transference of competencies, of which the least that can be said is that it is not according to good order?

It is certainly not no such defensive lines as these that the Church invites the faithful to stand today. Supremely exacting in whatever touches orthodoxy, ready to make any sacrifice so as to guard whatever comes from God or the tradition of the Apostles, she does not forget the inspiration that goes with her inner life: "Do not stifle the utterances of the Spirit," says St. Paul, "do not hold prophecy in low esteem; and yet you must scrutinize it carefully, retaining only what is of God." [82]

Tactical Integralism

But the world, it is answered, is evil; it is the empire of sin and error, the kingdom of Satan. There are therefore only two attitudes open to us, which Christ himself laid down: to flee it or to fight it.

To fight the world, by launching a crusade against the enemies of Christ, to answer their attacks and even go over to the offensive, that is the only course by which the Church will succeed in the face of evil, the argument runs. Giving way or perpetually resigning oneself to calumny and injustice is to forget Christ's violent treatment of the Pharisees. We must vanquish the world with its own weapons instead of compromising with it; the latter attitude will result in nothing but total loss.

But here also the Church reminds us of her mystery. It is true that she is "linked with the Eternal" by an alliance which is not of this world; it is true that she is the "Jerusalem without spot" which refuses to compromise with Samaria. But it is not by reason of her divinity that she has to stand out against the

[82] I Thess., 15:19-21.

world. Her transcendence is not of that kind. It is not because she is the elect of God that she has to harden herself and set herself against those still wandering far from the fold "in darkness and the shadow of death." The Church is not a party and Christians are not partisans. Nor will she win the world by stiffening herself in opposition to it, raising block against block. Undoubtedly, every error can be refuted and every injustice redressed; and there are violations of the imprescriptible rights of God and the moral law against which the Church rises, and will always rise, with the last ounce of her strength. Against the triumph of force she sets the shocked protestation of her conscience; and when the necessity arises she willingly sheds her blood. When a principle is touched the Church does not give way; she never swerves from a rigidity she holds as sacred. But when it is a question of methods, must she, for that reason, adopt the habits of her opponents? So as not to compound with their errors must she try to force upon them her Truth and her Faith? Does not history show, on the contrary, that methods of regimentation and recruitment which strike at the mind or are borrowed from the "secular arm" and man-made systems of propaganda, have proved themselves to be as unsuccessful as they were contemptuous of the liberty of the gospel? To what such misappreciation of the Church's "incarnate" aspect and of her living insertion in time lead can now be seen, namely, to the very error it was sought to avoid. Because we will have nothing to do with this world, we fight it; and in fighting it, we use its own weapons. Here also excess engenders its opposite, and "refusing" the world leads in the end to all the vicissitudes of "tactical Christianity."

Moral Integralism

Lastly, this same error is found among a third group of Christians who may be called Quietists or Jansenists according as they stress the uselessness of the world or its harmfulness. For the former, life on this earth matters little when compared with the city of eternity; what use is there therefore in the Church's concern with the world? God will see to it that His Church endures. Structures and adjustments should give way to prayer and trust in Him; the supernatural is quite able to do without natural means. And the same reasoning holds good of the Church.

Not only can the Church do without such means, argue the upholders of this system, but she is absolutely obliged to make a clean break with the world and that by the very fact of her transcendence. The world is evil; and, impervious to grace, it is equally impenetrable to the Church. The resurrection of the latter should not therefore be sought in methods of "immanence," which seek to incarnate her in a temporal civilization; for the "dialectical" process inherent in the development of technical and historical progress, which is a closed and inevitable system, does not admit of any such "revolution." The world and religion form two different planes, which necessitate "divorce" and not reconciliation. The duty of the believer is not to act upon events, but in his private life to be simply a faithful disciple of Christ. The Christian the Church looks to is not the "Christian of Constantine" but the "Christian of the Apocalypse and the Second Coming."

Is there any need, while saying nothing of the caution with which this view of the world and grace must be viewed, to point out here the presupposition on which it rests? This theory, like the others, has again retained only the transcendence of the Church. It is just this one-sided vision which gives the three forms of Integralism their common unreality;[83] And that arbitrary mutilation, as does Modernism its opposite error, needs to be corrected, and each of them reconciled, in a loftier vision.

[83] St. Augustine was well aware of the problem, and laid down the course to follow: "The City of God, or rather that part of it which lives by faith in exile in this mortal life, must use that peace of which I have been speaking. It must continue to do so until its mortal nature, which makes submission to that peace essential, has passed. And so the City of God lives in captivity and exile, as it were, in this city on earth, though it is all the time sustained by the promise of redemption; and it never hesitates to obey the laws by which the earthly city is governed. Such laws are essential for the maintenance of human life. And since the two societies are alike in being mortal, it is right that they should have a common policy in all that concerns this life." St. Augustine, *De Civitate Dei*, book XIX, chapter 17.

THE CATHOLIC SYNTHESIS

At this point, one thing needs to be made clear. The action upon the world which the Church has to undertake today is far too crucial for her to be satisfied with a temporary and local compromise. What is needed is a vast synthesis, and one which will provide Christians with the double answer they are awaiting: action upon society which will be successful, and a doctrine which is fully Catholic. Here again it is the Theology and the History of the Church which make the construction of that enduring system possible. In what we write we have no other object in view than to point out the road to the faithful and support them in the action they take.

A "*Summa*"

The complete working out of that double answer will be the result of a long process, and it will not be the work of one man. The hour has struck when the greatest service that can be rendered to the Church and her sons is the making of a "Christian Summa" of the world now taking shape. The greatest mistake the Christians of the XX century could make, one which their descendants would not pardon, would be to let that world come to birth and be unified without them, without God—or against Him; and they would do so if they were to content themselves, in their apostolate, with stereotyped methods and accepted ways. We have no wish to make that mistake. And it will perhaps be the great honor of our time to have undertaken what others will bring to a good issue, a humanism embracing the dimensions of the world and adequate to the designs of God. It is by that, and by that alone, that the Church will find it possible to soar, and become, in the near future, what she was in the Middle Ages for the West, the spiritual centre of the world. The spreading atheistic and anti-Christian civilization of our day can give way to a "sacred culture," to a Christian transfiguration of life.

Is there any need to say that it is to the intellectuals that this task belongs, as happened in the days of the great doctors of the Church? It is their province to lead, with all the power at their command, in the creation of a Christian society in which the Kingdom of God will be sought before all else. The first apostolate, at the crossroads where we stand, is the Apostolate of Thought. The Church is at a turning-point such that she can lose everything or gain everything, according to the spirituality she asks humanity to adopt.

That "vision of the world" can be grouped entirely round two principles which are in fact really one, and which sum up completely the mystery of the Church. They are the Mystical Body of Christ and His Kingship.

"Catholic" Spirituality

With the Mystical Body as its first principle, our spirituality will be first of all *"Catholic,"* that is, it will enlist the help of all the scholars, the philosophers, and the sociologists of every country, providing the theologians with the results of their findings. But above all it will be *universal* through the understanding it shows of the conditions, cultures and problems of our entire humanity. It will appeal to all men without distinction and without dealing with them all upon one level. It will be all the time directed towards completing the Mystical Body,[84] which is to be done by bringing in new members, all of whom share in the same divine life. It will be a spirituality proportioned to the dimensions of the world.

By that very fact, it will be all-embracing, open to a wide range of different values in which error is often mixed with good. For it to become so requires a complex effort: it will be necessary first of all to fight against a number of human tendencies, now general and widespread, which are evil, such as the exclusive concentration upon profit and enjoyment, the worship of force, a passive attitude to the propaganda of hatred and division, and others. But at the same time inside the perspectives opened up by religion, it will be necessary to find room

[84] "The Church continues Christ's mission on earth and seeks nothing else but to bring the whole human race to the knowledge of Jesus Christ, and to lead it, by knowledge of the laws of the Gospel, to eternal glory." Sacred Congregation of Propaganda to Missionary Superiors, December 7, 1929.

for human values which are good and authentic: the growth of social organization, the renewing and transforming of the world by the united efforts—intellectual, technical and aesthetic—which recent centuries have produced, the more and more conscious affirmation of the solidarity of mankind everywhere, etc. The ability to discriminate should start from two principles, first, the growth of the Mystical Body and the universality it has in theory and is meant to have in history, a consideration which will lead to an attitude of intellectual charity; [85] but secondly, and at the same time, the unchangeable consistency of the Church of God, which lays down a firm and inflexible line in matters of doctrinal truth.

Total Spirituality

With the doctrine of the *Kingship of Christ as its other principle* the spirituality which the contemporary world is looking for before it can be baptized by the Church without reserve will be truly "cosmic," that is, it will envisage the world in its totality and such as God wished to "re-establish it in Jesus Christ." Seen from that angle, the Christian system is a frankly optimistic one; it shows that the world has a meaning, that it is not the plaything of a blind materialist dialectical process, but is warp and woof of the eternal "predestination" of all things in Jesus Christ. It shows that nothing can be outside his Redemption, that everything has been washed in His blood: "*Terra, pontus, astra, mundus, quo lavantur flumine*" [86] and therefore, from that moment, that the world has been sealed

[85] "I could easily show that almost the whole body of truth is contained somewhere or other in the various philosophic sects. We do not wish to destroy philosophy, like the Academicians, who prefer to rebut any proposition that can be made. That is mere mockery and calumny. No, we believe that there is no body of philosophers however wrong, no individual however stupid, who has not had at least a glimpse of the truth. What is more, if there had been anyone with the ability to collect and systematize all the parts of truth which are so widely scattered up and down the various schools, then I am sure he would see life as we do. But no one could undertake such a task without a thorough grasp of truth: and this can only come to a man who is 'taught of God.' " Lactantius, *Inst. Div.*, VII, 7. (P.L. VI, 758).

[86] Hymn at Lauds, *Lustra Sex*, on Passion Sunday.

with love. The Christian, far from having to flee the world, has as his task to "complete" it and "assume" it. "*Omnia vestra sunt, vos autem Christi.*" [87] At once the road he has to follow is there before him, and his "insertion within the temporal" is justified. Instead of closing his eyes to progress, the Christian believes in it and works for it, so as to "complete creation" and bring forward the day of the "second coming," when the entire universe—the Mystical Body and the whole of creation—will show forth the triumph of Christ the King by realizing his "pleroma" and achieving the total Christ.[88]

Let no one think that this soaring conclusion is merely a flight of fancy; it is, on the contrary, an idea familiar to the early Christians, but in these days too much forgotten. It is by restoring this vision to its true value that the Church will once more gain a hearing from men today because it is a dynamic view of man and society that men today are anxious to accept. Shall the Church stand aside and allow a pale imitation to oust the finished model? And shall man accept contentedly his limits—*homo homini deus*—or be driven to despair—which is the new sickness of our century—when we can, through her, soar immeasurably beyond himself: "*Vos autem Christi, Christus autem Dei?*"

Humanism of the Person

Let us lay down, however, with the utmost clarity, that the humanism which the Church offers is not only different from the "messianic" humanism of atheism, as Jerusalem differs from Babel—and we mean in the organization of the City—but it differs from it above all *by the meaning it gives to the person.* For if society, its institutions and the universe of matter itself are meant to be redeemed, it is always *for* the human person that this is intended, and *by* him that it is to be done; and it is the human person, if we take the world as being ruled by God, who

[87] I. Cor., 3:23.

[88] The pages of P. Huby are well known: see his *Commentaire de Rom.* VII, 19 sq. (Collection *Verbum Salutis*), and II Peter, III, 13. See also the *Bible* by Pirot, who brings together Isaias, 65:67, 66:22, and Rom., 8:19, I Cor., 7:31, Apoc., 21:1, &c.

comes "first" in the creative intentions of God for Society. To forget that is to sacrifice the unique drama inherent in the life of the individual to the "eschatological" furthering of the collectivity, and to transfer unwarrantably to the group prerogatives and an autonomy which belong to man alone: "In any living physical body, the sole final purpose for which each and every individual member exists is the benefit of the whole organism, whereas any social structure of human beings has for its ultimate purpose, in the order of utilitarian finality, the good of each and every member, inasmuch as they are persons.[89]

To ignore that truth, by reversing the order of values, means to make possible and lawful slavery and sorrow of every kind. As against the encroachments of collectivism, that reminder is of great value.

Humanism of the Cross

On the other hand, a place, unfortunately very large, must be kept in our synthesis for sin. Against the myth of man's continuing perfectibility, we must set the dogma, and the experience, of man's fallen state and the redeeming value of suffering: our cosmic humanism will still be a *humanism of the Cross*. The Church is too keenly aware of the value of blood not to place sacrifice at the heart of her vision of the world.[90]

Salvation of the world and salvation of the person; love of creation and the meaning of the cross; progress and sin; the saving of the present and the making of tomorrow; city of heaven and city of earth: none of these antinomies can be resolved except by a theology grounded in the double reality which the

[89] *Mystici Corporis*, E.T. p. 23.

[90] "The ink of the scholars is more pleasing to God than the blood of martyrs," runs the Arab proverb. "Unhappy race," exclaimed Psichari, "who have not understood the value of a drop of martyr's blood. . . . and that the ink will fade but that the drop of blood will never be washed away . . . Unhappy race which has not realized the price of sacrifice, neither the sacrifice of a brother for his fellows nor that of a God for men. That is what it means not to have had a God who could suffer and who died on a cross of wood." E. Psichari, *Les Voix qui Crient dans le Desert*, pp. 213-214.

Church is; and they will only be resolved by much patient work. Eternal and Transcendent, she refuses to compromise or give way; incarnate in history, she puts on its changes in order to act upon it from within. The soul of each Christian is marked by the same mystery. As a messenger of the supernatural, he is not afraid to be a "scandal" and a "folly' in the eyes of men; as a citizen of this earth he will "give to Caesar the things that are Caesar's" and loyally shoulder the tasks of this life.

We now see, therefore, that the program before the Church, like the program before the Christian, is not a "choice"; it does not shut out another alternative and become for that reason partial and exclusive. It is a synthesis, and the simultaneous accepting of a double summons.

THE ENGAGEMENT OF CHRISTIANS

No automatic formula, no easy compromise between them will reconcile these contraries; they will be reconciled simply and solely in a right hierarchy of values. The re-emergence of the Church calls for an order and a proportion which shall guide the action Christians undertake, and which can be expressed in two principles: the primacy of the Spiritual, and insertion in the Temporal.

THE PRIMACY OF THE SPIRITUAL

The action of the Christian will be first of all supernatural. It will be an *apostolate,* that is, a spreading of the gospel and the communication of the divine life. What in fact is its purpose, if not to extend the Redemption and save souls? But only God can bring about conversion; and we cannot emphasize too strongly that the apostolate is essentially a work of God. It is God's love giving itself to the world by Christ and the Church. Being an apostle means, therefore, opening oneself to the gift God makes so as to be able, as a humble instrument of His work, to communicate it to the world. If, therefore, the decisive hour at which we live lays upon Christians a "Catholic" sympathy for a world in travail, it is vital, now more than ever before, to begin with the essential point: giving the life of God is the beginning and the end of the apostolate. A transcendent reality, which it is far beyond the possibility men have by themselves to acquire, is given to the apostle, and his abiding attitude ought to be one of humble acquiescence. Grace is a gift of God; it is not proportionate to the powers given us by our nature, Souls will not be brought to eternal life save by the cross of Christ, the only mediator: "I am the way, the truth, the life." [91] In this age of official and practical atheism, our Savior's prophecy is verified more than ever: "Without me you can do nothing." [92] What Benedict XV said to missionaries in distant lands can be taken by all Christians as said to them: "Let the apostle trust in God alone . . . . Everything in the missionary apostolate is divine, for only God can get within the soul, enlighten the mind . . . and fire the will; He alone can give man the strength he needs to enable him to follow truth and do good . . . The missionary, if the Lord be not with him, is beating the air." [93]

An Apostolate Founded on Holiness

But how can the "non-believers" be brought into the "kingdom which is not of this world" [94] without the use of transcendental methods? The Church's mission is not "to rebuild the kingdom of Israel." [95] Souls will be brought to the Cross—*spes unica*—by no means other than prayer and penance, and the long patience given by prayer and charity. "All true and permanent reform has in the last resort originated in sanctity, from men who were inflamed with the love of God and their neighbor, who by their great generosity in answering every appeal from God . . . have enlightened and renewed the times in which they lived. When zeal for reform has not sprung from the pure source of personal singleness of heart but has been . . . the explosion of passion, it has brought darkness instead of light, it has pulled down instead of building up, and has often

[91] John, 14:6.
[92] Ibid., 15:5.
[93] Benedict XV, Apostolic Letter *Maximum Illud.*
[94] John, 18:36.
[95] Acts, 1:6.

been a starting point for errors still more disastrous than the evils which it desired or claimed to correct." [96] Our Lord's teaching is in danger of being too much forgotten today: "There is no way of casting out such spirits as this except by prayer and fasting." [97] Our first duty is holiness; it is with God that we have to set ourselves to the task, and in particular, the conversion of the world has to start with our own. "It is not," says Pius XII, "that we underestimate human means, or that we blame the use made of them when they are enlisted to serve the apostolate . . . but the error consists . . . in basing ourselves on these things *first of all* . . . and not turning to supernatural forms of grace, by prayer and penance, except secondarily and as an addition." [98]

We cannot insist too strongly on the absolute primacy to be given to the supernatural values which are the very reason for our action. All other problems are clarified by it; and it is within that supernatural reality that all the rest, under the promptings of the Holy Spirit in the Church and in the soul of the apostle, acquires significance.

The Soul of the Apostolate

The inner life, therefore, provides the "soul of the apostolate"; [99] it is also the antidote to naturalism, the guarantee of our fidelity to the "one thing necessary" [100] as well as the underlying condition of conversion; for men today will never throw over their idealisms in favor of a debased faith. What they long for is the gospel, without compromise. "Those who think that man will more easily be brought back to the duty and the practice of religion by relaxing the Master's yoke are wrong, and do great harm to souls." [101] This does not mean, in any way, that the apostle ought not to make men love the "true devotion" of St. Francis de Sales. But "they are no less wrong who point out

[96] Pius XI, *Mit Brennender Sorge* (E.T., The Situation of the Church in Germany, C.T.S., section 22).

[97] Mark, 9:28.

[98] Pius XII, in a broadcast for *Le Grand Retour,* 1946.

[99] Dom Chautard.

[100] Luke, 10:42.

[101] Pius XII, ibid.

the hardness of the road and its thorns, and do not trouble to make men love it." [102]

Here it would be necessary to bring in the whole spiritual tradition of the Church, as it is taught by the Magisterium and mystical writers, to explain that without a close and continual contact with Christ there is no holiness and no apostolate. The apostle, whether priest or layman, must therefore put in the foreground the values which explain his being: prayer, silence, recollection, meditation, and all that nourishes it: retreats, days of recollection and the life of the sacraments. The breviary ought to be the daily food of the minister of God; from other sources of devotion also, and especially from a deep love of Our Lady, he will draw the nourishment his life needs. Mental prayer, spiritual reading, the Holy Sacrifice of the Mass and frequenting the sacraments are not merely "spiritual exercises" to which he must sacrifice, to a greater or less extent, part of the time he devotes to action, but they are the indispensable source and substantial food of the Christian life. It is thus not a question of our life having a surface veneer of spirituality; it is not an artificial regime to be followed or abandoned as we like; there can be no authentic apostolate unless the following condition is present, namely, that we draw from God, from Christ and from the Church, the divine life it is our mission to give.

Realistic Apostolate

Fully supernatural in this way, the *apostolate* must also be *adapted*. But there must be no misunderstanding about what is meant by that word. *Adaptation does not mean accommodation*, or systematically substituting the "new" for the "old," *still less mutilation of the Church's message*, but solely an integral and intelligent "Incarnation" of that message in the actual state of things we have to change.[103] The situation is not always and everywhere the same; and it is this which explains

[102] Ibid.

[103] "Adaptation is only a practical consequence of the Catholic conception of Nature. It is a specific case of the Incarnation." L. de Coninck, S.J., *Les Problemes de l'Adaptation en Apostolat*, Nouvelle Revue Théologique, October, 1936, pp. 686-689.

and justifies the fact that the methods of the apostolate change with the times. This fact is so important that it dictates the whole attitude we have to adopt today and the line we have to follow. The first duty which is laid upon us before anything is done is "to sit down and count," [104] so as to study the conditions which govern the re-Christianization of the world at this present time.

Missionary Apostolate

One fact strikes us forcibly from the very start. The methods necessary for the re-Christianization of the world are as different as they possibly can be from those that were traditional in the ages of "Christendom." In the Middle Ages, and even down to the XIX century, Christianity was everywhere localized and the missionary apostolate "geographical." Missionaries went from Christendom to preach Christ in pagan lands, paganism was outside the Christian world. Today, on the contrary, the two are no longer separate, but inextricably conjoined and closely interwoven. Pagan society everywhere comes into the daily life of the Christian. A Christian society, sealed off and sheltered from pagan influences, has become, it would appear, something which cannot be imagined at the present time; and France is not the only country which has become "a missionary country." The phenomenon is more acutely felt among us, but it is latent everywhere, and it is likely that it will more and more show itself and become more and more general. That situation, which has never before been seen on the world scale it has now reached, involves two consequences.

After the Manner of Leaven

The first is that the modern apostolate can in no way whatever be a negative attitude of withdrawal from, or protection against, influences which are harmful, no more than it can be

[104] Luke, 14:28.

"Becoming a master of the faith is a task which makes a Christian of our countries very like the missionaries who, on the furthest confines of the Christian world, bring the light of the Gospel into the darkness of paganism." Pius XI, speaking to the Bishops and pilgrims of Jugoslavia, May 18, 1929.

"propaganda" or even "conquest" in the sense of externally "annexing" men or the currents of their civilization. The "victory" of the Church cannot involve isolation: the Christian reality can no more be "isolated" than an organism can be withdrawn from the neighborhood of harmful bacteria; the body breathes them every day but its reactions save it from infection. It is the same with the Christian; and the part he has to play is thereby made clear: it is a "battle" of two conflicting "toxins," one of which, as we know, is immeasurably stronger than and different from the other. The Christian does not choose his method; it is imposed on him by the environment of which he is part, and it is the action of the leaven. Without moving from where he is, he is invested with a duty and a task, the duty and the task of a missionary.[105] His efforts will thus not be directed merely to recruiting others and making the unbeliever "come to him," but also, and above all, to identifying himself with them in order to save them as they are. It is a *centrifugal action*, by which the Church must be made into the ferment of the masses and the new blood which will restore their life.[106] This missionary activity of the Christian, in the circle of life where he is placed, has been too long forgotten and even looked on with suspicion, because of the dangers accompanying the prevalent secularism, by the Catholic community, which has not ceased sending its sons and daughters to distant lands; from that has come an attitude of defence which was expressed—and its expression is still strong today—in a formidable degree of inertia. And yet every Christian, according to the part he plays, can apply to himself the words of Benedict XV to a missionary superior: "To the furthest point of the territory given into his charge he is bound to work for the salvation of all who dwell there, however numerous they may be. To have brought a few thousand pagans to the faith

[105] *Ibid.*

[106] "The needs and the structures of the age have day by day enlarged the field of the apostolate; great new battles are taking place along the roads and upon the ground which the development of civilization has opened to us." Pius XI, Letter to Mgr. Skwireckas and the Bishops of Lithuania, December 27, 1930.

out of a countless number does not give him the right to rest."[107]

Witness

By what means will the Christian be enabled to become "a leaven"? Experiments in this matter, thank God, are no longer wanting today; and they provide the answer. The apostles to the deChristianized *milieux* find continually that if they are to announce the Good News they have first of all to live the same life as those around them, as Christ did who "dwelt among us" [108] and, like Him, share their joys and sorrows, their hopes and disappointments, and stand squarely with the just aspirations of those around them. For Christian truth is not a system which commends itself from without by the prestige of its teachers, nor even by its sole objective truth; it is first and foremost *witnessing*. But the presence, physical and moral, which identity of life supposes is essential for a witness; and that is the meaning of the formula which is sometimes only superficially understood, but which contains a profound truth: "the apostolate of like by like." It does not mean that those in a particular setting who are of a different race or class must be excluded from our apostolate, but it does lay upon the apostle who goes to them the duty of putting off what is particular to himself in order to become "all things to all men." The essential law of the apostolate is "Incarnation."

"An Ascending Incarnation"

There must be no confusion as to what this incarnation means. It does not consist simply and solely in an artificial and superficial adjustment; when the Word "became flesh" [109] He became "fully man" like us. Above all He did not restrict himself to a descending movement; He *took* our nature and "assumed" it, as it is—*absque peccato*—so as to bring it into the glory of the Father at His Ascension. It was an ascending movement which crowned and explained his coming on earth. "God became man so that men might become gods," and that,

[107] Benedict XV, *Maximum Illud,* ed. U.M.C., p. 163.
[108] John, 1:14.
[109] Ibid.

according to the Fathers, is the full circle of the Incarnation and the Redemption to which it led. That is the model the "incarnation" of the Christian must follow. Being an apostle means taking on everything and penetrating everything, in what can lawfully be assumed, belonging to man and the world he has made. Everything—that is, apart from sin, all values, even those which until now have been foreign to Christianity, when they are not in fact "its own ideas run wild." [110] Distinguishing between these fragmentary truths is a delicate matter; but it is essential for successful as well as lasting penetration; and this task is one of the most urgent confronting the Church today. This is the way in which her action as "the leaven in the lump" must be understood. The lump is not denatured but uplifted by the leaven. Similarly, adherence to the Christian religion does not mean that any authentic human value must be in any degree given up—no more than the missionary who brings the gospel to a people of an ancient civilization, such as the Indian or the Chinese, asks his neophytes to renounce their culture or their ancestral inheritance. Thus, nothing which is part of the legitimate appanage of the worker or the intellectual today must be foresworn—with the obvious exception of sin. For the gospel is meant for everybody: *praedicate omni creaturae.*[111] It is true that there is no action by men which is without danger or defect, and the path in which our lives are cast may sometimes incline us towards bias or timidity, towards weakness or complicity with wrong. But such individual failures ought not to make us misjudge the value of methods and the fruit they have already given. In no case can the gropings and mistakes of pioneers provide the majority of the faithful with a pretext for inaction.

From the "Law of Incarnation," understood in its integrity, we wish to draw two conclusions for the present.

Catholic Action

The first is that the Apostolate must be *based on Catholic Action.* We have indicated what the balance sheet of the latter

[110] Chesterton.
[111] Mark, 16:15.

is for France, with its results and its hopes. We remind you now of the great store we set on it and what we expect from it. The reasons which brought it about have since grown even more compelling; and the line laid down by Pius XI is still just as opposite: "Present circumstances therefore indicate clearly the course to be followed. Nowadays, as more than once in the history of the Church, we are confronted with a world which in large measure has relapsed into paganism. In order to bring back to Christ these whole classes of men who have denied Him, we must gather and train from amongst their very ranks auxiliary soldiers of the Church, men who well know their mentality and their aspirations, and who by kindly fraternal charity will be able to win their hearts. Undoubtedly, the first and most immediate apostles of working men must be working men, while the apostles of the industrial and commercial world should themselves be employers and merchants."[112] Such action will often be no more visible than that of the leaven which, when it has made its way into the lump, disappears and seems to be swallowed up. At the present time our Catholic Action movements, while still concerned with "producing a shock" and witnessing to the faith that is in them, understand more and more clearly the indispensable link there must be, if a better world is to be built, between their apostolate and the practical gestures of the charity of Christ. When religious vitality is on the wane, religious life confines itself to acts of worship; conversely, when it is mounting, it spreads from acts of worship into all the activities of the Christian, even to those which seem to be the most profane: "*Sive manducabitis, sive bibitis. . .*[113]

Rooted in the Working Class

The second consequence of that "realist incarnation" is that the apostolate of the present day, without forgetting anyone, will above all pivot on the workers; first, because it is without doubt the laboring masses who are at this moment cut off from

[112] Pius XI, *Quadragesimo Anno*, May 15, 1931. "Five Great Encyclicals," N. Y. Paulist Press, 1939, p. 166.

[113] I Cor., 10:31.

the Church, and because their evangelization raises problems which have to be solved at all costs if we wish the twentieth century to restore to Christ the masses the nineteenth century took from Him; but also because the Church is too clearly aware of human dignity not to encourage, and be farseeingly sympathetic to, the possession by the workers of their legitimate place in the nation. This calls principally for education, and the use of all means—work, leisure, family, the life of the spirit—to prepare for an "inner deproletarianization" which will be directed not to an elite among them but to the mass of workers; it is not a question of giving them a "second zone" religion or a sub-proletarian morality; but to them must be revealed their sublime dignity as sons of God.[114] "For the Church, having as her head the divine worker of Nazareth . . . by the force of her doctrine and persevering action freed the workers . . . from slavery and raised them to the dignity of brothers of Jesus Christ."[115] It is by giving the laity wider and wider responsibilities, and by associating them ever more closely with the work of the hierarchy, that the profound transformation indispensable to the Christianization of the modern world will be brought about.

A Communitarian Apostolate

The united effort this entails shows that the apostolate must be communitarian. It needs to be communitarian in two fields, first of all *among the apostles*—both priests and leaders—and this means that they cannot remain isolated without danger or their action will become sterile. The guarantee of their inner life, as also of their own private perseverance, and their mutual support, is the community. The latter does not necessarily mean that they must live together; but it supposes above all that a team spirit exists among them. It requires that the messengers of the gospel shall not act as independent skirmishers, but that they shall devote themselves to united action towards which all their views and methods converge. The return on their efforts

[114] Canon Cardijn, speaking to federal chaplains, November, 1946. In *Notes de Pastorale Jociste*, February, 1947.

[115] Pius XI, Letter to the Cardinal of Lisbon, November 10, 1933.

will be thereby increased tenfold. Isolated, the Christian is an island in a sea of indifference; and even if he lives his religion faithfully, he makes no impression on society.

This consideration helps us to see that the idea of community applies not only to the apostles, but also, and especially, *to all those whom they reach*. Doubtless, total conversion cannot be brought about without the private contact of soul with soul, and this supposes individual contacts. But we cannot confine ourselves to that. We must reckon with the community and count on the community. A group will only be transformed by a group, and for this it has the "grace of its state." Today above all, when social forms have assumed such great importance and exert such strong pressure, it is no longer only the individual but the group itself which has to become missionary; and it is the natural communities—families, a group in the same block of flats, at work, leisure or in a street—which should bear witness and hand on the message.

There is, however, one condition for all this, and it is that there be no giving in to what may be called the "*temptation of Thabor*": "Lord, it is good for us to be here" . . .[116]—that is, that the community does not look inwards to itself and thereby forget its essential mission. The communities we have in mind are not ends in themselves. They are at once a product and a starting-point of a missionary movement. It is their duty to nourish the life of the soul, but without holding back the members in their work: the latter refresh themselves and pass on. But to convert their devotion to each other and their apostolic zeal into the goal to be reached is on the contrary to lay the community open to a double danger: egoism, which is satisfied with what it has; and exclusiveness, which shuts out the souls beyond. That is not how communities are to be understood: they must welcome all and be open to all.

Parishes and New Communities

These communities will be of many kinds: parishes, missionary teams, teams of Catholic Action.

The parishes remain the basic communities of the Church,

[116] Luke, 9:33.

provided that they become more embracing and better adapted. The *Mission de France*, with other bodies, is working for this.

In the more paganized sectors which the parish cannot reach, the missionary teams have to create new communities, open to those who have "come from afar." Such attempts are being carried out by the Paris Mission.

In conjunction with all three, Catholic Action teams are making the Church actively present in the institutions inside their various environments.

It is our wish that the parishes shall work more and more with these advanced groups, and by contact with them intensify their missionary outlook.

Criteria of Orthodoxy

New problems demand a new apostolate. The door is always open to new formulas of research and penetration. But such attempts require a guarantee. By what marks will they be recognized as reliable? A supernatural feeling for souls and the spirit of faith; humility and a continuing charity; these are already their own criteria, as are common sense and an accurate appreciation of realities. But above all, the touchstone will be found in love of the Church and that will decide if the attempts proposed are well founded.

A Filial Sense of the Church

Those who undertake these ventures must not only be "*in*" the Church but "*of*" the Church. At present such a reminder is highly important; for nothing would more compromise the mounting movement of conquest than chaos and dispersion. It would prove a serious danger to a number of undertakings if their bonds with the Hierarchy were not strengthened. Cut off from the Hierarchy, they would soon end by going astray; while on the other hand "as long as the limb is still part of the body its health must not be despaired of; but if it be cast away, it can neither be cared for nor cured." [117] The great guarantee is thus the Church.[118] "No man can call God his Father unless

[117] St. Augustine, *Serm.* CXXXVII, 1.

[118] It has been written, without, of course, injuring the primordial autonomy of the person, and envisaging solely the action of the Christian,

he acknowledge the Church to be his mother," says St. Cyprian . . . "He that gathereth not with me scattereth . . . It is a revealed truth that the Father, Son and Holy Spirit are One Being. Now the Church is one, because God is one. Hence to deny the Church's unity really means to deny the law of God, to refuse obedience to the Father and Son and to throw away life and salvation." [119]

Devotion to the Hierarchy

But where is the Church? She is to be found *round her bishops*. Her Hierarchy is not simply and solely the visible authority which can be recognized in her, which, in its externals, can be likened to other human powers, but a "mystery" like the Church herself: *Ubi Ecclesia, ibi Christus; ubi Petrus, ibi Ecclesia*. The Sovereign Pontiff is the summit of her unity; but each bishop in union with the Pope is himself a successor of the apostles and a direct representative of Jesus Christ. Thus "where the bishop is, there also are his people; just as where Jesus Christ is, there is the Catholic Church." [120]

Without a deep and filial respect for the bishop of the diocese—*Sacerdos et Pontifex*—who expresses completely the Pontificate of Jesus Christ, and without loyal obedience to the directives coming from the Pope, the Vicar of Jesus Christ, there can be no apostles. The laity have no meaning apart from this background, by which good order and an ideal are made one in the person of the Pastors. Let us therefore have neither "laicism" nor "clericalism"; all, whether priests, religious or lay people, must nourish a filial spirit of obedience for the Hierarchy, in mutual trust. In signs such as these will the seal and the influence of the Holy Spirit be recognized.

---

that this action can be explained only "as a function of the hive . . . To transfer to the bee the rights of the hive is to kill both." P. Charles, *La Robe sans Couture*, pp. 129-130.

[119] St. Cyprian, *De Catholicae Ecclesiae Unitate*, cap. 6. (Sancti Cypriani Opera Omnia, ed. Hartel, vol. 1, pp. 214-215).

[120] St. Ignatius of Antioch, *Smyrn.*, 8.

URGENCY OF TEMPORAL ACTION

Is the mission of the Church confined to the apostolate? There are some who think it is; and we have seen the objections they raise to her being "embodied in the temporal." According to these theories, embodying the Church would constitute a betrayal of the Kingdom of God, which is not of this world, and a compounding with the present-day self-worship of society. We have already dealt with the false ideas such arguments involve.

Work in the World Legitimate

Let it be enough to recall briefly here that without "incarnation" the Church ceases to exist, and that an attempt to deny man's life "according to the flesh" ends in destroying the supernatural itself and becomes Protestantism. For if it be true that the Church is the kingdom of souls, that her end is absolutely supernatural, and that thereby she does not directly pursue the happiness and civilization of man in this world, she is none the less concerned with them from another point of view. Because man is body and soul, mortal and immortal, she is concerned with whatever in him serves as a natural ground for the supernatural; for "grace does not destroy nature but elevates and perfects it." Further, as the messenger and an instrument which is "one with the redeeming Christ" of whom she is the living incarnation,[121] she owes it to herself to extend the benefits of the Redemption to the whole created world. Christ did not come to excommunicate the world but to baptize it in His Blood. From that moment the Christian has not only the right but the duty to "complete" creation, and to work at the

[121] "Our Saviour acts as God but also as man. . . . Remaining man he continues to act in the way men act and not solely as God acts. In our world, He uses not only His divine omnipotence, or purely spiritual forces, but also all the resources . . . of nature . . . which he created. The whole of humanity, that is, all the human, can be and ought to be employed by Christ. Every noble human activity should become 'sacramental,' that is, become supernaturally efficacious." L. de Coninck, *op. cit.*, p. 686.

city of this world. "The Temporal is a wounded reality and it must be loved with a redeeming love." [122]

Christian Optimism

It will be seen how far we are from the false picture men choose to make of the Christian: mistrustful of the present, unarmed against it, useless to society.[123] Yet it is precisely by our works, effective and real, that we shall be judged. "I was hungry . . . and you gave me food . . . a prisoner and you came to me . . ." [124] The path the Church invites us to follow is no other: it is an authentic "engagement," to "increase and possess the earth" [125] by our work and our discoveries, and then make of that an offering to the Creator—what could be more religious than this? "The Creator of all things himself placed in the heart of man those irresistible aspirations towards finding a happiness on earth which is consonant with them; and Catholicism approves all the just efforts made by our civilization and progress properly understood for the perfection and development of humanity." [126] And Pius XII writes in the same vein: "It would be a wrong interpretation of our words to take from them a condemnation of technical progress. No, we do not condemn what is a gift of God who . . . at the time the world was created . . . hid in the inner recesses . . . of the earth treasures . . . which the hand of man had to draw from it

[122] "To love the creatures of God, human joys, human effort, is not only allowed but ordered: it is necessary if we are to be like Christ and perform our duty. . . . The Christian loves the temporal as something which is meant to help him to reach God . . . What Christianity therefore energetically condemns is not love of the temporal but idolatry of the temporal." J. Mouroux, *Le Sens Chretien de l'Homme*, p. 16.

[123] "The Christian is not a coward afraid of facing life, or a weak ling who shrinks from joy, or frustrated. He is lucid and decided and knows that everything has to be purified—nature, love, even the person; and that with Christ he is capable of so doing." J. Mouroux, *op. cit.*, p. 21.

[124] Matt., 25:31-46.

[125] Gen., 1:28.

[126] Pius XI, *Caritate Compulsi*, May 3, 1932, Huslein, *op. cit.*, p. 268.

for his needs . . . and his progress."[127] Do not therefore be afraid that you will be less of a Christian the more you are a man; and each fresh conquest of the earth is a new province you bring within the universal domain of Christ the King. The words of the Pope are categorical: "The Church cannot shut herself up and remain inert within the secrecy of her temples and by so doing desert the mission laid upon her by divine Providence, to form man and form the whole man."[128]

"Set yourselves therefore to the task . . . do not stand idly by in all this destruction. Step forward and rebuild a new social order for Christ. . . .[129] The question has been settled: not only must we be "present in the world" but we must embrace progress. "There can be no question for a Christian who weighs history with the Spirit of Christ of returning to the past, but only of the right to advance upon the future and of going from strength to strength."[130] These last words we here make our own, and in the most categorical fashion we say to you: Go forward, work at the building of the new world. It depends on you whether it will be Christian or not. The world will belong to those who conquer it first. Upon you therefore depends the task of securing the Second Spring of the Church.

In the real life around you, what are you to do? It is the question St. Paul asked, on the road to Damascus: *Domine, quid me vis facere?* He received the prompt answer: *Surge, ingredere civitatem*.[131] Entering Society, becoming an active citizen within it, calls for a two-sided program.

THE TASK OF THE INTELLECTUALS

We have explained the general part to be played by the intellectuals in drawing up the "Catholic synthesis" which shall reconcile tradition with progress, transcendence with incar-

[127] Pius XII, Christmas Broadcast, 1941, *Catholic Mind*, Jan. 8, 1942, pp. 8-9.

[128] Pius XII, speaking to the new Cardinals, February 20, 1946.

[129] Pius XII, Christmas Broadcast, 1943, *Catholic Mind*, Vol. XLII, p. 72.

[130] Pius XII, May 13, 1942, *Catholic Mind*, June 8, 1942, p. 7.

[131] Acts, 9:8.

nation. It remains for us to set out here the particular tasks their important mission lays upon them.

Their Rightful Autonomy

We remind you first of all that their work is to be done in independence: "The Church has no intention of taking sides against any of the individual and practical forms by which peoples and States are trying to solve the gigantic problems affecting their domestic organization and international collaboration, as long as these solutions respect the laws of God."[132] It is not her mission to resolve directly problems which belong to the technical sphere. She leaves to the specialists their rightful autonomy; she is not held in fief by any system, in science, social questions, or politics; and she gives her children freedom to follow their choice and pursue their researches. The latter have their own methods and their own object. It is necessary to make this distinction so as to avoid any confusion of "spheres." Let no one therefore expect from the Church what it is not within her power or duty to give; she will inspire everything, but she does not herself fashion civilization.[133] It is not for her to lay down what the structures of tomorrow shall be: she respects too highly the rights men have and their freedom to initiate.

Initiative of Thinkers

But what she cannot herself do Christians can do and must bring to pass; because, being also of this world, they have an equal right with others to share in the search for truth and to

[132] Pius XII, Christmas, 1942, *Catholic Mind*, Jan. 1943, p. 46.

[133] "Within the limits of the divine law, which is the same for all and whose authority binds not only individuals and nations, there is a wide field and liberty of movement for the most varied forms . . . The sole desire of the Church . . . the guardian and mistress of the principles of faith and morals, is, with the educational and religious means she possesses, to transmit to all peoples without exception the clear stream of their inheritance and the values of the Christian life so that each nation, in the measure suited to its particular needs, may use the doctrines and the ethical and religious principles of Christianity to establish a society worthy of man . . . the source of true well-being." Pius XII, Christmas, 1940. *Catholic Mind*, Jan. 8, 1941, pp. 4-5.

take part in all the debates and transformations of a City to which they belong. The "children of light" are only too often less clever than the "children of darkness"; and that fact, when it was voiced by our divine Master, was not given as a precept. That Christians have been behind-hand in ideas may be a fact, but it is no virtue.

We therefore tell you, Christian thinkers, that your duty is not to follow but to lead. It is not enough for you to be disciples; you must become masters. It does not suffice to imitate; it is necessary to invent.

In Research: Disinterestedness

Your researches will deal first of all with Truth simply and solely, and with disinterested knowledge. You will pursue Truth for its own sake and without anticipating its applications. You will penetrate the secrets of nature more and more deeply; and the unique mystery they constitute is a constant appeal to climb higher in your search, even to God himself. You will put together the conclusions you arrive at in your specialist sciences and will endeavor to build up a cosmic vision of the universe. In doing all this, you will allow no consideration of interest, not even of apologetics, to enter in: you will seek only for what is. Your loyalty will be equalled only by your openness of mind and the effective cooperation you show with all those, believers or non-believers, who pursue Truth "with all their mind." You will have no hesitation in devoting yourselves, with all your powers and in the "delight of knowing," to your "vocation of scholarship." [134]

In Building the Future City

Along with this, you will not hesitate to apply your researches in another sphere also, that of civilization. What in fact is the question at issue? It is a question of building the

[134] P. Termier. On this subject, see the words of His Holiness Pope Pius XII to a group of French professors and students April 24, 1946, on "The Joy of Knowing." "That happiness is offered to you: do not despise it . . . You will be more eminent, even in your own line of study, the more you know how to enlarge your outlook."

new world, of specifying and preparing the structures which will enable man to be fully man, in a city worthy of him, of transforming all things to make of them a Christian world.[135] This is a vast program, far beyond the capacities of one generation, and one which demands two things. First, a process of analysis: you have to pronounce upon our present civilization to judge it for its condemnation or its correction. As we said recently,[136] you must draw up an objective balance sheet of our urban civilization today with its huge concentrations of human beings and its continual growth; the black spots of its inhuman production, unjust distribution and exhausting leisure. Then, secondly, by a process of synthesis, beginning with the weaknesses of the present order, but above all starting from its aspirations and the promise it contains, you will draw up a plan of urban civilization and of humanism on a vast scale, seen in relation to the nature of man, his capacities and his needs. The whole sum of your accumulated labors is to be directed towards that gigantic synthesis of the future world. Do not show yourselves timid in this task; but in the name of science in which none should be your equal, defend, exact and impose your masterly vision, which shall liberate man and the world.

The Recognition of Man

In the researches you make and the reforms you propose, you alone will be the best humanists, for you alone have it in you to provide the emerging civilization with a standard which will be complete, namely, the right conception of man. It is the Christian conception of human nature, and it alone, which will save man from being dehumanized. Instead of leaving him to be crushed by technical developments which profess to liberate

[135] "You must use all your natural gifts in the service of Christianity. And so I hope you will not hesitate to have recourse to those parts of Greek philosophy which may help; for this branch of knowledge is part of one's general education, a preparation for higher studies." Origen, *Ep. ad Greg. Thaum*, 3. (Bibliotheca Veterum Patrum, Venice, 1788, tom. III, p. 436).

[136] To the doctors and students of the Conference Laënnec, November 15, 1946.

him,[137] and instead of beginning with technical progress as though it were a good in itself and justified all the sacrifices individuals and our society now make, you will invariably begin with man himself and recognize him as a "person" and independent. It is for him that the City is being built. It is the City which is made for him; *it* will some day end, but *he* will continue to live by his soul, which is immortal; and even at the resurrection of the dead, his body will continue the body he knew on earth. It is perhaps not necessary, in undertaking to elaborate social life, to be a Christian; but it is necessary to be a Christian to succeed completely in making man and his society; for only the divine view of men can bring God's creatures to the supreme development He intended them to reach. For it is this view which reminds them that their "aspirations are infinite" and ever unsatisfied until they have been transcended; and that to stop short at a point of development and name it the "golden age" is imprisonment and death. From that aspect, it is part of the Church's mission to remind the world—as she has repeatedly done in the past and continues to do today—of the requirements its temporal organization must recognize, if it is not to disfigure in man the image he bears of God.

It is for this reason that today, in social questions, the Church equally rejects a liberal economy which converts struggle into a law of progress as well as theories of the State which would swallow up the freedom of the individual in favor of an anonymous power, and in their stead puts forward solutions in which the organizing of the City comes from the united efforts which all together contribute freely and willingly with respect for natural societies: the family, contracts, the various professions, and others.

The Structural Reforms Necessary

Your mission at this present time, therefore, carries with it the duty of research into, and a profound reform of, the struc-

[137] The "Catholic Centre of French Intellectuals"—C.C.I.F.—took man and the questions which the development of technical progress raise for him as the subject to be studied in 1947. Individual groups are already at work on this very real problem.

tures of society, and that in every sphere. The most urgent need is in social and economic life. We are aware that courageous leaders of industry, in close contact with the working classes, have listened to the pressing appeal the Church in France addressed to them only recently, when we reminded them "simply but firmly" that the principle governing the relations between capital and labor should be "directed more and more plainly towards partnership." [138] They are working boldly, as can be seen by their ideas and by what they have already accomplished, to find a new outlook and to organize their factories along these lines, by associating the workers in them with administration, ownership and profits. We are also aware from other sources that large numbers of the laity are anxious to promote genuine professional organizations which, in their right proportions, shall unite accepted members of the profession who are representative of its interests with adequate control by the public power. Such reforms in their application involve technical questions of many kinds upon which it is not for us to pronounce. But they are in line with the ideas already put forward by the encyclical *Quadragesimo Anno*. They are necessary if the problems of economic and social life are to be solved, and they lay down the conditions without which there can be no transformation of the proletariat. We therefore warmly encourage those of the laity whose responsibilities allow them to act in this matter, to take part in this development, and to persevere in it without being discouraged by the difficulties of all kinds which they encounter.

What we have said here of industry we apply to all the other sectors of public life: civic life, economic life, "political" life in its wider sense, international exchange, culture, education, leisure, the arts, and others. Christians must be present everywhere; that is the watchword we continue to give you and in the clearest terms we can. Let Christians become the "leaven" and the mass will be transformed.

[138] Statement by the Assembly of Cardinals and Archbishops of France, February, 1945.

A Threefold Plan of Action

But it is necessary, as has been very truly said, that the mass must be the real mass and not an artificial one.[139] It is precisely here that the problem of the Temporal joins that of the Apostolate. The conditions prevailing in what we call "modern civilization" are no longer human; and the message of the supernatural, even when it is brought by the most competent and fervent elites, no longer encounters "the natural" but a body of dissimilar and chaotic elements which, in the generality of cases, can no longer serve as a ground for grace, still less as stepping-stones for its action. It is for this reason that the task of the Christians is so obvious; for if they do not provide a cure, if they do not take our institutions in hand, if they do not replace the corroding environments of this "soulless world" by an atmosphere it is possible to breathe, their efforts to evangelize are in grave danger of failure. To convert the world, it is not enough to be a saint and to preach the gospel; or rather, it is not possible to be a saint and invoke the gospel we preach without doing all we can to assure for all men conditions of work, housing, food, rest and human culture without which life ceases to be human. The mission of the Christian is thus not just an *Apostolate*; it is the product of simultaneous and converging lines of action in three fields: religious, civic and social. That task is so large that the Christian, isolated, is helpless; and to have realized that is the honor of Catholic Action. Catholic Action teaches its members to judge civic, economic, and social problems by their faith, and prepares them to shoulder the responsibilities in the City which that Christian faith lays upon them. Finally, by its own life, it claims living conditions for men which are in keeping with their sublime destiny as sons of God. That such simultaneous action is necessary is a valuable conclusion, because it shows that the facts confirm the Catholic conception of "incarnation" and makes it possible for the Church to direct her development.

That development on all fronts must find its starting point

[139] P. Desqueyrat, *L Apostasie des Temps Nouveaux*, in *Travaux*, October, 1946, p. 22.

once more in an effort of the mind. It will only be made possible by the establishment, in every branch, of research centers, cultural institutions and the like. Much has already been done in this direction;[140] and we give wholehearted encouragement to them. But we wish to see these bodies grow more and more numerous, and especially to see a close coordination unify their activities; for otherwise they run the risk of dissipating and losing their energies. It seems that the moment has come when the need of centralization is being intensely felt, perhaps even an organic centralization, which shall nevertheless respect their indispensable pluralism, and the autonomy each specialized center needs to enjoy. From the vast inquiries made by scholars, sociologists and technicians, the philosophers and the theologians, step by step, have in their turn to build up a constructive synthesis; and the signs that it is on the right lines consist in its continual growth and the way in which it submits its conclusions to the judgment of the Church.

A CALL TO ACTION

Do not think, however, that the building of the future City belongs to the intellectuals alone. It is not necessary to be a scholar before you can share in this great work; and every Christian is called to it. Each one in his sphere of action can bring an influence to bear. "The duty of this present hour is not to wring our hands but to act. Let there be no repining for what is or was, but reconstruct what is emerging and what must emerge, for the good of society."[141]

Indeed, except he shut his eyes, who can not see the sorrows which surround him and the evils to be relieved? "What priest, what Christian, can remain deaf to the cry coming from the depths of the masses who, in the world of a just God, cry for justice and brotherhood? . . . The Church would be denying her own self, she would cease to be a mother, if she remained deaf to the cry of anguish which reaches her from every class of humanity . . . For us, *misereor super turbam* is a sacred

[140] In this connection we note the *Centre Catholique des Intellectuals Francais.*

[141] *Ibid.*

watchword."[142] "Before He began to teach the people, Jesus Christ used first to tend the sick . . . and He even gave a similar power to his apostles, with the command to use it."[143]

Thus, let each one set to work and drive his roots ever more deeply into the surroundings in which his life is cast. For one it means work in a welfare organization, or one which aims at securing better conditions of housing or of work; for another, action in a trade union or a profession, or accepting his responsibilities in a family association. Some will enter town-planning, others youth movements or rehabilitation schemes. And by the living experience we have of them, we are certain that those of the faithful who are active in Catholic Action or who have been trained by it, are particularly fitted for these many different tasks. Day by day, each can contribute his stone to the edifice all are raising together. It is enough to do this without heeding criticism or obstacles, with the "faith that moves mountains." "You say," exclaims Tertullian, "that we are not men of the world. What do you mean? Do we not eat like you, dress like you? Do we not share the same way of life, the same human needs? Do you take us for aboriginals and savages, roaming the woods and exiled from civilization?"[144] Do not have any doubt about the results which will come from action thus immersed in life. At the time, you will not see the results of your groping and perseverance; but a day will dawn when your children and your grandchildren will thank you for the earthly dwelling you prepared for them.

Do you now see the lines of opportunity opening before you? Are you going to remain timid and despairing when such a splendid field of construction awaits you?

Beyond Outward Appearances

We know that some are tempted to consider the task impossible. Never, perhaps, has the world lain so heavily upon our hearts; and there are undoubtedly days when everything seems dark. A world without God, the rising tide of sin everywhere,

[142] Ibid.
[143] Pius XII, quoting Math., 8:16; Luke, 10:8-9; 9:6.
[144] Tertullian, Apol., XLII, I. (P.L., I, 490-491).

the repeated threat of collective suicide, the cries of distress assailing us wherever we turn, these are indeed enough to unnerve us. The anxiety which each feels in his own heart, how can he not extend it to the Church? What can she do, what is to become of her, in a world which has moved far from her and is bent on striking her name from the list of the living? Yes; it is indeed true that the task can appear beyond the power of men and impossible even for the Church, seemingly outflanked everywhere, and submerged by the deluge of the age.

And yet, look beyond the appearances; and we know, even now, that in the struggle which has been joined, the Church is victorious already. Without illusion, and having calculated the price she will be called to pay, she repeats to us the words Christ gave her to say: "Have courage, I have overcome the world." [145]

Beyond False Systems

Our faith in the Church is grounded first of all in the insufficiency inherent in all that is not herself. The new messianic systems now being put forward, or which are trying to hoist themselves into power as the answer to our hopes and our ills, always fall short in one respect or another. At the very time when the attraction they exercise is strongest, they provide obvious signs of decline to those who have eyes to see. It has been said that the body takes its revenge; today we ought to speak of the spirit taking its revenge. The world cannot expel God with impunity; and the hour of His return has sounded at last. The body of man can be broken and ground to powder; but no one has the power to stifle and kill his soul; and today his soul has begun to speak. That can be seen in the disillusioned masses and felt in the eager searchings of the intellect. Never, perhaps, have the systems of men felt the craving for God to the degree they do today. So that when we look upon the Church, it is not doubt which assails us, still less fear or a feeling of shame, but joy and pride. For these are systems and promises which pass, whilst the Church outstrips them all. She

[145] John, 16:33.

would stifle in such messianic theories, closed and mutilated as they are. Her youth withstands their power to grow old.

The Immortal Youthfulness of the Church

Ever youthful and undying always, such is the lesson of the past as well as of the present. What age before our own has known such hopes as these? If there is no effect without a cause, it is equally true that there are no causes without their effect: and how can what is being sown today not flower and bear fruit tomorrow? Whatever may come about, we know now that in every class of society there are Christians who, in spite of error, opinions and perhaps persecution and death, will witness to Christ and His undying Church. We know that whatever may be done or said against God will be answered in the hearts of others whom love of Him inspires. Anything may happen, persecution, heresy, war; but we believe, more than ever, in the undying youthfulness of the Church. Here, how can we do other than make our own those words of Newman, when he spoke of the Church's Second Spring? "Yes, my Fathers and Brothers, and if it be God's holy will, not Saints only, not Doctors only, shall be ours—but Martyrs, too, shall reconsecrate the soil to God. We know not what is before us ere we win our own . . ." But the call to joy follows the call to courage: "We are engaged in a great, a joyful work"; and if we are to escape our present ills it must be by going forward. "The world grows old, but the Church is ever young." [146]

Of the youth which is the ground of our hope we now know the secret: it is the Mystery of the Church. "One of the qualities of the Church which Scripture praises most," says Bossuet, "is her perpetual youthfulness and her ever-enduring newness. And if you are perhaps astonished that instead of the novelty which is receding at this moment, I speak of a newness which does not end, it is easy for me to satisfy you. *The Church of Christ is always new, because the Spirit Who is her soul is always new.*" [147]

[146] Newman, The Second Spring, in Sermons Preached on Various Occasions, Longmans, 1898, pp. 178, 176.

[147] Bossuet, *Sermon pour le Temps du Jubile*, Metz, 1656. It should be noted how the Fathers always go back to the mystery of the Church

. . . and Her Second Spring

With such a vision before us, and hopes such as these, we are now in a position to conclude.

What is to be thought of this Church which was called dead? The storms which men and ages have known have been unleashed upon her to engulf her; and like the Ark she has weathered their violence and has each time found new shores for a wider growth. Today as in the past the world will not be saved from the deluge without the Ark.[148] Today as then "the Spirit hovering over the waters" sends out to it the dove, His living symbol, which bears His olive branch; and that witness to an unexplored continent in no way resembles a handful of withered leaves. It has the grace and damp freshness of Spring.

Prayer

"Let us pray, dearly beloved, for the holy Church of God: that our God and Lord may be pleased to give her peace, and union, and preserve her throughout the world . . . so that, spread over all the world, she may persevere with a steadfast faith in the confession of Thy Name." [149]

"O God, unchangeable power and light eternal: mercifully

---

when they forecast her permanent youthfulness: "What makes you say 'the Church has vanished from the world?' She will vanish only when her foundations fail. But how can Christ fail? And while Christ stands firm, the Church will never waver till the end of time." St. Augustine, *Enarr, in Psalm, CIII, Sermo* II, No. 5. (P.L. 37, VI, 1353).

"The world," he says in another place, "believes that Christianity will be short-lived and soon forgotten. On the contrary, in the words of the Psalmist, "it will endure as long as the sun endures." As long, that is, as time lasts, whose measure is the rising and setting sun, the Church, Christ's body on earth, will never fail." *In Psalm*, 71, (P.L. 36, V, 906).

"Never leave the Church, for she is the strongest force on earth. She is your hope, your refuge, your salvation. The Church is higher than the heavens, broader than the earth; never growing old but always in full vigour." St. John Chrysostom, *Hom. de Capto Eutropio*, No. 6. (Opera Omnia, Paris, 1721, p. 391).

[148] "*Haec est arca quae nos a mundi ereptos diluvio, in portum salutis iducit* . . ." Proper of Paris, Dedication of a Church.

[149] Prayer from the morning office of Good Friday.

regard the wonderful mystery of the whole Church, and peacefully effect by thy eternal decree the work of human salvation: and let the whole world experience and see that what was fallen is raised up, what was old is made new, and all things are re-established, through Him from whom they received their first being, our Lord Jesus Christ, Thy Son. . . ." [150] Amen.

[150] Holy Saturday, prayer after the second prophecy.

THE MEANING OF GOD

Transcendence and Immanence are also two notions in the theology of God. In our pre-occupation with the brotherly aspect of the Son of Man we dare not lose the mystery of the Son of God. To forget that God created the world out of love and saved it out of love would be to lose the meaning of man and of God.

Contents

The Meaning of God

I. THE ABSENCE OF GOD

The contemporary world has been often defined as the age of the machine and the age in which everything is relative; but the civilization of the present day can be defined more accurately by a feature which marks it off from any civilization which has preceded it. It is an age without God.

IN CONTEMPORARY SOCIETY

This absence of God causes contempt today among the most diverse kinds of men. It is not an evil on the surface of life; nor is it a geographical absence, as though God were missing from certain regions only. It is a chronic and universal absence, at one and the same time a fact and a deliberate intention. God is absent, banished, expelled from the very heart of life. Society has closed up on that exclusion and the resulting emptiness, a desert without God, is a void from which it is dying.

It would take a book, not merely a letter, if we were to try to enumerate all the forms of contemporary atheism. It is enough to realize this if we look at the posters in the streets, the pictures in magazines, the headlines in the press, the publicity given to certain films and novels. Nor could we hope to carry out such an analysis in a few pages, as much qualification would be needed.

We are concerned more with making Catholics realize this absence of God acutely and even painfully than with enumerating its different aspects. We must escape the slow movement of asphyxiation, and the need is urgent, by one of indignation. "God is absent from the towns, the countryside, laws . . . manners . . . art. He is absent even from the life of religion in the sense that those who still wish to be his friends do not need his presence." [1]

This last assertion may cause surprise. But need we be surprised if this universal atheism affects Christians themselves? Because they have to breathe that atmosphere they are in the end impregnated by it. The subtle poison is drawn in through

[1] Léon Bloy.

all the senses, the deadly peril being that it does not kill its victims but immunizes them against itself. Thus we do not have to go far to find the godless. They are found at every step. A large number of baptized Christians, while they are not genuine atheists, in practice live and act like atheists.

The Nominal Catholics

The first group among them is made up of the nominal Catholics, who only go to Church on big feasts. Can they really be said to know the meaning of God? They do indeed perform religious acts at certain times of the year, through family ties or because such acts are traditional; but can they really be said to have the faith? Is not their religious life an empty formalism? That this is so is shown by their conduct—it is no different from that of the unbelievers around them. They read the same books, patronize the same amusements, share the same judgments on life and events. But it is above all in their family life that the poverty of their religion appears. In relation to divorce, free unions, abortion, and birth prevention they are almost incredibly indulgent when they do not actively sponsor these doctrines. If this judgment be thought severe, think of the education parents of this kind are liable to give their children. Every day, even in the poorest homes, the greatest efforts are most touchingly made to obtain for the children everything they need: but only for the body. Health and hygiene have become idols to which everything else is sacrificed. All that relates to the formation of a Christian—conscience, religious faith, spirit of sacrifice, apostolate—is unknown or even despised. In the opinions of parents such things are superfluous. We need not be surprised therefore when adolescents systematically left to themselves on the plea of unshackled freedom swell the rising tide of juvenile delinquency or at the very least lead purely material lives, the end of which in their eyes and in those of their parents is death, beyond which there is nothing. How many baptized Christians weep over a grave "like those who have no hope"?

Practicing Catholics

Although they do not go to this degree of complete materialism, practicing Catholics themselves have also seriously lost the meaning of God. Sunday Mass and often the reception of the sacraments are for them a routine with which they are content and in which they settle themselves as in some privilege. Religion is for them an insurance against risk, a certificate of good education. Its obligations are performed as though thcy were a boring but necessary formality to which sacrifices must be made, just as sacrifices are made to other social conventions. Moral judgments are doubtless stricter and conduct more frequently inspired by duty. But what becomes of God in all this? It would be unjust to say that he is utterly forgotten; many belong to him more than they think or lead us to imagine. Their faith is awakened at intervals by some great happening in the Church or by some historical event. Nevertheless, in their lives as a whole God has ceased to be a personal God; he is a principle, a colorless abstraction. The awful and overwhelming words of Christ fall unheeded on their ears, the Gospel does not enter into their lives. Need we be surprised if the lives of so many Christians which proclaim Christ so slightly or so badly are barren or a scandal to the unbeliever?

THE ATTITUDE OF CHRISTIANS

Christians have felt this scandal painfully. Having begun to understand the meaning of the present crisis through a profound training in religion, they have chosen God and engaged themselves in the Church's service with a generosity admired in France and throughout the world.

Values Gained

For some twenty years—in practice since Catholic Action began—a magnificent effort has been made to bring the spirit of Christ into all the aspects of life. After a long period during which the Church was absent, some of the barriers between the contemporary world and the Christian tradition seem to have been lowered. A renewal of married and family life can be seen everywhere. Many young families show daily that an integral Christian life is possible in the ordinary conditions of life. In the field of education, among other successes it is enough to mention that of the Scouts. Boys who sought strength and the spirit of chivalry have been taught by this movement to find in union with Christ the impetus they needed to build up their personality. Thanks to specialized and general Catholic Action and especially to the Young Christian Workers a genuine and authentic spirituality of work now animates the worker and the student. They know that the world will not be brought back to Christ and they themselves be sanctified if they turn away from their daily tasks. They spontaneously transpose this mystique to social and civic action, and that not merely in order to make certain that the Church shall live in society but in order to establish among all men a union which shall reproduce on earth the image of the City of God.

Philosophy and theology, far from being closed to the perspectives of humanism, whether in literature or in science, have made a noteworthy attempt to integrate more fully a number of values—history, the idea of progress and others. Lastly, in matters of evangelization, a big advance has been made with the promotion of the laity. There remains of course much routine and habits of exclusiveness which belong to another age. But an immense movement to renew all Catholic institutions and especially the parish can now be seen. It shows that a number of routine attachments are merely temporary hardenings which will in due course be taken in hand and remolded by the life which is reaching them from every side.

It can thus be seen that by these concerted efforts a vast field has been withdrawn from the profane and placed under the prompting of the Holy Spirit. "Everything is grace . . ."—these words may serve as the banner and the conclusion for a development the like of which has never been seen.

Values Forgotten

Without indulging in the morbid form of disparagement apparent for some time and very frequent among ourselves, let us loyally recognize none the less that a serious overhaul is necessary. We invite all our militant Catholics to make this examination of conscience, but this in no way affects the fact of their engagement. What we asked from them last year as one of the conditions essential to the Growth of the Church we repeat just as insistently this year. The world will be saved only if Christians are present in it. More than at any other moment in history they ought to animate existing institutions, foresee and provide the reforms which must come. It would thus be contrary to our deliberate intention for anyone to avail himself of the analysis we intend to make as justifying his destructive and sceptical outlook or culpable escapism. The critic who never acts easily avoids mistakes—mistakes only come from action.

Further, it is not always a question of actual errors; the loyal examination we ask you to make concerns possible dangers, tendencies, or lines of experiment just as much as what has been achieved.

In any case everything comes back to the central question: do we possess the meaning of God? In other words, do the paganising surroundings imperceptibly color us? Have we kept the notion of God sufficiently high and sufficiently pure? We are engaged in the temporal—is our engagement sufficiently situated in the perspectives of the faith?—for without them our reforms would be neither legitimate nor successful. Does the meaning of man eclipse in us the meaning of God? Is God for us always God?

A Weakened Belief

The first danger concerns the very notion of God. The accent is put on everything that brings Him near to man: God as Father rather than God as Master. He is "Our Father," but on earth rather than "in heaven," a good God rather than the Sovereign Judge. Of the Word of God we have especially retained the adjective "Incarnate," and Christ has become the Friend, the Confidant, the Elder Brother, the model of life for multitudes of souls. But his Sacred Humanity, which was wholly referred and absolutely faithful to the Father, the Lord who grafts us upon the intimate life of the Love of the Three Persons—all that takes second place. Our age has fortunately rediscovered the extraordinarily brotherly character of the Son of Man but misses the mystery of the Son of God. We regard the coming of God into the world as a prodigious event and point to his action in history as at once directing it and giving it meaning. But not to see beyond that role, to forget that God has raised man towards himself, comes near to making God a means for the service of the world rather than a Being sufficient to himself apart from us. In short, we keep the Immanence of God [2] and are in danger of forgetting his Transcendence.

The "Meaning of Man" . . .

What is happening? Without our realizing it the great systems of philosophy and the great currents in the modern world with which our intelligence and sensibilities are entangled, inevitably exercise a contagious influence and penetrate the very bases of our faith. All the time the "meaning of man" tends to take the place in us of "the meaning of God."

Scientific discovery is directing everything towards technical achievement and the domination of material forces, and in the battle against all forms of enslavement *homo faber* expels *homo sapiens* and any form of disinterested contemplation. At the same time as man's power over things increases so also do his liberty and his autonomy. Man has the knowledge and the power; he is self-sufficient and has become his own center of interest. The majority of the modern tendencies in philosophy lead to atheistic humanism; and this is an abuse. In former days the attacks of heresy were directed against a dogma; during the

[2] Even though this word was recently disputed we use it in the meaning given to it in contemporary writing and in connection with the ideas of St. Thomas, expressed for instance in the title he gives to question 8 of *The Existence of God in All Things.*

last century they envisaged all dogmas. But at the same time a certain deism was still tolerated. Today the denial is the most radical of all, for the besetting sin of the modern age, as it was in the Old Testament, is idolatry, the idolatry of man.

. . . Has taken the Place of the Meaning of God

This conclusion clearly applies to the atheist; it applies also in a lesser but more subtle degree to the children of light themselves, for whom concentration upon man threatens to become a fatal poison. It consists in a reversal of values, in grafting God on man and not man on God. "What interests us is not God as he is in himself, but man, the world and its explanation, an answer to which must be found. Once the explanation has been given there is no need to look further . . . We have ceased to be aware of God in himself but only of God in us, that is of ourselves in our relation with God." [3] Everything is done as though God were at the service of man, as though he had a part to fulfill in relation to man, namely, the perfecting of the individual or of society.

Such a reversal of viewpoints, if it were once accepted, would destroy all religion. It would also contradict the whole of Scripture as well as the tradition of the Fathers and the Doctors of the Church. God made to our size, God in this human form, would cease to be God.

Lest these conclusions be thought to be too theoretical we will examine various aspects of contemporary Christian life; it will be seen to what lengths in tangible consequences this latent danger leads.

Contemplation is Misunderstood

The first consequence appears in the life of religion itself. Prayer of adoration and praise is little appreciated because the value of the virtue of religion and of the philosophical virtues is admitted only grudgingly. In some cases faith rather easily appears as no different from the contemporary idealistic systems by which their followers pledge themselves to a completely

[3] H. Paissac, "L'Athéisme des Chrétiens," supplement to "La Vie Spirituelle, May 15th, 1947.

human cause. Christians are aware of God in themselves but "they shrink from thinking of him in himself as though the question were unreal." [4] The prayer of contemplation is willingly reserved to religious as their special province, while the laity find God everywhere since he is immanent in the world.

The Sacred is Forgotten

It thus happens that sacramental and liturgical life suffer since their mystery is reduced. Because the only aspect seen of God is his familiar aspect, the sense of the Sacred has been lost. The pastoral clergy and chaplains unanimously find that one consequence is a weakening of the sense of sin along with an attendant distaste for the sacrament of Penance. Even among the best the feeling of guilt attaching to sin and the necessity of contrition in order to repair an ingratitude to God have become overlaid; we are close to ranking humility with natural moderation, purity with hygiene, charity with philanthropy. The expansive phrase is often repeated, and rightly, *sacramenta propter homines*. But it is not sufficiently realized that if the reception of the sacraments must always be made possible to the faithful, the reason is that they can thus the better appropriate them and be carried along in the great movement of praise and thanksgiving rising from this earth to God through His Son. If the sacraments are emptied of this essential content they will soon become lifeless rites.

The same is true of the Priesthood. Because some are tempted to make the priest the same as the militant—the best, it is true, and the most thoroughly committed—his particular function in the offering of the Sacrifice is no longer properly understood, with the result that the part played by the community is emphasized onesidedly. Is not the crisis in religious vocations due in part at least to this, that perhaps a plus value has been given to marriage (the high dignity of which can never be sufficiently stressed) while at the same time the consecration of the priest or religious is insufficiently emphasized and celibacy is not properly viewed as choosing God alone?

[4] H. Paissac, *op. cit.*

The Mystery of the Liturgy is Lost

This wrong idea of the minister of God is in reality nothing else but one aspect among others not infrequently met with of how the sense of the sacred in the liturgy has been lost. If the liturgy fortunately no longer keeps the laity as strangers to the wealth of the Church's official texts and gestures, it is on the other hand sometimes emptied of the essential element of mystery which has been sometimes excluded from too many ceremonies. The whole congregation making the Mass a dialogue is a real progress, just as long as too many mediocre commentaries, by destroying the silence, above all during the Canon of the Mass, do not intrude on too many of the faithful.

"Active" Holiness

The loss of the meaning of God is shown secondly in action, which tends to assert itself not only over contemplation but over sacrifice. Holiness is sometimes regarded as a beautiful flowering of humanism or the ultimate unfolding of the personality. In reaction to the negative moralism which was the vogue recently, the range of the active virtues is what is now offered to the young believer. To avoid formalism all spiritual constraint and often asceticism are condemned, for the reason that love covers everything and is everywhere sufficient. The primacy of charity was never before asserted as strongly as it is today, often enough because St. Augustine's *ama et fac quod vis* is interpreted too widely.

In fine, mortification—and even more readily obedience—are confined to those in religion, for the Hierarchy has become a stumbling block to many of the laity. Instead of seeing in the Hierarchy the emanation and the astounding prolongation in time of the mystery and the very person of Christ, they now see only the machinery of a complicated administration. It is not surprising therefore if a reckoning is demanded of an authority which is conceived as being built on merely human lines. Instead of seeing God they merely see man.

Success the Criterion

It is to be feared that in their determination to save all men, their brothers and especially those furtherest from them, Christians who are admirable indeed in generosity may fall into one of the dangers of our time, namely activism. What matters, what comes first, is action, and the dividend received; while the gratuitous gesture, the "useless" service from which nothing can be expected "historically" is looked down on and the profound value of failure is rarely understood. People are tempted to make another principle, the criterion "does it work," the matter of the apostolate, when the latter ought to be a disinterested communication of the integral message of the gospel. This is easily explained in an industrial age such as our own, in which everything is weighed, everything counted, everything measured, and belief is wrung from the mind by repeated publicity and propaganda. It is quite natural for such an influence to extend to the world of souls and for the messengers of Christ to be tempted to employ methods and even techniques which succeed. Do not many rely more on their own powers than on grace? And does not the lowered understanding of the sacraments everywhere noticeable derive from that? Natural methods are often preferred to the incomparable spiritual means, Penance and the Eucharist; and this is a new proof which cannot be gainsaid that even among the best there is a weakened sense of God.

THE CHOICE BEFORE CHRISTIANS

This somewhat long analysis has only touched on one or two of the main features in contemporary religious life; but it makes one thing quite plain: such deviations, which we warn the faithful exist and are possible dangers, have well known and interchangeable names: naturalism, pragmatism, subjectivism, secularism, and the like. That is no mere coincidence; there is a chain of cause and effect. The systems just mentioned, when they spread in the West, did not afterwards become extinct; they left behind them seeds which grew in the free atmosphere of the unbelieving world and in an underground but no less real manner in the Christian world.

From Philosophy . . .

In each of these worlds the systems mentioned were united by one common feature: they all had a philosophy of man. This philosophy, understood in two different ways, has divided contemporary thought into two distinct streams.

One, of optimism, believes that the indefinite progress of the universe by technical achievement due to an inherent law of dialectics will result in absolute happiness for humanity. The first duty is thus to believe in the future, to advance, to dedicate oneself unreservedly to the possession of the world.

A second broad current, the opposite of the first, moves towards pessimism. Everything is brought back to man considered in his concrete existence as a free being. But that existence, since it has no reason which explains it, is absurd, has no given direction, no meaning; and of this the actual bankruptcy of science and of civilization is sufficient proof. The attitude men must take is thus not a confident forward movement towards a better future but a conscious and despairing leap into nothingness.

. . . to Theology

Whether by effect or by coincidence, the minds of Christians deeply involved in the movement of the world hover between these two extremes, but on a different plane. They also can be summarily divided into two tendencies, or rather in both conscience is challenged by a different alternative. We exposed this dilemma a year ago in the measure that it affects Catholics in the matter of the Church. Confronted by the modern world what should be the Church's attitude: rupture or adaptation?

The problem thus appears here once more, but enlarged and more essential because it raises the whole question of humanism as well as the whole question of God. How much room does the meaning of God leave for the meaning of man? What rights does the kingdom of God leave for the city of man?

Transcendence or Separation?

At one extreme are those for whom they leave nothing. This world of ours must not only not be pursued for itself but we must not try to make it better or transform it. It is corrupt beyond redemption, an evil world, a closed system, the plaything of the dialectics of history and of technical change, and thus it admits of no "conversion." The world and grace are two different planes which call for divorce and not for reconciliation. The duty of the Christian is not to shape events or structures but to witness to the transcendence and the eternity of God, even to scandal.

This theoretical position is really based on two facts. Its followers point first of all to the many deviations we have just mentioned in the religious life of the present day and conclude that humanism has failed spiritually: it is an obstacle between the soul and God. To attempt to put God into the world is a hopeless task, the eternal temptation of making heaven on earth, the sin of idolatry. There is one way only of escaping from it, namely to return to a transcendental outlook and to find asylum unconditionally in the mystery of a sovereign and absolute Being compared with whom any interest taken in the things of this world is necessarily missing the point and procrastination.

In the present distress of the world is not this precisely what is revealed by the unconquerable instinct impelling man to seek outside himself the achievements larger than himself which he needs? With the unbeliever this instinct emerges in obscure substitutes for God, entities touchingly and defiantly deified such as Fraternity, Progress, Peace, Humanity; all of them impersonal substitutes for the God they do not know and think they do not seek. Next, how can we explain the extraordinary fascination now obvious among many Catholics for some Eastern religions except because they find in them a sense of the absolute and of divine contemplation which Western Christianity, too geared to natural methods, does not, they think, give them to the same degree?

But it is not merely in the attraction of Hinduism and

Theosophy that the need for a return to transcendence is shown; it is found in the Church itself. Among the faithful, opinion is on the watch for fresh apparitions and mystical phenomena. The appetite for manifestations of the supernatural and the deliberate absence of a critical sense in their acceptance, in contrast with the rightful prudence of the *magisterium*, is proof enough that many souls experience a hunger which a too human Christianity no longer satisfies.

. . . *Or Immanence and Incarnation?*

Against this exalted idealism and a supernatural position which looks elsewhere, the upholders of Immanence bring forward the great fact of the Incarnation. If God has sent his Son into the world and made him the model of the perfect man, he intended thereby to show us the road to follow, namely that we must reach God through man, through the holy humanity the Word assumed. If he shed his blood on earth, how is it possible short of blasphemy not to maintain that he did so except to redeem it? Ought not the efforts of the disciple of Christ be efforts in the world, in order to complete the Redemption done by its Head?

Even those however who have chosen to engage themselves in the temporal (and we remind you here, without repeating the reasons we have already given, that this is a pressing duty for every Christian) are anxious. For they know only too well that those attempting to complete creation—to "increase and possess the earth"—and to organize the world to the image of the Kingdom of heaven are in danger of becoming so enamoured of their task that they may forget the other city which it ought to mirror and towards which it should lead. A degradation of values is thus caused whereby what is specifically Christion loses its savour and disappears. The spirit of the apostolate can become proselytism or recruitment, charity can become philanthropy or party comradeship, hope merely trust in the indefinite possibility of progress; faith in man deprives man of that in him which makes his genuine nobility, namely, that he is incapable of completing himself except by going beyond the possibilities within him and by embracing vistas larger than his own.

There is undoubtedly no more cruel disillusionment for a Christian or for a movement a more searing failure than the hackneyed experience countless times repeated in the past: the apostle sets out with enthusiasm, the carrier of the Good News; he knows that a long road stretches ahead of him before he can come up with the shepherdless masses, that prejudices have to be overcome, aspirations shared, a destiny to be shouldered in common. And when the long effort has been accomplished and he has made his way into the heart of the problem, when contact is re-established and he feels he is quite close to those he sought and similar to them . . . he suddenly finds himself with nothing to give. The message he bore has grown dim and the treasure scattered. The apostle has done the opposite of what the merchant did in the gospel, when he sold all he had in order to obtain the pearl without price; [5] he has let the divine treasure slip through his fingers and all he now has to offer are human things. He may be utterly devoted and a friend to all—it is no use; for he is incapable of satisfying the expectations of those he hoped to save. For "man cannot live by bread alone," [6] nor by improved conditions of living, nor by human affection. By whatever name he may call it, man's hunger is for God.

Return to the Doctrine of God

Those Catholics who are most deeply involved in action feel this acutely and are made anxious by it. Therefore we intend this year also to point out what road should be followed by those who are scrutinizing their conscience and loyally wonder which direction to take.

To those who rightly rebel against a naturalistic system which reduces God to our human measure and who therefore refuse to see him in this world, we wish to show that the Infinite Being is present to his creatures and relies on our labours for the world to be dedicated to him.

[5] Math., 13:45-46

[6] Math., 4:4.

To those on the other hand who are in danger of losing sight of the absolute transcendence of God in the eagerness of their engagement in the temporal, we point out that he who made himself one of us nevertheless remains apart from us and unique.

Only the theology of God, by showing that these two unilateral conceptions are complementary, will make their reconciliation possible, and only it will enable us to save the meaning of man by returning to the meaning of God. In the third section of this letter we will lay down the resolutions which should direct an impartial examination.

II. THE TRUE GOD

What are the sources from which we draw a proper knowledge of God? The Church formally says there are two, the first being reason, which proves to us that God exists and can moreover tell us something authentic about his nature although in a very summary fashion. The Vatican Council enlarges on this double power and duty of the human mind. "Whoever says that the one and only true God, our Creator and Lord, cannot be known with certainty by the natural light of the human reason by means of created things, let him be anathema."[1]

But in reality and by right such meagre knowledge yields place to an infinitely deeper and warmer knowledge, that of revelation. "God," says Pascal, "speaks well of God" but man does not. It is therefore in the bible that Christians will find what God teaches about himself, as well also as in tradition, in the writings of the *magisterium* and the Doctors of the Church, which form the complementary and living source of faith.

It need scarcely be said that in these pages it is not our intention to recall or even to sketch a treatise on God. Our purpose is to take some of these inspired texts and show that in them God appears constantly and at the same time in two aspects which are apparently contradictory: he is sometimes transcendent and apart, at others present to man and immanent in the world.

[1] Denz., 1806

THE MOST HIGH GOD

We advise all who feel hemmed in by a closed and stifling world to open the Old and the New Testaments. They will there find vistas which will liberate them, and the excellent food of the only true God.

The Mystery

The first element when we meet God will be that of mystery. God is the Inaccessible, and he is inaccessible for all. "No one has seen God," says St. John; [2] and even for those to whom God gives himself to be known he remains the hidden God. "Show me thy face, that I may know thee," asked Moses, only to receive the categorical answer: "Thou canst not see my face: for man shall not see me and live." [3] No illusion is therefore possible: God remains the incomprehensible, and the human mind possesses no key which can unlock his secret. All that the human mind at its best can experience is fear and consternation at the impenetrable mystery. Of God man knows that he does not understand him, and that all he sees of him is his shadow falling on the things of this world: he remains inaccessible, in his intimate reality, to the eyes of the spirit. "Verily Thou are a hidden God." [4] "We realize how majestic the nature of God is," says St. Gregory of Nyssa, "not by understanding it but because it cannot be proved by any demonstration or grasped by our intellectual powers," [5] and St. Augustine insists just as much: "God is not what you imagine or what you think you understand. If you understand you have failed." St. Thomas in his turn does not try to feed our pretensions or our flippancy.[6] God is darkness. To know God is to realize that we do not know him.

[2] John, 1:18.

[3] Exodus, 33:13, 20.

[4] Isaias, 45:15.

[5] Greg. Nyss., *In Cant. hom.* 12.

[6] "*Dicimus in fine cognitionis nostrae Deum tanquam ignotum cognoscere.*" (*In Boet. de Trinitate,* 1, 2; *primum*). God remains quite other: "*Neque intelligitur, neque dicitur, neque nominatur, neque in aliquo ex-*

Analogical Knowledge

This conclusion does not mean, as some philosophers maintain, that God cannot be known by reason; it merely makes clear that the created mind is too small to encompass and seize the Infinite Being. God is utterly beyond any ability of ours. Christian philosophy tells us that there are two ways of reaching him. The first and royal road consists in saying of God all that we know of created perfection and developing this to an infinite degree, and by extension to the *n*th degree to try and gain some idea of a perfection that is infinite and uncreated. We arrive at it by the principle of causality and analogy; and our knowledge of God is thus neither a myth, nor false, nor exhaustive; it is meagre and relative.

Negative Knowledge

But the mind has a second road to God, the way of negation, the opposite of the first. In order to be certain that we do not contradict the infinite, by bringing him within our categories, we deny of him all that we affirm of ourselves, and we define him by all that we ourselves are not.[7] The philosophers and the theologians, but especially the great spiritual writers, thus sought to know God by denying any common measure between his being and the world. "All the being of creatures is nothing when compared with the infinite being of God . . . Not one of them comes even close to God, or has any likeness to his being." [8] "There is not merely a difference of degree but of essence: I am who am, thou art who art not," our Lord said

---

istentium cognoscitur, omnia est, et in nullo nihil et in omnibus cunctis cognoscitur et ex nullo nulli." St. Thomas took these words and commented on them in his *Expositio super Dionysium de divinis nominibus*, c. 7, *lectio* IV.

[7] "The God of St. Thomas," says M. Gilson, "is even far more inaccessible than the God of Aristotle, who was quite inaccessible enough already. All we can situate is his metaphysical position without being at all able to conceive what he is, but only 'what he is not and the connections everything else has with him' (St. Thomas, *contra* Gen., I, 30)."—Gilson, *Le Thomisme*, p. 150.

[8] St. John of the Cross, Ascent of Mt. Carmel, I, 6.

to St. Catherine of Sienna. "Every created thing considered in itself is nothingness"; [9] and St. John of the Cross goes even further: "the beauty, the grace and the attractiveness of creatures, when compared in their entirety with the beauty of God, are utterly ugly and horrible."

These phrases and many another are not rhetorical developments, nor are they condemnations of the work of our Creator; their whole aim is to isolate for us the absolute transcendence of God.

God is Holy

At the very moment God allows himself to be known to us, he remains separate, quite other from us. Between his immaculate pureness and man, infirm, weakened and sordid, the gulf cannot be bridged: "Come not nigh hither; put off the shoes from thy feet," God ordered Moses from the burning bush [10] for he is "the Holy One of Israel." [11] Respect and trembling are the sentiments which are least adapted to recognize his mystery.[12] Adoration is the inescapable condition always, even in heaven: "Holy, holy, holy is the Lord God, the Almighty." [13] Faced with God, the children of Adam know they are radically impure and are thereby unworthy to continue in life. God has no equal: "To whom then have you likened God? Or what image will you make for him?" he has himself asked.[14]

Sovereign

He is for this reason the Sovereign Lord: "I am the Lord, and there is none else: there is no God besides me," [15] the Living God, self-sufficing, in no way bound to explain himself

[9] St. Thos., Ia IIae, 109, 2, 2.
[10] Exodus, 3:5.
[11] Isaias, 1:4.
[12] Yahweh was "feared" by Isaac: Gen., 31:53, Jacob "trembled," Gen., 28:16; cf. for the same meaning Heb., 10:34.
[13] Apoc., 5:8.
[14] Isaias, 40:18.
[15] Is., 45:5, 43:13; &c.

to us, to whom must go all obedience and all homage: "I am the Lord thy God, mighty, jealous." [16]

He is the master and free: his revelation erupts into the life of man and disturbs our established institutions. Abraham had to leave Ur of the Chaldees,[17] Moses to lead his people through the desert in spite of his attempt to avoid the task,[18] for God's interests take first place over ours. He has his plan and his ways are beyond our scrutiny. He is the master of time and of history; he manipulates both as he wishes: "for my thoughts are not your thoughts; nor your ways my ways." [19] This mastery of God over the development of the world is beyond the ability of man to grasp, for we look upon the events of time as we would wish them to be.

What is true of the Old Testament is true also of the New. "Mosaic and prophetic revelation was not destroyed, it was consummated in the gospel. The affirmation that God is one, that he is the sole Lord and loved above everything created, was to be as sacred to the Christian as much as and even more than it has been to the Jew." [20] Our Lord did not cease to point to the infinite majesty of his Father: "Why dost thou call me good? None is good, except God only." [21] His sovereignty was without division: "You are not to claim the title of Rabbi; you have but one Master, and you are all brethren alike. Nor are you to call any man on earth your father; you have but one Father, and he is in heaven." [22] Our Lord mystified his contemporaries as much as Yahweh had mystified their ancestors: Israel expected a victorious Messias and the Son of Man told them of the ruin of Jerusalem and of the Cross. The mystery of God's ways remains inscrutable to man: there also God is apart from man.[23]

[16] Exodus, 20:5.
[17] Gen., 12:1.
[18] Exodus, 4:13-14.
[19] Isaias, 60:8.
[20] P. Lebreton, *Lumen Christi*, p. 5.
[21] Mark, 10:18.
[22] Math., 23:7-8.
[23] The teaching of the Church is no less clear: "The Holy, Catholic, Apostolic, and Roman Church believes and confesses that there is one

The End of Humanism . . .

Having reached this stage in his researches, it seems that the Christian has no need to choose; his road seems inexorably laid down; to divorce himself from the world and take refuge in transcendence, with the two consequences which are inevitable in relation to actual life, the end of humanism and the end of history. How should humanism be other than blasphemy when every created value is worthless and there is not merely an abyss but a contrast between the High God and the worthless dust we are? [24] How can any interest taken in this fleeting life be other than madness if our last end be considered, and an inexcusable frivolity with the eternal? How can man's attempt to constitute a human order not escape the charge of idolatry—that sin which more than any other calls down the anger of Yahweh? Since God is the great one apart, since he is not "immanent" in his creature, the latter cannot as such situate itself outside him without being against him. Whatever we do, the "meaning of man" goes directly against the "meaning of God," and the meaning of God is precisely the greast lesson and the constant reminder of the whole of the bible.

. . . and of History?

The same is true of history. Since God seems to despise "our ways" and bothers with them merely in order to upset the normal course of events by disconcerting interventions, we can no longer talk of the developments in time or of the progress

---

only true and living God, Creator and Lord of heaven and earth, all powerful, eternal, immense, incomprehensible, infinite in intelligence, in will and in every perfection who, being a unique spiritual substance by nature, absolutely simple and unchangeable, must be declared distinct from the world in fact and by essence, happy in himself and by himself, and lifted above all that is and can be conceived outside him."—Vat. Coun., const. *Dei Filius*, cap. 1.

[24] St. John of the Cross says so: "All the wisdom in the world and all human cleverness compared with the infinite wisdom of God is sheer and extreme ignorance. All the riches of the world and the glory of creation, compared with the wealth of God, are extreme and abject poverty."—Ascent of Mount Carmel, I, chap. 6.

of society and of human institutions. God does not act from within but from without, in a completely external way. He does not arrive from this side of things but from the other. An "eschatological" direction must therefore take the place of the views of history. Our Savior did not teach us to say "Our Father who are in our hearts" but "Our Father who art in heaven," and it is there and not here that we must look for him and find him in pure faith and contempt of the world.

GOD WITH US

But is this notion of God complete? He is apart. But is he not also the everywhere present? Scripture and tradition with equal certainty show this second aspect of God. He wished also to be God with us, a God who gives himself.

The Two Alliances

The revelation of this began in the Old Testament with the idea of an alliance,[25] which lays down from the beginning and with growing clearness that God is not only a mystery of infinity but a mystery of love. He calls Israel, then all the nations, to community with him, first in the imperfect reconciliation made by the first "testament," then in the pardon and the intimate union of the new alliance in Jesus Christ. What else do the prophets proclaim if not the rigorous and tender love of "the God of Israel"?[26] Because if God seems to deny or upset history, this is not the contempt or the cruel game of a despot, but a tireless appeal to us to enlarge our vision.

He intervenes from without in order to transfigure us from within. Abraham had to leave his own country, but it was in order that he might become the father of those who believe; Moses had to obey even against his own will, but it was in order to save a people; St. Paul was thrown to the ground on the Damascus road, but it was in order to become the apostle of the Gentiles. God uses men and events to fulfil his plan of

[25] Gen., 17:1; Exodus, 32:10.

[26] Cf. Isaias, 43:4; 49:10; cf. also the words of Jeremias in the Office of the Sacred Heart.

salvation. Can we say after this that he does not lead history? Will anyone say that the God Apart is not also everywhere present?

Everywhere Present

But this presence of God in its turn is merely a particular case of a more universal fact and intention, that God, by the fact of their creation, should be present in all creatures. "In Him we live, move and have our being," says St. Paul.[27] In some splendid pages of the *Summa*, St. Thomas takes up this statement of "God existing in things."[28] "As long as a thing has being, God must be present in it . . . it is a necessary conclusion from this that God is in all things and in an intimate way."[29]

What reason teaches on this matter is exactly what is taught by scripture: not pantheism, not the God of Aristotle wholly apart from a world he does not know. "The God of the Christians," writes Pope Pius XII, "is not an empty phrase . . . or an abstract idea decked out by thinkers. He transcends all that is, and everything that exists owes its existence to him . . . millions of men can hurry through the streets . . . absorbed by their affairs . . . without ever thinking of God. Yet it is he who keeps them in existence."[30]

What then must we say of God's presence by grace in the soul, a presence which is not merely that of God the Creator immanent in his creature, but the intimacy of the three divine

[27] Acts, 17:28.

[28] Ia., Q.8, a.1.

[29] "Our very being," says P. Sertillanges, "bathes in the being of God, who is the being of our being, if such an expression may be allowed; and there is immanence . . . On the other hand, St. Thomas again says: 'God is incomparably lifted above every form of being' and there is his transcendence. What isolates God and makes him 'the Holy One' is the unique plenitude of God . . . This plenitude is also the reason why nothing can subsist except in him, a conceptual relationship we express by the term 'immanence' or more currently by 'God being present in all things.' "—Sertillanges, *Dieu ou Rien?*: pp. 87-88.

[30] Pius XII, in a radio message to the United States Catechetical Congress.

Documentation Catholique, December 8th, 1946.

persons shared with us? "We will come and make our dwelling there." [31] The last word has been spoken, the very mystery made open to us: "God," says St. John, "is love." At once the double chasm is bridged; God's sovereignty is now seen to be love, seeking its own glory by communicating itself. God in himself and God given to us are one, the holy God is also Emmanuel, God with us. If we forget that gigantic reality—which is also certain—we lose sight of the meaning of God and fall into a Manichean conception of the relations between God and the world.

IN THE UNITY OF GOD

Transcendence and immanence are thus the two notions which the theology of God reveals to us and tells us never to separate. God is simple; but our minds are so made for understanding the world that they cannot imagine what the infinite is except by its relations with the finite, within or without, immanent or transcendent. A believer may try hard to convince himself of the shortcomings of his intelligence when confronted with the Absolute, and of the truth these two aspects simultaneously contain; but all he can do to express these opposites is to set them down side by side. The danger thereupon is great of retaining only one of the two terms: of seeing God only as opposite from the world, with the conclusion going with it that he must have nothing to do with the fatal and corrupt dialectic of this life; or on the contrary, of not seeing God except in the world and in life, with the danger of divinising one or the other. In each case the result is secularism: God in the world or the world in God, each being the end of two distinct processes.

Those who hold uncontaminated transcendence do indeed see the majesty of God but they at once contradict it and injure it by limiting it; for they withdraw it from creation, mistake the rule of providence over the world, and are quite blind to the fact of incarnation. At once, quite naturally, they tend in practice to isolation, to faith without works, to contemplation without the apostolate, to the Church deprived of her features

[31] John, 14:23.

in time. That attitude of refusal is the same which, according to the period and the problem, is called Quietism, Pessimism or Jansenism.

On the other side those who uphold an exclusive immanence forget the infinity of God. Their wish to put God everywhere ends in withdrawing him from everything; for what remains of a God who is present only in the world, a God who has ceased to be present to himself, a God who is no longer God? What meaning is there in an immanence which is the immanence of no one or of nothing? Incarnation pre-supposes being, and in the same way immanence postulates continuing existence and continuing self-sufficiency. It has been pointed out that the wish to humanize God in order to make him closer to man is an error; God is close only if he is the High God; and far from denying transcendence, immanence all the time supposes it. Without it the world, far from being intelligible, is absurd, inexplicable or guilty; inexplicable because it has no object, absurd because it has no reason for being, guilty because it sets itself up in competition with "him apart from whom there is no God." [32] We can indeed get rid of the problem by confusing God with the world, and at once the result is pantheism.

In Incarnate Love

We once more find that the truth lies in uniting and harmonizing these two symmetrical statements. The God of Israel has the right to be called "the true God" because, combining all perfections, he is both pure spirit and creator, him of whom it can be said "True praise of thee is silence," and "All ye works of the Lord, bless the Lord." [33] The problem is not solved by an abstract formula; the solution itself is alive and is found in a person, the Word of God. He is revealed to us by the Incarnation, "taking the nature of a slave," [34] come among men, at the same time the equal of the Father by his nature as God. The God of the philosophers is thus outstripped in grandeur, and that of the philanthropists in nearness to man.

[32] Isaias, 45: 5.
[33] Canticle of the Three Young Men.
[34] Philip., 2:7.

The Lord we adore is not a compromise of two extremes, but the completing of both in the mystery of his person.[35] Here again, and especially here, everything is unified and made perfect in love. Everything is explained by him . . .

Gratuitously Given

. . . on condition that this statement is at once clarified. The expression "synthesis" and "unity" in God of the two words making up transcendence—immanence is capable of being wrongly understood and of giving the impression that they are on the same plane, that thcy arc two complementary perfections inherent in the essence of God. It is quite clear that this is not true. Immanence is understood only of God's presence to created beings. Created beings, however, are not necessary beings; creation is the consequence of a free act in God, is not part of his nature, and adds nothing to him.[36] God continues independently of the world with his infinite perfections. The brief analysis just made from the bible and theology applies to a state of fact only, to a reality which is, but might not have been, or might have been different.

All the perspective which the meaning of an incarnate God causes to faith and humanism are admissable only in the hypothesis of the economy of salvation, which revelation presents to us as a fact. To forget that, to forget that God created the world freely and out of love, and that he also saved it by the same means by becoming incarnate out of love, would be to lose the meaning of man and the meaning of God.

Meaning of God, and Meaning of Man

Both are bound up together, not by their depending upon each other, for God suffices to himself, and immanence and

[35] St. Hilary thus describes God: "*Deus, totus intra extraque, supereminens internus, circumfusus et infusus,*" a double aspect of God much insisted on by the Fathers.

[36] It has been pointed out that St. Albert the Great, in an obviously expanded sense, calls the world "*accidens Dei*, an accident of God," meaning by this that the world is not essential to God but that he is essential to it, as substance is essential to accident and is part of the definition of accident.—Sertillanges, *Dieu ou Rien?* p. 87.

incarnation on his side are love absolutely and freely given; but in the sense that in its definition humanism is entirely dependent on the idea of God.

If God is only immanent, the consequence is pagan humanism; man is enclosed within himself, a prisoner in the world, and for ever incapable of going beyond himself.

If God is only transcendent, the world loses all meaning, ceases to be related to the mind and the heart, becomes night and sin; man becomes a prey to an unappeasable disquiet.

Condemnation of Humanism

But if God is "he who is," a High God as well as a near God, everything is different, and humanism is provided with two foundations.

The first comes from the fact of creation. To pledge oneself to action in the world is justified, because everything being upheld by the presence of God in everything, bears the imprint of the creator. That presence and likeness exist more deeply in man, since in virtue of his spiritual nature he has been created to the image of God. But God is present in things not merely to preserve them in existence; by pure love he decided to become incarnate in the person of his Son. This second degree of immanence draws God closer to man, and thereby the world and mankind are consecrated.

Thus by divine adoption in Christ man assumes an infinitely higher likeness to God, for God places in him by his grace his living imprint.

By this double title—man as citizen of this earth and son of God—the whole of Christian humanism is founded, and with that our temporal and supernatural engagement is entirely justified. On the one hand, man can and ought to root himself in the world, following the example of its Head; and that is a reason for his nobility. On the other hand, he is called to go infinitely beyond his own nature, and he already shares in the kingdom of Heaven: *Conversatio nostra in coelis est:* our true home is in heaven.[37]

The humanism of the Christian is thus founded in its whole

[37] Philip., 3:20.

extent, since it comes from the only lasting origin, that is, from God. The conclusion is crucial, and it does not appear as a new problem, but as the only solution for the theoretical and practical lack of certainty dividing Christians in the problem of their attitude towards the world. It is not a question, it need hardly be said, of exhausting here or even setting out the scheme of the vast problem of humanism. Others are busy in this matter, philosophers, theologians and saints, for it is one of the most urgent problems of our day. We cannot emphasize enough how urgent and fruitful such an examination is if it remains closely faithful to itself and docile to the suggestions of the Church's *magisterium*. Our only object, in the same spirit in which we write our pastoral letter, *Growth or Decline?* and in order to enrich from within the lines of action we then gave you, is to show that the meaning of God can alone safeguard the primacy of the spiritual and make legitimate and efficacious a wholehearted engagement in the temporal.

III. THE RETURN TO GOD

We are now able, in no arbitrary fashion, to see the ways this return to God must take; it is urgent and indispensable if the hesitations of Christians committed to action are to be resolved. The remedy is not far to seek, nor need we call everything in question and turn away from action. On the contrary, we cannot emphasize strongly enough the degree to which the methodical efforts of priests and militants are shown to be indispensable. It would be superfluous to insist upon a truth so evident and so often preached in recent years by the Holy See. We ask you to be more faithful than ever to your engagement in the spiritual order and the temporal order, as we invited you a year ago. There is a hierarchy of values to be saved, a spirit to be breathed into what we think and do.

IN FAITH

We must go to the root of the trouble, that is, the weakening of belief; as we pointed out at the beginning, this is the feature found in all contemporary errors.

Belief

Many who believe are convinced that they have the faith. In fact the God they honor is often a God created or modified by themselves. They do not accept, they choose they do not receive revelation, they elaborate a rational divinity, a dangerous counterfeit, a product of their own guilty errors.[1] God, we have seen, in Mystery, and his infinite being, escapes our grasp. The Absolute does not become known to us as the conclusion to a syllogism or as a clear and distinct idea. We shall only reach him by faith. That knowledge is certain knowledge because it is enlightened by love; but it will always remain obscure. The infinite is beyond our human experience; and the ineffable reality of a trinitarian God is larger than any gesture or intuition we can make.

Must we therefore refuse to use our reason?

The whole effort made by theology is a standing witness to the contrary. Its rational elaboration does not start with man; it starts with revelation and stands on the authority of God. We do not therefore deduce God from history or from man, we receive him as what he is, prodigious and free, as the Reality without answer or precedent.

The world and human life in this perspective are explained. "I am the First and the Last."[2] "I am Alpha, I am Omega, the beginning of all things and their end."[3]

It is not he who is at our service but we who ought to gravitate towards him as our lifegiving end. This straightforward reversal of direction eliminates any anthropomorphism from religious life and centres it truly on God by a surrender of self which is both respectful and disinterested. Where before we were sensitive to our rights we become receptive to the idea that we have duties to God.

This is not a matter of a mere verbal quibble or a sheer

[1] "Above all beings there is the unique being, God . . . It is not man's belief in God which makes God exist; it is because God exists that all men, if they do not deliberately close their eyes to the truth, believe in him and address their prayers to him."—Pius XII, *divini Redemptoris.*

[2] Isaias, 48:12.

[3] Apoc., 1:8.

mental exercise. Very real questions are involved and at once illuminated. Take Sunday as an example; for the majority of Christians it is undoubtedly a day of rest and rightly so. But for how many is this rest really concerned with God? Who among them, when they have once been to Mass, still feel that they continue to be involved in the Lord's day, a day which belongs supremely to him, a day which in the long continued story of our lives and cares he has reserved to himself in order that we shall turn to him in prayer, peace and praise?

Prayer

The return to God must show itself most clearly by prayer. We do indeed pray today, but we pray far too much for ourselves. Perhaps we also pray far too much for others, and then our prayer for them is spoilt by interest or takes the place of thanksgiving and praise. We must become conscious again of the grandeur and splendor of God, annihilate ourselves before his majesty, humbly recognize our sinfulness before his countenance, dedicate all things to his exclusive love.

An effort needs to be made to restore the sense of the sacred, the progressive weakening of which has been pointed out by many competent judges, to the external manifestations of religious life. In our Father in Heaven we are tempted to see merely an easy-natured providence, and in his eternal Son a companion like ourselves. Let us therefore restore to the centre of our own lives that "fear of God" and respect for actions and feelings which, far from harming the descent and intimate presence of love in the soul, on the contrary fittingly translate how deeply conscious we are of our smallness.

Return to Mystery

The liturgical revival which can be seen so successfully at work today will then produce all its fruits and will not be jeopardized by the obsession, lawful in intention but sometimes clumsy in procedure, of adapting it to modern society. The liturgy will undoubtedly be able to carry further all the values which uplift life, and harmonize the linguistic, aesthetic and community methods which are clearly necessary if we are to draw all men into a truly Catholic worship. There is no question of returning to the pernicious individualism which dried up so many generations; we must continue more than ever to promote a community worship. But we must not be afraid to bring silence into it, a silence which is not the collective dumbness of individual worshippers but a community silence which unites all as brothers and lifts the soul to God.

Contemplation

This collective prayer which is so productive of good ought however to be always accompanied by or rather express a more profound and more secret intercourse with God. All prayer is not on the same plane. The best prayer is the prayer of which our Lord said: "When thou art praying, go into thy inner room and shut the door upon thyself, and so pray to thy Father in secret." [4] A disciple of Christ should be capable deliberately and alone of paying homage to God by shutting himself off from the world and forgetting himself in prayer.

It is at this point that the phrase which will liberate us must be spoken. Admittedly the word contemplation sometimes frightens us and seems to provoke contradiction; it at once evokes an idea of exceptional lives, ecstasies, apparitions and mystical phenomena which ordinary Christians attribute to a few privileged initiates. It is, on the other hand, patient of various meanings and is not without prestige among the intellectual elites which are attracted by the alluring systems of the East. The reason for this lies in mere appearances: through not drawing sufficiently deeply on the springs of Christian life men set out to find springs or evasions which are less pure, and on their return are less ready for the sacrifices of ordinary life. All contemplation must be kept separate from the weakened forms and unhealthy substitutes in which religious feeling and highbrow talk delude their authors and others.

Contemplation and Inner Life

Contemplation contains two realities each of which is different. The first, that of the contemplative separated from the

[4] Math.; 6:6.

world, is directed to keeping ever present and fresh the dialogue which united Christ to the Father in his long hours of prayer. The contemplative, indispensable to the Church, is dedicated by his state to witness to the transcendence of God. The duty of the Christian is to understand the contemplative; and that of the contemplative is to remain faithful to his mission.

But in ordinary language contemplation also means a reality more readily accessible; and it is to this form of it that we invite you. It is not necessary to be a theologian or a great mystic to reach it; it is enough to enter into oneself and approach God as a present and living person. It therefore consists above all in an effort of *direction:* instead of turning our prayer towards things and men it is enough to turn it towards God.

Face to Face with God

The essence of contemplation is to make God our object, to place ourselves face to face with him, to direct ourselves towards him, as a river runs to the sea instead of wasting its waters in the sand or harmfully spreading them beyond its banks. When we look at God, who has no equal, all we need do is let the soul admire and be uplifted by his grandeur and his beauty. It is enough to let the soul sing and to tell God that we thank him for all his goodness, to offer him our work, our joy, our sorrow, and above all ourselves. The essential thing is to become humble before him and to open ourselves to him, letting him invade the soul with his strength and gentleness. Contemplation is thus not a matter of human ingenuity; we make ourselves over without holding back, like children and time after time, to that inner grace ceaselessly at work upon us and uninterruptedly calling us to turn ourselves to God.

This invitation is addressed in the first place to priests. The Church for good reasons enjoins this upon them;[5] priests are not merely the leaders of Christian society—they are dedicated to revealing the mysteries of the love of God.

[5] Code of Canon Law, 125, 2; 595, 1-2; 1367, 1.

The Spiritual Effort to Be Made

The lives of the saints, however, show that this grace is not confined to the clergy.

With some, circumstances willed by providence favor a life of intimacy with God, and more than one solitary soul can contribute for his fellowmen a witness which is far more precious than direct apostolic work. No special state of life is necessary to be thus dedicated to Love; and there is no life which cannot and ought not set aside some time for prayer and for attention to God. Closed retreats and spiritual reading will help to unite these souls even more to their Father in Heaven.

Return to the Bible

The effort at contemplation we ask you to make is in practice and first of all a return to the main springs of our religion. Instead of stopping at the many secondary works and anaemic commentaries, the multiplication of which stands between us and the parent texts, let active Christians go to these texts and re-discover the bible. In reaction against the Protestant doctrine built on private interpretation, Catholics were long severed from the infinite riches contained in the word of God. Today that danger has disappeared and we are glad to recognize the movement which grows stronger every day in favour of the inspired books. Brought up in a scientific, technical and materialistic world intellectuals of the present day have ceased to find God in the old framework. They will return to God active in history by returning to the plan of redemption contained in the bible. We encourage this movement, with the precautions necessary for it to remain in the truth of the faith committed to the Church.[6] This spontaneous movement is, we think, providential; for nowhere except in the Prophets, in the

[6] We remind you that in these matters no one may read a bible printed without notes. An annotated edition contains explanations which are indispensable to the vast majority of Christians. The modern culture they have received has not familiarized them with the history of the Jewish people, or with the question of literary *genres* which is so necessary for an understanding of the bible.

Gospels, in St. Paul and in the Apocalypse shall we find a witness to the Grandeur and the Holiness of God.

The Sacraments

We must also return to the sacraments, if we wish, in contemplation, to nourish it and to remain in the path of logic; because if the sacraments exist for man they also exist, and in the first place, for God. They are there so that we may be invaded by them and by them be dedicated to God; and if the sacraments of Confirmation, Penance and the Eucharist are looked at in this way they will undoubtedly assume an absolutely new meaning, indeed their whole meaning, for all who, exacting in their demands upon religion, had failed to realize, through the absence of this view, the depth and the finality of the sacraments.

IN ACTION

Belief, adoration and contemplation, these are the primary elements in a return to the meaning of God; but they raise once again the problem of action. What becomes of action in a religious life apparently wholly occupied by the values of contemplation? Ought it to be tolerated? It is not a matter here of again questioning its theoretical value—on this we have sufficiently insisted; but many wonder how in practice these two forms of Christian life can be reconciled. Some wonder if Christian life and contemplative life are not necessarily in opposition or mutually harmful.

Primacy of Contemplation

One thing is certain: contemplation comes first by right and must come first in fact; for contemplation, that is the inner life, is nothing else in man than the free and deliberate manifestation in us of God's own life, begun on this earth at the first Pentecost and in us on the day we were baptized. It is not limited to pious exercises but is to be identified with the living faith so frequently inculcated by the scriptures.[7] By it, and by

[7] "The just shall live in his faith." Hab., 2:4; Rom., 1:17; Heb., 10:38; Gal., 3:2.

the theological virtues of faith, hope and charity, man enters into communication with God present in it; and by them man's powers of action are mysteriously assumed into that stream of love which St. John uses to define God.[8] Inner life is the eruption of faith into all our powers, the unfolding of the state of grace and of the indwelling in us of the three divine persons; in short, the soul living under the motioning of the Holy Spirit.

What runs counter to contemplation may be called "activism," that is, procedures and systems applied externally which, because they are artificial, are for this reason bound to fail. But it is not action,[9] for action is merely the external manifestation or overflow of a superabundant life of faith and love, a thin screen pierced by the light of God. "The Holy Spirit, shining in those from whom all stain has been purified, makes them spiritual by contact with himself. Similarly, just as transparent substances, when subjected to light, themselves glitter and give off light, so does the soul, illuminated by the Holy Spirt, give light to others and itself become spiritual."[10]

Contemplation and Apostolate

Far from being enemies, action and inner life thus complete each other and mutually continue each other.

A return, in action, to God does not mean a greater degree of action; it simply supposes—and this can take us all our lives—that at the heart of his engagement the Christian places a passionate belief in the transcendence of God and is convinced that thereby the adaptations necessary will be made possible.

In the apostolate such as Christ instituted it, there must

[8] 1 John, 4:16.

[9] "The danger of exclusivism takes two forms. The heresy of action arises when the apostolate is confined to its external element, to a naturalising and superficial task. The apostolate may also be limited through timidity to its inner element, piety, an attitude which scarcely conforms to our Lord's words: 'It is fire that I have come to spread over the earth, and what better wish can I have than that it should be kindled?'—Luke 12:49."—Pius XII, radio message to the Barcelona International Congress of Sodalities of Our Lady.

[10] St. Basil of Cesarea, *De Spir. Sancto*, IX, 22.

therefore be as much living faith as technique, as much prayer as natural ability—or rather the first two are the condition of the second. The road to man is through God; and in that sense it is possible to say that the apostolate is beyond contemplation. It begins in it and ends in the redemption of others, which is done with God and under his influence. Far from hindering the apostle, contemplation provides him with his motive power. The apostolate therefore does not come primarily from the needs of souls but from the love of God. "The reason we have for loving our neighbor," writes St. Thomas, "is God; and what we must love in him is that he may be in God." [11] St. John of the Cross says the same: "The great love the soul has for God places it in great pain and sorrow for the small amount it does for him; and it would be largely satisfied were it allowed to die a thousand deaths for him." [12] It is this love of God impelling us to wish him to be known and loved which drew from St. Paul his cry: "*Caritas Christi urget nos:* With us, Christ's love is a compelling motive." [13]

The Saint a Living Synthesis

The two terms action and contemplation, so wrongly considered to be mutually exclusive, will not be reconciled by an abstract mixture of varying proportions. There exists a living synthesis—holiness.

The radical difference between the apostle and the propagandist is that the latter persuades and recruits whilst the former witnesses and transmits life. The abyss between the two is vast. "The Church," says Pope Pius XII, "is in greater need of witnesses than of apologists." [14]

The saint, by rigorous recollection and absolute renunciation, has stripped himself of self and allowed God to invade him; at that price and because of it he is a reminder in all circumstances of God's transcendence and of the consequences it entails. Because he has preferred the folly of Christ to ordinary

[11] Summa, IIa IIae, 25, 1.
[12] St. John of the Cross, Dark Night of the Soul, II, chap. 19.
[13] II Cor., 5:14.
[14] Radio speech to the Nantes Eucharistic Congress, July, 1947.

means and has left everything, he manages to regain everything.[15]

Renunciation

We remind all who, continuing the direction given to their lives by baptism, wish to dedicate themselves to action, that one condition remains indispensable to Christian asceticism. Let them remember the universal mediation of the crucified Christ. "Never seek Christ without the Cross," writes St. John of the Cross. If we follow this counsel we avoid finding a cross empty of Christ, and it is this which causes so many of our contemporaries to despair.

One primary renunciation consists, not in self annihilation, but in so living that our tendencies to evil—fatal seeds we bear within us of death—are neutralized; and for those in the world this is an asceticism as constant if less radical than a life of mortification in religion. But it is not enough for us to repair our falls by becoming more virile. The cross was not given us in order to perfect our humanism; it exacts sacrifice, a sacrifice made, by love, for God. Human failure with all its meaning must be brought into our action. Why does the latter often end in mediocrity or lack of success? Because we count solely on our own abilities instead of on supernatural means. Instead of preaching the cross, sacrifice and penance in union with our Savior, we sometimes employ methods of persuasion which succeed in obtaining us a hearing but which cause no change in the soul. Let us by all means love our brothers, and with all our strength; but let us not rest until we have prevailed on them to be converted to him. No day will end without our experiencing how true are the words of St. Paul: "It is when I am weak that I am strong. I can do all things in him who strengtheneth me." [16]

[15] "If spiritual men realized how much they forfeit in the abundance of the spirit and in spiritual goods through allowing themselves to indulge their appetite for useless things, they would at once find in the simple food of the spirit the attractiveness of all the things to which the will obstinately clings."—Ascent of Mount Carmel, 1, chap. 5.

[16] II Cor., 2:28.

The Remedy for Activism

The remedy for activism is contained in these last words. Beginning with a full conception of grace and of human freedom, under the name of "the heresy of action" it opens up errors which are much more ancient.

We shall have no reason to fear this error if in what we understand and do we daily have regard to the true notion of God. Because he is transcendent and his ways are past finding out we will accept failure, delay and obstacles which are seemingly impassable without surprise or discouragement. Far from crushing us, his immensity becomes the very motive of our security, our hope and our daring: "because he who is mighty has wrought for me his wonders."[17] God dwells in us and is doubly immanent in us, first as our creator then as our adopter; and for this reason we cease to count on our own weakness, the failures of which make us despair, but on Love dwelling within us who is more part of us than we are ourselves. It is his discreet and irresistible strength which works in us: "Both the will to do it and the accomplishment of that will are something which God accomplishes in you."[18]

TWO TRUTHS TO BE REMEMBERED

The saint in his own being thus succeeds in harmonizing the wealth of the two; he witnesses to the transcendence and the immanence of God, is at home in the two worlds of heaven and earth, is the man of God and a man among men. Neither an escapist nor an introvert he embodies in his own person the living image of the living God. Holiness thus becomes not merely the model but the one and only condition of a genuine and successful engagement by the Christian.

This engagement must turn on two essential realities, which form the two conditions of Christian humanism. They are the Incarnation and the Redemption.

[17] Luke, 1:49.
[18] Philip., 11:13.

Dedication: a Humanism of Incarnation

The Christian need not wait until he is a saint before engaging himself. It is enough if he is already trying, for him to have the right, the duty and the grace. Let it be clearly said once more that his title as a creature endowed with reason and placed by God as the crown of the material creation by itself gives him the right to exercise a command which must not remain merely abstract. The Gospel has not destroyed the precept which stands at the beginning of the book of Genesis: "Increase and multiply and possess the earth." [19] Man's duty is not to allow the forces of matter and of life to master him. Disorder for him would consist in his becoming their slave; it does not consist in his possessing the world; indeed from this angle possessing the world becomes for him an obligation.

Here the direction we are giving meets and repeats the appeal we made last year when we asked Christians to enter wholeheartedly into the temporal. We then grounded it on the double nature of the Church, as being unchangeable and contingent. This duty is now strengthened even further in depth and in extent by the mystery of God, as being transcendent and incarnate.

The Christian is asked not to destroy or belittle the world but to assume it and sanctify it in order to offer it as a homage to God. It is in this that real incarnation resides, in the strength of God invading humanity in order to lift it up and bring it within the sphere of the life of God; and an understanding of his transcendence illuminates this incarnation and gives to it significance and meaning. For creation itself is from him, and the element which constitutes creation is that it is a reflection and image of him. Far from despising a work as valuable as this, the Christian understands creation because he sees it with the eyes of God and loves it dearly. He makes no gesture of refusal, utters no scarcely veiled regret for the attractiveness of human values—it is more a matter of his unconcealed joy sweeping him onwards to the triumphant plenitude of the infinity of God. No humanism can be complete without faith,

[19] Gen., 1:29.

for it alone enables us to view the world from the standpoint of God; and we owe to this theological virtue, which in some way assimilates us to God's own knowledge, that we can see the created world with the eyes of its creator.[20]

We at once see on what conditions human endeavor is made possible and legitimate; it is not a question of how much, or of where, but of the spirit. Everything must be assumed in order that everything may be offered, and the movement of incarnation must be made to emerge in consecration; thereby we restore to God the universe he has entrusted to us and at once stamp this world with the sacred sign that it is meant to be ordered to him.

We find that Christ himself perfectly expressed this consecration in his prayer after the last supper: "I am not asking that thou shouldst take them out of the world, but that thou shouldst keep them clear of what is evil . . . Keep them holy, then, through the truth . . . Thou hast sent me into the world on thy errand, and I have sent them into the world on my errand; and I dedicate myself for their sakes, that they too may be dedicated through the truth."[21]

The feature which saves Christian humanism and differentiates it from atheistic humanism is the object towards which we try to direct it. In atheistic humanism everything is made for man and stops at man; Christian humanism, on the contrary, is theocentric: everything goes towards God, everything is for God.

Redemption: a Humanism of the Cross

The dilemma which as we saw tormented Christians, whether to be present in the world or to shut themselves up in God, thus disappears. In the terms in which it is expressed there is no solution; it has to be seen in the light of what scripture and theology teach us about God.

All however has not been said. If we were pure, if we were established in the sole love of God, our journey in the world

[20] "*Fides est quaedam assimilatio ad cognitionem divinam.*"—St. Thos., *In Boet. de Trim.*, qu. 3, A. 1.

[21] John, 17:15-19.

would resolve itself into nothing else than pure praise of our Creator. But ever since sin occasioned in us a tendency to seek ourselves as the end in all things, all our relations with created things can become a temptation to self-centred enjoyment, to the detriment of the rights of others and of the exclusive love to be given to God. When we forget this, we start once more a wholly material messianism, for no humanism can be built except on the recognition of sin. There can be only one legitimate humanism in the actual condition of the world, and that consists in redemption made incarnate. There can be only one humanism for the Christian, and that consists in the humanism of the Cross.

All we have said about the saint, his soul and its mortification applies here to all the dimensions of man's effort. We must remember that man is not infinitely perfectible; the dogma of original sin and the experience of actual sin are a witness to this truth. The sacrifice of Christ is at the centre of the visions of mankind. Any other solution is precarious, for it is constantly the prey to and disturbed by the disordered tendencies in man. The engagement of the Christian will only be a realistic engagement if he all the time remembers not only the "greatness" but also the "misery" of man, whom he has undertaken to serve and save.

There is only one way to correct the tendencies which constantly impell us to seek ourselves, and that is to aim straight at God by an act of filial and exclusive submission, and to prove that we choose Him before all else by accepting and choosing the road of sacrifice.

But it must not therefore be thought that in doing this the Christian renounces joy. The lives of the saints, on the contrary, show that the kingdom of God is the place of happiness in this life, and that all we may have given up for his sake will be given back to us a hundredfold. History shows how the saints who have the most died to themselves exulted at the end with love and gratitude. By firmly embracing the cross they found hope.

CONCLUSION

Having reached the end of our examination let us now turn again to the world and calmly survey it with the eyes we have been fixing on God. What we see has little relation to his peace and serenity. Confusion is everywhere, for no age has been more marked by terror than our own; and it is not easy, in these conditions, to keep the mind clear and the will calm.

Everything is in preparation, everything is in process; nothing is completed, nothing solved. Systems are built up, plan succeeds plan; so also do anguish and revolution. When order seems to reign in one place we know that in another it is attacked. The recent wars have been followed by rumors of new conflicts, and all over the world the minds of men are torn by this double madness. It is indeed stupid; but some turn this absurdity into a philosophy whilst the vast majority of men are driven by it to despair. They find no consolation after the breakdown of the ideal they had formed that progress would continue indefinitely; and they conclude that nothing can be hoped for in a world in which man is evil and fate is master.

The most tragic feature of our present distress is its silence. Millions of men are suffering, millions more expect to suffer tomorrow, yet among them there is no complaint and even surprise has ceased; they are silent. The world over, there now obtain a lassitude and a mystery which are very like the threatening calm before the fierce outbreak of the storm. No one fails to feel this anguish; we hide it, but it is there. Many of us brace ourselves in silent agony before a hideous future, and many others when told that this future is not inevitable, refused to be impressed. The evil is already vast when it grips those not yet reached by the Gospel; but if it were to conquer Christians it would constitute a scandal.

The Salvation of Man Is by God

You to whom we speak will not, we know, be among their number. Your hearts remain sensible to this universal despair, to the bloodshed and the rising tide of distress everywhere. You are aware of what your fellowmen are suffering, their sorrow possesses you, you suffer with them in the most secret places of your being. Since you feel what they endure, you can the better share their burden.

But do not fail to learn one lesson from this, that man is not saved by man alone. We do not mean that human effort is useless to cure and uplift the world; we have already said how noble is the task men on this earth perform. But the evil must be cured at its root; and since the world's sickness is not due to the absence of God, the solution necessarily lies in a return to God. The appeal we therefore make to you is thus a call to faith and a call to action.

To Action . . .

. . . because, unlike those who believe in nothing, you have no right to wait upon events when it is events which are waiting upon you. If you are absent anything may happen, because nothing stands in the way of the forces which threaten you. But if you are present you will, on the contrary, contribute by influencing the path of development, in full submission it need scarcely be said to the eternal will of God.

We say again that this is a call to action, and we ask that the return to God shall serve no one as a pretext for doing nothing or as a ground for criticizing those who devote themselves to action. Without works, faith, let it be remembered, is dead. There is no question of our doing less; we must, on the contrary, commit ourselves to the limit to action, and that everywhere. An hour when the world looks to the Christians and the Church looks to her sons is no time for the latter to betray that expectation and that confidence. Priests and layfolk are faced with a task which contains enough material to satisfy completely all their powers of love, action and self-giving.

. . . and to Faith

But before all else we must return to God in faith and never allow our trust in him to falter. We know that history is neither blind nor driven by fate—we believe in Providence. We know that evil will not triumph everlastingly over good—we believe in God's justice and goodness. We know that if we are weak, he is strong. At a time when everything seems leagued together to drive us into fear, the example of St. Teresa of Avila encourages us to let nothing trouble us, to let nothing worry us, because God knows all, sees all and can do all—and loves us in addition.

The highest mission Christians have at this time is to pray. Do not let yourselves tire therefore in spite of the apparent silence of God, but continue to act "as though prayer were not enough" and continue to pray "as though action were useless."

In Hope

Thus instead of going from one extreme to another at the whim of propaganda and disillusioned prophets, you will never show yourselves to be "men of little faith." [22] Listen to the burning words of the prophet Isaias: "Be converted to me, and you shall be saved, all ye ends of the earth; for I am God, and there is no other," [23] and allow them to enter today into your hearts. That mighty prophetic voice reminds you, as it reminded the people of Israel, not to put your trust in Assyria or in Egypt, but in God.[24]

Confronting the rising danger and while not neglecting temporal helps, whether these come from themselves or from others, Christians will resist any attempt to reduce the present crisis to purely human alternatives. They will not look to one particular part of the universe, or rely upon another for help; they would learn too rapidly that walls of that kind crumble in their turn, and cause more ruin than they had sheltered illusion. Light and strength, they will find, stretch before them and above them, for the cure to the evils which oppress them and the secret to a new future will be found only in God. Placed by Providence on the frontiers of the world where two civilizations meet, they will be able to choose; and instead of the fickle promises of men they will prefer the pledge and reality given by God, Hope.

[22] Math., 14:31.
[23] Isaias, 45:22.
[24] Isaias, 28:33.

Prayer

"O God, who dost prepare us for the Mystery of Easter by the lessons of the Old Testament and the New, give us the grace to understand your pity for us, in order that what we now experience of your gifts to us may firmly establish our expectation of those that are still to come." [25]

[25] Holy Saturday.

PRIESTS AMONG MEN

Christ did not simply fulfill the function of a priest. He was Priest. He is, essentially, Priest.

From this are consequences concerning the priest's mission in the social order. He remains a priest in all that he is, in his most humble as well as in his most sublime act.

The Priest must be a man of God and a man among men, if he is to be a real mediator of human society.

Contents

Priests Among Men

During this Holy Week which sets before you the whole mystery of Salvation, we invite you once more to look at the world. Look at it as a whole and take a profound view. Our prophecy has not proved false: a new world is in the making, emerging faster than we suspected. Of the force which drives it, we can only be certain that it is moving towards a complete re-casting of civilization.

Modern inventions which have increased at an ever-growing pace cannot be for Christians just another news item or a mere scientific curiosity. They have their value as pointers and they must henceforth be integrated into the Christians' apostolic vision of Redemption. For they are something more than empty symbols: they are making a new universe. And this is the universe which we are called upon to save.

Outlook Unsettled

We have to save it, for its salvation is not yet achieved. Neither is its salvation impossible. We Christians know that this changing world is neither wholly good nor wholly bad. As realists, we know that by itself it is tending neither towards the golden age nor towards annihilation. It has within itself, as has man its designer, a strange dualism: it is capable of grace or of sin. The City which is in the making can be either the City of God or the City of Satan.

The dilemma is not new. Since the Cross, history has continually presented instances of this fundamental choice. But this is the first time it has been presented on a world-wide scale, because, for the first time, the world is one.

Who then is going to rescue the world from this innate duality? Whose task is it to save it from catastrophe, to bring it to a unity of truth and love? Christ, for He is the one Mediator. But Christ is given to us only in and by the Church which continues Him. Hence, two years ago, we told you that the salvation of the world is bound up with the "Growth" of the Church. The specific task of the Church is to effect a penetration, both extensive and intensive, which will leave no territory untouched by the baptism of its grace.

But this labor of total consecration pre-supposes that the Church, in its "Growth," always preserves the true "meaning of God," that she does not naturalize herself in seeking to supernaturalize this world's values. She must at all costs remain what she is—transcendent, the bearer of a mysterious message. This is a complex task, at once difficult and exalted. Negatively, she must oust atheism; positively, she must satisfy that relentless desire for the things of the spirit which appears almost everywhere in a humanity tormented by the absence of God.

This is where the priest comes in. He enters the scene, sent by God from on high, to fulfill the anguished need of men here below. He is present in the Church always; he is, with the Holy Ghost, the enduring source of her permanence and of her life.

The World and the Priesthood

The world and the Church, dependent on the priest? At first sight this seems impossible! This man, without arms or money, facing the gigantic labors that lie ahead. He who has turned his back on normal community life, to be accepted as the norm for thought and action? What irony, or what an imposture! What are atheist thinkers to make of him, or even the sincere adherents of a future humanism? He is an exasperating witness to former times; an unproductive parasite in a society in which each man works and creates; a second-rate citizen, either to be classed as unfit, or else to be fought as a hypocrite for his alleged intention of enslaving the working masses.

Thus is he attacked by his adversaries, but what does he mean to Christians? Many love and follow him. Many others respect him, sometimes through a sub-conscious self-interest, because to them he gains support for the established order, and is the representative of what is permanent in a changing society. Others again have a secret human respect for the priest. Such people, engulfed as they are in modern life, think of him as having power over public opinion, and sometimes find fault with him—unsparingly—for his inefficiency or for his out-of-date loyalties. Like the Word coming into this world, the priest is often not recognized by his own: *Et sui eum non receperunt.* (John, 1:2)

The Mystery of the Priesthood

Surely the unanimity of critics so diverse proves clearly the ridiculous disproportion between the end to be reached and the means proposed? Is it not criminal folly to leave the fate of the present and the future in such frail hands? Certainly, if the priest is no more than what he appears to be. Those who reject him, atheists or shallow believers, sin alike in common ignorance. They see the man, and they measure him like economists; while his hidden work and invisible efficacy escape them. They remember only a derived aspect or accidental characteristics of the priesthood. They do not see it as a whole. They do not set it in the context of its mystery. All this is only the logical consequence of the pervading atheism. Our age has secularized, naturalized, and humanized the priest. To get back again to the meaning of God, it is necessary to get back again to the meaning of the priesthood. There is no return to God without a return to the priest.

Therefore, my dear brethren, you will understand why the subject of this Pastoral Letter appears to Us a logical sequence to the other letters and an answer to modern needs. It is certainly a logical step: if "the growth of the Church," the condition of the universal redemption, is to be realized without deviating from "the meaning of God," a divine craftsman is needed; and that is the priest.

And that he may be "the priest in the world," and all that that connotes, it is indispensable to rehabilitate him with his detractors, and to revalue him in the eyes of the faithful and perhaps in his own, by recalling the infinite grandeur of his powers and of his mission. In so doing, it will become apparent that a world without a priest is a dead world, a civilization which makes no sense and achieves nothing.

Writing thus in all the fervor of our recent priestly Jubilee, We address this letter particularly to Our dear sons, the priests of the diocese of Paris. After them, We write for the consecrated religious, men and women, whom a common vocation in the service of Our Lord calls to a more intimate understanding of the Sacrament of Holy Orders. Finally, We write for all our faithful, to give to them, or to increase in them, an appreciation of the ideals of the priesthood.

Let Us make it clear that, long as these pages already are, We have with reluctance omitted a number of questions, theological or practical, relative to the priesthood. We shall not even consider all the problems to which the position of the priest in the world gives rise. In the first part We explain what will always form the essential and immutable nature of the priesthood. In the second part We show what this constitutive mission implies in the modern world. Then in the third part, we indicate some of the necessary links created between the priest and community by his unique position in the human picture.

I. THE ETERNAL PRIESTHOOD

At the outset it is essential to clear up a misunderstanding. Some people would believe that of the two terms, "priest" and "world," the first is subordinate to the second. Value in a priest would depend on his usefulness to men at a given place and time. By a meticulous analysis of human needs, one might outline an imaginary portrait of the priest, conceived, in accordance with the dictionary definition, as "the Minister of a religion." It is as well to insist on this point. Many minds, even cultured minds, have a very vague idea of our priesthood. When they think of a priest, they begin with a blurred generic definition and see in the Catholic priesthood an example and a particular instance of an institution which is found in all social groups at all ages of history. Seen in this light, the priest is merely one of the representatives of the world; its deputy in the presence of God. He receives his powers from below; he does not transcend what is human.

This conception, by no means imaginary, is at the root of all the confusion, and of all the secularization of the priest. If the priest is only the image of the world, there are as many types of priests as there are civilizations. Likewise, if he depends on superstition or philosophic systems, there will be as many priests as there are hypotheses. Lastly, on these grounds, the priesthood can be conceived only as an exterior function, or as a transitory and secondary role belonging to the man whom the group has selected as its delegate. Such a man is not a priest; he is a man who takes on a religious function, much in the same way as he would take on any public office. So, is it surprising that so many Christians regard the members of the hierarchy as no more than functionaries and consider the priesthood as a profession, the highest of them perhaps, but nevertheless one of the professions?

The Plan to be Followed

The approach to the question must be quite the reverse. The priesthood is not a function derived from society. It is not constructed artificially at the whim of our confused and lop-sided systems of society. It is not a non-essential, an outer ritual vestment. It affects the priest in his very being, within. It is given from on high. It is unique, permanent, eternal. It must be taken for what it is: not the result of a deduction from all the imperfect outlines shown by the history of religions, but their original source and their supreme fulfillment. This priesthood is the Priesthood of Jesus Christ, the Son of God. Being a priest in the world does not consist in inventing functions but in continuing, by His grace, the unique Priest in His Mystical Body which is the Church.

It means continuing Him just as He is, through time and space. It means preserving Him unchanged through the changing course of history, identical under the most diverse forms of life of human society, subtracting nothing, adding nothing, rendering Him *plain* and communicable. For there is an essential distinction to be made, similar to the one we made with respect to the Church: just as there is in the Church a transcendent aspect, that of its mystery, and a contingent and temporal aspect, that of its successive incarnations, so it is with the Priest. He has an eternal, and a temporal, aspect. To be a priest in the world is to perpetuate what is immutable and essential in the Priesthod of Christ—i.e., His mysterious mediation, under the constantly renewed forms of here and now.

Leaving controverted questions on one side, We would like to show, from Scripture and Tradition, what is the priesthood common to all priests; what gives them all their unity in Him; and what makes them all consecrated: their participation in the unique Mediator.

THE PRIESTHOOD OF CHRIST

When you hear Us speak of Christ the Priest, dear brethren, you at once think of a new devotion, of another title given by spiritual fervour to Jesus Christ, as, for example, devotion to the Sacred Heart. For most of you, Christ is, together with the other functions of His ministry, a priest. You make no mistake, especially if sermons and spiritual reading have familiarized you with the beautiful traditional formula: Christ is Priest and Victim, *Sacerdos et Victima.* We insisted on it in explaining to you how the Sacrifice of the Mass renews the Sacrifice of the Cross. Nothing could be more just and commendable, provided that this word, "priest," is well understood, and provided that you do not see in it only an added and provisional function, as though Christ had been first of all a man and then a priest. It was not only in the Cenacle and on Calvary that Christ was a priest. He was a priest from the first moment of His mortal life, intrinsically and in all His acts. We must insist on this point because it dominates the rest of this letter.

Christ has not merely *fulfilled the function* of a priest; He was Priest; He is essentially Priest.[1]

[1] This doctrine may appear abstract and difficult. In fact it is hardly surprising that the faithful are not used to it, for the Holy Scriptures they know best are the Gospels. Yet, more than once Our Lord lays claim to this title of Priest. Other writings, especially the Epistles, barely make allusion to it. It is only in the last of the Pauline Epistles, to the Hebrews, that this essential doctrine is expounded "ex professo."

How can this silence be explained? As the deliberate intention of Our Lord and the first Apostles. For the priesthood which existed in their time was the Levitical priesthood. Its members represented the priesthood of Aaron which had had service as its purpose, since God Himself had instituted it through Moses. But after the coming of Our Lord, it had no

The Plan of Love

To understand the plan of love it is sufficient to recall in a few words the plan of the redemptive Incarnation. "God is love" (1 John iv. 8). To raise us to His divine life, He created the world of which man is king. Man is an intelligent being created in the image of God. He is to be the adorer of the infinite Being in his own name and in the name of all creatures. But Adam wanted no other ruler than himself: that is his sin. Relations are broken. The original order is destroyed. Who is to re-establish the bonds with the Creator? Man is incapable of it. But God "Who wonderfully created everything, in His mercy wishes to restore everything still more wonderfully." [2] He decided to send to men His own Son, as Pontiff, *Pontifex*, which is translated "the bridge-maker." He will be their ferryman for the passage between God and man. Christ Himself acknowledges it explicitly: *Ego sum via* (John xiv 6). He is the only way—i.e., the unique Mediator between creation and its Creator, and thus the unique Priest.

Priest by His Incarnation

This teaching has been magnificently illustrated by all patristic and theological tradition. Both show that the Priesthood

---

meaning any longer, since the Son of God came to replace the bloody and necessarily inefficacious sacrifices by the only perfect Sacrifice, that of Calvary. To have compared this new Priesthood with an old and abolished institution, which moreover the greedy and sectarian Levites had discredited would have seemed a contradiction on the lips of the Messias, the messenger of the Good News, and a blasphemy in the mouth of the Apostles.

The author of the Epistle to the Hebrews does not prove this interpretation false. For if he based his sublime theology about the Priesthood of Christ upon a comparison with the Levitical sacrifices, it was only to demonstrate how the New Testament surpasses and abrogates the Old. But the most profound reason is far simpler. The sacred authors do not stress the Priesthood of Christ, because it already formed part of the redemptive Incarnation which is the whole substance of their preaching. The title of priest has not to be added to that of Christ; it is already included in it.

[2] Offertory of the Mass.

of Christ is derived directly from His Incarnation—i.e., from the hypostatic union.

St. Augustine says it formally: "In as much as He is born of the Father, God is God. He is not a priest. He is Priest because of the flesh which He has assumed, because of the victim He received from us to offer." [3]

"In fact, Christ is formally priest only according to His human nature, for priesthood implies a real submission to God. Yet the human nature in Him possesses the sacerdotal dignity only because it subsists in the Person of the Word, in such a way that His Priesthood draws from the hypostatic union its existence, its dignity, its power, its superiority. It belongs to the human nature of Christ by the title of sacerdotal consecration which was conferred upon Him at the moment of the Incarnation in the womb of the Blessed Virgin Mary; and since this hypostatic union is indissoluble, it is also the reason why Christ is the Priest for ever." [4] The Priesthood of Christ which is destined never to end had a beginning in time. The Word, the only Son of God, was not a priest before coming among us: It was at the moment of the Incarnation that the Incarnate Word became priest; as long as He remains in the bosom of His Father, He cannot abase Himself, nor adore, nor pray." [5]

Priest by His Own Nature

The French school of spirituality has done magnificent work in throwing light on this "ontological" character of the priestly consecration of Christ. Beginning with the etymology of the word Christ, which means anointed, it has shown that the consecratory anointing which was the priestly ordination of the Savior, was not secondary nor derived but proceeded from His double nature. "The unction by which Jesus Christ was consecrated Sovereign Priest is the Divinity itself, which from the moment of the Incarnation filled and sanctified His sacred Humanity, just as balm or perfume penetrates the paste with which it is mixed, or as fire enters and penetrates hot iron, or

[3] Enarr. in Psalm 110:3—P.L. 37, c. 1459.
[4] Galtier, "De Incarnatione et Redemptione," p. 424.
[5] Tanquerey, Dogmes générateurs de la piété," p. 455, et seq.

finally as the sun would penetrate and set ablaze with its splendor a crystal globe (the Fathers use these examples). Similarly, as the Apostle bore witness: *In ipso inhabitat omnis plenitudo divinitatis* (Colos., 11:9), the Divinity is united to this humanity; it dwells in it as a permanent abode; it sanctifies it, consecrates it, deifies it. Hence Jesus is anointed and consecrated, so as to remain a priest forever (Heb. vii); and hence He is the first Christ, and therefore the source of the grace and sanctity of the priesthood, the one and only founder of the priesthood in His Church."[6] Thus, "He is not an agent, deputed by the crowd; He is of Himself priest. . . . His consecration is nothing other than His personality, and His anointing, it is Himself: He is anointed because He is the God-Man."[7]

Invested from On High

The dependence is ontological; one could even call it necessary, at least in the *de facto* economy of the Redemption: "The Word Who is at once the perfect image of the Father and the exemplar of creation, from the time of the Incarnation cannot be other than the Mediator, the religious bond between God and man, and consequently the *Priest*."[8] But it is not an inevitable dependence, as if the Father and the Son had of necessity to submit to it. On the contrary, each is expressly and freely the cause: the Father, because He decided to send His Son on earth and to accept Him as the atoning Victim; the Son, because He consented to it. The Epistle to the Hebrews has clearly emphasized this investiture: "The purpose for which any high priest is chosen from among his fellow-men, and made a representative of men in their dealings with God, is to offer gifts and sacrifices in expiation of their sins. . . . His vocation comes from God, as Aaron's did; nobody can take on himself such a privilege as this. So it is with Christ. He did not

[6] "Oeuvres de Bérulle, Préface," p. 103. Cf. Bourgoing, "Méditations sur les vérités et excellences de N.S.J.C.," t. 1, p. 188, quoted by Pourrat, "Le Sacerdoce," p. 28.

[7] P. Mersch, "Morale et Corps mystique," p. 143.

[8] G. Salet, S.J., "Le Christ notre Vie," Casterman, 1937, p. 53.

raise Himself to the dignity of the high priesthood; it was God that raised Him to it, when He said: Thou art My Son, I have begotten Thee this day, and so, elsewhere, Thou art a priest for ever, in the line of Melchisedech." (Heb. 5. 1:4-6.)

This doctrine is emphasized unanimously by the commentators. "The priesthood, being a public office, belongs legally only to him who is accredited by God and who has received from Him an official investiture. The priesthood of Jesus Christ is no exception to the rule. The unique Person, Christ, constantly hears spoken the eternal word of divine generation: 'Thou art My Son.' This divine decree constitutes Him at the same time Mediator between God and man. There is the metaphysical root of the Priesthood of Christ, its eternal foundation." [9]

On the other hand, the Word is not the passive instrument of the divine will of His Father. On entering into the world, Christ says: "No sacrifice, no offering was Thy demand; Thou hast endowed Me, instead, with a body. . . . I said, See, My God, I am coming to do Thy will." (Heb. 10:5-9) Christ made Himself our Brother and our Ambassador in complete freedom and purely from love.

Born in time, Jesus has yet been in existence from all eternity: *ante luciferum genui Te*. (Ps. 109, 3.)[10]

This doctrine, dear brethren, may seem rather abstract; but, in fact, as you will see, it is the foundation of the mission of the priest in society, even in its most practical aspects.

One Priest Only: Christ

The first consequence is that there are not many priesthoods but only one, that of Christ: "Others have had some participa-

[9] Bonsirven, "Epitre aux Hebreux," pp. 40, 41 et 267.

[10] "Jesus is man . . . this man is God. There lies the investiture of His priesthood. . . . The divine word which constituted Him priest of humanity was that which, at the Incarnation, raised human nature to God . . . and made it enter into the person of the Word . . . : 'Tu es sacerdos in aeternum.' This word, in fact, which made of God a man and of man a God, made of this God-Man the mediator between God and humanity, the born priest who gives God to men and men to God." (P. Bouesse, O.P., "Théologie et Sacerdoce," p. 97).

tion of the Priesthood; He has it in its entirety, or rather it is not so much that He has it as that He is it. He is the whole priesthood. . . . Thus He is not a priest among priests, greater than them or more holy. He is the unique priest. . . . He includes all priesthood in Himself." [11]

There do not exist, then, different types of priests, different degrees of priests, as if each were derived of itself. *The priesthood does not originate itself: it is.* And even, in one sense, it is not some-thing; it is some-one: Christ.

Christ, Priest; two interchangeable titles. At once this priesthood is complete and perfect; nothing can be added to it.[12]

It is a permanent mediation, accomplished on earth on the Cross, consummated in Heaven where Christ "lives on still to make intercession on our behalf." (Heb. 7:25.)

Given from On High: Sent for Salvation

The second consequence is that this priesthood does not originate here on earth. "This priesthood . . . does not originate in the Christian community, nor is it derived by delegation from the people." [13] The priest's mediation is not a bilateral contract by which he would impose conditions on God. It has been given from heaven, just as He is, by a purely gratuitous love.

The priesthood is inseparably connected with the redemptive Incarnation and, like it, is a divine "mission," using the word in the profound sense that theology gives it—i.e., the extension in the world of the eternal birth of the Word in the bosom of the Trinity.

The priest is then an envoy, a messenger, an official delegate of God among men. Thus it is clear that the apostolate is based not so much on a command of Christ, as on His very Being:

[11] P. Mersch, o.c., p. 143.

[12] "Our High Priest is different from the priests of the Old Law, who, being men, had to succeed one after another, and who, being sinners, could offer to God only imperfect sacrifices. He, on the other hand, is unique, because He is eternal; and His sacrifice is also unique, because it remits all the sins of the world and constitutes the definitive act of religion." (Bardy, Supplement to "La Vie Spirituelle," April–May, 1936.)

[13] Encyclical, "Mediator Dei," section 44.

"I came upon an errand from My Father, and now I am sending you out in My turn." (John, 20:21); "When God sent His Son into the world, it was not to reject the world, but so that the world might find salvation through him." (John, 3:17.)

Priest and Savior, here is a new meaning of the greatest value.

Yet One of Us, Our Real Representative

Yet if this Priest, given from heaven, is to be our Mediator, He must not be a stranger to us. He must be truly our representative, for every union supposes two terms.

The Sovereign Priest fulfills these conditions: He is one of us, not merely one of those who knew Him or one of His compatriots, nor even of those who loved Him. If He were only a legal delegate, He would be only the ambassador of the race or of the sect which had accredited Him. But He is ambassador by nature, by a "designation not only verbal, but real, arising out of the very constitution of Christ . . . composed of two natures in one person . . . and consequently His sacrifice is social; it is the sacrifice offered solemnly by the whole of humanity . . . in its Head, in its nature." [14]

An equally important consequence is that Christ is the Mediator not only of the just, but also of sinners, of all those who at least for a time have neglected or even refused His saving intervention, crying out with the deicidal Jews: "We will not have this man for our King." (Luke 19:14.)

The mediation of Christ does not coincide with the extension of sin over the earth; it exceeds it on all sides. The Sovereign Priest has no need to await a mandate from His brothers. By nature and by office, He has the right to save them. For the priest this is the unassailable foundation of his missionary duty.

Priest by Status as well as by Sacrifice

If Christ is Mediator by the very fact of His birth, what of Calvary? And what of the Cross and the Eucharist? All that We have said, dear brethren, might indeed in some way prove disconcerting to you. Traditional doctrine of the Church as it

[14] P. Charmot, S.J., "Le Sacrament de l'Unité," p. 114.

is, it does not remind you of the theology which you have been taught. Until now, you have associated the priesthood with the Passion of Christ; with Maundy Thursday, for its origin and institution by Our Lord as the Sacrament of Holy Orders; and with Good Friday, for the redemptive sacrifice in which Christ on Calvary was at once Priest and Victim.

Is it necessary to say that there is no opposition between these two theologies, but rather an intimate liaison? We always celebrate the feast of the priesthood on Maunday Thursday. Actually it has an anniversary also on Good Friday and on the feast of the Annunciation—i.e., the mystery of the Incarnation of the Word in the womb of the Virgin Mary. Though they do spring from the one design of love, the Priesthood-Sacrifice and the Priesthood-Incarnation are yet two intellectually distinct aspects. They have given rise to complementary and invaluable spiritualities. The commentators of St. Thomas and of the Council of Trent have associated the Priesthood more particularly with the Sacrifice of the Cross, prolonged in the Sacrament of the Eucharist and the Sacrifice of the Mass.[15] Some of the Fathers, followed by the French school—St. Vincent de Paul, M. Olier, Berulle, Bossuet, &c.—have preferred to emphasize the permanent and ontological character of the sacerdotal Mediation of Christ. There is no question here, you will understand, of emphasizing a controversy, but only of re-uniting two realities which are complementary. Having firmly laid down what is a truth of faith, that the Sacrifice of Calvary and the Eucharist which is its efficacious and lasting sacramental sign are the crown of the sovereign pontificate of Christ, surely there is something to be gained by showing that He "is substantially priest, by all that He is, by the whole of Himself . . . that all His actions will be, and will be necessarily, sacerdotal." [16] "Jesus Christ is not Priest only in the Cenacle or on

[15] It should be noted that the Epistle to the Hebrews does not mention the Eucharist in its doctrinal construction; the Eucharist does not in fact enter St. Paul's argument. This silence shows, nevertheless, that an argument to prove the sacerdotal character of Jesus Christ can quite naturally be based on the Hypostatic Union alone.

[16] G. Salet, o.c., p. 53.

Calvary. He is Priest always, since His Priesthood is co-extensive with the Incarnation itself. Perpetually He exercises His mediatory functions. He is the living and substantial Sacrament. He is Priest also in all his relations with God and with men." [17]

Here again is a consequence of great importance for defining the mission of the priest in the world. For he should not only be "the man in the Upper Room," that is, of the Eucharist and of all the sacraments which complement it. He will not only be the minister of worship; his priesthood will not only be ritual nor his ministry exclusively sacramental. To put it another way, he will not be priest only by the acts which he exercises intermittently by virtue of powers he has received. He will live his priesthood in an uninterrupted, and even, invisible fashion, by all that he is. He will be priest at every hour of his life, in the humblest of his occupations as in the most solemn act. His ministry will be of worship but also "prophetic." He will be consecrator, because he is consecrated, always able and always ready to sanctify human values.

Mediator: Synthesis of the Function of Salvation

This consequence involves another. In the religion of Jesus Christ, "or at least in His person . . . the Priesthood is total. . . . It assumes at once all the mediatory functions which could not be dissociated in His mystery: those of Moses, of Aaron, of Abraham, or Melchisedech." [18] Because Christ is Mediator by all that He is, all the functions that He exercised in His hidden life and His public life will find place and be renewed in the life of the priest: spiritual head, pastor, preacher of the kingdom, benefactor of men, contemplative servant of the

[17] Masure, "Prêtres Diocésains," p. 27. In this excellent work, the author develops this distinction and correlation: "the notion of priesthood is larger in time and in metaphysics than the idea of sacrifice. The priesthood lasts; it is a state. The sacrifice is offered and completed; it is an act. But on the other hand, even if the priesthood is logically anterior to sacrifice in order to make it possible, what kind of priesthod would that be which never realised itself in the offering and the immolation of a victim? That is the way by which it justifies itself, fulfils itself, and . . . in a certain sense passes from potency to act."

[18] Masure, "Prêtres Diocésains," pp. 27-28.

Father. All that is inferred from His Mediation must be present, at least in some degree, in his continuers, the priests of the world.

THE PRIEST IN THE CHURCH

Christ lives on in time. Risen again, He is not satisfied with living His Priesthood in heaven, where "He lives on still to make intercession for us." (Heb. 7:25.) He has expressly chosen to exercise it upon earth in a visible way until the end of time.

Through whom? The answer is so obvious, dear brethren, that without a second's thought you can say: through the priest. For you the mystery of salvation is summed up as a rule in this elementary scheme: God—Christ—the Apostles (i.e., the bishops and priests)—souls. But the reality is at once richer and more complex.

The Church, the Extension of Christ

One should not think of the priest as a kind of isolated person to whom Christ has entrusted individually and directly the mission of prolonging Him—*Sacerdos alter Christus*—and who will use his powers as seems good to him. It is impossible to imagine the priest thus cut off from the Church, not only because he is already incorporated in the Mystical Body by his Baptism and because the sacrament of Holy Orders by which he was made priest is a sacrament of the Church, but also and above all because his mediation thus understood would be counterfeit. For, as we saw two years ago, it is the Church which prolongs Christ on earth and continues Him. If He is the unique Mediator, she is the unique mediatrix. This is the meaning of the axiom: Outside the Church, no salvation.

But the Church, being the Mystical Body of Christ, continues Him in all things. By her own being and then by all her members, she shares in the sacerdotal mediation of Christ. And so it is nonsense to imagine the Priesthood as something apart from the Church, as if the priest were another intermediary between the soul and God. The ground of this conclusion is in Scripture and Tradition.

A Priestly People

Even in the Old Testament is found the announcement of a "priestly people." [19]

The prophecy is fulfilled not only in heaven, as the Apocalypse shows,[20] but even on earth, where Christians form "a spiritual fabric . . . a holy priesthood" and constitute "a chosen race, a royal priesthood, a people God means to have for Himself." (I Pet., 2:5 and 9.)

The Fathers and the Doctors of the Church have often taken these texts and applied them enthusiastically to all who have been baptised.[21]

[19] As far back as in Exodus (19:5-6) God announces His designs for Israel, the type of the Church: "Keep your covenant with me; and I, to whom all the earth belongs, will single you out among its peoples to be my own. You shall serve me as a royal priesthood, as a consecrated nation." Isaias (61:5) is still more precise: "For you, a higher name, a greater calling, priests and chosen ministers of the Lord Our God."

[20] "Out of every tribe, every language, every people, every nation Thou hast ransomed us with Thy blood and given us to God. Thou hast made us a royal race of priests." (Apoc., 5:10.) See also Apoc, 1:6 and 20:6.

[21] St. Justin ranks the faithful among the true race of archpriests of God. (Justin c. Tryph. cxvi, 3.) St. Augustine, commenting on Psalm xxvi affirms clearly: "It is not only the Head which has received the anointing, but also the body, and this body is us . . . Jesus Christ incorporates us in Himself, making us His members, that in Him we may be Christ as well. So the anointing which makes priests and kings belongs to all Christians. . . ." (Enarr. in Ps., 25:2-2.) Origen shows equally how the Christian belongs to "the priestly race" and so must "offer up to God the sacrifice of its prayers." (In Levit. Homill. lxi.) St. Leo calls on "the people of the divine adoption, the whole of which is priestly and royal," and he explains himself: "As the Apostle says, we are all one in Christ . . . in the unity of faith and Baptism, the society is undivided, its dignity extends to all according to the word of St. Peter the Apostle. (Here, he cites I Pet., 2:5-9) . . . All who have been regenerated in Christ are consecrated priests by the anointing of the Holy Spirit . . ." The anointing is of such kind that "in the entire body of the Church is celebrated the unique mystery of the priesthood which, after the outpouring of the blessed oil, has communicated itself more abundantly to the higher parts, but has also descended lavishly upon the rest of the body." (Sermon iv L.P. 54-108.)

The explanation is always the same: Baptism makes us members of the Body of Christ and admits us also to His priesthood.

These assertions, dear brethren, may upset all our habits of thought. If it is the whole Mystical Body which shares in the priesthood of Christ, you may ask yourselves what becomes of the ministers of God? If all Christians are mediators already, how are the priests mediators? Your surprise would be perfectly legitimate, if this doctrine meant that each Christian is individually a priest, and that all are equally priests. This theory has been formally condemned by the Council of Trent.[22]

The Baptismal "Character"

What the sacred authors and the Fathers mean is that baptized people are no longer profane but are already consecrated, and that, on this title, they share, although in a very humble way, in the Priesthood of the unique Priest.

Theology, and especially St. Thomas, gives it a more systematic explanation. Three sacraments, Baptism, Confirmation, and Holy Orders, imprint a seal on the soul, traditionally called the "character." This mysterious imprint which is the distinctive sign of God's ownership of us, assimilates, "configures," the soul, invisibly but really, to the Sovereign Priest. Thus the Encyclical *Mediator Dei* states that "by reason of their Baptism, Christians are in the Mystical Body and become by a common title members of Christ the Priest: by the 'character' that is graven upon their souls they are appointed to the worship of God, and therefore, according to their condition, they share in the priesthood of Christ Himself." [23]

[22] Session xxiii, can i. 8.

[23] "Mediator Dei," Section 92. This doctrine of the character is classical in Theology. In spite of its abstract nature we think it useful to give here a summary exposition of it for the benefit of those of our layfolk who love to find in Theology a foundation for their obligation.

The existence of a sacramental character is defined by the Council of Trent (Session vii, can. 9): Three Sacraments, Baptism, Confirmation, and Holy Orders, impress a character on the soul, that is, a spiritual and indelible sign in virtue of which these sacraments cannot be repeated.

The Council, far from innovating, was only summing up the sacramen-

Sharing in Priestly Worship

"According to their condition": that is the essential qualification. For it would be wrong to imagine that the character of Baptism, that of Confirmation and that of Holy Orders, are simply three degrees of the same kind, a direct and so to speak quantitative extension of one another. What unites them is an analogical relation—in other words, an ever more vivid resemblance and an ever more real participation in the priesthood of the Incarnate Word. The idea of the priesthood implied by the baptismal character is not of a complete priesthood but of a priesthood on a reduced scale. This, Confirmation and Holy Orders will enlarge, just as a statute reproduces in greater size the original model. The baptismal character is simply the character of a member, a simple "delegation to divine worship." It is simply the right, and the fact, of being incorporated in Christ the Priest and of entering into His

---

tal doctrine and practice of fifteen centuries. Greek and Latin Fathers compare these three sacraments to the picture of a king on a piece of money, to a military badge, to the mark of possession with which a master branded his sheep.

This effigy makes the soul like to God, and more particularly to the Incarnate Word. Although this transforming imprint may be, like grace, the sign of the gratuitous good will of God, it is distinguished from it: grace can be lost; the character remains always even in the apostate or the sinner, just as the brand remains on a deserting soldier.

The seal, which is at once a sign of recognition and a likeness to Chirst, is represented by St. Thomas as a sharing in the sacerdotal power of Christ: "Character sacramentalis specialiter est character Christi, cuius sacerdotio configurantur fideles secundum sacramentales characteres qui nihil aliud sunt quam quaedam participationes sacerdotii Christi ab ipso Christo derivatæ." (iii. Q. 63, 3.)

The character imprinted exclusively by these three sacraments—which explains why they alone may not be repeated—is not some vague kind of participation in the priesthood of Christ; it is the participation in this priesthood in so far as it expresses itself by the worship of the New Law: "Per quaedam sacramenta, quae characterem imprimunt, homo sanctificatur quadam consecratione, utpote deputatus ad cultum divinum." (IIIa, Q. 63a. 6 ad. 2.)

"Consecratione," "deputatus," these two terms indicate the double effect of the character. It consecrates, i.e., separates from the world and the

eternal mediation of religion and salvation. After the fact of union with the Savior by grace, it is the reason why it can be said that the Christian is another Christ. This real consecration does not confer on the baptized the power of representing the Church, but that of being represented. It does not give them the power of being consecrators but only that of uniting themselves to the oblation and of consenting to the consecration.

The Primacy of the Priest in the Church

Therefore, dear brethren, you see the place of the priest in the Church. On the one hand, against an opinion which is too common, he must not be set over against the faithful, as if they had nothing in common with him and were as different from him as pagans are. If he is consecrated, so are they—although in a different manner. See how close this brings the pastor to his people and how it confers on them a dignity of the first order, and at the same time a missionary duty. For, by this consecration which incorporates them into the Sov-

---

devil (Q. 63a, 3 ad 3), and sets apart for God, by transforming the soul interiorly. This it does by conferring a capacity, a "power of being subjects or ministers—i.e., the instruments of the sacerdotal power which Jesus Christ Sovereign Priest will exercise in them and by them" . . . "deputatur quisque fidelis ad recipiendum vel tradendum aliis ea quae pertinet ad cultum Dei." (Q. 63, a. 3.) They become then, in different degrees according to the character received, like members in which and by which Jesus Christ acts, the invisible Head of the Church." (Moureau, "Dic. Theol," col. 1704.) Wherefore the baptised can be ministers of the two Sacraments: of Baptism by way of exception, and Marriage as the rule. Wherefore also they can say the Divine Office together with a priest without the priest being obliged afterwards to repeat the alternate verses.

Theology finds support here in Scripture and Tradition. For example, "No one shall eat or drink of your Eucharist except those baptised in the name of the Lord." (Didache ix, 5. Cf. Ephes. 5, 12, 16; 4, 30.)

By the character one becomes able to share validly in Christian worship, in the liturgy of the Redemption. "Character importat quandum potentiam spiritualem ordinatam ad ea quae sunt divini cultus." (Q. 63, a. 2.)

In the Second Part, when we speak of the Mass, we shall deal more exactly with what distinguishes the simple baptismal power of worship from the priestly or hierarchical power of worship.

ereign Priest, all the baptized must share also in His Mediation of salvation with regard to all the human race.[24]

But, on the other hand, the priest is no longer merely a baptized person. He is not a layman invested with a temporary function, but a man separated from the faithful, endowed by God with transcendent powers and marked with a consecratory character which, in setting him absolutely apart, makes him at once pontiff and head in the society of the baptized. This is what we learn from the unanimous testimony of dogma, history, and theology.

The priest is set apart from the faithful first by the divine power which the Sacrament of Holy Orders confers upon him: [25] to baptize, to remit sins, to administer the sacraments, but above all to offer the Eucharistic Sacrifice by consecrating the Body of Christ. The words of M. Olier come to mind: "Jesus Christ alone can do in the priest what the priest does every day in the Church." [26]

The affirmation of this miraculous power is not a late contribution of theology. Already in St. Paul we see the teaching, when he exorts Timothy not to neglect the "special gift" which he received with "the imposition of the presbyters' hands." (I. Tim., 4:14; II. Tim., 1:6.) This power is closely connected with the indelible "character" of which We have already spoken. What distinguishes this sacerdotal character from that of the baptized and the confirmed is that it confers on the ministers so invested the capacity of representing the unique Pontiff and of acting in His name and in His stead.

This power and this "ontological" differentiation which sin cannot destroy—for they are ordained above all for the common good of the faithful—carries with it an essential consequence: the priest is more than just consecrated, he is consecrator.

[24] Cf. Encyclical "Miserentissimus Redemptor" of Pius XI. (Roman Breviary, Feria II within the Octave of the Sacred Heart of Jesus, Lesson VI.)

[25] "Ordo potestatem principaliter importat." Summa Theol. Supplement Q. 34, a. 2. ad. 2.

[26] "Traité des Saints Ordres," III, ch. II.

Unique Consecrator

Sole consecrator, for as the Encyclical *Mediator Dei* says with great precision: "The unbloody immolation by which, after the words of consecration have been pronounced, Christ is rendered present on the altar in the state of a victim, is performed by the priest alone, and by the priest in so far as he acts in the name of Christ, not in so far as he represents the faithful." [27]

The superiority of the institutional priesthood is thus indisputable.[28]

While the priest, then, is the only qualified minister of "worship in spirit and in truth," he appears from the very beginning also as the *spiritual head* of the community. This community was never unorganized. The first care of the Apostles was to establish "elders" (Presbyteri) at the head of the churches. They were at the same time ministers, as we have just shown, and "over-seers" (Episcopi). The man of prayer, and the sign and cause of unity: these two aspects of the priesthood do not extend in two parallel lines; they converge in the person of the priest.

[27] "Mediator Dei," Section 96.

[28] ". . . that the priest acts in the name of the people precisely and only because he represents the person of Our Lord Jesus Christ, considered as Head of all the members and offering Himself for them; that the priest, therefore, approaches the altar as Christ's minister, lower than Christ, but higher than the people; that the people on the other hand, because they in no way represent the person of the divine Redeemer and is not mediator between itself and God, can in no way possess the priestly right." ("Mediator Dei," Section 88.)

As has been justly remarked, "the Pope uses a particularly illuminating argument: the priest is the representative of the people, not because he holds his priesthood by delegation of the people, 'but because he represents the person of Our Lord, who contains and recapitulates in Himself the whole body of the baptised.' This priestly power comes entirely from above."

As for the expression "the priestly power," it means here, evidently, full priesthood; for the Encyclical shows elsewhere, as we have seen, that the faithful "according to their condition . . . share in the priesthood of Christ Himself." (Section 92.)

Artisan of Organic Unity

The Encyclical *Mystici Corporis* shows that the character of the Church must always be juridical and mystical and that the same is true of the character of the priesthood of the New Law.[29] Just as with a natural body, *unity* is the condition *sine qua non* of the life of the Church. It is not sufficient for it to have a "head" and some "members"; they must form an organic whole. The Church marvellously fulfills this living unity in an harmonious diversity of functions. Without the priesthood—which represents and continues in particular the Head, Christ, the Head of His body—the Church would no longer be a society but a mob or an anarchy. Nevertheless, the role of the hierarchy is not merely to ensure order, least of all by coercive means. It is the instrument, mysterious although visible, of the "physiological" functioning of the Body and of its permanence.

In the Church—which here as elsewhere completely transcends temporal societies—Christ Himself creates His Body and makes of it *a community of love*, by working in it continually as Principle of cohesion and life. This He does by His Spirit and by the Holy Eucharist, but also by living on in His Priests.

And this, dear brethren, is what gives a transcendent character to the authority of your priests. Far from being purely an honor, it is a *power* given from on high and a mission constitutive of the Church. "Bound up with this power and with the grandeur of the acts which it permits is a pre-eminence

[29] It shows how there is no opposition between the authority of the Church and her inspiration by the Holy Ghost. "It was one and the same purpose . . . which caused the divine Redeemer both to give the community of men founded by Him the constitution of a society perfect in its own order, provided with all its juridical and social elements and also, with that same end in view, to have it enriched by the Holy Spirit with heavenly gifts and powers. . . . Hence there can be no real opposition . . . between the invisible mission of the Holy Spirit and the juridical office which Pastors and Teachers have received from Christ. Like Body and Soul in us, the two realities are complementary and perfect each other." ("Mystici Corporis" Section 63).

over Christian peoples. Holy Orders gives them at the same time office and status . . . it organizes the Church."[30]

The power does not exist by "immanence," but as a gift of God. "Only the Apostles and those who since have duly received from them and their successors the imposition of hands possess that priestly power in virtue of which they stand before their people as Christ's representatives and before God as vicegerents of the people. This priesthood is not transmitted by heredity or blood relationship; nor does it originate in the Christian community nor is it derived by delegation from the people. . . . Therefore the visible . . . priesthood . . . is imparted to selected individuals by a sort of spiritual birth in one of the seven Sacraments, Holy Orders." [31]

So we may understand the recommendation of the Roman Pontifical: *sacerdotem oportet praeesse:* it is necessary that the priest rule, and not merely as the first of the faithful but as one who is delegated and consecrated.

Source of Life in the Church

As head of the community, the priest has not only the common good as reason for his existence, as have other heads on earth; by his powers he is at the same time the source of life in the Church.[32]

This role is seen most easily with regard to the Eucharist, of Which he is the exclusive consecrator.[33] It is equally clear

[30] Perinelle, o.c., p. 237.

[31] "Mediator Dei" (Section 44).

[32] The Encyclical, "Mystici Corporis," draws an extremely significant parallel between the two social sacraments of the Church, Holy Orders and Marriage: "For the social needs of the Church, Christ has also provided in a particular way by two other Sacraments which He instituted. The Sacrament of Matrimony . . . ensures the regular numerical increase of the Christian community. . . . And Holy Orders consecrates to the perpetual service of God those who are destined to offer the Eucharistic Victim, to nourish the flock of the faithful with the Bread of Angels and with the food of doctrine, to guide them by the divine commandments and counsels, and to fortify them by their other supernatural functions." (Section 19.) Cf. also S. Th. IIIa, Q. 65, a. 1, c.

[33] Theology sums up the powers of the priest in two essential prerogatives: "the power of order" and "the power of jurisdiction." St. Thomas

in the other Sacraments which are reserved to him or habitually entrusted to him, and likewise in all his pastoral and doctrinal ministry, as we shall see later.

So he transmits the gifts of grace. He does more than that: in one sense the priesthood is the source of life in the Church, as it perpetuates in her the sacraments and the Sacrifice of Jesus Christ. At each moment of time the Church is brought into being both by the Holy Ghost and by the priesthood which continues Christ, the chief and Head of His Body. But on the other hand, one can say that the priesthood, even while it is the source of life, is at the same time given life by the Church. For in as much as she is the Spouse of Christ and universal Mother—*Mater Ecclesia*—she is anterior to it; like all baptized people—and moreover as such—priests are her children.

* * *

And that clearly defines the position of the priest in the Church; far from being an arbitrary dispenser of gifts from heaven, all that he is has its *raison d' être* only in the Church, by the Church, and for the Church.[34]

Aquinas and the majority of theologians consider that the power of jurisdiction derives from the power of order. "The priestly power according to St. Thomas, has as its first object the dispensation of the Holy Eucharist . . . for what it contains is not merely a power derived from Christ, but Christ Himself. . . . It is moreover the sacrament of the Sacrifice of Christ. . . . Its second object, assuming this first, is that (the spiritual power of order) should extend over the Mystical Body of Christ, in order to prepare it to receive the Eucharist (Périnelle, o.c., p. 238).

Scripture, on the other hand, seems to place the power of jurisdiction in the first place. The official Code of Canon Law also puts the power of jurisdiction first: "Holy Orders sets aside in the Church and by the institution of Our Lord, the clergy from the laity, to 'govern the faithful' and carry out the divine worship." (Can 948.)

We do not pretend to take any part in this controversy as to the primacy of the power of Orders over the power of Jurisdiction. What is more important is to note the indissoluble bonds which unite these two powers in the person of the ministers of God.

[34] On Christ everything depends. His historic sacrifice and priesthood prolong themselves by His sacramental sacrifice and priesthood, and find their pleroma in a mystical sacrifice and priesthood. And none of it leaves Him; everywhere He is Himself, but everywhere differently; here as Head,

Priesthood and Church are but one and the same legacy of love from Jesus Christ.

THE PRIEST AND CHRIST

Such is the priest's position in the Church and such must be his position in relation to Christ. But at once, dear brethren, a question will occur to you: If Christ be the only priest, how can there be other priests on earth?

Many Priests

The question is in fact obvious; but the answer once more is furnished to us by the mercy of God. Because He knows what man is, He knows that we need tangible signs. And what signs can be more living than human beings? That is why Our Lord, Whom only the inhabitants of Palestine two thousand years ago could have seen and touched (I John, 1:1.), wished to continue Himself throughout space and time by priests who are visible and like ourselves.

Besides, in order that "worship in spirit and in truth" might be truly the social worship of the whole human race, it would have to be expressed by exterior and public rites. Such is the double reason why Christ has chosen human helpers.

One Priest Only

Thus called and delegated by Our Lord, those who continue Him on earth do not therefore constitute so many distinct and autonomous priesthoods. Of themselves they have no stability, nor do they add anything to Christ. For "it is not His inadequacy that makes other priests necessary to Him; they are necessary to us because of our penury. Precisely because He is Priest in a unique, unparalleled, transcendent way, He is Priest therefore in a universal, mystical, overflowing way: *fons totius sacerdotii* [35] as said St. Thomas; *catholicus sacerdos,*[36] as Tertullian put it." [37]

---

there as an efficacious sign, there again in His members; yet nowhere is He divided." (Mersch, o.c., p. 160.)

[35] Summa Theol, IIa, Q. 22, a. 4c.

[36] Adv. Marcionem, iv, 9.

[37] Mersch, o.c., p. 144.

To describe human priests in relation to the Sovereign Priest, St. Paul employs a formula which indicates at once their nature and their function. They should be regarded, he says, "as Christ's servants, and stewards of God's mysteries." (I Cor. 4:1.) This formula, used by the Encyclical of Pope Pius XI on the priesthood, shows at once the penury of the priest in relation to Christ and his mysterious grandeur in relation to men.[38]

Penury of the Earthly Priest

In reaction against the heresies which made the priest merely a powerless juridical agent, certain oratorical effusions would have it that the priest is identified with Christ, that he is Christ Himself. Is it necessary to say, dear brethren, that this error arises from confused thinking? The Sacrament of Holy Orders means to the priest no loss either in nature or in person. The traditional formula, the priest is another Christ, is quite legitimate when it is properly understood; but it must not terminate in pantheism.

Christ alone is the Man-God. He alone, consequently, is intrinsically priest. The priest himself is only the man of God; in a real sense he perpetuates the presence of Jesus Christ.[39] His priesthood is not essentially connected with his person; it is a participated priesthood. The priest needs investiture from God in order to operate.

But, among these operations, a distinction is to be made.

The Priest, Minister of the Sacraments

In so far as he administers the Sacraments—i.e., with regard to his power of Orders, the doctrine of the Church has never varied. "The priest," writes Pius XI, "is the Minister of Christ, an instrument, that is to say, in the hands of the Divine Redeemer." [40]

[38] "The Catholic Priesthood," p. 9.

[39] "It is not a question of a sacramental presence: the substance of man has not disappeared, it has not been changed into the substance of Christ. . . . The priest is a consecrated ambassador." (Charmot, "Le Sacrament de l'Unité," p. 164, note.)

[40] "The Catholic Priesthood," p. 9.

On this title his role then is one of complete effacement; he no longer acts in his own name: it is Christ Who acts in him. St. Augustine had already said it with regard to Baptism: "When Peter baptizes, it is Jesus Who is baptizing; when Paul baptizes, it is Jesus Who is baptizing; when Judas baptizes, it is Jesus Who is baptizing."[41] This instrumental role appears still more clearly in Penance and above all in the Eucharist. The priest does not say, "May the Lord pardon thee," but "I absolve thee"; he does not say, "This is the Body and the Blood of Christ," but "This is my Body, This is my Blood." "At the Consecration," says a contemporary of St. Ambrose, "whose are the words? Those of the Lord Jesus. . . . It is the word of Christ that accomplishes these mysteries."[42]

Instrument of Christ

The efficacy of the sacramental rites, then, does not depend on the minister. He may be a sinner or an ignoramus; the effect is nevertheless completely produced. For it is literally an act of Christ. "Earthly priests do nothing but lend their hands and their lips, and however unworthy they are, the grace which comes through them is neither less pure nor less august. Someone else, the Priest, acts through them; in the acts which they do in His name, their power is equal to His and their baptisms, their absolutions, their consecrations, have the same value as His, because in actual fact they are His."[43]

The priest, then, is both instrument of Christ and distinct from Him; but he must not be thought of as a material and inert instrument. He is an instrument which is alive and rational. Further, out of respect for the dignity of the minister and of souls, God has willed to make the validity of the Sacraments depend on the intention of those who confer them; but that means only that the ministers must intend to act as Christ and the Church wish.

[41] Saint Augustine, "Tract 6 in Joann." Ante med.
[42] "De Sacramentis," Lib. iv, Cap iv.
[43] Mersch, o.c., p. 155.

The Priest, Pastor and Teacher

When he acts as spiritual head and pastor of the faithful—i.e., with regard to his power of jurisdiction and teaching,[44] it does not happen in quite the same way. There God leaves real scope to the moral qualities and the human gifts of the minister. When he preaches, or gives spiritual direction, he pledges Christ, in the sense that he speaks in His name and that he is His agent, His witness; but he does not efface himself before Him to the extent of becoming a mere instrument. In the exercise of sacramental power, one can speak of the substitution of Christ for His ministers. Here it is necessary to speak rather of co-operation; their human activity works with grace to influence and convert the faithful. It is the same with their share in the government of the Church;[45] when they take decisions, they can make mistakes, they can administer their parish or their diocese better or worse. Their ignorance or their faults will diminish the effect of the message which they transmit; on the other hand, their sanctity will impel souls to conform themselves to it. But it is evident that, even in all those acts which are dependent on their power of jurisdiction, priests have only a modest part in the work of salvation, which has as principal agent the grace of God.

They are multiple and transitory in their sacerdotal mediation, where Christ is unique and eternal; sinners, where He is "holy, guiltless, undefiled" (Heb. 7:26); instruments—or simply helpers—in the almighty hands of Christ, human priests are clearly poverty-stricken in comparison with the Pontiff of the New Law.

[44] It will be remembered that by divine institution the simple priest belongs to the hierarchy of orders, not to the hierarchy of jurisdiction, which contains only "The supreme pontiff and the subordinate episcopate." (Code, Canon 108, 3.) The bond of origin between the simple priesthood and the episcopate is always so intimate, that one cannot say that the simple priest is purely and simply a stranger to the divinely conferred power of jurisdiction.

[45] With the reservations made in the previous note.

Grandeur of the Priest

But what makes them insignificant when compared with Him constitutes their grandeur when compared with their fellow human beings. Because they do nothing by themselves —or only in the measure of their infirmity—they are strong with the very strength of God. Let us dare to say: "there is not less in our sinful hands, when the words have been spoken over the bread and wine, than there was in His own hands . . . on the evening when He instituted the Eucharist. Unheard of dignity of the Christian priest: he has Jesus Christ and he gives Him; still more, it is Jesus Christ Who gives Himself . . . with a giving which never ceases." [46]

Consecrated and Consecrator

Even if the priesthood is not "intrinsically" connected with the person of the priest, yet it is—by the free disposition of God—part of his being. It is not an official "vestment"; it is a permanent disposition, the mark of an appurtenance and a mission "Thou art a priest forever in the line of Melchisedech" (Ps. 109: 4). [47] Here again is an explanation of the "character." This seal which is not effaced by death or sin or heresy, is not just a kind of sign; it is a transforming reality which consecrates the very being of the priest and renders him consecrator. No doubt this prodigious faculty—which uses the powers of the human soul without destroying them—is not constantly in action. But it remains always capable of action. For "the priest," says Fr. Bourcoing, "is clothed in the very person of Jesus Christ." Also it is his unique responsibility that he remains free to make use of this permanent capacity whenever he wills.

From now on you will understand better, dear brethren, the unparalleled dignity of the priest: all the sacerdotal power of Christ, is, so to speak, at his discretion. It depends on him, as a free and conscious minister, whether the eternal mediation

[46] Mersch, o.c., p. 155.

[47] Ps. 109, 4. This word, which is addressed properly to Christ, can also be applied to the priest of the New Law, whose character is indelible.

of the Savior is to reach the souls of his brethren or not; it depends on him also whether the world renders to God the homage which is due to Him, by the sacrifice of the Cross, the renewal of which is his unique privilege. The whole of Redemption and the whole of the Church have been put into his hands.

* * *

Minister of Christ; dispenser of the divine mysteries. These titles show well enough that the priest is at once and inseparably the priest of Christ and the priest of the Church. His priesthood, shared with the Unique Priest, is also ordained for the sanctification of the faithful. Because he prolongs the Sovereign Priest, according to all that he is—the priest is another Christ—the human priest will reflect in his being and in his ministry something of the mystery of the Unique Priest. In other words he will not only offer the Eucharistic sacrifice, he will be priest as Christ is—i.e., in a permanent fashion, priest by all his acts, priest by his state. Like Christ again, and by the mission received from Him, the priest will unite in his person the prerogatives and the functions traditionally attributed to the Incarnate Word: Pontiff, King, Prophet—i.e., he will have "to offer," "to rule," "to teach." [48]

But these ministries, which must be separated and distinguished, are reunited in their turn in a function which sums them all up, that of Mediator.

This conclusion, dear brethren, is not artificial. It is deduced, as we said in the beginning, from the simple fact of the Incarnation of the Word. It proceeds no less rigorously from the reason why the Church exists, the extension of the Unique Priest. Wherefore, We can without being arbitrary, define—in its essential features—the role of the priest in the world.

This will not consist—let Us repeat it—in "inventing" or in *choosing* in the priesthood whatever aspect appears better

[48] Strictly speaking, the bishop alone shares in His royal function of governing, since only the jurisdiction which belongs to him is of divine right. (Cf. Note 43 above.)

adapted to our contemporaries. It will consist—for all priests wherever they are and in whatever age—in being faithfully what Jesus Christ was: mediators of salvation.

II. THE PRIEST IN THE WORLD

"What properly speaking constitutes the office of the priesthood," writes St. Thomas, "is to be mediator between God and the people in that he communicates to the people divine realities." A little further on, in speaking of Christ, he specifies: "Insofar as He is man, it is his work to bind men to God, by offering to men the precepts and the gifts of God and by satisfying and interceding with God for men." [1]

The reality which the word mediator covers seems simple. Actually it gives rise to ambiguities which it is necessary to dispel at once.

Mediator

When one speaks of the priest being the mediator between God and men, some people conjure up a kind of Jacob's ladder with three steps: at the top is God; at the foot is humanity; in the middle on the rung in between is their common delegate, the priest. The image is good in that it includes the two extremes and a middle term which unites them; but it is false and dangerously so, in that it places the priest half-way between God and man, as if in the hierarchy of being he were a being apart, neither God nor man.

A prime error is *angelism*. Let us admit that a certain amount of rhetoric is used here. In their praiseworthy zeal to enhance the greatness of the priest, people rank him among the immaterial adorers and servants of God, sent like them, to be a guardian angel of his brethren. Like the angel, the priest would be an intermediary between God and the human race.

We cannot say often enough, dear brethren, how false and dangerous is this manner of speaking. The priest is not an angel. First because of his nature, for an angel is a pure spirit confirmed in heavenly beatitude, sheltered always from the sin

[1] Summa Theologica IIIa. Q. 22, 1; Q. 26, 2.

which he once refused. As for the priest, he is a man like other men, composed of soul and body. He feels hunger, fatigue, the burden of age. He has experience of sin (Heb. 5: 1-5); and though we can rightly speak of his holiness, it is a struggling, fighting virtue, a holiness mobilized in combat.

Different Functions

The priest and the angel are just as different in the parts they have to play. By function both are undoubtedly adorers and servants of God and both are delegates, charged with a mission to men. But while the angel is a temporary messenger limited to an occasional task,[2] the priest is invested with a continual mission inherent in his priesthood; he is, permanently and in every sense, the way of access to God.

Scripture shows us this. The heavenly messenger is endowed with miraculous powers. He guides and preserves Tobias; he stirs the water in the pool at Siloe and gives it the power of healing, &c.[3] The powers of the priest may not take in these exceptional effects,[4] but they go infinitely beyond them: no angel is capable of doing what a priest does. For the power of the priest is the very power of Jesus Christ. You can see the meaning of the much quoted sentence attributed to St. Francis of Assisi: If I met a priest and an angel, I should bow to the angel, and I should go on my knees to the priest.

From Above and Below

But these two messengers differ most of all in their origin. The angel comes from somewhere else, from on high. He comes from God. He is a messenger from His right hand, a legate *a latere*, who intervenes in our human business in the name of his Lord and Master. We welcome him with respect and love, for his Lord is ours; but not without a certain amount of fear, for this spirit of light even when he is our

[2] Or permanent, but only auxiliary, like an Angel Guardian.

[3] Tobias 5:20; 6:4; John, 5:4.

[4] The miracles of the Curé d'Ars and of so many other priests do not conflict with this rule; they reveal the holiness of these servants of God, not their priesthood as such.

guardian angel remains for us something of a stranger. The priest is also the legate of God. He also comes from Him. But, if he is invested from on high, he is yet drawn from here below. He is "extracted" from humanity. He comes from God; but he comes, he is, he remains, from among us. He does not come down to the earth from heaven, as one to have charge of the divine rites. When he prays, we all pray with him, and this prayer is a cry from here below: *De profundis clamavi ad te, Domine* (Ps. 129, 1). He does not need to be taught our business or our distress; he knows them well enough; they are his own.

The Encyclical on the Mystical Body recalls this in quoting Saint Thomas: "He does not take hold of the angels, but of the seed of Abraham he takes hold." All the more reason why his minister should not seek to escape it. To "angelise" the priest is not only to incur the fate foretold by Pascal to those "who would be an angel. . . ." It would prevent the priest in a radical way from being the mediator of men. For men would never recognize for one of themselves so ethereal and imperceptible a messenger. And God will not accept him either, not recognizing in him a flesh and blood son of Adam, an adopted brother of His Son. The first condition for representing humanity is to be one of it. No angelism—whether old or new—can be preferred to Christian realism, born of the Incarnation.

Neither is the priest a magician. Nor should we count on his being a wonder-worker in the world. God has entrusted to him divine powers over His Eucharistic Body and His Mystical Body, which is the Church, but not over material things. The priest is not a man of miracles, like an intermediary god, the ancient "demiurge." And it is a good thing that he is not. For all power is a temptation; for him who has it, a temptation to abuse it; for those who benefit from it, a temptation to expect everything from it.

The priest is the trustee of an unequalled power of transformation—Transubstantiation and the Sacraments; for him the peril of a sacrilegious line of action is no illusion. He always runs the risk of using his prodigious gifts for his own ends and of attempting by their means to control persons and things. The Second Commandment of the Decalogue is always directed to him: Thou shalt not take the name of the Lord Thy God in vain. In modern terms this means that the priest will never invoke his priesthood to establish a despotic clericalism or to lay claim to honors and gifts meant for God. It means also that the priest will not consider his part finished, when he has validly pronounced the sacramental formulæ. There is no question, as We have said, that it is Christ and He alone who gives them their efficacy; but that in no way releases the minister from the duty of preparing the souls of the faithful who are not, and never can be, inert and passive subjects.

The Priesthood and Magic

But it is especially with regard to the faithful that this duty must be recalled. For they particularly might be inclined to see the priest as a well-meaning (or even wicked) wizard, to turn the sacraments of which he has the monopoly into infallible charms. Ethnology and the history of religions show us that this error in the interpretation or the exercise of the priestly function is not a product of the imagination. In a number of primitive societies or so-called primitive societies, the sorcerer is seen to arise by the side of the priest or in his stead. Peter and Paul, as the Acts of the Apostles show us, had seen and pointed out such a peril with regard to Simon the Magician (Acts 8:8-11). But in our own day we are given new proof in the superstition which technical progress seems to have the effect of releasing. Among the ill-informed faithful, it is passive credulity. Among non-christians it shows itself by an innate revulsion arising from the obscure fear aroused in them by the very sight of a priest.

Finally, and this proceeds from what has gone before, the priest is not a "superman," the messias of modern days. Here especially lies the eternal temptation. The myth of Prometheus, who stole the fire of heaven from the gods, raises its head everywhere under one form or another. Our Lord encountered this foolish hope in the Jewish people, and this brought about His death. His contemporaries did not forgive Him for having refused to be their temporal king. They wanted a conquering Messias who would free them from the Roman occupation: Christ gave them their answer: "My kingdom does not belong to this world" (John, 18:36).

The Temptation in the Desert

Like Christ, the priest will experience the temptation in the desert. The Tempter will ask him, as he asked Christ, to make "these stones turn into loaves of bread," and will suggest that he submit to his rule "all the kingdoms of the world." Insidiously, Satan would persuade him that it is his duty, because it is in his power, to make himself the moulder of earthly progress, and then according to circumstances, to become the defender of the established order or the champion of revolutionary causes. The priest will need all his lucidity and all his detachment to turn a deaf ear to these appeals, for what gives them force is that they are directed to his heart. It will be urged as a pretext that he has the duty of using his reputation and his position, not for himself, but to safeguard culture or for the masses without shelter, home or bread. He will be expected by his influence to procure without delay, ease, instruction and security. It is indeed his duty to do so, more than anyone else's, but not like that.

For Jesus worked miracles—miracles which established Him as the Son of God. But He did not heal all the sick, did not feed all the hungry, did not raise all the dead. The blind to whom He gave sight or the deaf to whom He gave hearing were only a small handful of men in comparison with the enormous crowd of blind, deaf, crippled of His own time and of all other times. Why? For lack of love? Who would dare to say so, when He consented to be nailed to the Cross for us?

To overcome suffering, the consequence of sin, He did not annihilate it by magic: He took it upon Himself to transform it. He did not invoke His divine nature. (Phil., 2: 6.) Humbly He made Himself one of us; He willed to take human nature as it is; "He suffered for our sakes, and left you His own example; you were to follow in His footsteps." (III Pet., 2:21.) For He did not come to found a new earthly Paradise but to introduce man—persons and society—into the kingdom of God and "His marvellous light." (I Pet., 2:9.) Christ was not a magician but a Savior.

Priesthood and Messianism

The disciple is not above the Master. What Christ Himself has not done, the priest will not do. The mystery of Christ will remain the mystery of the priest. The priest is a Redeemer, not a temporal Messias. Following the example of the "Son of man," he will always reject the role of "superman." He will not allow his message to be naturalized, or the word and the powers of God to be reduced to a humanism of progress or to a philosophy of human transcendence. This is a much-needed reminder in an age which aspires to the exaltation of the intellect and of flesh and blood: "I teach you the Superman," cries Nietzsche. "Man must surpass himself . . . the Superman is the reason why the earth exists . . . God is dead! Now we will that the Superman live." [5]

Angel, magician, superman; the three counterfeits which have in common their reduction of the priest to one of themselves, or which place him in their midst. But the priest is not a hybrid. He is not a "neutral," etymologically "neither one thing nor the other." In fact, *far from such cynical indifference*, he has a foot in both camps, so to speak. He is zealous for each. Christ is Mediator because He is at once God and man: "He first effected this junction of finite and infinite. . . . Priests, in the image of Christ, reconcile in themselves God and men, as if they were two natures." [6] The priest must not restrict himself to distributing the gifts and the word of God, or to transmitting correctly the prayers of men. *He must make their salvation his own* to the extent of feeling the agony of their redemption even more than they do themselves.

The Man with Two Instincts

Such is the mystery of the priest: what he unites in himself at the same time tears him apart: at each moment of his life,

[5] Nietzsche, "Zarathustra."

[6] Charmot, *op. cit.*, p. 164.

he must follow two instincts. He must satisfy each completely without ever renouncing either. "These two tendencies seem contradictory. They are, at least, opposed to each other and imprint on one's nature a kind of violent and grievous tension which can only end in death. The Priesthood mirrors martyrdom." [7]

Transcendent yet incarnate: here again we find the two fundamental words which, as We said in previous Pastoral letters, constitute the mystery of the Church and the paradox of Christian humanism. In this case, scripture affirms the fact and the necessity in a well-known text which will serve as the framework for our survey of the functions of the "Priest in the World" because it defines *the priest in his inmost nature;* his role of mediator.

"The purpose for which any high priest is chosen from among his fellowmen, and made a representative of men in their dealings with God, is to offer gifts and sacrifices in expiation of their sins. He is qualified for this by being able to feel for them when they are ignorant and make mistakes, since he, too, is all beset with humiliations. . . . His vocation comes from God, as Aaron's did; nobody can take on himself such a privilege as this." (Heb. 5:1-4.) The whole transcendence of the priest is here affirmed; but he is thus separated and kept apart from his fellow-men in the name of his brethren: *pro hominibus constituitur.*

To be the world's real mediator, the priest must be at one and the same time a man of God and a man among men. We shall say in due course what each of these two aspects of the Christian Priesthood means in the world of today; and we shall prove that it is in the Sacrifice of the Mass that they find their living synthesis and their highest reconciliation.

THE MAN OF GOD

"Chosen from among his fellow-men": these words speak of the human origin of the priest; but they show, too, that he has been separated from men: "The power of the consecrating

[7] Ibid., p. 167.

word makes the priest august and venerable, separating him from the crowd by a new blessing. Only the day before he had been indistinguishable from the people; and now suddenly he has become pastor, doctor, presiding at the sacred mysteries. In his exterior appearance, nothing is changed; but from henceforth he carries with him a soul interiorly transformed by an invisible power and grace."

Separated

We showed how the "character" marks with a distinctive sign the soul of him whom God has chosen for Himself. By his consecration the priest becomes the man of God, His thing, His property, His servant. Christ Himself tells us: "They do not belong to the world, as I, too, do not belong to the world." (John, 17: 16.) Long before, the Old Testament had given the reason: "And now the Lord set apart the tribe of Levi, to carry the ark that bears the record of his covenant, and to minister in his presence, and to impart blessing in his name; that is why the Levites have no lands assigned to them like their brethren, the Lord Thy God has promised them that he himself will be their portion." (Deut. 10: 8-9.) No priest has any doubt about it. The first word which accompanies his first gesture on the road to the priesthood, on the day he is tonsured, is a spiritual testament: he renounces the world and chooses God: *Dominus pars haereditatis meae.* The Lord will assure my inheritance to me. (Ps. 15, 5.) This is how he becomes one of the clergy. "This word cleric," writes St. Jerome to Nepotian, means both that he possesses God and that God becomes his owner.

Dead to the World

Every Christian already by the fact of his baptismal consecration is no longer of the world in St. John's sense; but the priest quits it in virtue of his state and in a radical fashion, not indeed, as we shall say, to flee or to condemn society and human values, but to renounce them for himself. Henceforth he will use them "not taking full advantage of them." (I Cor., 7: 31.)

From this point of view his relations with the world will be those of the dead with the dead: "The world stands crucified to me, and I to the world." (Gal. 6: 14.)

This voluntary detachment, which will be his calvary and his joy until the day of his death,[8] is itself a death which leads to life; leaving everything, the priest finds all. Introduced into the divine intimacy, he becomes from henceforth a member of God's dearest family: "I do not speak of you any more as my servants . . . and so I have called you my friends." (John 15: 1, 15.) From now on despite his limitations, the priest has by his vocation become bound up with God's companionship. "God is my lot," the Cure d'Ars used to say.

From this you can see how he is "placed at the head of God's affairs." "His function has for its object not human and transitory things, however lofty and respectable they may appear to be, but the things that are divine and eternal."[9] The priest becomes the natural champion of God's interests. His whole life is specialized and determined towards the promotion of His kingdom. His ministry, of which one usually considers only the human exterior, is first and foremost turned towards God. If he gives himself to souls it is to give them to God. His apostolate is not mere philanthropy; it is eminently theological. One can say of him, from a completely different point of view, what St. Paul says of the ordinary faithful: "Whatever he does, he does for God's glory." (I Cor., 10: 31.)

The Man of Sinai

It is here that the "character" plays its profound part: in all that he does, in all that he is, consciously or not, the priest represents and pledges His Lord and Master. Freedom leaves him forever. He is a tied man. Should he forget it, public opinion will not. Indisputably it sets the priest apart; it ranks him in the category of "sacred." For the crowd he is not a man like other men. Even, should he seek, as we shall declare it to be his right and his duty to do, to make himself one with "mortal men like themselves" (Acts 14: 14), he will always

[8] "Lætus obtuli universa."

[9] Encyclical, "The Catholic Priesthood."

remain "quite different," a "solitary." Like Moses, the priest is the man of Sinai. Like him, and more so, the Lord has made him "powerful and solitary." The priest must always remember it: when the time comes to fight on the plain, one part of him, the higher part, must remain upon the mountain in the cloud.[10] Until the end of his life, unto the end of time, he will be a man of mystery.

PROPHET

First he is God's prophet. Scripture and the Fathers insist on the fundamental dignity of the "ministry of preaching." (Acts, 5: 4.) St. Augustine dares to say: "The word of God is not less important than the Body of Christ." And St. Gregory compares the preaching of the Gospel to childbirth. "Whoever is brother and sister of Christ in believing, becomes His mother in preaching; one can say, in fact, that he brings the Lord to birth, whom he has infused into the heart of his hearer, and he becomes mother by his preaching if, by his voice, the love of God is engendered in the soul of the neighbor." [11]

Dispenser of the Word

So the priest is a dispenser of the Word, not only at the sacred Table but each time he preaches the Gospel.

He will not turn a deaf ear to the injunction of Isaias: "Cry aloud, never ceasing, raise thy voice like a trumpet-call, and tell my people of their transgressions." (Isaias 58: 1.) In season, and out of season, he will carry to his human brethren the word of God, eternal and always efficacious. His must be no timid voice; it must make no concessions and permit no reticence, such as might be allowed in human pleading. As minister of the Word, the priest will not "like so many others, adulterate the word of God," but he will "preach it in all its purity, as God gave it to us . . . in Christ." (II Cor., 2: 17.)

The first loyalty of the prophet is to add nothing and subtract nothing from the force of his message; it is to receive it from heaven to spread it on earth.

[10] Deut. 9:9-11; 25; 10:1, 10, &c.
[11] St. Gregory, Hom. III. in Evang.

Witness of the Truth

One of the principal services the priest renders to the world is to tell the truth. Amid the babble of propaganda and the clamour for a following, his voice must resound, intrepid and grave, bearing witness to the truth . . . to the light.[12] Since God "has seen fit to entrust us with the work of preaching," he will be able to speak so as to "earn God's good opinion, not man's, since it is God who scrutinizes our hearts. He will never use the language of flattery . . . nor will it be an excuse for enriching himself; he will never ask for human praise." (1 Thess., 2: 4-7.) Cost what it may, cost his hearers what it may, he will dare, when he must, to upset idols, to denounce injustice, to beard established powers. He must remain in the great line of the prophets. His voice must re-awake the terrible and heartrending accents of the great "seers" of days gone by. If there is one thing which the New Law has not come to abolish in the Old Law, it is that spiritual liberty, that right of speaking in the name of the Only Truth. "There is no imprisoning the word of God." (II Tim., 2: 9.) It is not for nothing that the deacon, the official reader of the Gospel in church, should receive the virtue of fortitude; he knows to what he is exposing himself, when in the society of men, he opens that Book which is like no other.

Minister of Disquietude

If Christ "makes of his ministers a burning fire" (Ps. 103, 4), it is "to cast fire" (Luke 12: 49) on the earth." "I come not to send peace, but the sword." (Matt. 10: 34.)

The priest, like Christ, brings to humanity a gift without compare, that of *disquietude*. He must be the minister of disquietude, the dispenser of a new hunger and thirst. Like God, he calls "a famine upon the land." (Ps. 194, 16.) Obviously he does not act thus to sow a morbid fear in consciences already exacerbated by modern life. The disquietude that the priest must spread is that fear of God, that torment for the infinite

[12] John, 18:37; 15:26-7; 17.

which has brought forth from the mystics and thinkers of every age such convulsive cries for relief.

The revolt he preaches is the insurrection of consciences; the order he comes to disturb is the calm surface overlying evil and hate. Like the hero and the saint, the priest in the world is no passive, docile citizen; he is not of the common mould. For all his genuine obedience to the civil authority, his way of being a good citizen is to be the eternal "malcontent," not to trouble social peace, but ever preparing for its deepest fulfillment. It is a paradoxical function which makes him the prophet of perfect *Being*, to reflect God's sovereign peace and stability in passing civilizations. As a prophet of the *Living* God, he cannot tolerate that calm which means death. He must shape the new age, as it comes to birth in the hearts of individual men and as it unfolds in history. And so We can say without contradiction: his way of spreading order is by calling it in question. His own way of obeying the laws of men is to recall them without ceasing to the Law of God.

WITNESS

If the priest is the prophet of the Most High, he is even more His witness; not on his own initiative but as sent by Christ: "that I may single thee out to serve me as the witness of this vision (Acts 26:16: cf 1:8), not only by his sword, but also by his life. He is the living sign of God.[13]

More precisely, the priest is the "Sacrament of Christ," that is, he is His efficacious sign among men.[14] One can even say, in a sense which will be understood after what We have

[13] Before representing the people before God, the priest is the *envoy* of the divine Redeemer, and because Jesus Christ is the Head of that Body of which Christians are the members, *he represents God* before the people over whom he has charge. The power entrusted to him has thus nothing human about its nature; it is supernatural and comes from God; "As my Father has sent me, so I also send you" (J:20, 21); "Go into the whole world and preach the Gospel to every creature" (Mk. 16:15-16) (Mediator Dei, p. 20).

[14] It is always from the "character" that this conclusion flows. While it is a reality, this character is also *an efficacious sign*. . . . It marks and makes recognizable the ministers of Christ the Priest. When it is exercised

been trying to explain, that the priest is "Jesus Christ among us," Jesus Christ "diffused and communicated."

Reflection, sign, proof, presence: all these functions the priest fulfills. Since his whole body is consecrated, even his gestures are not and cannot be merely profane. All that he touches is, so to speak, exorcised and blessed. By everything he does, by everything he is, he must convey a sense of the sacred. By his mere presence, he declares the existence of an order of invisible and superhuman values to a world which fails to recognize or attacks them. You might say that, as he reflects its mystery, he makes tangible God's infinity.

First of all by his prayer. By this he is defined by believers and unbelievers: in many languages the missionary is called "the man of prayer." His prayer ascends and offers to God the substance of the adoration of men. God condescends to give to men grace and pardon in return. We shall come back later to this essential function when we speak of the Mass.

Yet, even when the priest is not speaking to God of his brethren, or when he is not speaking to them about Him, his very existence is a living sign. He fulfills, even in his flesh, the folly of the Cross. Obedience, chastity, poverty; whether the priest has pronounced these three vows or not, whether he is secular or regular, he keeps them every day. For by such virtues, which once staggered the pagan world, he has permanently broken off relations with the world. We shall come back to this point later. But here and now we must see their loftiness, their transcendent origin, above all, their value, as a sign.

(at the Consecration, for instance) it causes the Priesthood of Christ to be present sacramentally under the sign of the celebrant.

"Christ is Priest in a sacramental way, not in a natural way as he was Priest in a natural way on Calvary. He is Priest as far as he is represented through the character of Order in the human priest, and as far as he acts through the human priest; in other words, if there were no sacramental priesthood in the Church there could be no sacramental sacrifice. If Christ such as he is now, in his natural state in glory, were directly the sacrificant, there would not be a correspondence between the priest and the victim, as the one would be in the natural state and the other in the sacramental state." (Vonier: "A Key to the Doctrine of the Eucharist," pp. 233-4.)

Poverty, Obedience

By *poverty* the priest first of all renounces money, and thus defends monotheism against the idolatry of human values. But in sacrificing such cultural and æsthetic values and such efficiency as gold affords to the privileged few, his priestly poverty becomes a manifest *sign* of the providence of the Father Who can be trusted unreservedly to look after future needs and to provide daily bread. In imitation of Jesus Christ, Who "had nowhere to lay His head" (Matt. 8:20), the priest's detachment manifests with silent dignity his complete belonging to God, and complete independence of men.

Obedience strengthens this testimony. By his ready and willing acceptance of the precepts and suggestions of the Church which are expressed through the Vicar of Christ on earth and his bishop, the priest signifies his unshakeable confidence in the Holy Spirit, the Guide and Inspirer of the Mystical Body of Jesus Christ. His humble yet proud submission as a free agent becomes also—in the face of the unbridled individualism or the despotic totalitarianism of this age—the sign of a Sovereign Authority and of an order found nowhere else, at once perfect and considerate of our most intimate desires.

Chastity

But above all the priest bears witness by voluntary chastity. Usually one bases ecclesiastical celibacy upon the service of souls and upon the service of the altar: *Imitamini quo tractatis*, says the Pontifical: "Be virgins, like the Immaculate Host which your consecrated hands touch." These reasons alone are most noble, but they do not seem to exhaust the full reality. Chastity is Love and a sign of Love; the watchful and absorbing. Love of the "jealous God" who has set some of his sons apart for Himself; the exclusive love of these "consecrated" men for Him Who infinitely surpasses all created beauty, all created love.[15] For there is only one force in the

[15] Of course celibacy is not in itself necessary for the priesthood. It became general in the West only from the commencement of the 5th century. In the East—in the Uniate churches, which alone we are here

world which is strong enough to overcome love; it is another Love, a stronger Love. By giving up human love, the priest gives to such souls as are not blinded by prejudice—and even in the long run to them—evidence of a unique discovery of Happiness that is possible and can be found. *Deus meus et omnia.*

You see, then, dear brethren, the height to which sacerdotal chastity is raised. It is not merely a form of asceticism, adopted to make the apostolate more effective; it is the gauge of a future Kingdom in which God will be all in all, it is the anticipation of a spiritualized humanity.[16] It is the sign of the *Alliance* of love which unites men to God in a mystical marriage. This is partly the meaning of the bishop's pastoral ring. It is what is symbolized by the wedding ring which nuns wear as the seal of their spiritual marriage with the Lord Jesus.

It would seem beyond the possibilities of flesh and blood that men who, like the rest of mankind, are gripped by the desire to "possess the earth," by the joy of being free, by the

---

considering, a married clergy has continued up to our own days, except for Bishops, who are chosen from among the monks. But this example of the Eastern Church, which is always brought up against the celibacy of the Latin Church, provides on the contrary a new argument; for far from entrenching themselves in this traditional discipline, an ever greater number of priests and aspirants to the priesthood are renouncing marriage of their own accord for the reasons we have given above. Whatever there may be in this comparison with our brothers of the Eastern Church, what is to be stressed is this precise teaching: there is not, historically or theoretically, any essential incompatibility between the priesthood—which is a power and a function—and marriage—which is a state of life, and a means of sanctification. But there is, in the light of given psychological and sociological laws, a proper suitability, and, so to speak, a "pre-established harmony," between divine investiture and total consecration of body and soul.

It can be seen how much this doctrine and practice of the Church is bound up with Saint Paul's explicit and well-known teaching affirming the superiority of the state of virginity over that of marriage (Cor. 7:25), a doctrine that echoes the suggestions of Our Lord Himself. (Matt. 19:12; 22:30.)

[16] "Our chastity is not a mutilation, nor a throwback to a primitive civilisation, but on the contrary, an immense advance towards the future; it has an eschatological value and draws the present world, where we remain, towards that future world, to which we already belong." (Gray, "Priestly Love and Chastity," Masses Ouvrièrs, August, 1948, p. 16.)

need for being loved, should voluntarily give up their independence, submit their wills, and live a celibate life. The miracle lies in this: they are in the world and see its attraction, while at the same time they feel its temptations within themselves, and yet they are neither faint-hearted, weak, or callous, although they have renounced honors and the happiness of family life. The most telling lesson the priest can teach is taught by his own life.

SIGN OF CONTRADICTION

That this man does not live like others, this legate who speaks with a royal authority, is a challenge to other men; he is the *sign of contradiction*. Let him appear, and passions crystallize and coalitions form. He instantaneously lets loose "complexes" of revulsion or of love. He is the touchstone of conscience.

First because he intrigues them. He mixes with other men; he is like them in everything. Yet nevertheless there is something in him which escapes them; a secret that daily proximity does not fathom. Though near at hand, he is yet inaccessible; though completely open, he is yet mysterious. People think they understand him; he escapes all definition. He is adaptable, yet he always remains himself in a changing age; while he mixes with his fellow-men, no one weakens his consistency.

But this strange man is no stranger. Whether men open or close their souls to him, he is always present (even though unknown to them), like the prick of conscience or an appeal from God. A man thinks he is at peace, that he has done enough, and then the priest upsets his calm tranquility. You wish to escape him; he is met without fail on every road. You may think yourself autonomous, you may want to be free; suggestions and commands still come from the priest. That is why the priest in the world will always and everywhere be its adversary. He will never be forgiven for revoking and perpetuating, generation after generation, the One they thought they had suppressed for ever. Like Christ, the priest is the corner-stone, the living corner of the Kingdom of Heaven. The priest is no paternal counsellor or compliant citizen; he is like God, a being of terror.[17] He is the man of battle. As Jacob fought with the Angel until dawn, so the priest is at death grips in the lists with the Angel of Darkness until the dawn of endless day. Like St. Michael he engages the Dragon, and drives him out from his lair in hearts, crushing one by one his ever-resurgent heads. And this is not mere fancy. For, although too often forgotten, one of the orders he has received makes the priest an Exorcist; he has the power and the mission to expel the devil.[18] "Let him do it," the Ritual commands, "with a sovereign authority. . . ."[19]

Suffering Servant of Yahweh

"But also," the same text continues, "with much faith, humility, and fervor." These last words, dear brethren, show us the nature of the battle. If the priest is the hero of the drama, the champion of giant stature, he is not armed with the rage of the proud man nor with human strength, but with the humility of the Gospel and the folly of the Cross. He is the man of "contradiction" and the herald of the Kingdom of Heaven on the world—after the example of His King—through gentleness and the acceptance of suffering.

Attacked by "an enemy of his' '(Matt. 13:25), men hold it against this brother who excels them for telling them the truth. "Truth engenders hate," remarks St. Augustine.[20] "If the world hates you, be sure that it hated Me before it learned to hate you." (John 15:18.) The priest will not be surprised at lying accusations.[21] He will see in them a proof that he is walking in Christ's footsteps. (Gal. 1:10.)

"It is because you do not belong to the world, because I have singled you out from the midst of the world, that the world hates you. No servant can be greater than his master. They will persecute you just as they have persecuted me."

[17] Ps. 46; Cant. 6:3.

[18] "Exorcistam oportet abjicere dæmones" (Pontificale, Ordination of Exorcists).

[19] "Exorcismos faciat cum imperio et auctoritate" (Ritual).

[20] Serm. 10 in Nov. Serm.

[21] Ps. 69; John 15:25.

(John, 15:19, 20.) Relentless in the spiritual combat, unyielding in the defence of those entrusted to him, the minister of Christ when he himself is attacked reveals the tragic image of "the servant of Yahweh," spoken of by Isaias and fulfilled by Jesus.

He is "despised and the most abject of men, a man of sorrows . . . he is wronged and he submits, not protesting but like a lamb is led to the slaughter." (Is., 53:3-7.) He holds his peace, because he understands. He knows that his fellow-citizens "oppress the just man because he is contrary to their doings." (Wisd., 2:10-12.)

Above all, he knows that the Redemption is entrusted primarily to him, and that it does not operate without the Cross. A mediator, he has to offer himself, like Christ, as an expiatory victim. "Surely he hath borne our infirmities and carried our sorrows . . . he was wounded for our iniquities . . . and by his bruises we are healed." (Is., 53:4-5.) Read this chapter of Isaias again slowly and you will see whether it has not come true in many dramatic ways in ancient and modern history.

In human society the priesthood has fulfilled, and will unfailingly exercise, with a continuity which by itself alone would be an apologia, a new function, an office of its own, than which there is no greater love (John, 15:13): the function of suffering persecution, the office of martyrdom.

Artisan of Peace

The priest on earth, because he belongs to God, belongs to no one else. At the service of all, he belongs strictly to no one. He belongs to "the order of Melchisedech" and is, like him, "without father, without mother, without genealogy." (Heb., 7:3.) Witness of the Father, "who makes his sun rise on the evil and equally on the good" (Matt., 5:43), he is no one's prisoner: family, race, nation, none have the right to monopolize him. He is the "universal" brother;[22] he has his duty to all alike, hoping to reconcile all in Jesus Christ. Thus—and there is no gainsaying it—because he is no one's, he belongs to

[22] So Père de Foucauld styled himself.

all. Mediator in the sight of God, logically he becomes the mediator among men.

In our days—the vestige of an age-long impregnation of consciences by the Gospel—popular feeling has a very vivid appreciation of the fact that God is for everyone. God does not take sides. So it is with the priesthood. It is above class, party, divisions. This is an important message for our modern world where so many antagonistic ideas are mutually exasperating. In the subconscious mind of the masses, and despite their opposition—there is a "priesthood category," a common idea which is vague but moving in its implications. He is conceived as an asset held in common, an undivided inheritance, who is brought in at times of crisis or of joy, national or individual. This point of view is based on reality. The priest, by affirming unceasingly the common destiny of us all, in contemporary society is, and must be, the artisan of Peace.

Model and Something More

A craftsman of peace yet a minister of disquietude, an apocalyptic warrior and yet a suffering servant, the priest is an enigma to the world. He is at once "alike" and "quite different," in turn a model for his brethren—*forma gregis ex animo* (1 Pet., 5:3), and a scandal (1 Cor., 2:23), beyond understanding. Although by this mystery he baffles the world, he is thereby its salvation. If he is not its standard of human nature, it is because he is much more. His way of being an example and a "measure" among men, is to be "measureless," beyond measure. The priest's inestimable value to the world is that he obliges it to stop being self-sufficient and makes it seek elsewhere—in a higher World—the reason for its existence and Redemption. Strange destiny of the priest; to be of the World but not of it; to be of the world just because he is not of it. Until the end, this innate paradox will arm his brethren against him; he will be refused his rights in the world. Yet, till the end, this peerless "stranger" will be the salt to combat insipidity, the hope of rescue from the wreck. The first function of the priesthood in the world is to prevent it from becoming a closed society. Its first duty is to remain transcendent. The world can only save itself by becoming superhuman. It can only become fully the City of men by becoming the City of God.

MAN AMONG MEN

"Chosen from among his fellow-men . . . made a representative of men." This is of central importance. The priest is taken from his fellow-men in order to be sent back to them. He is the man of God, so as to become the man of men. There is no mediation without these two aspects together. We must repeat it: a priest's powers are not given to him for himself; they are powers "ordained," ordered to the redemption of the world. The priest is bound to God, but he is also bound to mankind.

One of Them

This means two things: that he is a man; and that he must act like one.

He is man by his origin. As he comes from every social milieu, he knows their limitations and failings through his own limitations and secret desires. He, too, knows "what is in man" (John, 2:25), for he is made of body and soul; a confused mixture in which the soul only slowly becomes "mistress of the body which it animates." One can never say often enough: "He is *altogether* like his brethren." Like them he feels hunger, fatigue, joy, discouragement; he is subject to sickness and death, to error and even to sin. But it is just this that gives him his letters of credence. "He is qualified for this by being able to feel for them when they are ignorant and make mistakes, since he, too, is all beset with humiliations." (Heb., 5:2.) Thus he has "put on our ills not as fortunate men have pity on the unfortunate, but as the unfortunate have pity on one another by knowing a common misery." [23]

Throughout history—from the time of the "care upon tables" (Acts, 6:2) until the time of St. Vincent de Paul and St. John Bosco—the priesthood has never stopped caring for the suffering and the sinful with a special solicitude.

[23] Bossuet, "Meditations on the Gospel," 25th day.

Eternal Aspect and Temporal Aspect

But a full share in the lot of humanity involves another consequence: the priesthood has an eternal aspect and a temporal aspect. It is transcendent and timeless, yet contingent and variable. It is unchangeable in its nature, but unstable in its frail forms. The priest, though marked spiritually with the arms of God, is also visibly marked by his century, his surroundings, his heredity. Clothes, language, culture, hardships encountered: all these, according to epoch and country, distinguish the ministers of Christ. And rightly so! Otherwise we are likely to fall into the double mistake, already noted in Our pastoral on the Church, of confusing the priesthood with its temporal forms. It may mean "canonizing," in the name of a badly-understood tradition, a temporary adaptation of method. This is pastoral, "ultra-conservatism," or it may mean sacrificing the priest's essential role of mediation for some passing means of expression. This is "evolutionism."

The Duty of Adaptation

To be a priest of the twentieth century, therefore, does not demand a slavish imitation of methods that were once valuable, nor in introducing new forms as a matter of principle. It means translating the message into contemporary terms. In a word, the priest must adapt himself. It would be a sad mistake (though it is sometimes made) to imagine that this adaptation consists in *imitating* slavishly contemporary manners. It does not follow that because a priest uses the latest refinements of technical invention or is up-to-date in the latest publications, that he will have the attention of his people. No doubt, today more than ever, he has the duty of being in the *avant-garde* of thought and culture. But if this knowledge does not proceed from, and is not accompanied by, a deeper understanding, which makes him one with the trials and the hopes of his fellow-men *from within*, they will never recognize him as one of themselves.

But while guarding against a too literal conception of adaptation, we should not fall into an opposite and more serious error; arguing from the fact that because the priest must be all things to all men, that he must remain apart from human particularities. This would be the negation of the principle of St. Paul: "With the Jews I lived like a Jew, to win the Jews . . . With the scrupulous, I behaved myself like on who is scrupulous, to win the scrupulous." (1 Cor., 9:20, 22.)

Renunciation and Acquisition

These words, often quoted, define the double task which falls on the apostle in general and the priest in particular: renunciation and acquisition. It means *renunciation* of his own particularities, of what is peculiar to himself: education, tastes, culture, and even mother tongue; but it means also *borrowing* from those he wishes to evangelize. He gives to them the essentials: the Gospel and the divine life. He takes what they have to give: ways of understanding and feeling previously unknown. As he is faithful in giving, so he should be docile in receiving. He must not think his message betrayed because it is translated into a new language; he must not consider it a weakness if he makes himself acceptable to them. Although he is a "sign of contradiction" he does not have to stir up trouble. The opposition he meets as God's witness should not arise from any clerical inflexibility, or vindictive bitterness, or obtuse sectarianism, all of them as useless as they are ridiculous. Far from maintaining a breach, the priest will do all he can to make them love in him the true likeness of Christ, to break down "the wall that was a barrier." (Eph., 2:14.)

The Priesthood and Sociology

It is a fact that this wall is still standing. It is a long and thick partition which divides into two closed camps the Church and the City of men. The first priestly duty of our days is to appreciate this fact and look straight at the world. It is an anxious moment.

The development of the Church will depend, probably for a long time, on this stopping for a moment, this pause for silence and prayer. The priest of today, whether after fifty years of the priesthood, or on the morning of his ordination, must ask himself what he is to do, confronted with an horizon dark with the smoke of factories, in the face of universities and laboratories, which produce as many problems as discoveries. The workers he sees at the factory gates, how can he become like them, how can he become their brother?

Hundreds of priests are asking themselves this question. And many have already found the answer. Salvation does not come from techniques and stunts. This is not the time for harvest, but for sowing, and, to do that, therefore, for understanding. A magnificent effort is already under way. Plans, at once objective and the fruit of fervor, sketch, though still tentatively, the outline of priestly action in the modern world. You will understand, dear brethren, that this letter expressly avoids any attempt at synthesis. If attempted too soon, it would be erroneous and need endless revision. All that is needed now is to make it a matter of conscience not to launch out into an adventure without taking good care to understand.

The Barrier

Though too few have so far drawn the inference, the evidence of the existence of two Cities is clear. Albert de Mun had already seen it, for he wrote: "There is an abyss between the priest and the people, and that is why the Christian life no longer thrives in France. . . ." Without going so far as to say, as he did (for happily the situation has improved) that our meetings, and even our social activities "attract only converts," we can apply to a great number of our Christian activities, the remarks of de Mun that "around these little circles, deluded by their warmth, there swirls and lives and moves, and suffers and frets an entire people, knowing nothing of what is done or said or taught in them." [24]

This is borne out above all in the world of work; the more manual the trade, the more the worker is cut off from the Church. The Christian message strikes him as completely foreign. True he keeps a real nostalgia for the Gospel, but the Church has the appearance of being no more than a political

[24] Albert de Mun quoted by Brugerette. "The French Priest and Contemporary Society," III, 35.

power, and its actions tactics of self-interest. This indifference which is so manifest in the world of work is equally to be noted at every social level. Many men take their stand on a placid irreligion. They pretend they find in a completely secular life a sufficient justification of living. So on the social plane there is a divorce between the two societies. At one time parish and neighborhood group had the same name, because they coincided at every point. Today they have neither the same shape nor the same extension.

For something fundamental has happened: as in the beginning the Church again finds herself in a world that is partly paganized. But with this two-fold difference: on the one hand today's paganism is no longer like that of antiquity, primitive and still religious: it now has an organized mystique: atheistic humanism; and on the other hand, the Church is no longer young; she has centuries of Christianity behind her. Hence we can understand the difficulty. Our structures and methods are still for the most part those which were valid in the context of a completely Christian community. Our parishes, activities, and institutions have not grown as rapidly as have social entities and groups, especially in these last few decades. Nor have they moved in the same direction. They are turned inwards, and not outwards towards the humanism which is in process of development. Contemporary life flows on apart from Christianity; a great number of modern values are not touched by it; the current no longer runs through the Church. All develops as though Christianity were only concerned with a "dream world."

The Priesthood and the "Real World"

This separation applies even more to the priesthood. The sorrow and anguish of modern priests is to feel that the "*real world*" exists and is being built without them, and that they are strangers to it. When they examine their life, they realize that the greater part of their ministry is devoted to the faithful flock. But with this difference, that the right proportions are reversed: whereas they should be seeking the lost sheep, in fact it is the lone sheep in the fold that occupies the greater part of their day.

Apart from the Eucharistic Sacrifice and Baptism, are the priestly functions—distributing the Sacraments, preaching, community prayer, parish works, teaching the catechism—to be performed only for the Christian people? Are they only meant for the faithful? It is true that at one time the only problem was that of preparing them for or bringing them back to the practice of the Sacraments. But today, in a secular world, does such pastoral activity attain its end?

Given this change of circumstance, must not methods be changed, too? Should we give up the emphasis on sacramental worship in favor of evangelization, or, on the contrary, whatever happens should we restrict ourselves to sanctifying those who are already baptized, so as not to interrupt the homage of adoration due to the glory of God, and to saving what we can? In short, must the priest of today be minister or apostle? That is what priests are asking themselves.

Without anticipating the answer, We can say that the first duty of a priest in the world is to be obsessed with the idea of making his work productive of good.

Whatever be the mission entrusted to him, in the Holy Ghost, by Holy Mother Church, he must each evening, before God, set out once again on his desk or his poor table two maps of the parish, with its districts, schools, or factories that he has received as his portion. Patiently and zealously he should compare, detail by detail, these two "master plans." The old one will be that of the Church in the Christian community, with its islands of influence, its acquired positions, its habitual practice. The other, that of the new society, with its swift expansion, its centers of spontaneous interest, its unexpected seethings. This priest, be he parish priest, curate, professor, or Catholic Action chaplain, should have no rest until the two plans overlap, and the two coincide to become but one City in truth and love.

This man will spend every hour of the day and night in planning the City to come on the basis of the City that is. No one can now accuse him of having no part in it. Men can no longer refuse to accept him as one of themselves. This "universal brother" has left everything that he may belong more fully to everything. God has only taken him to return him more completely and to free him, unreservedly, for all men, without exception.

The priest has understood this investiture, and heard this call. By his powers and by his whole life, he will truly be a savior, not only in the plan of the invisible Kingdom, but also at the heart of temporal civilizations.

The Two Plans of Salvation

It is in respect of these two plans, overlapping but distinct, that he must exercise his function of mediation. But, it is essential to recall, this mediation means nothing outside of the Church. It can only be exercised, by right and in fact, in her and through her. The priest is not an autonomous and extra mediator. It is the Church that is responsible for the salvation of mankind.

This means two things: an eternal Redemption and a temporal salvation. The former consists in causing men to be born again to the life that comes from the Son of God, by making them members of the Mystical Body, and by leading them, as a body, towards the "Parousia." This is the establishment of the Kingdom of God already on earth. But, while waiting for the heavenly Jerusalem, mankind has a temporal destiny. Gathered together in communities, national or otherwise, it strives to "possess the earth" and to create civilizations. It is the vocation assigned to it in Genesis (1:28.) In the fulfilment of this mission it can never succeed, granted the existence of sin, unless it is saved by Christ, and is animated by Christian charity and Christian hope, which alone will prevent it from using for its own destruction those things which should make it great and free.

The Church, the living continuation of the unique Mediator, can alone accomplish this salvation, in its double perspective.

The Church in this effort is undivided: it is all that she is, for the whole Body of the Redeemed participate in the priestly mediation of Christ. Not alone the Hierarchy, but priests and people, inseparably united. These latter, Pope Pius XII recalled, "are found in the front lines of the life of the Church; *through them the Church is the vital principle of human society*. Consequently, the laity especially should always be conscious not only of belonging to the Church but of *being the Church*—i.e., the community of the faithful on earth under the guidance of their common head, the Pope, and of the Bishops in communion with him." [25]

The conclusion is clear: the world's salvation does not depend on the priest alone, but on the priest with and through Christians. He has, none the less, a specific role in relation to them which we have now to examine more closely, a role which varies according to the two redemptive missions we have just distinguished.

THE PRIEST AND THE PEOPLE OF GOD

The Church exists to incorporate and unite all men in Christ, in one single family for the glory of God and their own eternal beatitude. So its first mission is to announce the Gospel to men of every race, language, nation, class, and civilization, inviting them to share by Baptism in the divine Life which is in her.

This duty of "witnessing" and preaching is given in its fullness by the delegation of Christ to the Apostles alone and their successors the bishops, and then to priests, their "cooperators." [26] But, by their Baptismal character and their Confirmation all the faithful are called and made able to fulfill this religious function to humanity.[27]

[25] Pius XII, Allocution to the Consistory, February 20th, 1946.

[26] "Co-operatores ordinis nostri" (Pontificale, Ordination of Priests).

[27] In reality, if they are examined closely, it is the Sacraments of Baptism and Confirmation which impose, among other obligations, that of the apostolate, that is to say, spiritual help for one's neighbour. In effect, by Confirmation, we become soldiers of Christ. And by (Baptism) . . . we become members of the Church, that is to say, of the Mystical Body of Christ. Between the members of this Body . . . there must be a solidarity of interests, a reciprocal communication of life . . . one member must help another; no one can remain inactive; each receives, each must give in his turn." (Pius XI: Letter to the Patriarch of Lisbon.)

Priesthood and Laity

Based on the doctrine and tradition of the Church, this "participation of the lay folk in the hierarchic apostolate" has been consecrated and has, as it were, found a new reality in the definitions of Catholic Action given by Popes Pius XI and Pius XII.[28] Texts abound, but We shall do no more than refer you to them, for Our purpose is not to treat directly of the problem of the laity but only to show that only with them and through them the mediation of the priest has meaning and is complete.[29]

This is true even in the specifically supernatural domain of grace, the extension of the Kingdom of God. "Such apostolic labor done according to the spirit of the Church," writes Pope Pius XII, "in a way consecrates the layman and makes him a

[28] It is a matter of urgent necessity that the laity should in some way take their part in the hierarchical apostolate of the Church. Instructed by priests who also take care of their spiritual formation, and living an integral Christian life, these lay people prepare the way for the light of the Truth, and for the sanctifying action of grace in environments cut off from the Church or hostile to her action. . . . From this the fact clearly emerges that the mission of the laity is, in a certain sense, the very mission of the sacred hierarchy and of Jesus Christ, that is to say, to procure supernatural life for other souls, to make it grow, and to defend it. In consequence, their activity is a precious aid and a necessary complement of the priestly ministry. And it is by reason of this remark that We have addressed to both hierarchy and people, from the beginning of Our Pontificate, a paternal invitation for the faithful to be suitably prepared and organised in view of this apostolate, which We have defined as *the participation of the laity in the apostolate of the hierarchy*, and which We have called *Catholic Action* (italics in the text).—Pius XI: Letter to the Episcopate of the Philippines, January 18th, 1939.

[29] "For the Church consists of the faithful primarily . . . the laity, the Christian people . . . and the clergy have no raison d'etre in the community except to direct it, give it spiritual protection, and keep it in order. The clergy for the people, not the people for the clergy. Apart from the people, the clergy are inconceivable; they are surrounded by the community, formed in it, fed by it. The first and natural state of the Christian is to be a layman; the priest is a layman made a priest. . . . The Christian people is the nourishing soil of the Church. It is to them by definition that everything comes back, and on them all depends."—(Canon Leclercq: "La Vie du Christ dans l'Eglise," p. 185.)

minister of Christ in the sense in which St. Augustine explains it: When you hear, brethren, Christ saying, 'Where I am, there My minister is also,' be careful not to think only of faithful bishops and clerics. You also, in your way, should be the servants of Christ by living worthily . . . by preaching His name and His doctrine wherever you have the opportunity. . . ." [30]

An Undivided Apostolate

Thus, the apostolic task of the priest is clear. Faced with mankind which needs to be saved, he will not say "I," but "we"! The complete instrument of evangelization is not the baptized person, nor the priest alone, but the Christian community. The basic cell, the unit of measurement in the Apostolate, is everywhere like a kind of "organic compound," the inseparable duality priesthood—laity.[31]

Do not imagine, however, dear brethren, that they are on the same plane. On the contrary, they contribute realities and tasks that are complementary.[32] These do not result from the nature of the work, but, as we have seen, from the will of Christ, the depth and goodness of which the history of Christianity marvellously illustrates: the priesthood, given from on high, shows itself as a *service*.[33] The priest is at the disposal of his brethren. Whether believers or unbelievers, they have rights over him, and he has rights over them. In a word, he is their head, and he gives them life.

The primacy of the priest over the faithful, which we have seen to be derived from his power of Orders and his power of jurisdiction [34] is first of all a *function of mystical unity*, or-

[30] In Ev. Jo. tract, 51, 15 *seq.*—Pius XII, "Summi Pontificatus."

[31] Many texts of Pius XI on Catholic Action refer, explicitly or implicitly, to the doctrine of I Cor. 12:4-30, on the building up of the Mystical Body and the interdependence of the members on the head and on each other.

[32] At least in the Apostolate. Where the Sacrifice of the New Law is concerned, it is Christ Himself (and thus the priest, who alone, by the Sacrament of Order, is His "instrument") Who is the agent of the Sacrifice.

[33] Matt., 20:17-28.

[34] In what concerns the jurisdiction of the simple priest.

dained to the life of the "Christian community." It is not to be exercised in a despotic manner, but rather as an *efficient direction* which includes all the religious activities of the People of God; liturgy, Sacraments, instruction, services, &c., "so that," as the Apostle says, "all in the Church may be done with right order." [35]

"The Church can count on the collaboration of the clergy and of the laity," writes Pope Pius XII, and the "sovereign condition of all legitimate and fruitful collaboration in the hierarchic apostolate (is) a filial dependence in regard to those whom the Holy Spirit has appointed to rule the Church of God." [36] It was the last testament of Pius XI: "One thing which our already long experience has taught us is that in all countries the fate of Catholic Action lies in the hands of the clergy. . . ." [37]

Head and Giver of Life

The authority which links the Hierarchy with the Head of the Body is also its source of life.[38] The priest is neither the equal nor the delegate of Christians! He is their *Father*. First of all because he fathers them into divine life by faith and by Baptism, of which he is the ordinary minister.[39] Having caused

[35] "Cuique cœtui præsident sacerdotes, altari, sacrificio, sacramentis, exhortationibus, correctionibus, catechesi, divins præconiis et quibusque aliis ecclesiasticis, officiis ac sacris exercitationibus, ut omnia, sicut ait Apostolus, in Ecclesia *cum ordine fiant*. Ergo præesse in Ecclesia, absente Episcopo sacris quibusque officiis, proprium Presbyteri munus est." Catalanus, Pontific Rom.

[36] Pius XII: Letter to French Episcopate, March 4th, 1945.

[37] Pius XI: Letter to Episcopate of Philippines, January 18, 1939.

[38] Any opposition between the faithful, retaining the charisma and the "Spirit," and the Hierarchy as merely a juridical institution, subordinate and devitalised, is contrary to scripture, history, and experience.

[39] "The motherhood of the Church in the strict sense pertains not to the whole community, but to those persons endowed with the fruitfulness and the pastoral power by which the children of the Church are begotten, reared, and guided. In a word, it belongs to the fathers of the Church. We call them "fathers" because of their natural sex character, which in conformity with propriety is demanded by Christ for the carrying out of the higher offices in the Church. But if their function in the Church is considered formally according to its supernatural side, and if attention is

them to be spiritually reborn, he nourishes his children until their death. (I Thess., 2:7-8.) "Steward of God's mysteries" (I Cor., 4:1)[40], he feeds them unceasingly by giving them the Bread and the "Word," of which he is the minister (Acts, 4:4) and teacher.

Here again, there is no opposition: there would be no transformation of the world without the laity; but there would be no laity without the priesthood. The right and duty of Christians is to be apostles. But the right and the principal function of the priest is to father, train, and sustain a militant laity. In this the priest is irreplaceable. He is not merely an apostle: subject to the bishop, he is apostle *par excelence*, apostle by the duty of his state. Moreover, he is head and leader of the Church's priestly mediation, which belongs to him alone by his powers and his office, but in which all the people are allowed to share.

Minister or Apostle

Here We face the same dilemma, but now We can resolve it. It is always the same question. Faced by a growing mass of unbelievers, is it not sinful to reserve one's strength for the scattered flock, to devote one's life to a favored few? Should not things like Evening Service, processions, Benediction—and, much more, parish administration—give way to the "ministry of preaching" (Acts, 4:4)? The question goes even deeper: which comes first, administration of the Sacraments or spreading the Gospel?

The life of Christ, as well as the doctrine and the practice of the Apostles, shows that these two functions are not mutually exclusive but complementary. If the Gospel is preached, it is with the purpose of incorporating men into the Mystical Body

---

focused on their dignity rather than on their persons, they obviously have a maternal character. Thus viewed, their persons are seen in a special way to be wedded to the God-man in His Holy Spirit: they are persons through whom the God-man begets, rears, and educates His children."—(Scheeben, "The Mysteries of Christianity," pp. 555-6.)

[40] I Cor. 4:1; cf. Tit. 1:7; which the Vulgate translates as "Dei dispensatorem."

of Christ by Baptism. The Good News is the announcement of salvation, of the Fatherhood of God: expressions which imply two other realities: the forgiveness of sins, and the supernatural life. Since the apostle makes known and promises this life, he must give it. How is he to do so, except through the Sacraments, and above all else through the Eucharistic Sacrifice? It alone, and the public prayer which surrounds it, will enable newcomers to the worship "in spirit and in truth" (John, 4:24) to adore God worthily across the abyss which Christ alone can bridge. To put it in a better way, if preaching tends towards worship, as towards its ultimate end, it also finds its efficacy there. For the object of our preaching is to give the Faith, or to increase it. This is the divine work *par excellence*, and it means that the apostle must have an intimate contact with the genuine sources of grace.

Pastor of the Faithful

To be a pastor the priest must be both a minister and an apostle. But to whom? The faithful themselves need this double ministry: the Gospel and the sacramental life. So priests, already overburdened because of their small numbers, wonder whether they ought not to make a choice and confine themselves either only to believers or only to those outside the Church. The definition and experience of Catholic Action answers their doubts; not by a magic formula, in this realm of mystery and free gift, but by throwing a light on the way of solution.

The priest, as a minister of God, and the father of a community which, through him, must render to the Lord the worship which is His due, has charge of the souls of the people entrusted to him, whether they are "inside" or "outside" the Church.

He belongs to all, equally and without distinction. So he would have a poor grasp of what the Church expects of him, if he thought that the sad circumstances of contemporary atheism entitled him to neglect the faithful. Progress will not be made with unbelievers by jeopardizing the faith, charity, and moral life of believers, or by allowing the source of their apostolic generosity and spiritual energy to dry up. The care of the baptized must not be considered as a ministry of secondary importance, still less as a necessary evil. On the contrary, it is the open road, the predestined passage of grace, to the masses who are separated from Christ.

So the priest must devote all his efforts to the sanctification of Christians; by giving them, from the cradle to the grave, the sacraments of life; by visiting the sick, by preaching, by caring for the beauty and the intelligibility of the Liturgy and so on.

For the Unbelievers

Nevertheless, though the Word of God is always the same, those who receive it differ. The charity by which all must live is translated into the precise duties of fathers and mothers of families, of workers, of employees, of technicians, of business executives. Sanctifying them means helping them to discover their own vocation and to fulfill the responsibilities which Providence has given them.

Obviously this kind of formation does not affect only those whom it reaches; it is meant for those outside the Church, too. In this way the traditional ministry should be renewed. In everything and everywhere it should contribute to the creation and education of the faithful so that they will become the *Christian leaven*. If they are backed up by an understanding and realistic priest, who meets them on their own level in order to raise them by degrees to the point of giving themselves completely, the faithful will bring about a profound transformation of their whole environment.

In this pastoral effort, priests must guard themselves against two excesses. The first excess is that of restricting themselves to an indirect apostolate, as if their sole right and power were to form leaders, who should alone be the witnesses of Christ in the paganized world. Any systematic distrust of the efficacity of a direct priestly witness is mere prejudice, and should be treated as such. On the other hand there is a very real temptation for the priest, in view of the time-lag inherent in the methods of Catholic Action, of trying to by-pass it, and devoting himself exclusively to "the direct apostolate." Such an attitude is founded upon a false conception of the mission of the laity. They have their own vocation: to live their ordinary lives in a Christian way, and so be witnesses to Christ. This conception of a lone apostolate leaves out, also, the indissoluble link which must always bind the community to the priesthood, and bind him to them.

Indirect Apostolate and Direct Witness

These last two criticisms apply only to an idea of the ministry which excludes or neglects the collaboration of the lay people. They do not refer, on the contrary, to certain forms of immediate contact which the Holy Ghost Himself seems to have inspired in recent years.

The sacerdotal function, always in essence the same, can take, and has in fact taken in the course of the ages different forms and functions, in which stress is laid in turn on its royal, prophetic, or sacrificial character. Thus it is that a priest, and more particularly a bishop, has become at different times "paterfamilias," ruler, "defender of the city," regent, judge, and so on; in some cases there was an excessive encroachment on the temporal; in others he had to supply the lack of responsible people to serve the Common Good. The commitment of the "priests of the mission"—the poverty of our language must excuse the tautology—is to some extent bound up with present historical conditions and sometimes with local needs.

Essentially, however, it responds to a deeper need felt by the priest; the necessity of experimenting in order to understand and redeem the people. So, in certain circumstances, of which the Hierarchy is the sole judge, the need for an intimate penetration into certain areas of life from which the Church is excluded may lead to the seconding of priests, carefully *picked* and *trained*, for this difficult mission. The highest authority of the Church affirmed this recently to the Capuchin Friars Minor on the occasion of their General Chapter: "Modern times demand that this apostolate be exercised not only in the churches—too often deserted by those who would benefit by being there—but also whenever the opportunity is offered to priests, to exercise the sacred ministry, in the countryside, in workshops, factories, hospitals, prisons, and whenever they are in the midst of workers, becoming brothers among brothers, to win them all to Christ. Let them unite their apostolic toil with the sweat of the workers. . . . Commit yourselves to . . . this apostolate . . . without counting the cost. Penetrate to the heart of the mases as mediators of peace. . . ." [41]

The Priests of the Mission

In too many so-called Christian countries, and in France in particular, the Church, in spite of the existence of buildings and of priests, no longer exists for the majority of men. They no longer have the chance of deciding whether they are for or against Christ. An enormous accumulation of prejudices has completely deformed the face the Church in their eyes. The priesthood is even less accessible to them. Wherefore it is a work of charity for priests to become witnesses again, less to conquer than to be a "sign." It has been well said that to be a witness does not mean to spread propaganda, or even to create an impression, but to *create a mystery*. It means living in such a way that one's life would be inexplicable, if God did not exist. They are witnesses, much less by the external difference in their mode of life than by their firm determination to establish with the disinherited masses a genuine community of destiny. The life led by these priests is neither escapism, nor a means of social study, nor even an attempt at "conquest"; it is a vocation of redemption. Work is not for them a pretext or opportunity to make propaganda, but the "act of naturalization" made by a priest to join the people, among whom he will no longer be a foreigner; it means the suffering, painful sharing, of the human lot. Here indeed it would be well to recall and develop what We had to say of the priest as the suffering servant of the Lord.[42]

Only One Clergy

But the priest in taking on, by an act of complete renunciation, the whole of human distress and aspirations, is not ex-

[41] Letter of Pius XII to the Minister General of the Capuchins, December 12th, 1948.

[42] cf. also II Cor. 4:20 sq. Phil. 2:17.

empted—apart from exceptional vocations which only go to prove the rule—from gathering together and training and sustaining lay leaders, to help them become the leaven in their environment.

So there are not two kinds of clergy, one missionary and the other not. Those priests who are committed to sharing the full life of the people are not to be thought of as foreshadowing the future type of priestly ministry. But neither are they "no more than skirmishers; they are the spearhead of a whole army of clergy on the march. . . . Catholic Action laity, specially detached priest-missionaries, and missionary parishes [43] are thus seen to be all three necessary. *It all amounts to one great endeavor by the Church to become missionary*. There is nothing to suggest opposition between them. A missionary clergy or a missionary parish would both be inconceivable without the lay mission of Catholic Action." [44]

Thus the priest's normal relation with the people of God should be a complementary alliance with them as their father and their leader. His missionary task will show the effects of this. At first it will not consist of baptizing individuals, but, according to the well-worn phrase, in "planting the Church," right among the masses, in every milieu.

Pastoral Theology and Spirituality

Such a program pre-supposes a tremendous effort. To start with, it calls for mental effort. The christianization of this new world is going to demand a real intellectual renunciation. Possibly for a long time we will have to break down the habit of certain "methods of mediæval Christianity." It is painful

[43] And grouped together. We repeat here the importance we attach to missionary deaneries or sectors—i.e., a group of parishes corresponding to a real unity; district, suburb, industrial area, geographical grouping, &c. Action taken in common, and carried out in close collaboration, through groups of priests and laity, otherwise fully independent in their territorial ministry, shows itself capable of solving the problem posed by modern life in the matter of information, religious and social initiatives, relief both material and intellectual, and so forth.

[44] Masses Ouvrières, July, 1948. Collective Editorial: "Mission and Catholic Action," p. 4.

enough, and will become more so, to shake off the limitations imposed by methods, perfectly justified in their own day, but enunciated by a theology which could only generalize from a Christian society. The essential effort, therefore, of analysis and synthesis, remains to be applied to a theological deepening of the idea of the priesthood, and to a parallel elaboration of a pattern of priestly spirituality. We mean here merely to stress the urgent need for this without suggesting even an outline, for that would be premature.

* * *

In the meantime, *the practical groundwork must be attempted.* We must not attempt to reduce or to harm the integrity of dogma or the transcendence of missionary work; nor to destroy what wisdom has built and what experience will always, or at least for a long time, show to be valuable; nor again to anticipate the decisions of the official Magisterium, by presenting it with a *fait accompli.* But, with all due respect and objectivity, to keep lawful authority informed of the concrete reactions of the masses; to sort out every real need from the passing fads of an age which so quickly makes the novel into the archaic; to make careful localized experiments and wait for experience and authority to draw the broad conclusions. This action should go along with pastoral activity, inspiring it step by step. It means great vision, and large-scale calculation, but also counting and checking details, allowing for objections, obstacles, or complete deadlocks. Something new must be built before the old can be torn down. But at the same time We must build without waiting, using provisional materials, rather than offering the faithful and unbelievers nothing better than plans for a promised Cathedral. The task confronting the present generation of priests and those who come after them will be one of thinking and planning and loving, in terms of the entire world, while with humble submission accepting reality with all its obstinate conservatism and inevitable flaws. The presence of the Church in the world of tomorrow very largely depends on the clear-headedness, prudence, and breadth of mind with which this is done.

THE PRIEST AND THE TEMPORAL ORDER

Although he is an apostle and promoter of the apostolate, the priest is still not responsible merely for the salvation of souls.

To start with, this is so because there is no such thing as a soul in isolation; souls inhabit men of flesh and blood. The people he invites to the eternal kingdom live on earth while waiting for the kingdom; they have here no lasting city. Willy-nilly the priest would have to reckon with the temporal order, for he meets it everywhere; in himself, for he is not an angelic immigrant; in others, for his message can only reach them through the language of the senses. Finally, though the City of God and the City of Man are distinct and often today sorely at odds, they are not just parallel orders but are intimately mixed together.

The "Catholic" Mission of the Church

But does this incorporation into human affairs involve the necessity of saving it? Can such a "temporal" order, seen by its very name to be transitory, come within the scope of an everlasting Church? Why should the supernatural bother with the natural? Does not man's struggle to control the earth and to build civilizations demand independence in things temporal?

It is not in any way our intention here to elaborate a "theology of the temporal order"[45] nor to re-examine the legitimacy of Catholics being "committed" to the City of Man, for we have recently described this as the urgent duty of every Catholic. This right and this duty—more so for them than for others—of "multiplying, and possessing the earth" (Gen., 1:28) has of recent years been frequently emphasized by the Papacy.[46]

[45] Although this is one of the objectives of greatest urgency and importance for contemporary theology, in widely different countries new ideas are multiplying very pleasingly in this line. From now on they should be encouraged and followed closely.

[46] "It is the Creator of all things who put into man's heart the irresistible urge to find even on earth the happiness fitted to him, and Catholicism approves of every legitimate effort of true civilisation and progress, rightly understood, to perfect and develop humanity." (Pius XI,

Based essentially on the power over all creation given to man by the Creator, it is also founded on the catholicity of the Church. Her mission is to baptize not only the whole of mankind but the *whole of man,* and *everything else through him.* The Church has to penetrate and win for Jesus Christ the whole of humanity with all its diverse traits at every period of history. Her mission is abolutely universal; nothing can remain outside it. Thus St. Paul defines her task: "to restore all things in Christ" (Eph., 1:10).

Does this annexation of all things to the kingdom of Heaven (a process which while progressive in fact is indeed in its intention complete) mean the suppression of the kingdom of the world, or the confusion of the two kingdoms?

Legitimate Autonomy

The official teaching of the Church is clear: there is to be neither confusion of the two powers nor mutual interference. There exists an order of things for which man is legitimately responsible. Grace does not suppress nature. While too lofty thus to lower and demean herself, the Church has also too much respect for what is human to desire to absorb it by any kind of theocracy, or to treat it like a minor, with a disingenuous paternalism. Everybody will recall the distinction made by Leo XIII between the Church and the State, both "perfect societies." "The Almighty has appointed the charge of the human race between two powers, the ecclesiastical and the civil, the one being set over divine, and the other over human, things. Each in its kind is supreme, each has fixed limits within which it is contained, limits which are defined by the nature and special object of the province of each, so that there is, we may

---

Caritate Compulsi, May 3rd, 1932.) "It would be wrong to interpret our words against materialism so as to deduce a condemnation of technical progress. No, we do not condemn what is a gift of God Who . . . has hidden in the bowels . . . of the earth, since the days of creation, treasures which the hand of man should draw from them both for his needs and for his progress." (Pius XII. Radio Message, Christmas, 1941.)

say, an orbit traced out within which the action of each is brought into play by its own native right." [47]

This principle, though not directly applicable to "imperfect societies" and the other temporal groups, can be applied to them, in various degrees, on the sole condition that they respect the superior order laid down by God. "The Church has no intention of taking sides against one or other of the concrete and particular forms by which different peoples or States tend to solve the gigantic problems of their interior organization as well as that of international collaboration, so long as these solutions respect the divine law. [48] The Church thus owes allegiance to no scientific or social or political system; much less does she take over "in the technical field, in regard to which she lacks both appropriate means and competence." [49]

The Temporal Order at Stake

Yet, although the temporal order maintains its freedom in the realms of structure and technique, the Church does not thereby forego her redemptive mission. There is an order of transitory things which, while not destined to survive in the heavenly Jerusalem, still calls for salvation here below. And this for two reasons.

Firstly, because of the close link between the supernatural salvation of souls and human society, in other words, the social institutions and daily realities which condition the development of the human person, and which can lead to its fulfilment, or to its degradation. Since the Church is the mother of men, she cannot remain indifferent to those human factors on which depends in part the eternal happiness of those who are or will become her children.

But there is more to it than this. In their very nature these earthly realities call for "redemption": Christ the King has a right to them. For His universal dominion extends far beyond persons, and demands the collective homage of institutions, of all mankind, and of the whole created universe.

[47] Leo XIII.—"Immortale Dei."
[48] Pius XII.—Christmas Message, 1942.
[49] Pius XI.—"Quadragesimo Anno."

THE VOCATION OF THE LAITY

These are the two reasons why every Christian should be committed to activity in the temporal order.[50] All must be committed, that is, every member of the Church; but the commitment is not identical in every case. So the priest faces a new question: what is to be his specific mission, by contrast with that of the laity, in regard to earthly institutions and values?

It is not fitting for the priest to take over secular affairs; that is the laity's business. Nor is this an arbitrary judgment; it is founded both on facts and on rights.

Presence and the Duties of State

The fact is that only the laity are truly present in the temporal order, since they live in it, and are in continuous and immediate touch with factories, homes, and districts. But their irreplaceable role comes neither solely nor mainly from this reason—it comes from their *vocation.* Placed by God at the head of a family, or of a firm, a member of a profession, it is the *duty of their state* to direct these institutions to their proper end, and to infuse into them the Christian spirit. It means an eminently constructive work which falls to their special lot, a work of which we were recently reminded by the Holy Father: "One cannot hope to solve these (anguishing) problems (of the world of work) by a negative attitude or a simple warning against false shepherds. What is needed is the active presence in factories and workplaces of pioneers who are fully conscious of their double vocation—as Christians and

[50] "The Church cannot shut herself up lifelessly in the hidden interior of her temples, and so turn her back on the mission entrusted to her by Divine Providence, of forming the complete man. . . ."—(Pius XII: Discourse to the new Cardinals, February 20th, 1946) "To work, then, my dear sons . . . do not remain passive in the midst of the ruins. Rise up and reconstruct a new social world for Christ."—(Pius XII, Christmas, 1943.) Thus, not only "Presence in the world," but "Progress." "There can be no question for a human soul, who considers history with the Spirit of Christ, of any return to the past, but only of the right road into the future and of not going too fast."—(Pius XII, May 13th, 1942.)

as workers—and who are bent on assuming their responsibilities to the full, knowing neither peace nor rest until they have transformed the environment of their lives to the demands of the Gospel. The Church, by this positive, constructive work, will be able to extend her life-giving action to the millions of souls for whom she has a maternal and ardent solicitude." [51]

Taking Charge of the Temporal

"Transform the environment of their lives," "double vocation as Christians and as workers": such words provide a complete program for the laity.

First, it is a professional and human vocation; the improvement of hygiene, security, conditions of work, and housing; a better distribution of goods and of employment; the promotion of the arts and of culture and scientific research, none of these can be secondary and optional activities for them. The attainment of such human goals cannot be a matter of indifference. The true Christian will give himself entirely, and without any ulterior motives of proselytizing, to these human tasks, and to fraternal collaboration.

But there is a specifically Christian task: apart from a few exceptional personalities, man is the slave of his environment. The most spiritual apostolate cannot neglect this humble but daily dependency. It is the magnificent task of the laity to make their environment a favorable atmosphere which will predispose souls to receive and to live the Christian message.

The Salvation of Groups

This duty of humanizing institutions and of making the natural order receptive to grace has become today a compelling obligation. Society, as it exists today, is characterized by a new and universal phenomenon: "socialization." The different community groups of former times, guilds, towns, provinces, &c., have been succeded by a complex fabric of collective influences and new social structures. Man is much less alone in face of his destiny, less alone to meditate on it, less alone to pick and

[51] Letter of Pius XII to Canon Cardijn, Chaplain-General of the Y.C.W., March 21st, 1949 (*New Life*, Vol. 3, p. 82).

choose. The world of our time is a complicated place. It no longer consists of autonomous individuals; each one belongs to an environment which has its own customs, duties, and myths. The laity must face up to this highly organized society. The humanization and sanctification of individual life is no longer good enough; what must be done is to christianize all these "social institutions" which constitute district, class, leisure activities, culture, cinema, and radio. They form, in fact, an environment of life and constitute a *reality* which is independent of the individuals who compose it and come under its influence.

We must be quite clear about this: the salvation of individuals cannot be carried out without some "salvation" of the world. There can be no question but that the social order exists for persons and not vice-versa.[52] Nevertheless, one could say that civilization itself is in need of sanctification, in every one of its problems, and its trends, each of which constitutes in itself a collective reality. In particular there are certain human conglomerations,[53] such as the village, or the town, or the nation, which may be considered as "moral persons" and which, although transitory, must because they are human groups submit to the divine law and to the rule of Christ the King.[54]

The Laity are Irreplaceable

Such is the irreplaceable misison of the laity. They have their own witness to bear, their specific problems to solve and reforms to be undertaken, all on their own responsibility. By giving them a free hand, the Church is not making the best of a

[52] "The common good . . . cannot . . . find its primordial law in the material prosperity of society, but much more in the harmonious development and natural perfection of man, to which the Creator has destined society as a means.—(Pius XII: "Summi Pontificatus.")

[53] "Just as," writes Pius XI, "those who live together as neighbors come to build up cities, so nature inclines the members of one trade, of one profession, whatever it is, to create corporative groupings, so much so that many consider such groupings to be organs of society, if not essential, at least natural."—(Quadragesimo Anno.)

[54] "Te nationum presides—Honores tollant publico—Colant magistri, judices—Leges et artes exprimant. Let the leaders of nations do Thee public homage. Let masters and judges honor Thee. May laws and the arts show Thee forth. (Feast of Christ the King—Hymn at Vespers.)

bad job and using them as substitutes until such time as she has reliable priests to take over the direction of the temporal order. On the contrary, she fully intends, without any ulterior motive, to confide to the laity the full responsibility for human society. The specialized movements of Catholic Action are specifically designed to train such a leaven.

The temptation, however, can be great for the priest, to assume functions other than his own, and for which the laity have a special vocational grace. He will have to resist it, even if, for the moment, "efficiency" is somewhat reduced. For his specific role never involves running the temporal order. There his competence ceases.

But his mission does not do so. For if secular functions are normally barred to him, it is his business to *inspire* Christian leaders. Their action, to be efficacious, presupposes a spirit of faith and practical charity which demands the enlightenment of Holy Scripture and Dogma. Above all, "they will find the strength to accomplish this work, which must seem superhuman, in the practice of a sacramental and eucharistic life which becomes ever deeper . . . in following loyally and generously the directions of the Hierarchy . . . and in a fraternal and happy cooperation with the other movements of Catholic Action, with a view to submitting the whole of society to the rule of God." [55]

The Priest as Spiritual Educator

The priest, as head of the mystical unity, must be the soul of this community and must link it with other Christian communities. It is up to him to nurture the interior life of the apostles of the temporal order.

He can never give too much time to this. The formation of consciences is no easy task. To start with, there can be nothing makeshift about it; it rests on the unchanging principles of Revelation, transmitted by the infallible Magisterium. Neither does it mean deducing a ready-made mechanical solution for any given case. Blue prints have no place in the moving and constantly changing context of these problems. The advice

[55] Letter of Pius XII to Canon Cardijn.

the priest gives to the leaders will have to follow, hour by hour, the inspirations of grace and the lines of conduct suggested by the Holy Ghost. It means real "direction of consciences," calling the priest to respect their freedom, and exacting from him a deep understanding of the environment he has to animate.

Pastoral Mediation and Self-Effacement

The priest, by being the soul and as it were vital principle of the Christian community, fully committed to the broad stream of human activity, truly guides the world. He does it indirectly, but none the less really. He stays in the background, only so that he can be of better service. The priest is failing in his vocation if he confines his efforts to the salvation of individuals: his parishioners are not only souls, but problems, social structures, a given section of space and time of the earthly city. This holds good for all degrees of the hierarchy. Its responsibility is not merely "horizontal" or geographical; it is now, as it were, "vertical" and enduring. The priest who inherits a part of the Church, in a parish, or a school, and so on, will have to render an account to later generations for the situation he has prepared for them. By that he will be judged. Therefore, while every form of clericalism, that is every confusion of jurisdiction, must be ruthlessly repudiated, the collective salvation and human perfection of the world is imposed on the priest as a duty.[56] All this on one condition: he must seek to reform it not from without, as is the way with laws and constitutions, but from within, by encouraging, through Christian leaders, a deep and freely willed adherence. In this he will be following the example of Our Lord. Not once in the Gospels is Christ seen to concern Himself with questions of civilization or progress. But he provided a leaven for them, by preaching and living His Beatitudes.

[56] "Let no member of the Church imagine that such an action (that of a missionary of labour) is foreign to the priestly ministry, under the pretext that it is exercised in the economic field; for it is precisely in this field that the eternal salvation of souls is in peril."—Letter of the Sacred Congregation of the Council to Mgr. Liènart, repeating the letter of Benedict XV to the Bishop of Bergamo.

THE PRIEST'S PRIVILEGE

As well as his role as an educator of consciences, the priest possesses a unique privilege which compensates beyond all reckoning for his withdrawal from the ordering of secular affairs. He is the one who is able to give meaning and divine value to the whole of human reality. It is not that baptized people are radically incapable of doing so themselves, for their Baptism has given them a certain share in the Church's priestly mediation, empowering them to act as a ferment in the paste of human society, as the leaven of Christ. But they have to carry out this transformation of creation at the level of action. The priest's work is in the *ontological* order, at the very root of being. And his prerogative is summed up in two words which imply, one positively and the other negatively, the same power he has over things: *exorcism* and *blessing*.

When the priest is called an exorcist nowadays, dear brethren, you spontaneously conjure up the picture of a power once often used but now hardly ever exercised except in missionary lands. The exercise of this power over evil spirits is, it is true, reserved by the Bishop to a very small number of subjects and cases. Yet the statement of the Pontifical is precise enough: "*Exorcistam oportet abjicere daemones.*" This injunction should no more surprise the twentieth century Christians than it did those of the Ages of Faith.

Scriptural texts abound which show that sin, committed at the instigation of the serpent, put Adam and his sons under the power of the devil. (John, 8:34.) Our Lord called the latter "*the prince of this world.*" [57] He made use of this title in the desert to offer Christ all the kingdoms of the world, "with their power and their glory" which he claimed "were entrusted to him, with power to give them to whom he would." (Luke, 4:6.) Christ's victory is not only over sin but also over Satan. (Rom., 16:20.) The Christian life carries with it the duty of resisting "the devil, who is your enemy, who goes about roaring like a lion, to find his prey." (I Pet., 5:8-9.)

There would be no more point in multiplying quotations

[57] John, 12:31; 14:30; 16:11; I. Cor., 2:6, &c.

than in drawing a wrong conclusion from them: Manichean dualism. The devil is not God's equal. He is His creature, and has only received from Him permission to tempt free man. But, as he is deceitful (Gen., 3:1), he knows how to assume the most different and the most successful forms. The disguises he adopts in this age of rationalism and discovery are subtle. He no longer makes use of visible appearances as in simpler times, but insinuates himself into the threshold of the thinking mind, and into the hand that takes and shapes. For a technical and naturalistic generation the fallen angel wears the appearance of intelligence, culture, and progress. In a world in process of unification he promises a unity very little like that which Christ left us in His priestly prayer at the Last Supper (John, 17.)

The everlasting temptation nowadays takes two chief forms.

Denial of God

Of the two, the denial of God is the graver, but is the less deceptive even when concealed. It is as old as the human race. It perpetuates Lucifer's refusal to serve, and Adam's naive self-sufficiency. One may recognize here, in passing, the exploit of Prometheus, and nearer to our own day the myth of Faust; the self-contained universe, and the would-be self-sufficient man. The autonomy of temporal society, legitimate so long as it does not close itself to the workings of grace, becomes blasphemous and anarchical when it becomes an autarchy jealous of its own power.

This conclusion is not mere theory. The immense collective effort of humanity to improve the condition of mankind and to make this world a joyous place has suddenly, without time to reflect, become possessed of astonishing means of discovery and control, not only of the universe, but also of the human person himself. The possibility offered by recent biological and psychological techniques of influencing the spiritual faculties of man by conditioning them, offers to scientists and to leaders of men a temptation out of all proportion to anything ever known before; namely, of creating, without God, a new Adam.

It will be one of the great missions of the priesthood of our time, in which enthusiasm for *homo faber* is mingled with doctrines of despair, to preserve the world from the pagan optimism of the superman as well as from an equally destructive pessimism. Its mediation, to those who regard this temporal order as an end in itself, will consist of reminding them repeatedly that it is only a stage towards eternity, and that they possess only an infinitesimal degree of being. The priest should follow, with sympathetic attention, the evolution of material techniques and the sciences of man, whether individual or social, so to prevent the world from becoming an ants' nest of slaves, even satisfied slaves, whose life and spirit would be dominated by a minority of omnipotent technicians. From his place in the background the priest will have to take the lead in exalting the humble and securing independence for the weak.

The Naturalization of Christianity

However, the priest will have to apply his powers of exorcism to more than atheistic mystiques; he must purify the effort of Christians themselves to transform and spiritualize the universe. For an insidious danger may lurk in this task which, We repeat, is a grave obligation for Catholics.

God's eternal design, according to the teaching of St. Paul, is truly to "restore all things in Jesus Christ" (Eph. 1:10), "First-born of all creation" (Col., 1:15), "in Whom all things subsist" (Col., 1:20). The Church has not limited the scope of this program. But there must be no confusion about the purpose of this universal consecration. Its end is not to deify human values for their own sake. This would no longer be Christianity but pantheism; God would be immanent in things, and hence they would be self-sufficient. No doubt, as the Fathers repeat, "God became man that man might become God." But if the Word took our flesh, it was to draw it after Him in His Resurrection, into the very "fellowship of God" (I John, 1:3). The Fathers often emphasize this double movement of the Incarnation of the Word. He came on earth to assume our humanity, and with and in it He made a solidarity of all creation. But after this He ascended to His Father with all mankind, drawing with Him in His train, as it were, the whole created universe. If they are not careful, some Christians will remember only the first part of the Incarnation, the transfiguration of all profane things through Christ's descent on earth. But by stopping half-way they are involved in the danger of divinizing the earthly state of things, and thus reducing the mystery of Christianity into a self-contained humanism. Of course, most of them would not get as far as this idolatrous glorification of worldly values. But the danger would remain of being too much attached to them and of reversing the right order by making them an end and not a means.

The Conversion of Humanism

This seduction, so obviously proceeding from the Tempter, will accompany the Christian in all his undertakings. He will often run the risk of losing himself in the very act of trying to save himself. At this stage the priest must step in. His specific role will be to screen the inspirations of the men who are building and transforming the universe, and to purge from their undertakings every trace of pride and covetousness.

He will always remember that, although temporal realities have a real value, because they come from God, Who "saw that they were good" (Gen., 1:31), and have been redeemed in Christ, they still remain what they are, elementary and transitory. There is nothing in them to slake the thirst for the infinite of supernaturalized man. The priest especially will see them as they exist in reality, in the context of sin. In each human subject, worked on by the grace of Redemption, there are two men in conflict with each other; the "old man" and the "new man" (Col., 3:9-10; cf. Rom. 7). At every moment everyone is capable of being one or the other, a sad result of the division wrought in the world through original sin. Since the human being is essentially "ambiguous," capable of grace and capable of sin, the world is, like him "ambivalent," poised between failure and redemption.[54] The world is the stake in a superhuman struggle at every moment of development; it will belong to and resemble the winner.

The stakes are doubly grave now, when extraordinary tech-

[58] Cf. A. de Soras, "Neutralitè et laicisme," p. 121, *et seq.*

nological advances are in the process of shaping a new world. The danger is no longer localized; it is world-wide, and all will be saved or lost. The world's fate is literally in the hands of Christians. But it is even more so in the hands of the priest, for with them he must deliver this cosmic process from its dilemma.

As exorcist he will know how to make use of "the discernment of spirits," to "scrutinize it all carefully, retaining only what is good" (I Thess., 5:21), leaving to Satan what is Satan's, and to Christ what He has redeemed. Since he has by his duty and grace of vocation "power over unclean spirits" (Mark 6:7), he can root out and banish the covetousness and secret ambitions which would always tend to transform the Gospel into a messianism of self-interest.

Salvation Through the Cross

The great work of the priesthood is to remind people that the world is sinful and needs redemption. It neither is nor can be consecrated or restored directly and as it stands. Hence it is not just a matter of perfecting and developing temporal values by christianizing them. They must also be purified and delivered from evil, given direction and opened unceasingly to eternal values. They must be ordered by Charity, the one reality which will "never pass away" (I Cor., 13:8), since St. John uses it as the definition of the divine Being: "God is Love" (John 4:8).

Thus the temporal order can only be saved by conversion. The only way is the *via dolorosa* followed by Christ on the way to the Cross. The supreme act of the world's salvation, which alone can accomplish it by transfiguring the world, is the Sacrifice of Calvary; extended through time as the Sacrifice of the Mass.

The Cross of Salvation is ours, too; we carry it with Christ. There can be no salvation of the temporal order without asceticism and penance. There can be no access to grace without death to sin. There can be no life without mortification. This is the awful choice the priest presents to the world—the great recall—to accept the Cross or to refuse. By casting out the "old man" so that from the depths of the soul the eternal youth and baptismal splendor of the "new man" may rise up, the priest is the craftsman of the most essential unity. He will thus raise mankind to a higher level.

As the adversary and conqueror of man's enemy within, he is God's best ally on earth and the world's best citizen.

The ceremony of adult Baptism,[59] you remember, dear brethren, begins with a series of exorcisms. But that is only the beginning. Having cast out the evil spirit, the priest blesses the new Christian and invites him to enter the Church. "Enter the Holy Church of God to receive the heavenly blessing from Our Lord Jesus Christ. . . ."[60]

And so, though naturally only by analogy, the "baptism" of the temporal order has to start with a kind of exorcism. For it too, in St. Paul's phrase, is "condemned to frustration" under "the tyranny of corruption" (Rom., 8:20-21). It is awaiting a "return to grace," a reconciliation and blessing, and it is the priest who has the power to bestow this blessing.

Of course the power must here be understood in a broad sense, and is obviously outside the scope of liturgical words and gestures. But at the same time it is an authentic extension, and demonstrates the deep significance of blessings, which are so often reduced by the thought of our contemporaries to petty ritualism. This is because unfortunately people have forgotten the role of Sacramentals in the Church's work of sanctification.[61]

[59] As also with a new-born child, for although it has not committed actual sin, it is still in some way under the dominion of Satan, until the original stain is effaced.

[60] Ritual of the Baptism of adults.

[61] "At the moment when the Word was made flesh, the divine virtue was carried in some way into the very heart of the material Universe, to restore it, transform it, and sanctify it. It is not only Christ's bodily nature but also the whole of material nature that was invited to share in a dignity till then undreamt of. For while in the Incarnation it is Christ's Body, in the sacraments it is other material elements, of the vegetable or mineral or human order, water, bread, wine, oil, our bodily actions and words, which become the instruments of God's Spirit. You could say that henceforth the earth (which up till then had given man only his bodily life and nourishment) appears in the sacraments as the instrument of his spiritual life and nourishment."—(Journet—The Apostolic Hierarchy.)

Minister of the Ritual

When the Bishop exhorts the new priest to bless, *sacerdotem oportet benedicere,* he refers to a function constantly mentioned in both Old and New Testaments. This blessing (words and gestures calling down God's favor on a person or thing) was reserved, since the priesthood began, to priests alone, first of the Old and then of the New Covenant.[62]

The explanation is given by the Pontifical: only their consecrated hands can give a blessing.[63]

The Church has defended this power against two lines of attack; against those who maintain, with Pelagius, that nature is essentially sound and needs no blessing and against the opposite error of the Reformation, which made nature essentially corrupt, incapable of being blessed.[64]

[62] The power of blessing pertains only to God. He blesses the whole of creation (Gen. 1:22-3), Noah, &c. But he is very soon hands on this power to men; first to fathers of families and kings, and then to the priesthood.

The Gospels give us many blessings of people and things by Christ; children (Matt. 19:13-15), apostles (Luke 24:50), bread and fish (Matt. 14:19), &c. This power of producing divine effects by gestures Christ left to his disciples (Matt. 10:12-13). In the Acts the Church is already seen using this power. "In the thought of the Fathers the power of blessing is bound up with the power and mandate possessed by the Church of sanctifying the world. . . . The Church claims the power as the prerequisite of her priesthood. The *Apostolic Constitutions* forbid the laity to bless. . . . The priest is God's minister, and by way of sacerdotal blessing, the divine benevolence itself comes down."—(P. Beillevert "Catholicisme" art. Bénédiction, col. 1406.)

[63] "In order that all they bless may be blest, all they consecrate may be consecrated, and sanctified, in the name of Our Lord Jesus Christ."—(Pontifical.)

"Cum Sacerdotes consecrentur ut sint præcipui Christi ministri et dispensatores Mysteriorum Dei; ac præterea, cum per benedictiones dispensentur gratiæ et dona Dei, merito Ecclesia adnexuit Ordini Presbyteratus munus benedicendi, ita ut soli Sacerdotes sint ministri benedictionum: quare, cum ordinantur Sacerdos ejusque manus consecrantur, sic ei dicitur ab Episcopo consecrante: *Ut quaecumque benedixerint, benedicantur.*" (Catalanus, Pontificale Romanum).

[64] Pelagius was attacked by St. Augustine (Epist. 179, 4), and then at the Council of Carthage in 1416 by the Bishops of Africa. As for Protes-

Today the teaching of the Church must be held to more than ever, as something of great value and importance.

Craftsman of Universal Rehabilitation

From this it will be seen why the Ritual (the official collection of sacramental rites and blessings), takes on a fresh meaning. Because he alone is the "Ritual-man," the priest is invested with both a power over and a duty to temporal things: that of placing them under the guidance of the Holy Spirit "who gives life to the elements" (cf. Gen., 1:12).

In the Church he is responsible for this universal reconciliation of creation. It does not happen immediately or without effort, but progressively, commencing with the lowliest realities. One has only to open this wonderful book to be convinced. Nothing else in the Church shows more plainly her touching and maternal love for the passing companions of our earthly journey. The liturgy forgets nothing.[65] It blesses

---

tant errors, the Council of Trent demonstrated the value of blessings. (Denz., 856 and 943.)

[65] The Code of Canon Law (Can. 1148) ranges blessings, from the point of view of their effects, in two classes: blessings called *constitutive*, given in such a way that the persons, places, or things that receive them are given a kind of sacred character, and removed from the usage of common life, and destined for divine worship. Such . . . are the consecrations of Virgins, a Church, sacred vessels, &c.—(Mangenot, D.T.C. art. Bénédiction, col. 632.)

Simple blessings, on the other hand, "are invocations by which the sacred minister asks God to grant the person or thing being blessed some spiritual or temporal advantage, without these persons and things becoming holy or sacred, or changing their status, from the religious standpoint."—Col. 636.)

It is these latter we have in mind. Of these blessings the priest as we said earlier, is not a magical dispenser, but a minister—that is to say, the rite he accomplishes produces its effect "in virtue of the prayer of the Church"; but he remains judge according to circumstances of the opportuneness of carrying it out.

Thus understood in their usage, and especially in the context of the Church as "the Sacrament of Christ." Blessings can only contribute to the healing and spiritualisation of the bonds between man and the things of earth, to show that nothing is common or unworthy of consecration to God, and that the things of nature, or the works of civilisation, can share

houses, bread, eggs, fruits. It thinks of fountains, ships, stables, fields, sick animals, it remembers bees, wax, working tools. It hallows water, light, fire, and incense. Everything is greeted with sympathy, even tenderness. The latest discoveries do not surprise it: machinery, railways, cars, planes, telegraph, seismograph, and now television. It includes everything, admits everything, hallows everything, both for man's good use, and also, as related to his eternal end for which these mysterious elements serve (as the Liturgy emphasizes), by way of symbolism.

The Open Book

Like the Church, the priest rejects nothing in the temporal order. Known as a man who rejects the world, and rightly so in a certain sense, he is also the man who accepts and welcomes it. He is accused of withdrawal, yet he remains minister of universal integration. Thanks to him, "all is good that God has made; nothing is to be rejected; only we must be thankful to him when we partake of it, then it is hallowed for our use by God's blessing and the prayer which brings it" (I Tim., 4:4-5). How can he be accused of being out of date when his one care is to save progress, by preserving its meaning and proportion. Does he not give validity to human development by making it intelligible?

One of the most moving characteristics of the Ritual is its incompleteness: it is an open book waiting for new pages when mind and hand, tools and released energy will add new things to those already blessed by priestly hands. And just to make sure that nothing escapes his care, whether on earth or in the depths of the sea, the Church has composed this blessing as a wonderful indication of her great magnanimity and of her complete confidence in the grace of Christ the King, the blessing *ad omnia:* "O God, whose word hallows all things, pour forth on these creatures Thy Blessing . . . through Christ Our Lord."

When a priest blesses, dear brethren, you will notice that

in the coming of the Kingdom. They maintain in man a religious sense of the universe, and tend to characterise, in their own way, every epoch of Christianity.—(Beillevert, op. cit. col. 1409.)

he makes a sign, which never varies, though the words may change. Over the person or the object he wants to bless, he makes the sign of the Cross. This is no arbitrary sign, for this movement of a hand in the air is God's own signature, the essential seal apart from which none can be His true child or creature. This mark of the Trinity, Father, Son, and Holy Ghost, is an unchanging reminder for man today, just as for the men of yesterday and tomorrow, that for the things that pass and for immortal persons there is but one road and one redemption: "salvation through the Cross."

The Sacrifice of Calvary took place historically only once. By this unique act the Redemption was accomplished.[66] God willed "to win back all things, whether on earth or in heaven," through Christ, "into union with himself, making peace with them through his blood, shed on the cross." (Col., 1:20.)

Yet Christ wishes to renew this Sacrifice always and everywhere. This is the Holy Sacrifice of the Mass. We do not intend here, dear brethren, to give a complete exposition of the doctrine of the Mystery of the Holy Eucharist, even in summary form, but rather to deal with it from the point of view of the temporal order.

First, we shall contrast the official atheism of this age with the social worship of the ancient City-State. We shall show that what is lacking in the present world compared with antiquity can be supplied, in a transcendent degree, by the unique Oblation of the Priest of the Priest of the New Law.

WORSHIP AND THE TEMPORAL ORDER

"The human race has always felt the need of having priests, that is to say, men who, by an official commission entrusted to them, are to be the Mediators between God and men, and who, entirely consecrated to this mediation, make it their life's work, being chosen to offer God official prayers and sacrifices in the name of society. For society as such has an obligation of ren-

[66] In Part I We have already spoken of the links which bind together the Sacrifice of Calvary with the priesthood which Christ possesses by virtue of the hypostatic union.

dering to God a public and social worship, of recognizing in Him the Supreme Lord and first principle, and of tending to Him as its last end, thanking Him and seeking to propitiate Him." [67]

The history of the ancient City-State shows that in fact "worship was the bond uniting all society . . . the City was the gathering of people who shared the same protector gods and together accomplished the religious act on the same altar. . . . Nothing was more sacred in a town than this altar on which the sacred flame was always maintained." [68]

The Lesson of the Ancient World

Pagan society was thus essentially religious. It was so in domestic as well as social life. "There was not a single act of public life in which you did not have the gods intervening. . . . The people never assembled except on a day allowed by their religion. . . . The assembly began with a prayer. . . . The tribunal was a sacred place . . . and the meetings of the tribunes were held near an altar and began with a sacrifice. . . . During a campaign the army reflected civil society. It took with it a portable hearth where the sacred fire burnt day and night. . . . Thus, in peace and war, religion entered into every action. It was present everywhere, and surrounded man. Soul and body, public life and private, meals, feasts, and everything, were under the sway of this State religion. . . . It ruled the human person with an authority so absolute that it left nothing out." [69]

Shortcomings and Possibilities in Society Today

This provides a great lesson for our age, which in one sense, has both learned everything and forgotten everything. Temporal society, when it lost its cult and its priests and made both into a separate category, one profession among others, lost its

[67] Pius XI—The Catholic Priesthood.

[68] Fustel de Coulanges, "La Cité Antique," p. 166. Its quotations envisage directly only the Græco-Roman cities. But they can be applied analogically to all societies known to history, with their differences of cult, origin, divinities, &c.

[69] Fustel de Coulanges op. cit. pp. 193, 194.

soul, its unity, and its life. By becoming a closed society it has deprived itself of its relationship with the Eternal and the Absolute. By desiring to stand completely on its own feet, it has made itself inconsistent and unintelligible. It has cut itself off from the one element of truth in its history, the return of humanity to its source, *en route* to its final goal.

Society needs to find its soul if it is to come alive again. It is disturbed when a philosopher deplores "the disproportion between the way the spirit of all humanity remained practically unchanged, while its body has grown enormously." [70] Perhaps it is waking up to its troubles. Perhaps something more than regard for the past, or admiration for great art is drawing it to our churches with an emotion that borders on nostalgia. It would no longer dare to suggest that the Christian faith "resembles a Gothic cathedral in its greatness, emptiness, and lack of solidity." [71] For it knows that the cathedral would never have been conceived and could not survive, were it no more than an empty jewel case.

If it is going to fulfil this duty to God society need forfeit none of its own proper ends. Indeed these have value only if they are integrated into a unity, subordinate to the higher ends that society has to acknowledge by providing for man's religious needs. So worship and society, priesthood and community, do not add up like two separate entities; for here again the priestly function is not just one among many. It is on a level of its own. While respecting all other functions and values, its mission is to raise them up and convert them, not only by exorcising them and blessing them, but by *binding* them actively to God (that is the meaning of the word religion), by bringing them into the stream of adoration, praise, petition, and supplication for forgiveness, which draws humanity in the train of the High Priest towards His Father and ours.

When she does this, the Church obviously has no intention of encroaching unduly on any of the different temporal do-

[70] H. Bergson, in his letter thanking Norway for the institution of the Nobel Prize. An idea taken up again in "Les Deux Sources de la Morale et de la Religion," p. 335.

[71] Renan, "Souvenirs d'enfance et de jeunesse."

mains, the autonomy of which she expressly recognizes. In her respect for conscience she has no more intention of "requisitioning" or of circumventing, for the purposes of this homage, any expression or group which has not yet given its free adherence.

Local Worship and Universal Religion

In this way we can see how the narrow provincialism of the ancient city has been quite outstripped. "Each city had its corps of priests independent of any foreign authority. There was no link between the priests of two cities . . . no exchange of teaching, or of rites. . . . Religion was quite localized, and quite civic, in the original sense—i.e., proper to each city." [72]

Religion was local, and it was also materialist and ineffective, unable to offer to God more than the fruits of the soil or animals; a simple human sketch of the only worship really able to please God and draw men together in a universal sacrifice. What the pagan religion lacked, modern society has within its reach. Before Christ, "there was certainly an infinitely adorable God, but no infinite adorer." [73] Now, on the other hand, society can penetrate to the heart of Triune Love. "Our Lord came on earth as *the universal man* to render to God His father all the honor He should receive from creation. . . ." [74]

THE PRIEST, MINISTER OF WORSHIP

The culmination of this perfect adoration is the Mass. "In the divine Sacrifice accomplished at Mass the same Christ Who offered Himself once in a bloody manner on the Cross," is present and is immolated in an unbloody manner. Without adding any comment to this simple statement of the Council of Trent, we would like to speak, dear brethren, of the part you play in the Mass, and through it, of the power you have of offering the world to God. Though it should be understood that it is the prerogative of priests alone to consecrate it by the sacramental immolation of Christ on the altar.

[72] Fustel de Coulanges, op. cit., p. 173.
[73] Bérulle, "De l'état et des grandeurs de Jèsus." Discours 2, p. 129.
[74] Olier, Tr. des Saints-Ordres III, 6.

The encyclical *Mediator Dei* recalls that "the essential element of worship must be interior . . . the exhortation of the Apostle: 'Have in you the mind which was in Christ Jesus' thus demands from all Christians that they should reproduce, so far as is humanly possible, the sentiments with which the Divine Redeemer was animated, when he offered the sacrifice of His own self . . . that is to say, that they should adore, honor, praise and thank God's sovereign majesty." [75]

Here then is the way of it. Christians have themselves the duty of offering all they are, all they have, and all that is about them. They have no right to remain passive spectators of the Sacrifice. Otherwise "religion becomes an inconsistent and empty formalism." [76]

The right on which this duty is founded devolves from the real capacity conferred by the "character" on everyone baptized. "It is not only the ministers chosen . . . for the clean oblation . . . who participate in bearing Christ's mysterious priesthood . . . and Sacrifice . . . but also the whole Christian people called with good reason by the prince of the Apostles, 'a chosen race, a royal priesthood'; for whether it is for themselves or for the whole human race, in expiation of our sins, the faithful must concur in this oblation. . . ." [77]

In actual practice, the celebrant expresses himself in the plural most of the time.[78]

[75] Mediator Dei.

[76] Mediator Dei.—St. Thomas had already observed that "religion involves, in the first place, interior acts which of themselves pertain to it. Yet it adds, in a secondary way, external acts ordained to the first."(IIa IIæ, Q. 81, art. 7.)

It goes without saying that this exercise of the theological virtues, which constitutes spiritual worship, the "rationabile obsequium" that St. Paul speaks of (Rom. 12, 1) does not come first, in relation the sacramental rite of Transubstantiation, as if the latter were ordained to it. The contrast between interior worship and external worship envisaged here by St. Thomas, is applicable, not to Christ and the faithful, but to the essential role they have between them, and does not affect the respective role of Christ and the faithful.

[77] Pius XI: Encyclical "Miserentissimus Redemptor."

[78] "Pray Brethren that my sacrifice and yours. . . . We your servants and your holy people offer you . . . the pure host," &c. "The faithful are truly

Proportioned Oblation

The faithful will remember this; they must share in the offering actively. If it is to be honest before the Lord, it must be proportioned to the offerers. Christianity teaches that these are not scattered individuals; God has put them where they are and wants them in living communities such as the family, country, or the human race. For the same reason they are bound up with and responsible for them. And so, when you approach the altar, never come alone, dear brethren. You have the power and the mission to save along with yourself your household, your street, your town, and the whole of civilization.

The offering from Christians must not be uniform. To each vocation will correspond a special oblation. The worker will offer up the monotony of work on the belt, or the joy of the completed product; the mother of a family, her domestic worries, or her fears for an ailing child. The scientist will offer the world of thought, the universe made captive in breadth and depth. To scholar, philosopher, sociologist, artist, there falls the task of gathering up the world and raising it up to the Father, at this turning point of its destiny.

In this way the Mass, so unimportant in the eyes of those who disregard it, should rather take on for them the appearance of a tremendous ferment of human perfection.

Catholic Intellectuals and the Offering of Creation

The Catholic intellectual of today has an exceptional mission. He must replace under God's dominion culture, cut off piecemeal for so many centuries from theology. The Catholic must reply with Christian realism to positivist theories seeking to possess the world without offering it, or to jansenist rigorism,

---

consecrated . . . not in the manner of passive recipients undergoing the action without reacting . . . but in the manner of members forming one unit mystically with the one who consecrates." (Meersch. op. cit., page 156.) The liturgical rites express this participation well: the drop of water in the wine; the custom of offering bread and wine, now replaced by offertory collections and Mass stipends.

out to condemn the temporal order and humanism as sinful, and content at Mass to offer without possession. The Catholic's motto will be to possess in order to offer, to conquer everything—matter, without which there would be no bread, no wine, no host, and spirit, the basis of faith and love—in order to return everything to God. The universe is like an unexplored continent, going to the first occupant. Christian thinkers will have to be able to get there first to plant the Cross in it. The extension of the boundaries of the known world is an enlargement of the material of the Offertory and so of the Redemption.

The Mass and the Suffering World

At the same time, while our modern task means primarily the "recapitulation" of a universe in childbirth, it has thereby no call to be exclusive. Human distress and defeat, sin and error, moral corruption and sickness, social oppression, political and international hatred, cry out for deliverance, for purification, for consoling and healing. Flesh and blood humanity, full of its faults and sorrows, is what the Offertory has to gather together, and the Mass to lead to the heart of God. Yet here, even more than a dedication to God of the known universe, there is needed a consecration and a redemption, involving something extra; offering is not enough, for a sacrifice is necessary. And for this it is not sufficient to be baptized; a priest is needed.

When the Pontifical lays on the priest the duty of "offering" it means to reserve to the priesthood the celebration of the Holy Sacrifice. This does not exclude, as we have just shown, some kind of participation by the Christian people: "the faithful too offer the Divine Victim." They can do so by reason of the power of worship bestowed on them by the baptismal character, "though in a different manner." [79] "If the people

[79] Mediator Dei. "The faithful . . . relative to the official priesthood, are receptive: they do not give, they receive; they do not consecrate, they are consecrated." (Meersch. op. cit., p. 150.) We come back here to the doctrine of the Baptismal character, and can now complete it. The Church in all her being and in every part is penetrated by Christ's priestly power . . . which invests her, consecrates her, and makes her able to carry

offer at the same time as the priest, it does not mean that the members of the Church accomplish the visible liturgical rite in the same way as the priest himself, who is the only one delegated by God for this purpose. . . ." [80]

Being consecrated, and so fitted to offer, the laity remain radically incapable of being consecrators. Only the priest, by virtue of his power of orders, is Christ's "instrument," and acts in His name and in His stead. "The unbloody immolation by means of which . . . after the words of Consecration Christ is rendered present on the altar, in the state of a victim, is accomplished only by the priest, in so far as he represents Christ's Person, not in so far as he represents the person of the faithful . . . and this holds good . . . whether the faithful are there present . . . or whether they do not assist at it at all, it being in no way requisite that the people should ratify what the sacred minister does." [81]

The Priest and the World's Consecration

If there were no Mass, all the offering in the world would be in vain, all offering of creation pointless. The entire effort of mankind to bring back the universe to God stands revealed as powerless and incomplete. For the Sacrifice of the Mass, since it continues the Sacrifice of the Cross, constitutes the essential act and culminating point of Christ's redemptive mediation.

---

on validly throughout the ages the external worship celebrated by Christ. . . . But in one portion of her being . . . in that of her children who receive the power of Orders, she is consecrated . . . to exercise the outstanding acts of Christian worship, as an instrument under the movement of Christ. . . . Thus, above the power of worship, common to all the faithful and conferred by the Sacraments of Baptism and Confirmation, there is a hierarchical power of worship conferred by the Sacrament of Holy Orders. This power enables those who possess it to dispense all of the Sacraments (except Matrimony) validly, and to render the Saviour bodily present at every moment of time." (Journet, op. cit., p. 118.)

[80] Mediator Dei.

[81] Mediator Dei. The encyclical is here concerned with the validity of the Mass. But it demands, on the other hand, that the faithful "should be present in great numbers and fervour" at the Holy Sacrifice, and it develops this desire, at some length.

In this way, through his power over Christ's Sacramental Body, the priest becomes, by extension, the privileged craftsman of the world's consecration. In the restricted space where, holding the Host in his hands, he lets the Sovereign Priest pronounce the words of consecration with his lips, the poorest and the humblest priest embraces the universe and continues its redemption.

The modern priest must make this stupendous certainty his own more than has ever before been the case.

In this action and at this unique moment, he will, without any doubt, gather up all his pastoral intentions; all those he names in the two "Mementos," the parish where he is rector or curate, the work entrusted to him, the leaders he has to nourish with the living God. But he will not limit himself to his own sphere; he will extend his intention to the scale of the whole world.

To begin with, mankind must be put into perspective, allowing for all its optimism and for all its grind of misery. The priest could well repeat the fine prayer in the Breviary attributed to St. Ambrose, and suggested as a preparation for Mass: "I put before you, O Lord . . . the tribulations of the peoples, the perils of the nations, the groan of captives, the suffering of orphans, the destitution of the sick, the despair of the weak, the calm of the old . . . the tears of widows." [82]

Yet to be really co-extensive with the world's true dimensions, the priest's intention will have to become universal. It will not be satisfied with what he can see, or with what he knows. It will gather up more than the visible congregation. Beyond the limits of church or chapel, it will go seeking through time and space for every being, spiritual or inanimate, to bring them back from the four winds to the foot of the eternal Calvary. The Church herself sings in her liturgy: "Terra, pontus, astra, mundus—Quo lavantur flumine: Earth, sea, the stars, the universe, all are washed by this Blood." And it is to the priest that they owe this "Baptism"; he has exorcised them, blessed them, and baptized them in the Blood of Jesus Christ.

[82] Breviarium Romanum, Preces ante Missam, Feria Quarta.

The Sacrament of Order

It is easily understandable why the priesthood should well deserve—in a widened, if not actually the historical sense—the name of "Holy Orders"; to restore all things in Christ. To put the world back in order, restoring it to its beauty and its first promise of goodness; re-making it in its original purity and harmony. This indeed is the priest's mission and power.

This process of restoring order to a sinful world, however, cannot be done without a purifying "immolation." The priest must bring salvation to this guilty world, in which contemporary mankind is inwardly torn between the forces of love and selfishness, since he can bring about in them and for them that rending of the Cross which alone can mend the rents of selfishness and hate and sin.

In actual fact, through the consecrating priest, "the whole Mystical Body of Christ, that is to say, the redeemed City, is offering itself to God through Christ," immolating itself to the Eternal Father with the Head who suffered for it.[83] Wherever the influence of the Mass becomes efficacious, it invites such immolation, and mysteriously effects it.

At the altar the priest is a victim like Christ. But he is also the minister of the sacrifice, and then he is terrible, for he brings death; death for sin, which he burns away. He is crucified and crucifies, unable to save the world, or to consent to it, unless he nails it to the Cross. "Unless blood is shed, there can be no remission of sins." (Heb., 9:22.)

The Man of God

Here at Mass the priest's mediatory role is most fully exerted, and here his outstanding superiority in relation to the faithful is most clearly apparent.

When he speaks to God, it is in the name of us all; what he does—"for our salvation and for that of the whole world"[84] —he does as the ambassador of human society. He reunites it completely and offers it with the Host in his outstretched

[83] Mediator Dei.

[84] Offertory of the Mass.

hands in the name of the Church, to the Father, by the Son, and in the Holy Spirit; *the priest in the world,* but also the whole *world in the priest.* It is he who lifts it up to God. He introduces and accredits it to Him, not through his own power or by delegation from the people but by the enabling of Christ, the unique mediator, with Whom he is identified more truly at the altar than anywhere else. From this it follows that in carrying out this mission he is sure of being always acceptable, for when he expresses himself, not he but the Word Incarnate addresses His Father, "making intercession on our behalf," (Heb., 7:25), by showing his pierced hands.

The Man of Men

The answer makes no delay. And here again the priest is its conveyor. He alone has power through the Consecration, of rendering Christ present, "bringing Him down," so to speak. He alone, too, can distribute Him, and dispense His gifts to a needy world. He is "the steward of God's mysteries" (I Cor., 4:1). He gives in Holy Communion the Son's sacred Body. He perpetuates His real presence in the Tabernacle. By the Holy Eucharist, in which St. Thomas sees their final end, he opens the source of grace of all the sacraments. In him and by him the "given God" is received by men, to become present in the world and in the universe.

The priesthood thus has a two-fold aspect, though a unique mission. "Incorporated in Christ the Priest, priests will be called upon to enter successively the stream of His ascending mediation, to offer God, by Him and with Him and in Him, all the men of their generation; and the stream of His downward mediation, so as to give God, by Him, and with Him, and in Him, to all the men of their generation." [85]

As God's Ambassador, and representative of men, the priest is at Mass above all the mediator of the human race, and the "Defender of the City." He saves it, and brings it "home," with all its woes and all its worth, despite its faults, and beyond its dreams.

[85] Journet op. cit., p. 79.

The Priest as the Minister of Prayer

Immediately after Mass, the Church puts into the official thanksgiving of Bishop and priest in the Missal, the song of praise: "All the works of the Lord, bless the Lord." By inviting them to associate with their own gratitude that of all creation, of angels and men, the beasts and plants of the earth, the stars and all contained in the firmament, the Church definitely means to stress the universal character of the Redemption perpetuated by the priest at the altar.

Yet at every hour of the day the Church imposes on its ministers the duty of taking up again this divine praise. She entrusts them with a book of her official prayer, the Breviary. Whether the secular priest recites it under this abridged form, or whether the Religious sings it all as the primary function of his monastery, the Divine Office after the Eucharistic Sacrifice becomes the public link between humanity and God, in the Church and by her.

Here is a new facet of the priest's mission. He is to be the man of prayer. Not only an intimate prayer rising from his own person and catering for it alone, but an official and collective prayer ordered to the glory of God and the salvation of the human race.

This mission confers on the priest a power and a right when he recites these psalms and hymns and Scriptural texts and recognized commentaries, a power over God, Who never refuses the supplications of His Son or the "Voice of the Bride" of Christ. A power over the world, to keep it from sin and reconcile it to God.

Turned to God, ordained for men, the priest is a mediator. As a man of God he adores Him and thanks Him in the name of the whole world, in the name of those who know him and who pray; in the name of those who do not know Him; and, above all, of those who refuse and are sinking in the mire. Yet in this un-interrupted prayer of homage to God the Creator and the Savior, God's ambassador remembers also that he represents mankind, and then in their stead and on their behalf he supplicates and calls for help and pardon.

This is the reason why the recitation of the Office, in the eyes of the world an empty piece of formalism, or a useless relic of a bygone age, is really a "civic" function, an act of society of capital importance, an eminent ministry of the world of men. The useless individual reciting a disregarded book in the same language the world over, being occupied with the Unseen in the midst of human affairs, is no social parasite: at every minute his prayer is directed to transfiguring and saving society.

III. RECIPROCAL OBLIGATIONS

After taking up so much of your time already with this exposition, dear brethren, we have no intention of enumerating all its applications, and writing a treatise on pastoral theology. We wish to end with a few corollaries, showing the conditions required from God's ministers on the one hand and the faithful on the other, on which depend the possibility and effectiveness of the Priest's role in the world.

PRIESTLY SPIRITUALITY

The first condition of being a priest is to understand it. In other words, to become increasingly aware of the priesthood with which he is invested. No meditation is worth half so much. No amount of generous activity could ever replace it. Priestly effectiveness is first of all a matter of spirituality. Such spirituality is not to be sought in outward expedients or new-fangled devotion. The priesthood is sufficient in itself, provided always the priest makes it his life's center and aim; provided, to, that he always gets back to its as the original source—and one that always is original—of all his thought and action.

It is always necessary, but such priestly spirituality finds a new *raison d'etre* in modern society. The latter so often refuses priests not only their place but their rights, that it could eventually engender in them a vague feeling of uneasiness and defiance—an inferiority complex in fact. The right and only way for them to get rid of it would not be to seek diversion in other things, but to return to themselves and apply to themselves, with the necessary alteration, Saint Leo's celebrated exhortation to Christians: "Priests, know your own dignity!" [1]

It does not mean, needless to say, that they should indulge in vanity in their completely gratuitous privilege, but that they should enter more deeply into themselves, with a humility growing over the years, and with a profound respect for "the great things that He Who is mighty has done in them" [2] and have no more doubts that their ministry is possessed of genuinely divine powers. Each morning, as they start their day, priests will kneel before their Crucifix, weighed down possibly by the burden of the coming day; but when their prayers are done and Mass said, they will turn to men with the mentality of "conquerors," [3] born of the faith which moves mountains (Matt., 17:20) and a boundless hope in the victory of grace.

The priest does not, then, have to look far for this sacerdotal spirit; he has only to deduce it. If the definition of the priest lies in his mediation, his spirituality—and thus his concrete action in the world—will have to safeguard a twofold series of values; those which make him the "man of God" and those which really ensure he is "the man of men."

CONSECRATED

Priestly spirituality will mean first of all a spirit of consecration, a simple consequence of the real transformation of the priest's very being by the Sacrament of Holy Orders. If it is true that the character has marked his soul for ever with the sign of God, the priest will have to accept the consequences that follow—separation from men and resemblance to Christ.

Separation

The priest belongs to no one except to God, Who has set him apart to take him for His own service. So he will accept the fact that he cannot know and experience or taste everything human, even though he fully shares the human lot. He

[1] Office of Christmas at Matins.
[2] Magnificat, verse 84.
[3] "Have confidence, I have overcome the world." John 16:33.

will be truly "man," but not like others. He will know how to keep distinct, even though he may mix and be present. To stop short at certain responsibilities, even the most lawful, he will consider neither an inferiority nor a betrayal. One of his modes of action, indeed, is to abstain and thus cause surprise. One of his duties consists in a mission of variance, and an apologetic of dissassociation.

Resemblance

At the same time, the sacramental character of Holy Orders does far more than separate; it creates a resemblance. The priest must never forget it. His first efforts in the order of sanctity must be to accentuate the marks of this likeness. He will have to identify himself actively and daily more thoroughly with Him whose reflection he must be.

The interior life, with its intimacy with the High Priest growing through asceticism and contemplation, under the guidance of the Holy Ghost, as He quietly shapes his being, is the priest's daily duty. Without such an interior pursuit of Christ's true countenance, he would be a man of God by his powers and his calling, but not by his life. It would mean that inward divorce which underlies all pharisaism, and every apostasy. One who has given himself to God irrevocably from the day of his ordination would never consent to them.

Priestly Holiness

Ordination gave the priest a grace which is at one and the same time both a capacity for and a call to a sanctity beyond that of those who are baptized. "In order to acquit themselves worthily of their priestly functions, no ordinary virtue suffices; but an excellent virtue, which is required so that, in so far as those who receive Orders are placed above others in rank, they should be their superiors also by merit of their holiness." [4] This statement of Saint Thomas, who was merely repeating a traditional theological and historical truth, the Church has made into one of the precepts of the Code of Canon Law: "Clerics should lead a life interiorally and externally holier than that of

[4] Summa, Suppl. Q. 35, al, ad 3.

the laity, and should be for them a sublime example by the virtue and uprightness of their actions." [5]

Such perfection is required in some cases under pain of sacrilege: "those who are not holy are not to touch holy things." [6] If the effectiveness of the Sacraments is in actual fact always ensured by the part taken by Christ as the principal agent, whenever the rite is validly carried out, the sanctity of the human minister remains nevertheless bound up logically with the effect which is sought. And it is equally demanded for the world's sanctification. To be its "consecrator" the priest must himself begin by being "consecrated." He, first, must effect in his own person the triumph of the "new man." Before, and for the purpose of, "exorcising" human activity, and driving out its duplicity, the priest must start with himself, to banish his own ambiguities, and produce unity in his own person. It is easily seen how this ideal of identification with Christ, far from turning the priest away from the earthly city, leads him straight back to it. How in fact will he be able to refer humanity to God if he is not already first bound up with God himself? The human race will adopt his way and no other. The obstacles he meets will become the world's; his inmost victories will prepare the way for those of the universe.

Asceticism and Contemplation

The fact that this tremendous solidarity is still in the balance must not be an excuse for the priest to let go of the traditional means of sanctification for the sake of a system of spirituality based on the idea that action involves its own asceticism, and that the pastoral ministry provides all the strength necessary and sufficient for the priest. The Church's age-old wisdom knows well that contact with the human heart is a powerful stimulant of sanctity—"For them do I sanctify Myself" (John, 17:19). She knows, too, the dangers inherent in prolonged relations with a sinful world. Prayer, spiritual reading, days of recollection, retreats, adoration of the Blessed Sacrament, the Rosary, examination of conscience, regular Confession, a well-

[5] Code, Cn. 124.

[6] Decretal, dist. 88, can. 6.

said Office, Mass celebrated carefully and with deep recollection[7]—these are spiritual values no priest can neglect, much less despise, without an imprudence whose consequences could become gravely culpable.[8]

In order both to protect himself and preserve intact the "deposit of faith" which he guards, the priest will consider it "a grave error fraught with many dangers should he be carried away by false zeal and neglect his own sanctification, and become over-immersed in the external works, however holy, of the priestly ministry." [9] And if he wants the faithful to imitate him, in an age made sceptical by the abuse of propaganda, he will have to shine forth first of all by his own example and supernatural virtues. But these, if they are not to seem strange or despicable, in an age that calculates and compares, will have to rest more than ever before on genuine natural virtues, supernaturally practiced. Reception of the priesthood dispenses neither from loyalty nor courage nor broad-mindedness, nor a sharp sense of justice. Without these qualities the priest will never touch what is best in man and in contemporary humanism, and he should not be surprised if he does not.

Priestly Culture and Consecration

This ideal of consecration also involves the serious problem of the priest's culture. For if the priest must attain a high level of knowledge, it is not only to put him on a level with thinking

[7] We know how difficult it is to give all the time and silence desirable for the celebration of the Holy Sacrifice, in our churches, which are so small that they must have as many Masses as possible on a Sunday morning. All the same, we call the attention of our clergy and faithful—whose discipline and outward recollection has such great importance—to the complementary duty of good organization and comprehensive obedience in this particularly sacred domain. And we are sure that, especially during the week, real progress can still be obtained with a little goodwill from all (by dividing the Masses between different altars, &c.) to help the celebrant, even when he has to give out Holy Communion, to take all the time he needs for a decent and fervent celebration of the Eucharistic Sacrifice.

[8] The Code, Cn. 125-126, invites Ordinaries to watch over the fidelity of their priests to the spiritual practices mentioned.

[9] "The Catholic Priesthood"

people, or to make Christian dogma and morals acceptable, or even to acquire and give to souls an understanding of sacred doctrine. All this is part of his duty, but does not exhaust it. Without any doubt, "for the honor of the function he exerts, and for . . . the efficacity of his pastoral work, the priest must possess that heritage of knowledge (even though not strictly concerned with the sacred sciences) common to the cultivated men of his time; or in other words, he should be sanely modern."[10]

But this is only to help him to aim higher. If a priest wants to be not only a scholar or a learned man, but *the Teacher of the World*, as his priesthood has obliged him to be, he must acquire a culture which enables him to see the world, men, and things, *from God's angle*. That is, so that he may save them and "consecrate" them, in their entirety. It is in this way that his culture must be "theological." It will have to deepen dogma, without adding or subtracting anything. It will have to embrace all human knowledge, in that "none should remain with a standard of learning and culture which sufficed, perhaps, in other times. . . . They must actually attain a higher standard of general education and of learning. It must be broader and more complete, and it must correspond to the generally higher level and wider scope of modern education as compared with the past."[11] It is all too clear that this task will not be the work of individuals. It is incumbent on all the clergy collectively, though each priest must play his part according to his capacity, and consider it wrong to prefer on principle pragmatic and individualistic procedures to a serious preparation for the eventual and universal triumph of Christianity.

The Sense of Consecration

The priest's culture, like his sanctity, is thus no longer meant merely for himself, or to be confined to himself. Since both follow from his consecration, they are ordained to God's glory, and at the same time to the Redemption of the universe. You see how there is no paradox in the fact that the interior life of

[10] Ibid.
[11] Ibid.

the priest, like his personal learning, becomes literally a public function and a social ministry. The priest will have to imbue himself with this conviction. It will grow the more it penetrates to the depths of his personality. It will give meaning to his entire life, reconciling in a higher unity those two seemingly contradictory calls—the call of God and the call of men. When he contemplates God, in silent prayer, the priest takes all his people with him. Wherever he goes, he is never alone. He must not be, he cannot be. He does not say "My Father," but "Our Father." Even his personal prayer should have a collective character. Nothing now belongs to him exclusively. Even in the intimacy of his interior life, he is a man surrendered. And yet the opposite is, or at least should be, equally true. When he is in the midst of his brethren, taken up with preaching and activity, he is not on his own. Another lives in him, acts, speaks, radiates, operates through "the infirmity of his flesh" (cf. Heb., 5:2; 7:28). Whatever he does, he represents and involves God.

Thus the priest is, so to speak, always on duty. When God looks at him and hears him, he is the ambassador of men; and when men see him and hear him, he is God's envoy. Let him grasp and apply to his own life, with the necessary adaptation, the Venerable Bede's remark: "When Angels come to us, they fulfill their external mission in such a way that never for one moment do they interrupt their interior contemplation." [12]

The Sense of "Belonging"

The sense of consecration, which gives rise in God's ministers to a deep and humble respect for the divine dignity of their priesthood, and also a constant desire for holiness, and a perpetual anxiety that they should not dim what lies within them, must be completed, if it is to be truly a mediator's spirituality, by a sense of "belonging." Only by belonging to his brethren can the priest resemble Christ. Would the identification be complete if the minister did not continue and partake of His Master's own mission? And that was to be the

[12] Ven. Bede, Expositio in Lucam. 1, 11-20. Lesson 6—Matins of St. Gabriel.

Savior of Mankind. The Whole Christ, besides being the Adorer of the Father, "God's Religious," is also the Preacher of the Gospel, and the Good Shepherd.

Such community of destiny with Christ by which the priest makes his own, and takes in hand, all His redemptive intentions, is therefore not a work of supererogation. Nor can it be reserved for a particular class of priests: it must be common to all for it is an integral part of the priesthood. The priest is not a priest for himself, but for God, and for souls, simultaneously and inseparably. It does not imply that every priest will exercise this mediation in precisely the same way. A priest called to a religious vocation of contemplation and redemptive expiation, still remains truly, though in a cloister, "a representative of men in their dealings with God," since he does not cease "to offer gifts and sacrifices in expiation of their sins." (Heb., 5:1.) And the priest God has destined to be in charge of souls, whether in the diocesan clergy, or as a religious, cooperates in their salvation by making himself an apostle; he especially is "sent" to them.

AT MEN'S DISPOSAL

In the great human family, some are responsible for a home, for a trade, or for a nation. The priest has to care for all, especially for souls, the part of men that is destined not to perish. He is accountable for their spiritual failures and success. Through this they have rights over him. This leader who is over them, is dedicated, consecrated to them. He is their "servant." [13] Every day he will have to renew this total gift for the sake of all, and give to all, without distinction, the welcome of a father, a brother, and a friend. If "the most divine of all tasks that are divine, is to cooperate with God in mankind's salvation," as says Denis the Areopagite, it involves great asceticism for the priest. It is no common virtue to be always available, always present, and fully attentive to all that is said and heard and done.

Pere Chevrier's motto could never be repeated too often: "The priest is a man who is consumed." Not just because his

[13] Matt. 20:27; John 13:14-15; II Cor. 4:5.

occupations prevent him doing anything else, but because it is his duty as a father to give himself as nourishment for his children, like the sublime Pelican, to which both liturgy and the sculpture of our cathedrals liken Christ in His Eucharist Banquet.

The priest will find the strength for his deep-rooted refusal to accept what we may be allowed to call the spirit of professionalism, and his capacity for instant adaptation and an all-embracing active sympathy, from those virtues which—whether or not he is vowed to them—are specifically his: poverty, chastity, and obedience. We have said already that they have value as signs. Now We should like to show briefly how they are conditions of the apostolate, rendering the priest completely at men's disposal.

Poverty

Since he has no material interests to defend, the priest is free. He has no partnership to keep, no competitors to rival. His poverty allows him to arbitrate—he is no one-sided judge. A man who has nothing and asks for nothing is above suspicion. The more he despises "the treasures on earth where there is rust and moth to consume," (Matt., 6:20) the better he can speak of "the one Pearl of the Kingdom" (Matt., 13:46). He is believed, and envied. Not being a hireling, he draws souls. He is always the man of the sick, and the father of the poor. At certain epochs this function consisted of distributing the Church's alms. In our times, however, at least for most of our French clergy, it means a real share in destitution, occasionally beyond all tolerable bounds. There is no question, certainly, of us treating lightly our part in this painful plight, however silently and nobly borne, in which priests in town and country alike are living. Nevertheless, apart from the extreme cases in which destitution has become literally crushing, such voluntary practice of poverty, while creating a duty for the faithful, puts the priest at their disposal and service. It does not dispense him from a constant meritorious vigilance to make sure that he does not get attached to the little or nothing he has left. Much more must he resist the hidden snare of seeking riches under the pretext, or even for the sake, of apostolic efficiency. For if it is an obvious right and duty to look for money when it is the only means of attaining necessary objectives, involving publications, workshops, schools, equipping social or charitable undertakings, and so on, this does not exempt such clergy as may have to receive and distribute these donations, from the duty of never keeping any for themselves. Forgetting self like this must find expression throughout the priest's whole life, in his house, furniture, recreation, and the rest. Detached from the world because he is nailed to the Cross, the priest can radiate the Apostle's proud freedom: "disinherited, and the world is ours" (II Cor., 6:10). By it he will be, amidst the intrusion of daily cares common to families and societies, the sower of confidence, of optimism, and of abandonment to Providence. Like the poor man of Assisi, he will find in his daily meeting with Lady Poverty, less for himself than for the world, the "perfect joy" of the "Canticle of Creation."

Chastity

When he promises while still quite young to renounce for ever all human love, the priest is perfectly conscious of the sacrifice he is making. He is not forced into it as all too common belief would have it, or as a pseudo-scientific opinion would like to prove. He is neither weakling nor dreamer nor morbid victim of an out-dated tyrannical Church. Nowhere more than in this is he a free man. He must be so, to renounce lawful pleasures and the tenderest attractions of the human heart. To be still more free, he undertakes complete and perpetual chastity. It is virtue of so high an order as to permit of no rhetorical comment; but it is not an isolated separate virtue. Charity comes first. Without it, as says St. Gregory, "Chastity has no grandeur." [14] In one sense it is even quite insignificant. Only Love makes it worth while. It is its sign, it is rendered possible only by it, and above all, it leads to it.

It does so first of all, because it detaches the priest not only from the flesh and its allurements, but also from human love. This latter is a valuable and hallowed love, since Christ made

[14] St. Gregory, Homily 13. Common Conf. non Pont. Lesson 8.

it a Sacrament. But it is an engrossing bond. The husband belongs to his wife and his children. For any other he can henceforth spare only a part of his time, of his thoughts, of his heart. On the other hand, as St. Paul remarks in his praise of voluntary virginity, by detaching the apostle from a restricted home circle, it attaches him to all, without distinction or reserve. Men understand this. When they give the priest the noble name of "Father," it is because they know he has left all only to engender in them a higher life. Clerical celibacy was founded securely on the spiritual nature of the new religion—"God is a Spirit" (John, 4:24). It also helps the minister of Penance and Extreme Unction to keep himself from sin, with which he is in daily contact. But it finds a positive *raison d'etre* in an unconditional adherence of the entire personality to God and to one's neighbor for God's sake. You can only love once; the priest gives himself, and there is no taking back.

You can see how his voluntary chastity, far from being opposed, either violently or surreptitiously, to marriage, may be conceived of as its mystical extension.

Going beyond those human nuptials, which the priest abandons without in any way despising, he discovers the overwhelming union of the divine betrothal. This mysterious union of the soul with Jesus Christ is closely related with marriage on earth because it is, like them, a reflection, though closer and brighter, of the union between Christ and the Church, to which St. Paul likens the Christian union of man and woman: "this is a great mystery." (Eph., 5:22-33.)

Celibacy, offered to God as a holocaust and in expiation for the sins of the flesh of the world, has also the effect of uniting the priest inseparably with the community, and of putting him at their service with an ennobled fatherhood: "It is to the priests," wrote Saint John Chrysostom, "that the spiritual birth of souls has been entrusted. . . . Our parents engendered us to the first life; priests to the second."

Obedience

So by living his sacrifice through chastity, that is to say, in the etymological sense, *rendering himself and keeping himself sacred,* the priest becomes something more than fully man. Raising himself, he raises the whole world with him, and becomes for it a source of life. But he can do so only by his attachment to the Church, through obedience. Far from stifling his initiative, this gives him a two-fold benefit.

To begin with, in the same way as poverty and chastity, it detaches him from himself, and from his own will, and gives him to all. It puts him at the disposition of others. Because he no longer does what he wants, but what God wants, he is, or can become, capable of generosity bordering on the heroic. More important, what he will give to souls in his teaching will not be the doubtful interpretations of his own pride or imagination, but the deposit of faith, the Church's thought.

Yet priestly obedience infinitely surpasses ordinary submission to human authority. We have seen it is something more than mere discipline. It belongs to the mystical order. By it the priest becomes a public personage, not a leader without a mandate. His filial docility to the hierarchy will itself be apostolic; it will serve as an example in inciting the faithful to be of the Church, to do nothing apart from her. It will help them to understand that, cut off from the Mystical Body, they can do nothing and are worth nothing in the cause of the Redemption.

The Bishop

The apostolate must operate at this level. The only means of transmitting the Gospel, is to have received it, by "tradition." The priest is not to improvise his preaching of the Good News; he is sent by the Church, and more precisely, by the Bishop. For "the Church is in the Bishop." [15] He is not merely the head who ordains, controls, and reprimands. He is at once the symbol and the source of unity and life. "Let priests do nothing without the Bishop's approval, for it is to him that the Lord's people have been committed." [16] This is fundamental. If he is cut off from the Bishop, the priest will be cut off from the Mystical Body, "like the branch from the Vine." His apostolate is thus clearly traced out; as the Pontifical makes clear,

[15] St. Cyprian, Ep. 69, 8.

[16] Canon Apost. 39, 2.

he must be a minister; a "co-operator" of the Bishop.[17] It is evident that this important relationship to their "Ordinary" cannot be envisaged without some reference to the Supreme Bishop—that is, the Pope. For the authority of the Vicar of Jesus Christ extends, not only to the Universal Church, but also to all the individuals who make it up. He is eminently the Bishop of each and all, without in any way reducing the powers and authority of those he himself has designated as the successors of the Apostles.

The Church's Apostolate

Thus in every way the Bishop is first in relation to his priests. By uniting themselves with the fulness of the priesthood and participating in the pastoral charity of their head, they safeguard the noble structure of the work of evangelization, undivided and in community. The apostolate is the action of *the Church*. The Bishop and the priests joined with him in the work of preaching and the care of souls in a diocese, are not exercising a parallel ministry. They are very much bound together. The apostolate is not individualist, but is the collective effort of the clergy as a body and of the Christian community. It would seem that our priests have an increasingly clear grasp of this truth today. In any case the communal trend which is daily taking clearer shape on the practical level, looks like being something more than a formula for efficiency, economy of effort, mutual encouragement and moral security, and so on. It rather seems to indicate—like a breath of the Holy Spirit— a salutary return to the organic unity of the Christian community; to the communion of love in the Church.

One Priesthood

Yet this fresh realization of unity in its most intimate depths affects the priesthood still more closely, for two reasons. Firstly, it proves that there is not a "high" and a "low" clergy, as some people like to think. Being present at an Ordination should convince anybody. After the imposition of hands on the ordi-

[17] Cooperatores ordinis nostri (Pontificale, Ordination of a priest).

nands, all the priests present, imitating the Bishop's gesture, surround him like his family. Soon afterwards, the new priests he has just ordained, range themselves in their turn around him, in order to "concelebrate," to offer with him the unique Sacrifice. Here is proof tangible, and always most moving, of the one "Presbyterium," of one sole Priesthood. Again, the secular and "religious" clergy do not make up two parallel series unlinked together. We have no intention here of touching on the problem of their relations, and of their specific natures. Let us simply recall that if the Church has recognized for her own these differing vocations, it is because both are of value. Without doubt the diocesan clergy have, by right and by direct mandate, the cure of souls, in virtue of the territory for which they are responsible before God and the Church. But the religious have received both power and mission, whether from the Pope, or from bishops, to aid, in a complementary way, the secular clergy, in their complex tasks of study, teaching, preaching, missionary penetration, and spirituality.

The history of the Church, especially in our own times, shows the reciprocal gain to be drawn by both branches of the clergy from this fraternal collaboration—thus forming, as it were, the "seamless robe" of Christ's one priesthood.

With all this in mind, no one can say that priestly "obedience" is a secondary virtue. It does even more than make the priest accessible; it helps him, with God's grace, to perpetuate the Church and thus to save the world.

DUTIES OF THE FAITHFUL

And now We turn to you, dear brethren, to recall to your minds three duties you have towards the Priesthood. If We choose them out from among so many others, it is because they seem to be particularly appropriate at the moment, and follow right on from everything We have been saying.

UNDERSTANDING THE PRIEST

Saint Gregory of Nyssa's daring comparison, as you remember, between the Priest and the Sacred Species, is very enlightening. "The bread is first ordinary bread, but when the Consecration has sanctified it, it is called and really becomes Christ's Body." So with the priest. "He becomes, all at once, the head and the teacher set over the Mysteries. In his outward appearance nothing has changed; but by an unseen force and grace, he henceforth bears a transformed soul." [18] Like the Sacred Species, the priest is the sign of the divine reality; and at the same time he hides it. One could apply to him the thought of the "Adoro Te": before such poor and obscure appearances reason runs the risk of failing; but what is so hard for it to surmount becomes luminous and alive by faith. To recognize God in the person of His ministers, reason is not enough; belief is needed. You have to acknowledge that beyond the appearances there is something unutterable, surpassing infinitely anything you could see or imagine.

Understanding

Such a spirit of faith, which will be necessary for you "to see your priests as the ministers of Christ and the dispensers of the Mysteries of God" (I Cor., 4:1), requires first of all that you understand them. In other words, you should never forget that they are, and remain, men. God works no miracles to lift them out of the human state. The priesthood confers on them no capacity by itself to do everything or excel in all things. Let this be a reminder to you to avoid an ancient error [19]—and one that keeps cropping up—that of dehumanizing the priesthood, with the consequence of putting the priest outside life. By this, grave harm is done. By thus relegating him, as do unbelievers, to the exclusive domain of rites and ceremonies, people deprive him of a good part of his *raison d'etre*. If men refuse to make their way by him, he is no longer, at least, fully their mediator. A good many Christians think they pay their respects and services to the priest by thus pigeon-holing him in what they label "sacred." It is in fact only the "ecclesiastical" category, according, that is, to the usual meaning of a word robbed of

[18] St. Gregory of Nyssa. (Or. In Bapt. Christi. P.G. xlvi, 581.)

[19] Which its partisans, already attacked by St. John, apply to Christ by making Him a "phantom," a mere appearance of a man; whence their name of Docetists. (From the Greek—to appear.)

its original grandeur—a secondary and inessential trapping. They shut the priest up and imprison him in a network of prejudices or of pharisaical surprise, and then go on to criticize him for his inactivity in the world.

Respect

On the other side, the spirit of faith will prompt a deep respect for the man of God. Not a servile respect that would legitimize the idea of a clergy conceived as a caste, but a religious respect, given with honest simplicity. But this is not sufficient, for it . . . is a question of an act of deference due to God's Majesty, present in His ministers. It means an act of gratitude likewise to Our Lord, for the goodness which led Him to perpetuate Himself in the world under the form most accessible to us—that of a man like ourselves.

Such dispositions of faith must not remain purely interior, but must find a practical expression. Mothers of families must know how to get their children used from babyhood to marks of thoughtful courtesy towards the ministers of God. These are among the chief charms of Catholic countries. Christian parents will know how to give the priest a place of honor in their family circle. They will welcome him as they would Our Lord Himself. All Christians will remember that they owe logically to the ambassador of the highest Sovereign the honors which this world's Governments give to the representatives of earthly powers. They should from their hearts pay their highest marks of respect to the priest.

A great step will be made, dear brethren, when Christians, who usually know next to nothing about the priest (his material difficulties, isolation or psychology), do manage to see him in the context of his mysterious duality: at once one of them and the Lord's transcendent Envoy. One of the first duties of Catholics is to rediscover the meaning of the priest. It is through them—and through them only—that he will be given his true place in society.

THE NECESSARY COLLABORATION

"Since, dear Brothers, the pilot of a ship and the passengers share the same fears and the same hopes, having a common cause, they must also be of one mind." [20] These words which the Bishop addresses to the faithful before the Ordination of a new priest, We take afresh for our own purpose, as the foundation of a second duty We wish to propose to you.

"Common Cause." "We already know how in effect the Church is inseparably both Christian Priesthood and People. Without returning to these principles, We want to suggest to you by now, by way of corollary, two watchwords."

Take Care of Them

The first is to look after your clergy. The idea is not to change places, for the priest is still responsible for you. But to help him in this mission of authority and life. Your priests are poor; you must help them to live. They have left all for you, often renouncing a future comparable or better than yours; remember that. You should do all you can to relieve them of administrative tasks, or even the humble material jobs which hinder them, to the detriment of their interior life and their ministry. You will clear the path before them. You will offer them your hands, your time, your place, your culture. You will tactfully keep an eye on their health. Finally, when you have a better understanding of their material needs and the Church's, having seen them a little closer, you will be able to show your generosity in the fulfilment of that duty you owe, doubtless in charity, but much more in strict justice, of paying your dues. It is not for the clergy to ask, but for you to take the initiative in making your offering.

Yet you must not limit your co-operation to this material assistance, but you must create an atmosphere of spiritual affection, reserved yet sincere, which can do so much to encourage your priests, and also the seminarists of your parish, who may possibly owe their perseverance in their vocation to your understanding welcome.

[20] Ordination of priests. Preliminary exhortation.

Action by the Community

When you have thus freed God's ministers by undertaking that work which falls to the laity in both ecclesiastical and temporal matters you will still not be done. It will not even suffice, however excellent it is, just to pray for them and with them. The Church is waiting for you to join in a work done in common, a community apostolate. If you give yourself to it, you will be able to keep yourself from a double excess; that of leaving everything to your priests, from scruple or timidity, and that of wanting to supplant them, however good your intentions.

If clericalism is wrong, what has been called "laicism" is, too. The truth lies in the happy mean; respect for the priest's autonomy, where it is irreplaceable (spiritual direction, official preaching, &c.), yet with a determination also, to take your place, as a baptized person partly responsible for the Gospel in the section of society allotted to you by Providence. At the present time, in Our own diocese, two spheres of life call especially for this close collaboration with the priest. The middle classes, on one hand, need to eliminate a certain attitude of "paternalism" towards the clergy. On the other, the workers need to make sure they have that contact with them which is needed more than ever for instruction and spiritual nourishment.

It is very largely in the family, through action in the home, that each of these social spheres can put the priest right at the heart of its real life and of its specialized apostolate.

And so, by thus shouldering and taking their part in the apostolate, the faithful will enable priests to remain prayerful and generous souls, like comets on fire to draw men in their wake towards the God of love.

THE LORD'S CALL

In this vast world which is both crumbling and still coming into being, in face of the surging waves of paganism, the moment has come for the Church to yield not another inch. She must establish everywhere genuine Christian communities as islands of spiritual resistance peacefully ordered for human well-being. Here is one of her essential constructive tasks. Every Christian must feel himself responsible for it, with the serious enthusiasm he puts into every enterprise entrusted to him. But these dynamic centers which are to prevent the world from building itself up outside the Church, themselves suppose a more intimate center. Here once again, as always, we find the priest.

But here again also priests are lacking. We are short of priests, in France at least. Care must be taken, when this dearth is discussed, not to make statistical evidence worse than it is by exaggeration or by too hasty a survey. Yet even admitting that the evil is more of a menace than an accomplished fact, the figures still speak for themselves. Every year we lose about 400 priests in France, without others to replace them.[21]

The Duty of All

What are we dealing with? Something more than encouraging vocations, for from the start, we can be clear that the idea of recruiting priests is somewhat ambiguous. It could even be dangerous, if it implied a careless attempt to push a drive for new vocations. God alone calls the soul to His service. The priesthood does not come from here below but as a free gift of the Holy Spirit.

Yet grace takes root in nature, and in a concrete environment. It admits and presupposes the free play of our wills. Just as Faith comes to us through teaching—"through hearing," St. Paul said—so with vocations. This consequence in no way contradicts the freedom of the call. It merely emphasizes the human element in the response. "How can they listen without a preacher to listen to?" (Rom., 10:14.) The action of Christians is defined by this. It can, and it must itself be a preaching, or in modern terms, a publicity campaign. To be effective nowadays it will have to fulfill two conditions.

It must be unanimous, so as to create an atmosphere serving as an antidote to the reigning secularism, and so it should gather in all the living forces of the diocese, to strike at the

[21] This figure comes from statistics compiled some years ago, which need revising.

same point. To effect a breach, you need to charge. That means unity and collaboration from everyone, in his own degree.

This presentation of the priesthood must next be concrete, for our times, and especially our youth, need pictures as much as ideas. The notion of the priest must be incarnated in a real life lesson. Everything must be set going to show the splendor of the priesthood, not by stunts unworthy of such a great cause, but by letting the truth show itself and become accessible to all.

Literature, plays, films, and lectures will all have to be brought in to show the priest's great destiny, which certainly fascinates the public, Christian or pagan, providing art sustains thought. This presentation, adapted to each audience, would reach souls by its appeal to their deepest aspirations.

Duty of Families

Yet it is up to the family, most of all, to give the Church her priests. Not only because it is to his parents that every priest owes, along with his life, the best part of his religious education, but because, far from being in opposition to each other, the ideals of marriage, and of the priesthood complete each other, just, in fact, as they were equally associated in the mind of Christ.[22] It is true that the insistence put in recent times on the beauty of the Sacrament of Marriage may well have turned from God's service to a certain number of fervent Christians, but it is still a fact that homes thus founded on so high an ideal, prepare the way for future generations, and produce vocations both numerous and generous. So it is not by putting conjugal spirituality under a bushel that you can hope to exalt voluntary celibacy. The conclusion is quite otherwise. Young people must have put before them, when the time comes for them to choose, a picture of the priesthood as capable of arousing their enthusiasm as that of marriage. Experience shows, moreover, how to the extent to which the laity have discovered and lived their married state in all its Christian dimensions, that they realize how much they need the priest,

[22] We refer you again to "Mystici Corporis" concerning the two "social Sacraments" of the Church.

and call on him to exercise his essential role of spiritual fatherhood. The furtherest limit and highest peak attainable by the love of two human beings, is to give to God, for a higher service, the son He has given to them.

Vocations and the Church's Needs

Yet this common effort, if a greater number of more perfect vocations are to be made ready to follow God's call, must keep in mind not only or exclusively the surpassing grandeur of the Eternal Priesthood. It must be determined also by the concrete needs of the Church. In our days it is a fact of experience that the need is greatest in regard to the diocesan clergy. The shortage is greatest among parish clergy, and risks becoming much worse as time goes on. Leaving a district without a priest means depriving God of a living section of His Church. The diocesan clergy, in fact, make up the normal structure of pastoral organization. The organic community is the Diocese with its Bishop, and at a more elementary level, the parish with the one who rules it—the Pastor, helped by his assistants. A priestless parish is not just sick—it is dead. This is why We make bold to say, in a spirit of fraternal charity and esteem, the sincerity of which We hope no one will doubt, the most important effort must be made, at the moment at least, in the field of diocesan vocations. Most important, but not the only effort, for, on the contrary, we both hopc and pray that God will raise up religious vocations at the same time, and give prosperity to the Religious Orders, those high schools of sanctity and evangelical example. And this not only for the glory of God and the enrichment of the Church, but for that extension of the field of collaboration in the sphere of the apostolate which is so possible and desirable. All we ask, and it is vital, is that the renewal of the secular clergy should be safeguarded, whatever happens, and should grow.

But here, once again, we have to face facts. Quite a number of young men are turning away from the secular clergy, to which they have at least two objections. They reproach it with being too easy in comparison with the religious life, because of its humble daily tasks and the absence of the three vows; and with being too hard because of its contacts with the life of the world, and the loneliness of the life, found alike in country parishes and in the cities.

Spirituality of the Diocesan Clergy

No effort will be of any avail if it cannot be proved that by right and in practice the diocesan ministry has a grandeur all its own. Extensive developments will be needed before it can be done, and they would be out of place here. We cannot even list the main points in the argument and apart from this, it has been made the object of a very worthwhile study at the special request of the French Hierarchy. We can only refer you to it.[23] Nor shall We do any more to indicate what changes have been made and will be introduced into our own diocese in the daily exercise of the parochial ministry, in the light of principles and of prudent experience. While showing that every priest exercises in practice the virtues which form the object of the three vows, we have already partly replied to the first objection denying the grandeur of the parochial ministry. As for the second, that the ministry is *impossible*, it finds its best answer in the daily lives of our priests and in our religious history—especially during the past few years. Our clergy have had their heroes and their saints. We know the secret of their far from commonplace virtues. Priests of our land, they have been nurtured by the powers of its soil. They lived where they were born. As clerics they chose it—the Holy Ghost making the choice for them. As priests they gave themselves to it, with a mystical

[23] This research into a mystique for the diocesan clergy has given rise in the last few years, to a series of studies based on the methodical inquiry made by Mgr. Guerry at the request of the French Cardinals and Archbishops, on "the nature and spirituality of the Diocesan clergy." Other attempts have been made in the same direction with different starting points. Without prejudging the conclusions which theologians will soon have to examine with judicial impartiality, we can recognize the good effects already produced, on the practical level of pastoral life, by the light this has shed on the resources and needs of the diocesan clergy.

Regulars and Seculars alike, we are glad to note, have already drawn from these loyal fraternal contacts a mutual profit, which we are certain must grow. In any case we owe it to truth and gratitude to record here the benefit derived in the diocese of Paris from such close collaboration.

union binding them to a sublime contract; yet their bonds are dear to them, and the task transfigures them. By respecting their origins, they mapped out their destiny; when the oak falls, it is on the spot where it was born.

The Privilege of Mothers

Mothers of families, We turn to you for you have an exceptional privilege at your disposal to promote the coming of Christ's priestly Kingdom. Perhaps you are, you always can be, and should desire to be, mother to a priest. When you think about it, perhaps you fear for this son and for yourself. You suspect you will lose him; you fear he will spoil his life. When you hesitate like this, look at her who trod the same path before you. Like you, Our Lady was first troubled at the Angel's Salutation (Luke, 1:28-9). But when she said her "Fiat" her whole life was changed. For Mary there was nothing but to wait, desire, and offer the Unique and Eternal Priest. She was present at His every act. Having given Him to the world at the Nativity, she presented Him to God in the Temple; she stood near the Cross. But Jesus rose again, and His Mother continues in Heaven to intercede for us with Him as the Mediatrix of grace and forgiveness. Thus though out of all proportion with this marvellous privilege, your own, mothers of this earth, renders you likewise "blessed amongst women." What grace could be greater for you than to offer Christ, the one Mediator of men, a voice to become His own; hands to bless and consecrate as His divine hands; a body to be immolated with Him as victim in expiation in the work of salvation. Let these thoughts become part of you. If God speaks to the heart of your child, do not stifle that call. The day will come, without any doubt, when this child you love will leave his father's house, to go into the world in search of his brethren to be saved. You will suffer then, in your rended heart. They will be able to say of you, to some extent, the words of the Prophet: "By his stripes we are made whole." (Isaias, 53:5.) But by giving God the one he asks for, you will realize how much it will be made up to you. His heart will never know any love other than yours. No son will be nearer you than he. Your joy will never cease because you have given the Church a minister; the world a redeemer. The priest's vocation is a pure gift from God. Yet it passes through the heart of the mother, and that will give her greatness and cause for gratitude, for eternity.

Prayers for the Priesthood

You will not fail in the threefold task, dear brethren, of understanding, helping, and giving priests to the world. There is one more to be added—that of praying for them. Many never think about it. They find it perfectly natural to recommend their intentions to their parish priest or chaplain or confessor, but the idea never once occurs to them that priests, by very reason of their sublime mission, and of the great load of misery and sin men lay on their shoulders, should be the first object of the Church's intentions. Do not be like that. Join with the daily supplications and sacrifices so many cloisters and monasteries, with all their hidden powerful souls, offer up to God for the extension and holiness of the Priesthood on earth. Keep in your thanksgiving after Holy Communion, or in your family night prayers, a specially fervent mention for priests and religious and missionaries. You will also link with them all those men and women who support them with their contemplation and penances, all the Church's consecrated souls who really or mystically share in the burdens and powers of the priesthood—clerics, novices, and those whom Christian terminology calls so truly and so well, Brothers and Sisters in Jesus Christ.

CONCLUSION

At the beginning of this letter, We asked you, dear brethren, to take a look at the world. We assessed the terrible stakes of its present transition. For if on the one hand it is being carried away on a wave of discovery and conquest, in which the Christian recognizes with joy the lawful extension of God's creative activity, yet on the other, we see with anguish a gap running right across humanity from one end to the other, dividing it into two hostile camps. Inside the nation as well as internationally, a growing enmity threatens to change itself into open hostility. Minds are already at grips; souls already closed to one another. Europe, still bleeding in her mourning and her ruins, is like a frontier between two worlds, resembling an open wound which cannot heal.

What the world and its spirit lacks, is the element which it needs to be healed and to escape catastrophe. It needs a life-giving grafting on to man's deepest nature, which would enable him, the maker of the world, to realize his plans. It would elevate him infinitely, and destroy in him all impurity and sin.

Such a task of mediation and conversion can be accomplished only by the Church. And within the Church it is the priest who has to do this, pre-eminently by his powers and his mission. It is to help you understand this better that We have written this Letter.

In conclusion We would like to arrange Our reflections round a few *images*. We shall take them from the Sacrifice of the Mass and from the Ordination ceremony. There are certain gestures of the priest that will provide you with symbols of his greatness and of his role in the world in which we live.

PROSTRATION

The first symbol is the prostration ceremony. "Let all prostrate themselves," cries the Bishop's assistant to the ordinands assembled before him.[24] The priests-to-be with one movement stretch out on the sanctuary flooring, with the immobility and silence of death, a death which the Church herself has just made a duty for them. A death which, according to the individual, either gives joy or astonishment. The priest is dead! Let us live without him! We have no need of the Priesthood! The world can stand on its own two feet!

This annihilating gesture is one a priest has to renew every day of his life. Such "death to the world" is no transitory action for him. It is an enduring state, a prolonged holocaust. He hears at every hour the jeers which mock his sacrifice as a suicidal folly. While he offers himself as a victim, civilizations pass by, men go on their way, unheeding or haughty spectators of

[24] Ordination of Sub-deacons, Deacons, and Priests.

his voluntary annihilation. It is an enduring lesson: the priest is and always will be in some way dead among the living.

Yet soon, when the supplications of the Litanies have brought down on them the prayer of all the Saints, the ordinands, like Peter, James, and John, after the vision on Thabor, which made them "fall flat on their faces on the ground" (Matt., 17:6), stand up and "looking about them, see no one but only Jesus" (Luke, 9:8). After the Bishop's consecration has made them priests they go off into the world "transfigured" in the likeness of Christ, transparent with his beauty, bearing his divine powers.

The temptation will assail them, perhaps, of using their power, in order to burn up the world-wide sinfulness more quickly and more surely, "to bring down fire from Heaven" (Luke, 9:54) on the faithless town. But Christ through the mouth of the Church, will deter them from that. (Luke, 9:55.) For if the priest like Christ has the mission of driving all trafficking from out of the Temple, and all hypocrisy; if God has put him on earth so as to "destroy and sweep away" it is also in order to "build and plant" (Jer., 1:10). The Son of God did not call to his aid the legions of angels (Matt., 26:53). He made himself a servant and a slave to heal and to save. So with the priest; he will use his divine powers only in order to be the shepherd of the lost sheep, the doctor of wounded souls. He too, like His Master, comes bringing "the sword on to the earth" (Matt., 10:34). He too is to save by sprinkling blood. Yet this blood is not someone else's, but that of the one Redeemer, with which his own is mingled. As long as there are priests, the blood that baptizes the world will never cease to flow.

THE ELEVATION

The second symbol is given us by the Mass. The priest holds the Host he has just consecrated and lifts It up for all the world to see, as an offering to God, with a gesture that betrays all the intensity of his desire and of his prayer. What he offers is no longer wheaten flour but Jesus Christ. Yet not alone. With Him and by Him, Whose place he is taking, the priest stretches out his hands to take the whole world and lift it right up to God. He offers it to His light, His warmth, His grace, His pardon. He shows it to Him, for Him to wipe away every spot and every weakness. He begs the Supreme Majesty "to look not on his sins but on the faith of His Curch." [25] He recalls His creation to the Creator; His "children of anger" (Eph., 2:3) to the Father, to make them "sons of adoption." [26] He takes the world into his hands in order to give it up to its God, to renew its links with Him, to re-establish the passage and the bridge. This priestly gesture may be misunderstood or fought by the world; it remains the essential gesture of public Salvation; the providential shelter from the "anger that is to come."

In elevating the Host the priest elevates the world with It. He tears it from its corruption, and leads it to its highest end, to its destination in the heart of God through His own mercy.

COMMUNION

God is found, and the way to Him restored. Yet God is also given, distributed, "eaten." At the end of Mass the priest comes down among the ranks of the people to give them Communion. What he divides among them is not a feeling or a simple every-day affection. It is a Person, living Love. There are others who, moved by the hatreds or helplessness of men have taken on themselves the task of bringing concord to the human race. It is worthwhile work, but nothing more than a very rough sketch, a fragile erection often dangerous because of the illusions liable to follow the first fervor. The priest knows these good intentions and touching efforts to bring about universal understanding. He supports them and helps them. But he knows that they are only on the surface, while he holds in his own hands the vital Union. After devastating wars, national leaders appeal and search or prepare for peace; but only the priest can provide it, only he really makes it and preserves it. He goes from soul to soul, calling to the world's hunger, and satisfying it, while never exhausting the ciborium. These men

[25] Ordinary of the Mass, Prayers before Communion.

[26] Romans 8:15; 8:23; Eph. 1:5.

of every race and color and tongue, before entering the temple, were divided, and split into hostile camps. But the priest at the Sacred Table has made them brothers and friends. When they leave the cathedral, they have become one whole people. Through Christ, God uses the priest "to reunite Jews and Gentiles, and to gather together these two flocks under one and the same shepherd, by the unbreakable bond of charity." [27]

Can you call a man like this a deserter, who dies to make others live, who bathes the universe in the Blood of Christ, and makes it pleasing to His Father, whose ministry is one of unity and peace?

Civilizations follow each other, nations "with their power and their glory" spring up and disappear. The Priesthood remains. It perpetuates itself on earth, in all the lowliness of its outward appearances and yet with the nobility of a royal dynasty that has known no interregnum. This strange man, called old-fashioned by his contemporaries, is always up to date, always modern. They allege that the priest is behind the times. In fact he keeps ahead of them. He foresees and predicts and prepares. He anticipates and surpasses all progress and humanism, by the way he keeps showing men Christ, "the New Adam" (1 Cor., 15:45), and by engendering them into His transcendent Life. But because he speaks the language of eternity no one bothers to listen.

People find him distant, since he is outside customary conventions. They think him indifferent, since he keeps quiet and recollected, whereas he "considers the whole world as his parish." The ungrateful world has no idea he is watching over it (Is., 21:11). It has no concern for this guardian protecting it in the night (Is., 62:6). It derives no satisfaction from the fact that he gives his life for it.

Here is the everlasting paradox of the priest. He carries opposites within him. At the cost of his life he reconciles loyalty to God and man. He has an air of poverty and helplessness, and in actual fact no one is weaker than the priest. He disposes of neither political power nor financial resources, nor armed strength, which others use to conquer the world. His native

[27] Prayers for the dedication of a Church.

force is to be disarmed and "to do all things in Him who strengtheneth him." (Phil., 4:13.) That means going, with the independence conferred on him by his detachment, to the suffering and ignorant and falling. Nothing is more belittled or less understood or more attacked, in history than the priesthood. And yet only before it do people kneel. Those who would like to clear the world forever of God's Church well realize that. Till the end of time the priest will be the best loved and most hated of men; the one most incarnate and transcendent; the closest brother, and yet the one great enemy! Till the end of time, his mystery—which even for himself a sacred enigma—will traverse events and civilizations, to serve as the greatest witness to the unseen Kingdom. Priests know that; when they stand for the first time at the altar they are under no illusions, knowing that till the day of their death they are going to be the "sign of contradiction," light for the children of the light, and darkness for the sons of night.

Here We must finally conclude, by going back to where We began. The priesthood was founded by *Love*, it is *Love* itself, Our Lord's last great gift.

In the light of Love, everything becomes clear in the priest. Others in the world have chosen glory, or money, or pleasure. Others consecrate their life to knowledge, power, or conquest. The priest has left all, abandoned all, and given all. He renounces every good; he renounces even himself. Yet there is one thing he claims which no one will take from him; one good he wants for himself, with obstinate determination; in this human world he has chosen Love. He has desired it for himself more than anything else. He wants it for his brethren—become now his only concern.

This unrequited giving, this supreme good, which resolved the contrast to be found in the priest, is also the secret of his role here on earth. In his sacred functions everything rests on or merges into Love. It makes a unity of the priest. It gives him his drive. With it as lever he can raise the world.

The minds of our priests should be filled with this conviction; it should radiate from them infectiously. It should be light and life for Christians, and haunt our unbelieving brethren, so unconsciously affected with a nostalgia to return.

May Christ, to whom alone in justice belongs the title and reality of the Priesthood, deign to confirm in our priests on earth, and inspire in those who are to follow in their footsteps, the honor, and grace, and joy, of saving the world, by becoming for it the ministers of Love!

PRAYER

"Father, I have made Thy name known to the men whom Thou has entrusted to me, chosen out of the world. They belonged to Thee, and have become mine through Thy gift, and they have kept true to Thy word. . . . It is for these I pray. . . . Holy Father, keep them . . . that they may be one, as we are one. . . . I have given them Thy message, and the world has nothing but hatred for them, because they do not belong to the world. . . . I am not asking that Thou should take them out of the world, but that Thou should keep them clear of what is evil. Thou hast sent me into the world on Thy errand, and I have sent them into the world on my errand; and I dedicate myself for their sakes, that they too may be dedicated through the truth.

"It is not only for them that I pray; I pray for those who are to find faith in me through their word; that they may all be one; that they may too be one in us . . . so that the love Thou hast bestowed upon me may dwell in them." (John, 17).

SPIRITUAL DIARY

Thoughts taken from the retreat notes and spiritual diary of Cardinal Suhard.

"To be a saint, therefore, must be the unique objective. I pray that the Holy Spirit inspire me and especially recall to me this precept: I must be a saint in order to be a good archbishop."

Contents

Spiritual Diary*

I. THE INTERIOR LIFE OF THE CARDINAL

I need to open my soul to a more intense and enlightened devotion to the Most Holy Virgin.

I must contemplate Mary, remember that she is my mother, hold fast to her, love and resemble her more closely.

Then I shall have the right to address her with the assurance of obtaining all.

This morning at Mass I renewed my resolutions, and each day I will renew them: Christ must be satisfied with me.

An immense work of the apostolate must be organized in Paris . . . instinctively, I am fearful, but the work is a work of God. I am but an instrument, and that instrument which is saintliest is best.

To be a saint, therefore, must be the unique objective. I pray that the Holy Spirit inspire me and especially recall to me this precept: I must be a saint in order to be a good archbishop of Paris.

The task God has given me to fulfill is heavy with responsibilities, but despite all the human excuses normally present in human affairs, the task is of such a nature that it will not admit of mediocrity in the maner of its fulfillment.

The Christian faith alone is the source of greatness.

The exaggerated attention which we give to the judgment of people on our conduct is a kind of pride.

In fact, the real value is what we value before God, neither

* The thoughts taken from the retreat notes and spiritual diary of Cardinal Suhard were collected by Monsignor Pierre Brot, published in France by "Le Bonne Presse."

more nor less. Human evaluations are frequently opposed to those of God.

The weaknesses of others must always be excused, especially in the case of the good ministers of Christ.

Christ led the holiest of lives on earth, the most beneficent possible life. He reaped for Himself, however, only failures and disappointments. Through the Cross He meant to overcome the world: *cum exaltatus fuero, omnia traham ad meipsum.* "When I shall be raised up, I will draw all things to Myself."

Good works are necessary, but they are good only insofar as they are marked by the cross.

The cross, carried in union with Jesus, is the real means of success.

There is no need that he who sowed the seed should reap the harvest: *alius est qui seminat, et alius est qui metit.* "It is one who sows, another who reaps."

Where Jesus, where the Virgin watches, there strength and love are always found.

"Blessed are you, Mary, who have believed": Elizabeth's praise of Mary evolves around this leading point: Faith. Such is the foundation of all spiritual life, of all true Christian life.

The spirit of faith implies two essential things: first, to make place for God in our life; before every action we should be concerned with what God thinks of it, and direct it solely to His good pleasure.

Then, we must develop within ourselves a profound respect for God, a filial respect, considering all that happens as willed by Him for our welfare.

Father de Foucauld remarked that the spirit of faith is particularly praised in the Gospel: "*Go, thy faith has saved thee.*"

Occasionally humility and charity are praised, but first of all, faith.

The spirit of faith is the will to allow ourselves to be guided in all things by the spirit of God. Naturalism is indeed the most habitual and most dangerous tendency for the public, even for us priests: One must not yield to this tendency.

The spirit of faith is the evangelical spirit, the will to allow ourselves to be guided by the Gospels. It is the spirit of confidence in God, the spirit of prayer and contemplation, of filial abandon to God. Thus I will not give my confidence too quickly to those independent spirits who believe that all will be saved by human means; but I will put my full confidence in our generous priests who work hard, who apply themselves to their daily duty; in those who are *Faithful to Prayer*.

When we have done all that is in our power, let us abandon ourselves without reserve to Providence. "I watched the Virgin as long as I could," said Bernadette. Let us have the will to attach ourselves to God with all our strength.

Mary, our mother, was guided in all things by the spirit of God. She lived only in the atmosphere of God. She breathed for God alone.

Charity for our priests. Through them is produced all the good which we can accomplish. I must be very close to them, loving all sincerely, be very indulgent, yet inspiring them, help them materially in the details of their lives, and spiritually by conversations, recollections, etc.

In trying times, when people close their hearts and set up barriers, I must remember that Christ alone is working in me, achieving all by bringing me to nothing.

I must, then, be transformed into Christ; I must go to his

school to humble myself. Alas, I am most miserable, but what does it matter if Christ works through me?

He can do all, and even if I am impotent, His power and His glory will be that much the greater.

I must truly be, therefore, an instrument of Christ.

O Lord, make me love my duty, all my duty, and grant that I accomplish it always with joy and patience.

I must make the best use of my talent. No one has faith in mere external qualities unless these point to a true value—TO BEAR WITNESS.

Order and discipline must be maintained, but always with goodness.

I will not put off what needs doing, but I will do it at once, taking care to see it through to the end.

I will not be discouraged, but will remember that the virtue which tends to flatter our ego is more to be feared than certain weaknesses or faults which humble us.

I will not be discouraged by an apparent defeat, but will continue working. Does this mean nothing is accomplished? When someone climbs a mountain by a winding route, he passes again and again the same scenes, but this is necessary in order to go higher, to judge the distance already covered, and to reach the summit.

The priesthood is for the service of God. Christ rendered this service not only by His acts, but also by a gift of self, that is, by unending service.

The priest, elevated to the highest dignity, must give himself in the same measure. He must be sacrificed and consumed, for is not this a way of being crucified?

What a glorious perspective this is!

And though I be sacrificed by the faithful, what a divine thought if I could elevate them to God—if not to the heights, at least to that road which leads to God.

I must remember Our Lord's threefold question to Peter: "Simon, son of John, dost thou love Me more than these?" Throughout the course of the day I will repeat frequently: "My God, I love you."

Take as a maxim of life: *God first served.* We must do all things to His satisfaction.

One thing alone saddens our Lord: a listless heart without generosity.

Holy Confidence measures itself by the infinite, for the charity of God for us is infinite like Himself. We must expect everything from God within the bounds of saintly living.

What have I suffered, Lord? What pains or sorrows have I undergone? Is my life like Yours?

O Jesus, unite me to your sufferings; grant that I may promptly accept the cares of my daily duty. Give me the strength to bear them, or I will not resemble you.

What good have I accomplished, Lord, during the long period of my life? I know well that it is You who have upheld me despite my weaknesses and faults.

Can I redeem the time in the years remaining to me? I so greatly desire that you find satisfaction in me.

O Lord, make me understand that the secret of my success rests in your love, and that without it, nothing can be done for You. Let this love fill my heart with zeal.

The mission of the priest is to serve: how much more so, then, is it my mission, since I have the fullness of the priesthood?

To serve, then, must be the holy passion of my life.

"Thou art the Christ, the Son of the Living God." How good it is to be firm and not to conceal the truth. When Peter acknowledged the divinity of the Master, he became the "pillar" of the Church. Bishops also must be pillars by knowing, holding to, and proclaiming the truth. Courage, firmness, discreetness, and fidelity are the qualities expected of us.

O Jesus, how good it is to work with You! You do not spare your workers, though You show them your esteem and honor them by calling them to the glory of your service.

I will follow, Lord, through sacrifice even unto death; but I ask You to support me with Your grace, for without You, what can I do?

(On the Feast of the Presentation of Mary)

On the feast of the Holy Virgin, when under her patronage we renew our priestly vows, a thought comes to me: how necessary it is for us to hold fast to God, to confide in Him, to think and act only as He would have us do, to rise above the world's turmoil.

We seek the truth. Now, the truth is not to be found in the

tumult of opinion, and even less in the revolutionary turmoil which governs the world. Truth is in the reality of things, in the affirmation of this REALITY, acting through higher principles governing the world, principles which are centered in God.

The restlessness of the present should not dishearten us; it must be tempered by hope.

O Mary, Queen of the clergy, inspire us with the spirit of wisdom and integrity which, in our time, is the true spirit of Christianity.

I think of the parable of the seed. The divine seed has fallen in abundance upon me. Who, more than me, has been filled with the divine word? But I must understand clearly the conclusion of the parable: "He bears fruit in Patience."

I like this thought of Bossuet: "Men are embarrassed when they ask for something great because they are so small. God is embarrassed when we ask little things because He is so great."

Therefore, let us be hearty in our requests.

I beg Mary, to whom my priesthood and episcopacy are confided, to support and encourage me, to impart to us priests a stream of holiness.

I should always remember that the effectiveness of my life as Bishop is in proportion to my generosity.

January 1. Another year has passed, another one begins. What will I accomplish? That matters little. What matters is that I use the time to sanctify myself, to save myself, and to save souls. Time has meaning only in the use we make of it. This year begins in the dark night, in mourning: may we be able to see the light and to finish the years in joy. For a Christion the word of the angel on Christmas night is always true and of real value: "I announce a great joy to you, because today is born the Savior of the world, Christ the Lord."

Everything for Christ and everything through Christ. We are only His instruments. We must convince ourselves of this truth and draw the consequence that we are of some value. We must be in the hands of Christ, adapt ourselves to our task, and accomplish it. CHRIST IS CHARITY, CHARITY FOR ALL.

It is good to know how to moderate emotions and moods and not allow them to get the better of us.

Blessed are they who die in the Lord. To what avail is it to work for *earth* when only one thing matters: *Heaven.*

I must recall that salvation is in Christ only, and that every pact with error or evil is deadly. I must be in close and continual union with the crucified Savior, and avoid all occasion to do evil.

In these days of unrest, what formula must I adopt? One only: to be good to all.

Above all, Lord, I must be the good instrument of your mercy in the world. For that I must be united to You, without weakness and without succumbing. I must remain closely united to souls in order to win them for You.

Sin is little understood because it is a spiritual evil; sensual people boast of it; weak Christian souls understand it little enough. Saints alone understand sin, and the least offense shocks them. How I desire this delicacy of conscience which gives true value to life. Such sensitivity in the face of evil is absolutely necessary.

Only Christ can be a source of pardon, and that by the shedding of His blood.

My Savior and my Master, what can I do without You? With You I can do all things.

May God preserve me from evil. I belong to Him: whatever His demands, I will obey.

The whole design of God is to make saints. No other thought could touch Christ's heart than to sacrifice Himself for this purpose.

It seems that the way of Providence is to select certain souls, conduct them to sanctity, and through them sanctify others.

We will not depart from this way, for it is Christ's way.

Today more than ever before we need saints to entice souls. Atheism is active, ravaging and persecuting entire regions, enticing people to apostasy, and some apostasize . . .

The remedy lies in an interior life which raises up saints and through sanctity provides barriers to such inroads.

Only holy souls have a true uplifting influence on those around them.

I suffer from injustices, or at least misunderstandings, in my regard. May these sufferings at least be salutary for me. Through them I will comprehend the true value of life. I must learn to carry the all-embracing Cross, the Cross of Redemption.

Through an edifying life I should make myself worthy of the mission God has confided to me.

In my Thanksgiving, in spite of trials which have not spared me, I am one of God's privileged: what graces have I not received? How can I refuse to think of those sublime duties which Christ has been pleased to confide to me and which have placed me in high position?

How can I refuse to think of those successes which have been purposely tempered with failures, willed or permitted by God because we are only His instruments. (A pastoral letter for example). God realizes all this.

Through sacrifice, through the Cross, Jesus redeemed the world and perfected His work. So it is with those who collaborate here on earth, especially His ministers and those in high places.

The longer I live, the more I realize that the most effective works of my ministry were those works of mercy and of aid to the afflicted.

But how can one be compassionate if he himself does not know in an experimental way the price of suffering?

The occasion for suffering, however, has not been lacking to me.

There is an interior as well as exterior humility. No doubt the interior is more difficult to achieve, yet it is the more pleasing to God.

I realize full well that interior humility is the essential condition for success, since through it our role as instrument is caught up in Christ Who is the principal cause.

Are not the most sorrowful days the most fruitful? Strength is perfected in weakness.

We encourage the faithful to accept trials: should not we ourselves also accept them? Must we not try to catch the true meaning of trial and make it serve our perfection?

(Ash Wednesday)

My God, how I must convince myself that I am nothing . . . I have distributed ashes to mere infants: they are signed for death—how much more so am I? Am I prepared? Grant that each day may be an active, conscious preparation for the rendering of accounts.

I must work resolutely and joyfully at my task. It is ardent, self-giving work, based on an ideal, which gives value to our activity. Nothing is so sterile as complaining.

My poor health obliges me to withdraw from important ceremonies. No matter. There remains the charge of souls under my care, some faithful souls to be strengthened, some misguided souls to be won over, and some souls not of the flock who must be led into the fold.

Unable to be directly at my post, I must be present through Christ, the first head of the diocese, the irreplaceable head, whose unworthy lieutenant I am. It is He Who guarantees the success of the undertaking.

Placing myself face to face with my eternity, it will be what I make of it. Faced with my duties and responsibilities, which are huge, I must try to maintain the moral and spiritual health of Paris, even of France, under the eyes of an enemy who spies on us and besieges us. I must face up to Christ, Who made me His priest and His bishop, so that I shall be a good worker in His undertakings.

Lord Jesus, before this world of duties and responsibilities I feel very small, feeble, and helpless. Humanly speaking I should be filled with discouragement. Happily, You are there. I confide myself to You in whom I hope. Jesus, be for me a Savior. The Lord has preserved me from evil because He has shown in my regard infinite condescension.

(Last Retreat, 1948)

Would that this retreat be the most decisive one in my life. It may mean my salvation. At my age death can come unforseen.

I must look to my conversion; what motives propel me: personal responsibilities and graces received; pastoral responsibilities: five million souls, more than two thousand priests . . . the duties imposed on me on a national plane: the gravity of the times. The present shapes the future. It depends on us, it depends on me.

To realize it we have at our disposal our works of zeal, our personal initiatives, all this human element which must not be taken lightly. But especially there is sainthood, our sanctity, for it is God Who works and guarantees our success. He sees, in particular, interior holiness. All that matters is—will I be a saint; but it does matter.

The means of sanctity is to be a good servant of God: "Behold the good servant." I do not belong to myself; as Bishop I am the servant of God. Therefore, I must be at work. The task may sometimes appear heavy, but is it not my joy? What an assurance to realize that in performing the good designs of God I sanctify myself authentically and, you might say, automatically.

II. THE BISHOP OF THE CITY

(After a pastoral retreat)

I felt a true opening of souls and confidence. Can I merit such confidence, merit, too, the grace to do good for this community of priests, which is truly very exalted and very precious?

For this, one ought to be a saint. May God aid me to be just that.

Now is the moment to choose. Humanity either will be given a body without a soul, an organization in which force will replace love, or it will be incorporated in the Mystical Body of Christ, which is the Church, and there rediscover liberty and unity of purpose.

Nothing is more opposed to the notion of the Mystical Body than a man of caste or of party. We do not gain souls by excommunicating them or in bullying them by force, even when this be done in the name of truth.

We must persuade our people that they must fashion and enlarge the Mystical Body and that they will accomplish this through their conscious presence, through the example of their lives, not noisy lives but beneficent.

I am more and more concerned about my apostolate. I state a fact when I say our whole population no longer thinks in a Christian way. Between them and a Christian community, there is an abyss. This obliges us to forget ourselves and reach out to them. Such is the true situation.

Until now our efforts have brought but few results; even general Catholic Action has declared itself unsuccessful. It is an "action geared to Catholics," not an action geared to the pagan world.

The house trembles and risks falling if we do not strengthen it by infusing faith in these deChristianized souls. Today they are the majority. Tomorrow they will be a power because they are susceptible to a strong faith which stimulates them. We do not see how our present Catholic leaders can have any influence on them.

To consolidate the Church we need a "missionary Catholic Action," for we must reach out to souls in their own environment, with their customs and their good and bad habits. We must also keep in mind what constitutes their opposition to the Christian community and what makes them distrustful of it. It is a question, then, of infusing a Christian mystique in them, in such fashion that they are reached and that they understand.

For this "missionary Catholic Action" we need dedicated and convinced priests, priests of supreme value—saints. God will not make this a fruitful work unless faithful and responsible priests are employed. The action of the priest is of first importance here: "to be a missionary to a pagan people." The need thus arises that he be specially applied to this work outside the Christian community: hence, a special missionary of Christ, wise, apostolic, prepared to reconcile two worlds.

That we might have such priests some day, we need good seminarians today, who know how to give themselves, who believe in conquering action for Christ, who strive to prepare themselves for it by a profound doctrinal formation, by a formation in prudence and in the special missionary life, with a clear insight into the world of the faithful which they must not, for all that, neglect.

The essential element in our revival appears to me to be a clergy sufficiently numerous, devoted, and apostolic, resolved to remain close to the people in order to feel their pulse, resolved to remain dignified in poverty or at least in a modest life.

More and more I consider the apostolic works which present themselves; in spite of the zeal of our priests, I do not think Paris is sufficiently evangelized because of the lack of an effective attention to non-Christians who are in the majority here.

It behooves me to consider this to which I must direct myself, our priests, our faithful and our lay apostles.

We must effect a turn-about; a world must be raised up, and God alone can do it by his direct and efficacious action on souls.

Can I obtain this through my prayers, my sacrifices and my personal action? To do so I must become a saint.

Can all our works and projects measure up to Paris? There are immense resources here. The question is to improve and utilize them wherever possible. Grant that God give me grace, as I have emplored Him each day. Let us get to work.

France will not return to Christianity unless she prepares priests sufficient in number and saints who will lead her along the straight path. The need is immense, and it requires total dedication to the task.

More and more I see the foolishness of using human means for building the city of God.

Decidedly, it is the divine element alone, applied opportunely to the temporal, which is efficacious; but on condition this this element lose nothing of its divine vigor and that it is well applied to the temporal.

Our aim is to cure a sick world through Redemption.

Let us hope that our Christians are not Christians only for the sake of themselves, or of their families, or of their social or cultural standing in society. They must not be clannish or drawing-room Catholics. They must be vital Catholics, open to all, associated with the daily life of men, sharing and understanding their cares, their affairs, their thoughts and undertakings. The Church will not grow unless she takes deep roots in the pagan world.

When you enter a church, you ought to have: a spirit of integrity and simplicity, which is that of little children, because this spirit presupposes purity; a spirit of love, of love of God and man, since He Who resides in the tabernacle is present there only to give Himself unceasingly; a spirit of zeal and generous dedication, because when love is pure, it leads us infallibly to this; finally, a spirit of sacrifice, because love gives itself through sacrifice.

To form apostles we need cultivated men and women. The apostle is human and must remain so. He must neither scorn knowledge nor destroy it, but perfect it.

Those who labor in our undertakings must be faithful to them. An exterior ardor will not suffice. The flame of fidelity, discipline and perseverence must burn.

Our works are works of "Catholic Action." Now, one is a Catholic in the intimacy of his soul by his knowledge of Christ, by union with Christ, by the practice of Christian virtues and by observance of the laws of the Church.

We must give the truth to souls, the pure and whole truth undiluted. Is it not so that truth defends itself? We must strive to make others act instead of attempting to do all ourselves.

For that purpose I must group my clergy in priestly families, where each will find a warm welcome and encouraging atmosphere. How many priests would find their salvation there!

Let our parishes be open and receptive to everyone: let each person judge himself answerable for another and be sympathetic to all those living with him under the same sun—believers and non-believers. Let each one, when he comes to the altar to receive the Body of Christ, receive it not so as to keep it for himself but to radiate it to others.

We must go out to souls to save them, and we must, when necessary, earnestly apply ourselves to the temporal and the social, because there also the divine will, the law of the Gospel, is found. This is the way to reach many souls and to save them.

We radiate Christ, make Him loved, gain souls for Him, once we ourselves are filled with His life, example, and spirit of justice.

To establish a climate of redemption, we must believe that each Christian, redeemed by Christ, has as his first duty the redemption of others in cooperation with Christ.

Every Christian rooted in Christ, must give witness to Christ by righteousness and loyalty, by justice and charity to all, by respect for the poor, by protest against oppression and exploitation of the weak. Such a testimony will make non-Christians eager for conversion.

Such must be the witness of the Christian laity. It is not new, but springs from the Gospels and was lived by the apostles themselves.

Each Christian must become a witness, not only individually and for himself, but even collectively and for the sake of others. The families of France, if they are Christian, inspired by the Gospel and conformed to the spirit of Christ, constitute her most precious treasure.

We must always be attentive to the events about us: needs, aspirations, institutions to reform or to improve. The policy of presence is a good one; we cannot systematically turn away from official happenings.

Never exceed the limit, even in zeal. The excessive is automatically suspect: moderation in everything. If we keep within just limits, there is nothing to fear; the wind of persecution may blow but it will subside, and French opinion, which is normally just because resting on good common sense, will have the last word.

We must give ourselves whole-heartedly to conquering souls; the ideal of missionary conquest will preserve us from stagnation.

Several dangers threaten the work of Catholic Action: first, a *dissipation of forces*, which paralyzes action and which is caused by each movement developing individually without sufficient co-ordination with other movements. Secondly, *isolation*, which means a development of action outside real life, apart from the institutions and organizations of the people, without taking into account living realities. Thirdly, *complacency*, which leaves us with an attitude of indifference, with no concern for others, instead of making us think of possible areas of attack. This fact leaves us open to criticism, all the more dangerous since public opinion is always ready to blame. Fourthly, *conservatism*, which makes us satisfied with results obtained, does not make us feel the need for progress. It is a false optimism; we turn about in circles; we are not militant.

It may also happen that instead of gaining new ground, we waste all our efforts fighting internal quarrels among different movements, each seeking to take over his neighbor's field of action.

To meet these dangers there are two possibilities:

One is to reflect on these diverse movements and not launch new adventures. Our attention should be given to the actual development of these movements and their attitude. This groundwork of analysis must be done first of all by the clergy who have authority and responsibility, then by laymen, equally responsible but better informed in the ways of the world.

Another possibility is to integrate the various movements on a parochial or diocesan level, where they will have more unity and greater strength, since they will share in the forces of the parish and the diocese. In this way, too, they will fulfill their true purpose better in giving a renewed life to the parish. Another benefit will be in establishing a beneficial control over them and giving them encouragement.

The common reflection on the movements will lead to a Federation of good works, without absorption, with a common goal and a common point of view.

(For the orientation of the young)

We need an activity more intense than ever before, not by display but in depth by way of formation.

There must be a certain independence and autonomy in action: We must beware of falling prey to opinion. The value of our action surpasses the value of opinion, which is often without comprehension, reflection, or consistency.

To work effectively we must know how to remain calm. There is the danger of permitting excessive concessions, which would be injurious to the character of our movements and compromise them.

Especially, we must hold to the Christian formation of the young through a sound training which always must have doctrine, order, and conformity to the Church as its basis.

We must be on guard and arm ourselves against isolation. Our movements must develop in the framework of our institutions and in the service of the nation, as well as in the service of religion. Isolation could lead to our ruin. We form our young for a spiritual radiation, and this runs counter to isolation. We must make contact, therefore, adapt ourselves and work together in all things. The means are at our disposal; we must use them without losing any of our doctrinal, moral and even civic integrity. And finally, we must give confidence to our youth.

(On the lay apostolate)

It is indispensable to recall that the laity must participate in the apostolate of the hierarchy. But in maintaining and even in suggesting the initiative to laymen, we must make them realize that they must receive and hold fast to the dogmatic and moral directives given them by the priests. On their part, the clergy must make sure they give these militants the authentic teaching of the Church, adapted and made appropriate to them, without ever abandoning the proper role and function of the laity. It is important to reject certain equivocal expressions which could lead to regrettable deviations: *clarify your expressions.*

An apostolate of conquest is necessary: we need only to look at the deChristianized masses; hardly a tenth of the population practices Catholicism; demoralization has given way to degradation. Without excluding direct action on the masses at large, such an apostolate will concentrate on forming select leaders. Without doubt we must not neglect the general apostolate (catechism, etc.), but we must remind ourselves that the priest will reach only a pitiful few by direct action alone . . . the rest are too far gone. Only action of like on like will be successful.

The formation of an elite for conquest calls for a development, an intense education and enlightened specialized movements. Such an elite, well formed, can be the leaven in the mass. One can do effective work in an environment only through men of the environment, and this cannot be done without preparation. On the other hand, we must acknowledge that these specialized movements already have shown their effectiveness.

The formation of this elite of leaders calls for a fuller Catholic Action than the specialized movements; that is, a union of parishoners in the apostolate. The specialized movements, although dynamic, are not numerous enough, and outside of them there are souls of good will precious for utilization. Thus we need a Catholic Action in the parish, which alone is objective, coherent and lasting.

The formation of leaders calls for a social formation, especially for a concentration on social reforms. We must work on the masses, and this is possible only if they realize that we work for them and wish their good. The Gospel makes justice and charity obligatory for all.

A professional formation is equally necessary, since professional competence alone inspires confidence and bestows a right to act.

To form an elite, we need a sufficiently numerous clergy, carefully selected, who are close to the people, since priests are the shepherds of souls, and they must form the militants of Catholic Action. But these priests must be sufficiently instructed in order to teach others; they must adapt themselves to the intellectual environment of the militants, it is their office to spread the doctrine of the Gospel by adapting it to the level of the people.

Normally the elite should be selected and formed, in France, at least, in the Catholic schools.

It is a question of reviving the soul of a nation; this will come about by recruiting generous, dedicated souls geared to an ideal and given to the concern of other souls.

The soul of the apostolate is the manifestation of the soul of Christ, above all, through obedience. You never go wrong when you obey. The soul of the apostolate is also the manifestation of the soul of Christ through kindness.

Christ has been blamed for everything, but no one could ever reproach Him for being hard-hearted. He was good, and this is the distinctive note of His heart: good, sympathetic, merciful.

Devotedness, all devotedness, comes from God, and even in those souls far from Christ we seem to see this same quality.

Dedication to the apostolate is the highest expression of divine love.

The motives of self-dedication are, on the one hand, the immense love of God for all men, and this leads each one to sacrifice himself for others; and on the other hand, the immense needs of men who have lost themselves and are on the road to damnation.

Effective dedication can be exercised only when it is united to an intense interior life; otherwise, it is purely agitation. This is dedication after the fashion of Christ and the apostles, notably that of St. Paul, who wished to become "Christ." As St. John Chrysostom says, Paul's soul was the soul of Christ.

It is good to feel this contact with souls; to do this we must follow the way of the heart. It is the only way which succeeds: be sympathetic to their needs and especially to their sufferings. *My God and my all.*

We must understand that we must take people as they are if we are to guide them to higher paths.

I would like to give a more precious and more determined activity to my life. I have the impression of doing nothing when there is so much to accomplish. Grant that God magnify my effectiveness.

The changes involved in a different orientation do not come about immediately; they require attention, effort, and tenacity of purpose in that effort.

The final absolute victory is had only through a whole series of partial victories.

The world can be saved only by the presence of Christians in every walk of life, Christians who are the leaven.

Now, these special Christians will never develop unless they are formed by priests conscious of their tasks and who are imbued not only with the needs of their priestly ministry, but also with the needs of the lay apostolate.

As a consequence our seminarians and young priests must cultivate this role and form themselves in it; first of all, by their engagement in temporal affairs, then by their conviction of the supremacy of the spiritual.

The Mission of Paris is close to my heart. It is well noted in the diverse environments and is considered as a precious leaven.

But it is also on parade. We cannot afford to have this work of the first order compromised through pure negligence or bad will.

And so these priests, obliged to assume certain secular positions, must never be secularized in spirit or in heart.

Let them remain more and more attached to the heart of the priesthood, notably to the breviary. They must hold fast to it in spirit, heart and will.

The Mission of Paris is a great work, not only for what it can immediately accomplish, but since it furnishes the principle of a conquering apostolate in the areas outside the Church's influence.

It must succeed; otherwise there will be a relapse harmful to the present and to the future which it conditions, and this is a particularly grave epoch in the history of the world.

Present opportunities will perhaps never come back.

The Mission of Paris must succeed: but this requires faultless workers, dedicated, disinterested, ready for sacrifice, qualities which truly mark the Church. Still more, the Mission of Paris requires the true ecclesiastical spirit, residing in souls and shining through them. (I am thinking here of the fidelity to ecclesiastical obligations such as reading the breviary and wearing the cassock).

These workers must realize that the eyes of the world are on them. In accomplishing this new work they must remain totally faithful to the requirements of the Church.

This is the price for disarming the criticism which will undoubtedly be expressed.

(On the Feast of St. Denis and his companions)

What do the Apostles wish of us? They wish us to realize the blessings of the faith they brought and all the wealth which it contains. They also wish us to understand and appreciate the way in which this faith has come down to us. This I see:

The doctrinal truth which the Apostles assimilated in their integrity (the true message of Christ).

I see the Mission needed, and the apostle to whom it is confided, accepting it.

I see the direction of this task, with all that it entails in disinterestedness and personal dedication.

I see the anxiety for saving souls, and the "shuddering" of the apostle upon seeing idolatry (indifference and false ideology).

I see the anxiety of making the Christian truth enter into souls in such a way that it becomes spirit and life to them.

I see the effort of the apostles in mastering themselves and remaining calm when facing the huge wall of paganism.

I see the effort of the imagination for discovering that point where contact can be made and where souls can be affected.

I see the concern for means of reaching souls and making indispensable contact with them (reunion in a tavern or at a pagan's home, etc.).

I see the willingness to risk, within the framework of prudence and zeal.

I see the willingness to throw oneself against obstacles, against dangers that may arise, even at the peril of death.

I see all the risks of persecution (chaffings, deceptions, attacks, calumnies).

The apostolate is made of all these things, and he who hasn't experienced all this is not an apostle in the highest sense of the word.

To see in the apostolate only a "communication of the truth," even authentic and integral truth, would be to limit its power for good.

Without doubt this aspect merits retention, but there is a "subjective" aspect of the apostle who makes a gift of himself. In all necessity it must be considered.

(the last page of his diary)